THE CHANGING FACE
OF CANADA

THE CHANGING FACE OF CANADA

ESSENTIAL READINGS IN POPULATION

EDITED BY
RODERIC BEAUJOT
AND
DON KERR

CANADIAN SCHOLARS' PRESS INC.
TORONTO

The Changing Face of Canada: Essential Readings in Population
Edited by Roderic Beaujot and Don Kerr

First published in 2007 by
Canadian Scholars' Press Inc.
180 Bloor Street West, Suite 801
Toronto, Ontario
M5S 2V6

www.cspi.org

Canadian Scholars' Press Inc. gratefully acknowledges financial support for our publishing activities from the Government of Canada through the Book Publishing Industry Development Program (BPIDP).

Library and Archives Canada Cataloguing in Publication

The changing face of Canada: essential readings in population / edited by Roderic Beaujot and Don Kerr.

Includes bibliographical references.
ISBN 978-1-55130-322-2

1. Canada--Population. 2. Canada--Population policy. I. Beaujot, Roderic P., 1946- II. Kerr, Donald W., 1959-

HB3529.C426 2007   304.60971   C2007-900598-5

Cover design: Aldo Fierro
Cover photo: Healthy Images, 0010, Health Canada Web site and Media Photo Gallery, Health Canada, http://www.hc-sc.gc.ca. Copyright © Her Majesty the Queen in Right of Canada, represented by the Minister of Health, 2005. Reproduced with the permission of the Minister of Public Works and Government Services Canada, 2007.
Interior design and layout: Brad Horning

07   08   09   10   11   5   4   3   2   1

Printed and bound in Canada by Marquis Book Printing Inc.

Canadä

TABLE OF CONTENTS

PREFACE

• •

SEVERAL MEDIA STUDIES RELATED TO CANADIAN DEMOGRAPHICS caught our attention on this weekend when our publisher assigned us the task of writing this preface.

The Globe and Mail carried a "Focus" section on "Boomers Turn 60" (June 24, 2006: F1–F17). Of course, it is over the period 2006 to 2026 that this large generation will turn 60. While this is a fertility story of times past, for many years it has been a story of the changing age structure, with implications for individuals and society. The leading edge of the baby boomers were advantaged as society made room for a large cohort. They were also advantaged by having even larger cohorts follow them.

When the senior author was at university in the 1960s, it was popularly said that if all else failed, one could always get a job as a teacher. In effect, the generations born in the late 1940s could teach the even larger generations of the 1950s. Things were somewhat different for those born in the latter part of the baby boom. They had the disadvantage of following a large cohort who had taken all the good jobs, and of entering the labour market in the less expansionary times after the mid-1970s. The baby bust, born in 1967–1979, should have had the advantages of being a smaller cohort, but they had the disadvantage of following the large preceding cohort. It is only since the mid-1990s that the labour market has become more favourable to young people who are also benefiting from their greater distance from the baby boom.

Another demographic story on this same weekend carries a policy proposal on immigration from Maurizio Bevilacqua as contender for the leadership of the Liberal Party of Canada (*The Globe and Mail*, June 24, 2006:A7). Bevilacqua proposes an "expansionist" policy that would go beyond filling holes in the labour force to deliberately expand the population. Since he proposes to do this by "bringing in far more foreign relatives of Canadians," the author of the article observes that this "relational immigration" is "probably good leadership politics."

In *The London Free Press*, columnist Lyn Cockburn expresses disgust at the narrow-minded view of her plumber who, on hearing of the head tax for which the prime minister was apologizing, proposes that such taxes seem like a good idea (June 24, 2006:F1). While the plumber is concerned about the competition brought by immigration, the columnist observes that "notions of inclusion go down the drain." This is but one example of the lack of meeting of minds on immigration. Could it be that immigration serves the interests of those who want cheap services, and those who benefit from the expansion of the population, including relatives of recent immigrants, while it makes for wage-depressing competition for workers in areas of the economy who are not able to isolate themselves from this competition?

While demographics can be cold aggregated phenomena, we hope that this book will incite thinking on how demographics come to be, and on implications that may differ for various parts of society.

We also wish to thank the various authors who have allowed us to use their work in this collection. The editors are especially grateful to Donna Maynard for her careful work on the bibliography, Jane Philbert for her translation of Chapter 7, and to Megan Mueller who has been a most encouraging and supportive receiving editor. This book is her idea!

Roderic Beaujot and Don Kerr
June 25, 2006
London, Ontario

A NOTE FROM THE PUBLISHER

Thank you for selecting *The Changing Face of Canada: Essential Readings in Population* edited by Roderic Beaujot and Don Kerr. The editors and publisher have devoted considerable time and careful development (including meticulous peer reviews) to this book. We appreciate your recognition of this effort and accomplishment.

TEACHING FEATURES

This volume distinguishes itself on the market in many ways. One key feature is the book's well-written and comprehensive part openers, which help to make the readings all the more accessible to undergraduate students. The part openers add cohesion to the section and to the whole book. The themes of the book are very clearly presented in these section openers. The part openers also contain recommended readings and relevant Web sites.

Further adding value to the book, the editors have composed critical thinking questions to close each chapter. They have also added an appendix containing Canadian Population Estimates (1971–2005) and Projections (2005–2035).

CHAPTER 1

POPULATION CHANGE INTO THE 21ST CENTURY

Don Kerr and Roderic Beaujot

• •

THE STUDY OF POPULATION PHENOMENA AND DEMOGRAPHIC EVENTS are central to several different academic disciplines, including sociology, geography, economics, epidemiology, and history. Clearly one of the most fundamental features of any given society is the number of people in its population, and how this is changing with time. When populations grow or get smaller, direct repercussions follow with sometimes dramatic effect. As a result, the study of demography is not only of interest to academics but is also of fundamental importance to those who have a more applied orientation, including those involved in public policy and administration.

Population-related questions are relevant to many of the issues that social scientists are examining today, and is likely to become even more important into the future. For example, what is the impact of slowing population growth on socio-economic development, or how might changes in population age structure have an impact on public policy? In the Canadian context, there is considerable interest in international migration and the integration of new Canadians, as few societies are as heavily influenced by immigration. On a global scale, there is much interest in the relationship between population growth, the environment, and the sustainability of natural resources. As the world's population has recently bypassed 6.5 billion, it continues to increase by about 200,000 people daily (UN, 2006). The behaviour, choices, and social activities of individuals can have a major impact collectively.

THE STUDY OF POPULATION

In terms of definition, demography can be defined as the study of populations, their size, distribution, and composition. This includes the study of the immediate causes of population change, including births, deaths, and migration. By population composition, demographers study a variety of characteristics, including age, sex, marital status, education, ethnicity, income, family composition, and so on. Population processes correspondingly bring about changes in population states from one point in time to another as people are born (fertility), they move around (migration), and they die (mortality). Population states and processes are interrelated: For instance, lower births (process) produce an older population (state), and an older population tends to have a lower birth rate.

The links between population processes and states become obvious when we formally consider how population processes influence population size. More specifically, a change in population size can only be a function of intervening births, deaths, immigration, and emigration. This can be formally represented by what demographers refer to as the basic demographic equation:

$$P_2 = P_1 + B - D + I - E$$

where P_2 is the population at a given time, P_1 is the population at an earlier time, B is the number of births in the interval, D is the number of deaths, I is the number of immigrants who arrived in the interval, and E is the number of emigrants who departed. Births minus deaths ($B - D$) is called natural increase (or decrease), and immigration minus emigration ($I - E$) is called net migration. It is a combination of natural increase and net migration that fully accounts for total population growth for a specific nation-state over time. In the Canadian context, natural increase has been declining in importance as of late, as about two-thirds of total growth is currently being maintained by net international migration.

When we consider the distribution of a population over space (as, for example, across Canadian provinces or cities), the analysis becomes more complex. For one thing, international immigrants tend to settle in certain parts of the country more so than in others, as Canada's largest cities are growing at a much more rapid pace than elsewhere. For another, internal migration is not evenly distributed throughout the country. Furthermore, regions and provinces differ in fertility and mortality rates such that the rate of natural increase is not homogeneous. The analysis becomes even more complex if we further subdivide the population in terms of sex, age structure, and various other population characteristics.

Besides the relationship between population states and processes, there is also considerable interest in the relevance of demographics to other changes in society. While births, migrations, and deaths mark an individual's life course, these events, added together, also demarcate the development of societies over time. At the group level, fertility and immigration are the basic mechanisms through which populations, countries, societies, and communities are regenerated. Not only do these regenerative processes add numbers to the population, ensuring demographic continuity in the face of departures through death and emigration, but they also change the character of the population and, consequently, of society. The character of the population is changed in terms of age and sex structure, socio-economic composition, cultural makeup, and regional distribution.

The study of population also has a practical importance. To plan public services, it is important to know the nature of the population groups that need these services. How many people are at retirement age, and how will this change in the future? How many children are of elementary school age, and how do we expect this to change over the next several years? How many single-parent families are there? These are among the host of questions that are important to the structuring of social programs. Several chapters in the current collection explicitly address these sorts of issues. In our concluding chapter we will return to them by considering in greater detail various consequences of demographic change for both public policy as well as for Canadian society more broadly.

CANADA'S CURRENT DEMOGRAPHIC SITUATION: SUSTAINED POPULATION GROWTH INTO THE 21ST CENTURY

Nationally, Canada's population hit an estimated 32,422,900 as of January 1, 2006, up by about 1 percent from the previous year (Statistics Canada, 2006). While many Canadians think of this as relatively slow growth, this rate is actually greater than in most other developed nations and only slightly down from the rate of growth that characterized Canada throughout the last several decades. For example, the average growth rate of Canada's population over the full period of 1971–1991 was 1.15 percent annually, only to drop slightly to 1.0 percent over the 1991–2001 period (Statistics Canada, 2002). In drawing some international comparisons, the annual growth rate for all of western Europe in 2003, taken together, was only 0.24 percent, less than a third of the current Canadian growth rate.

While Canada's population is growing more rapidly than in Europe, its pace of growth is comparable to its neighbour and major trading partner, the U.S. This is true even though fertility is significantly lower than in the U.S.—at about 1.5 births per women in comparison with about 2.1 births in the U.S. (U.S. Census Bureau, 2004; Statistics Canada, 2003a). In explanation, the relative impact of immigration on both countries is fundamental. Much attention has been given to the large numbers who migrate to the U.S., which in absolute terms admits more immigrants than any other receiving country. Yet there are relatively very few countries in the world that accept more immigrants on a per capita basis than does Canada, a fact which we will return to repeatedly in the current text.

DECLINING NATURAL INCREASE

Population growth is expected to slow considerably, although there is a lack of consensus as to the extent of this slowdown and its timing. Due to what demographers refer to as population momentum, past growth will continue for some time to come despite below-replacement fertility. The momentum of population growth is the potential for future increase in population size that is inherent in any present age and sex structure even as fertility levels drop to replacement level. In effect, births in Canada continue to outnumber deaths, as the relative number of adults at ages when mortality is low outnumber by a substantial margin those in their latter years of life where the risk of death is high. In addition, even though Canadian women are having fewer births than needed for replacement, the relatively sizable cohorts at reproductive ages have ensured more births than deaths, and this is expected to continue for some time to come.

According to Statistics Canada's medium growth population projection, births will continue to outnumber deaths in Canada until 2030 (see Figure 1.1). This scenario is considered realistic as it assumes that Canada's fertility will continue at current levels (at about 1.5 births per woman) while the annual immigration target will gradually increase

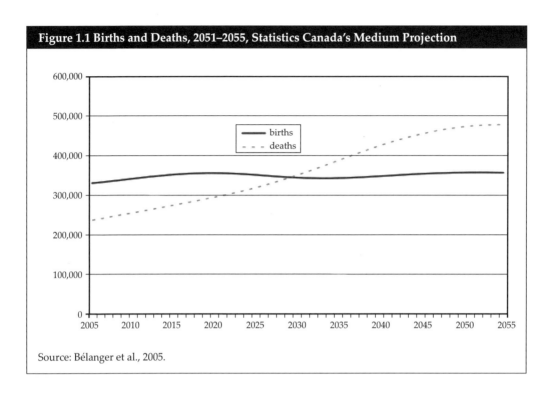

Figure 1.1 Births and Deaths, 2051–2055, Statistics Canada's Medium Projection

Source: Bélanger et al., 2005.

from about 240,000 in 2005–2006 up to about 280,000 by 2030–2031. According to this scenario, Canada's population is expected to increase by just over 30 percent over the next 50 years, which is lower than the growth experienced over the previous 50 years (as Canada's population has doubled since 1956). In other words, while demographers do not anticipate eminent population decline, the pace of population growth is expected to slow considerably.

As fertility has declined, so too have we observed major changes in terms of mortality. We have witnessed considerable gains in longevity and health care over recent decades, and most demographers project further gains well into the future. In a review of mortality in advanced countries, Oeppen and Vaupel (2002) see no reason why the future would not see continued increases in life expectancy, which have averaged 2.5 years per decade over the past 150 years. Average life expectancy at birth in Canada has reached about 80 years, which is on average about two full years greater than in the United States. By sex, Canadian life expectancy in 2002 was 77.2 for men and 82.1 for women. Only a few countries had higher life expectancy than Canada: Japan, Sweden, and Switzerland for men and women; France, Spain, and Italy for women; and Iceland for men (Bélanger, 2002). The climb in deaths as forecasted in Figure 1.1 is not the by-product of climbing mortality (but rather population aging), as age-specific rates are expected to continue declining into the future. This forecasted climb in the number of deaths in Canada is the by-product of both population growth and the movement of the large baby-boom cohorts into their high-mortality ages.

IMMIGRATION TO CANADA

Relative to its overall population size, Canada receives a substantial share of all immigrants to North America. Currently, the admission of over 200,000 immigrants annually represents well over half of Canada's overall population growth (Statistics Canada, 2003a). On an annual basis, since 1994, net international migration has comprised a larger percentage of total population growth in Canada than has natural increase (births–deaths). This situation has contributed to a sizable share of Canada's population being foreign-born—18.4 percent according to the 2001 Census (Statistics Canada, 2003a). The comparable figure in the United States is 11.1 percent foreign-born (U.S. Census Bureau, 2004), which highlights the relative importance of immigration to Canada's demographic and socio-economic development.

As depicted in Figure 1.2, immigration and emigration levels have varied considerably over time, as year-to-year fluctuations have followed the path of events both inside and outside of the country. In the early 2000s, immigration targets have consistently been set above the 200,000 mark as Canada continues to receive far more immigrants than it loses through emigration (hovering at about 60,000 emigrants annually). Unless fertility returns to higher levels, net international immigration will likely climb in importance in maintaining population growth with the prospect of higher immigration targets in the near future. While government policy on immigration is of fundamental importance in this context, politically, the federal government has followed the social climate and does not deviate excessively from public opinion on this issue. In the current set of readings, Green provides a careful appraisal of immigration policy in Canada, as demographic analysis has much to offer in terms of informing public policy debates.

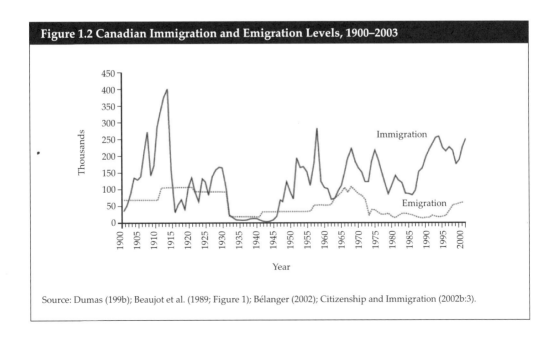

Figure 1.2 Canadian Immigration and Emigration Levels, 1900–2003

Source: Dumas (199b); Beaujot et al. (1989; Figure 1); Bélanger (2002); Citizenship and Immigration (2002b:3).

The success of immigrants in settlement, in gaining employment and/or the necessary skills for employment, has long been a central priority in developing Canada's immigration policy. With this in mind, the federal government introduced the points system in the 1960s in promoting the selection of immigrants on the basis of education, occupational skills, and knowledge of official languages. While a substantial proportion of all immigrants continue to migrate to Canada under the family reunification class (and, to a lesser extent, political refugee class), the federal government is committed to increasing the share of all immigrants that migrate to Canada on the basis of skills and education. As a result, immigrants admitted to Canada over recent decades have had educational levels significantly higher than that of other Canadians.

Despite these rising levels of educational credentials, the earnings and employment success of recent cohorts of new immigrants to Canada have declined in quite a pronounced manner (Abbott and Beach, 1993; Baker and Benjamin, 1994). While the introduction of Canada's point system was initially met with success, there is a growing body of evidence to suggest that migrants who immigrated to Canada during the 1990s have not fared nearly as well as those who migrated earlier in the 1970s and 1980s. While Canada has a reputation for its success in terms of integrating new immigrants, the economic difficulties as experienced more recently by immigrants to Canada have undermined this reputation (Li, 2003).

POPULATION AGING

In addition to the decline in population growth, Canada's population is aging. Population aging typically takes the form of an increase in the number of elderly, and a decline in the number of children and young people. This aging of Canada's population is represented in Figure 1.3, which presents the population pyramids for Canada in 1985, 1995, and 2005. In inspecting these age pyramids, there are a few features that are particularly striking, including (1) the relatively large size of the baby-boom cohort (currently in their forties and fifties) and (2) the rather pronounced shrinkage that has recently occurred at the bottom of the age pyramid.

Due to its mere size, the baby-boom cohort has had a major impact on various societal institutions. Figure 1.3 demonstrates that many of the largest cohorts born during the baby boom were in their young adult years in 1985, were well established in the labour market and family life by 1995, and in 2005 were moving into and through middle age. The shrinkage at the bottom of the population pyramid is seen in the 2005 pyramid by comparing the relative number of teenagers to the number of preschoolers. This major contraction that is currently occurring at the bottom of the age pyramid has received far less attention than the baby boom, partially because Canadians have not thought through the long-term implications of this decline in births. In addition, the U.S. has not experienced the same sort of contraction in the number of births.

As a by-product of below-replacement fertility, annual births in Canada have been steadily falling for well over a decade. Since 1989, this number has fallen by almost 20 percent, from about 403,280 in 1989 down to 327,187 in 2002 (Statistics Canada, 2003a). This is fully 32 percent less than the 479,275 births that characterized the height of the baby boom in 1959. With the passage of time, both of these features of Canada's population

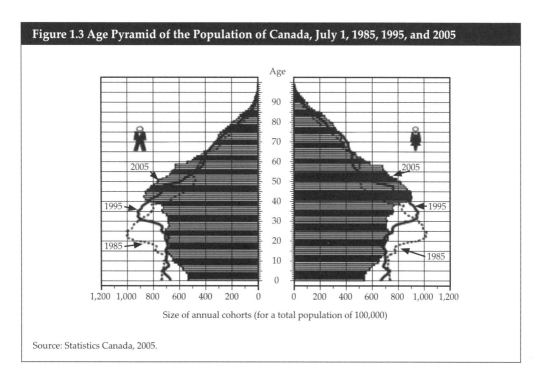

Figure 1.3 Age Pyramid of the Population of Canada, July 1, 1985, 1995, and 2005

Source: Statistics Canada, 2005.

pyramid (i.e., the baby boom and the contraction at the bottom of the population pyramid) will have several ramifications on society. As merely one example, consider the fact that the 1959 cohort will be reaching 65 years at about the same time as the 2002 cohort enters the labour market (in 2024).

In drawing a few international comparisons, population aging is at a more advanced stage in Europe, where Chesnais (1989) speaks of an "inversion of the age pyramid." At the turn of the century, the proportion over 65 is already over 18 percent in Italy and 16.4 percent in Germany. The figure for Canada (at 13 percent) is lower than the average for the more developed countries, and it is not expected to reach 18 percent until after 2016. Nonetheless, the Canadian change is now as rapid as that of European countries, and it will be more rapid once the larger baby-boom generations move into retirement ages. Whereas just over one in 10 people were over 65 in 1986, some 50 years later, in 2036, the medium projection suggests that almost a quarter of the population will be at these ages. Along with a median age of some 45 years, and more than 12 percent of the population aged 75 and over, this will make for a rather different demographic profile.

DEMOGRAPHIC CHANGE AND FAMILY BEHAVIOUR

While much demographic analysis begins with the individual as the unit of analysis, families and households are also directly relevant. There is much interplay between families and demographic change as what is happening in families affects the population, and population change affects families. Family behaviour influences demographics in a variety of ways. Fertility, for instance, is lowered by later marriage, more divorce, and more cohabitation. The geographic mobility of at least one adult, and often the person's children, is affected by the entry and exit from relationships. Morbidity and mortality are also affected by changing family patterns: for instance, married people benefit from the social support they receive from their spouses.

In documenting family change in Canada, reference is often made to two rather broad transitions. The first transition, which began in the 19th century, was the rather pronounced decline in fertility and mortality that accompanied Canada's modernization. Whereas fertility declined through to the mid-20th century (prior to witnessing an unanticipated baby boom), mortality decline continued unabated through to the present. The second transition, which occurred more recently, has involved some rather dramatic changes in the flexibility and stability of marital relationships (Lesthaeghe, 1995).

Whereas the first transition brought with it smaller families, the second transition brought with it dramatic changes in the nature of marital relationships, manifested in terms of increased cohabitation, divorce, and remarriage. While the first transition occurred over an extended period, this second demographic transition was much more rapid from about 1960 through to the present. While the first demographic transition was temporarily halted by the baby boom, the second demographic transition began in earnest only toward the end of the baby-boom era. As the timing and stability of marital relationships began to shift during the 1960s and 1970s, the total fertility rate in Canada returned to its longer term downward trend, and has since fallen to a near all-time low of only 1.5 births per woman (Statistics Canada, 2004).

The first demographic transition involved a change in the economic costs and rewards to couples of child-bearing and child-rearing, which is due to the absence of children's productive roles in the family with the advent of (prolonged) formal education. The second demographic transition is marked by greater flexibility in entry into and exit from conjugal relationships as evidenced by the pronounced rise in cohabitation and divorce. Even though most Canadians marry or will marry, the common-law union is increasingly challenging marriage as the pre-eminent context in which to pursue conjugality and, for a growing number of Canadians, parenthood. While most marriages last until "death do us part", divorce is ever more defying the definition of marriage as a permanent arrangement.

While the institution of marriage has been changing quite rapidly, it is quite hazardous to forecast future family change, particularly since past efforts to do so have at times been spectacularly wrong. For example, there was not one demographer in either Canada or the United States who accurately projected the baby-boom era. As a general rule, demographers and other social scientists usually forecast or anticipate a continuation of past trends, and past trends about a half-century ago suggested that fertility would continue to decline unabated. In addition, counter to expectations, the baby-boom era also saw a decline in the average age at which people marry and a higher proportion marrying at least once in their lives. Virtually no one anticipated either this marriage rush or subsequent baby boom of the 1950s—all in a context of an unanticipated return to domesticity.

Lesthaeghe (1995), who first introduced this idea of a second demographic transition in collaboration with Van de Kaa (1987) identified three rather broad stages. While there was clearly considerable variation in the timing of some of these changes across nation-states, Lesthaeghe developed three stages in order to provide for the broad contours of this transitional period. In Canada, the first stage can be identified as the period from about 1960 to 1970 that witnessed the end of the baby boom, the end of the trend toward younger ages at marriage, and the beginning of the rise in divorces. The second stage from 1970 to 1985 saw the growth of common-law unions and eventually of children in cohabiting unions. The third stage since 1985 includes a plateau in divorce, an increase in post-marital cohabitation (and consequently a decline in remarriage), higher proportions of births after age 30, and a stabilization in fertility rates well below replacement. These changes in births, marriage, cohabitation, and divorce have brought fewer children but also a higher level of diversity in the living arrangements and family life of Canadians.

As relationships are now less permanent and more flexible, child-bearing is often delayed, there are fewer births overall, and many children are born outside of legal marriage. As conjugal relationships have been altered, the level of diversity in the family has risen. Family life in Canada may or may not involve parents who are legally married to one another, just as it may or may not involve children who are biologically related to both parents. Step- and blended-family living arrangements are becoming increasingly common, as is childlessness among both cohabiting and legally married couples. In addition, as cohabitation has become more widespread, it is increasingly influencing post-marital relationships (i.e., remarriage in the event of divorce).

ORGANIZATION OF THIS BOOK

This book includes five major sections.

Section 1 begins with four chapters on fertility. Given the importance of fertility differences and trends, few areas are as well researched in demography. Yet even though this is a key component of population change, it has been particularly difficult to explain and predict fertility patterns. In reviewing this literature, much uncertainty continues to characterize explanations as to why young Canadians are increasingly delaying fertility or, for that matter, deciding to forego having children altogether. As Canada's birth rate currently hovers at about 1.5 births per woman, it is far from certain as to whether fertility may actually fall further and, for that matter, if it does, how low Canadian fertility can actually fall.

Section 2 includes four chapters on mortality, another core area of demography. Overall mortality patterns and trends are examined among populations, as are mortality differentials across population subgroups. In considering trends in mortality, patterns of health and disability, and the socio-demographic profile of mortality and morbidity, these readings demonstrate the considerable progress Canada has made over recent decades in extending life expectancy and reducing the risk of premature death. As each successive generation of Canadians has been somewhat healthier than its predecessor, with consistent gains made in terms of reducing the risk of premature death, the question remains as to whether this trend will continue into the foreseeable future. An informed analysis of past mortality and morbidity trends allows for more informed debate in terms of Canadian health policy, a debate that need be considered in a context of population aging and escalating health care costs.

Section 3 includes five chapters on international migration, domestic migration, and population distribution. Among the three demographic processes of mortality, fertility, and migration, the most explicit attempts to influence population trends have occurred in the area of international migration. Starting with a brief history of immigration trends, this section also considers the demographic, socio-economic, and socio-cultural effects of immigration. Past trends in terms of international migration have a direct impact on change in the distribution of Canada's population, as are past trends in internal migration and natural increase. The interplay between migration and regional disparity is of fundamental importance in considering Canada's demographic development.

Section 4 includes three chapters on the topic of population aging. Having studied the components of population change (mortality, fertility, and migration), the current section moves on to consider population aging as one of the most fundamental consequences of past change in terms of these components. At the national level, this transformation in age distribution has had and will continue to have profound consequences for Canadian society. While there is little doubt that population aging will add to the costs of health care and social security, there is considerable uncertainty as to the extent to which this will occur and our ability to accommodate this shift. As demonstrated in the chapters selected for the current text, there is considerable disagreement as to the seriousness of current trends toward an older Canadian population.

Section 5 includes five chapters on Canada's population composition. By composition, we are referring to not only the age and sex structure of Canada's population, but also marital status, household and family structure, living arrangements, ethnicity, language, education, and income, among other socio-economic variables. The popular term "demographics" has been used widely by non-demographers to denote population composition, as there has been a growing appreciation of how a society's demographics can hold fundamental implications for individuals, families, social groups, markets, and governments alike.

In our final chapter, we will be particularly concerned with Canada's demographic future, population forecasts, and the policy implications of current trends.

In the appendix, we include some recent population estimates and projections from Statistics Canada.

RECOMMENDED READINGS

Beaujot, Roderic, and Don Kerr. (2004). *Population Change in Canada*. Toronto: Oxford University Press. This text provides an overview of recent Canadian research in the field of population studies.

Bélanger, Alain. (Annual). *Report on the Demographic Situation in Canada*. Ottawa: Statistics Canada. Cat. no. 91-209. This annual publication gives data on the changing demographic situation in Canada. Each issue also focuses on a topic of special interest.

Bélanger, Alain, Laurent Martel, and Eric Caron-Malenfant. 2005. *Population Projections for Canada, Provinces and Territories, 2005–2031*. Ottawa: Statistics Canada. Cat. no. 91-520-XPE. This publication, which can be easily downloaded (free) from Statistics Canada's Web site, is the most recent set of population projections for Canada, the provinces, and territories.

Foot, David K., and Daniel Stoffman. (1998). *Boom, Bust and Echo*. Toronto: Macfarlane Walter and Ross. This bestseller reflects on how the age structure affects individual opportunities and how population change is transforming Canada's social and economic life.

Poston, Dudley L., and Michael Micklin. (2005). *Handbook of Population*. New York: Kluwer Academic/ Plenum Publishers. This handbook provides a comprehensive overview of recent work in the area of demography, focusing on definitions, methods of analysis, theoretical arguments, and interpretive examples.

Trovato, Frank (ed.). (2002). *Population and Society: Essential Readings*. Toronto: Oxford University Press. This collection contains 25 well-chosen articles on the ways in which population and society are related. The readings include a wide array of research and theorizing in population studies.

RELATED WEB SITES

Demography Program, Australian National University
<http://demography.anu.edu.au/VirtualLibrary/>

A comprehensive collection of demography links, as maintained by the Demography program at the Australian National University. This site includes links to several other relevant Web sites, ftp sites, software, and datasets.

Population Information Network
<http://www.un.org/popin/>

The Web site of the Population Information Network (POPIN) of the United Nations Economic and Social Council provides international, regional, and national population information, particularly information available from United Nations sources.

Population Reference Bureau
<http://www.popnet.org>

A Web site maintained by the Population Reference Bureau, Washington, D.C., PopNet is a source of population information. Here you can browse the most comprehensive directory of population-related Web sites available by organization, region, and country, or topic within countries.

Population Studies Centre, University of Western Ontario
<http://www.ssc.uwo.ca/sociology/popstudies/>

The Population Studies Centre at the University of Western Ontario has produced a wide variety of studies on demographic subjects, including several detailed monographs on Canadian fertility. This site also includes an online discussion paper series, as well as the Automated Bibliography of Canadian Demography, and an online catalogue.

Statistics Canada
<http://www.statcan.ca>

This is the Web site of Canada's national statistical agency. The user can browse by subject or do automated searches on a wide assortment of statistical data collected on Canada's population and economy. Most of Statistics Canada's publications are now available, free of charge, to be downloaded from this site. A free e-mail subscription to The Daily is also available, which informs subscribers of all of Statistics Canada's data and publication releases.

SECTION 1
FERTILITY

● ●

THE FIRST CHAPTER, BY BALI RAM, places Canada's current situation into a broader international and historical context. More specifically, he sketches some of the most salient changes that have occurred in Canadian birth rates over recent decades and how they compare with other nation-states. As Canada's fertility rate has fallen to an unprecedented low level of about 1.5 births, women are increasingly delaying their fertility, and the level of voluntary childlessness has risen. Fertility rates have similarly fallen below replacement throughout most of Europe, Japan, Australia, and several of the most rapidly expanding economies of southeast Asia and the Pacific Rim.

This review of the international evidence suggests a host of contradictory trends and pressures that will reshape our societies and economies as we move into the 21st century. For example, while we continue to have rapid population growth throughout many less-developed countries, many of the most affluent industrialized nations of the world face the prospect of population implosion (or a significant reduction in population size as a direct consequence of prolonged below-replacement fertility). The United Nations projects a world population of perhaps 9 billion in the 21st century, which might arguably be considered one of the most fundamental challenges currently facing humanity. Yet demographers point somewhat ironically to a whole set of additional challenges that may surface as a by-product of very low fertility and a population implosion among the most industrialized nations. Fertility differentials can influence social change in many fundamental ways, including important differences in the rate of population growth, modifications in age structure (and population aging), and changes in the family structure and living arrangements. Shifts in fertility have important implications for societies, particularly over the longer term, a theme to which we will often return through this text.

Torrey and Eberstadt's chapter focuses on what they label the "Northern America fertility divide." They begin with the observation that while Canada and the United States seem to be remarkably similar nations (both culturally and in terms of their degree of economic integration), they have diverged in their fertility behaviour over recent years. The U.S. fertility rate is about 2.1 births per woman, above replacement, and fully half a child more than in Canada's 1.5 births. In addition, Canadians marry later than do Americans, do so less often than their southern neighbours, are more likely to cohabit, tend to delay their first birth, are less likely to have an abortion or a child as a teenager, and are less likely to divorce or separate.

Torrey and Eberstadt's chapter reviews different theoretical arguments relevant in the explanation of fertility differentials. While North America has become more integrated economically (with NAFTA and the associated major expansion of trade), Canada and the United States appear to be diverging at the micro level of individuals and families. This seems to fly in the face of those who argue that as the world becomes more economically integrated, a homogenized culture with similar values and behaviour is the result. Various factors are considered, including differences in income and labour force participation; government policy on income support for families and children; differences in the incidence of abortion, ideational change, and secularization and religion (among other contributory factors).

Cultural values, such as religion and/or language, are often raised in explaining fertility differences. The importance of culture is obvious in Gervais and Gauvreau's contribution, which summarizes qualitative evidence on attitudes toward birth control in the province of Quebec in the decades leading to Quebec's Quiet Revolution (1940–1970). As Canada's only province that is majority French-speaking, the fertility transition occurred relatively late in Quebec, and at a much slower pace than in most industrialized countries. Interviews with Catholic clergy and physicians provide insight as to why this was the situation, including evidence as to the pronatalism of Catholicism and the profound impact this had on family life. Couples were strongly discouraged from using birth control, whereas physicians, most of whom were believers themselves, allowed religious morality to override the expressed concerns of women and couples to control births. This was to all radically change during the Quiet Revolution as civil society broke its ties with religious authority in shaping the decisions and day-to-day experiences of young adults.

Just as language or religion is relevant to fertility differentials, demographers have also systematically considered the fertility of immigrants. This issue is of some relevance to Canadians, as few other societies in the world are as heavily influenced by immigration. For example, about 18 percent of Canada's population is foreign-born, which compares with only 11 percent in the United States and fewer than 10 percent across most nations of the European Union. In light of the importance of immigration to Canada, Bélanger and Gilbert's chapter estimates the fertility of immigrant women, drawing distinctions according to country/region of origin. The differences as observed are relatively modest, quite similar to the fertility of the Canadian-born, yet related to the source countries of immigrants (i.e., immigrants from selected high-fertility regions of the Third World tend to have slightly higher fertility). Demographers have long understood that the fertility behaviour of the foreign-born tends to converge with that of the native-born as a direct function of integration and acculturation to the host society. As a result, immigration, even in a major immigrant-receiving country like Canada, tends to have a relatively modest effect on overall fertility rates.

RECOMMENDED READINGS

Balakrishnan, T.R., Évelyne Lapierre-Adamcyk, , and Karol J. Krotki. (1993). *Family and Childbearing in Canada*. Toronto: University of Toronto Press. An important contribution to the demographic analysis of fertility in Canada, this book summarizes the findings from the 1984 Canadian Fertility Survey.

Bélanger, Alain, and Geneviéve Ouellet. (2001). "A Comparative Study of Recent Trends in Canadian and American Fertility, 1980–1999." *Report on the Demographic Situation in Canada 2001*. Ottawa: Statistics Canada. Cat. no. 91-209. A summary study of the fertility differential that characterizes North America, this chapter provides possible reasons for the significantly lower fertility in Canada.

Health Canada. (2005). "Changing Fertility Patterns: Trends and Implications." *Health Policy Research Bulletin*, Issue 10. This issue examines the complex dynamics behind recent fertility trends, including transformations in family structure, gender roles, and life transitions. It also explores the implications of these trends for women, men, children, the health care system, and society as a whole.

Henripin, Jacques. (1968). *Trends and Factors of Fertility in Canada*. Ottawa: Dominion Bureau of Statistics. This classic study of fertility charts the baby boom in Canada and the beginnings of the baby bust using census data and vital statistics.

Romaniuc, Anatole. (1984). *Fertility in Canada: From Baby-Boom to Baby-Bust*. Ottawa. Statistics Canada. Cat. no. 91-524. This comprehensive study details long-term fertility change in Canada, with considerable discussion as to causes and consequences.

RELATED WEB SITES

Inter-university Centre for Demographic Study, Université de Montréal
<http://www.cied.umontreal.ca/>

The Inter-university Centre for Demographic Study at the Université de Montréal brings together demographers across several Quebec universities. Its main fields of research include contemporary transformations in families and fertility.

Planned Parenthood Federation of Canada
<http://www.ppfc.ca/>

This is the Web site of the Planned Parenthood Federation of Canada, which is an organization dedicated to promoting sexual and reproductive health and rights in Canada and developing nations.

Popline
<http://db.jhuccp.org/popinform/basic.html>

Popline is a bibliographic link, with over 280,000 records representing published and unpublished literature in the field of population, family planning, and related health issues.

Population Studies Centre, University of Western Ontario
<http://sociology.uwo.ca/popstudies/>

The Population Studies Centre at the University of Western Ontario includes an online discussion paper series as well as the "Automated Bibliography of Canadian Demography." This bibliography has a listing of virtually all Canadian research ever published on the demographic analysis of fertility.

Topics Related to Reproductive Health, Contraception, and Fertility
<http://www.rhgateway.org>

This site is a gateway to Internet information on various topics relating to reproductive health, contraception, and fertility.

CHAPTER 2

FERTILITY DECLINE AND SOCIAL CHANGE: NEW TRENDS AND CHALLENGES

Bali Ram

● ●

INTRODUCTION

Ever since the publication of Malthus's *An Essay on the Principle of Population* in 1798, books have been written about the social and economic effects of population growth. Following principles observed in nature, Malthus prophesied that populations had a natural propensity to grow "beyond Nature's ability to provide subsistence. Population would expand in geometric fashion, but food, only arithmetically." Malthus's name has come to be synonymous with a pessimistic view of population, which received a major boost by a proliferation of neo-Malthusian writings on the negative consequences of population pressure in academic and popular literature. Terms such as "population explosion," "vital revolution," and even more ideologically tainted "population bomb" were coined to describe the rapid growth of population.

The picture has changed over recent decades following fertility declines across both industrialized and less industrialized countries. As early as 1967, Bogue predicted "the end of the population explosion." Initially, this prediction was partially ignored, perhaps due to an overemphasis on the role of family-planning campaigns in bringing about fertility decline. However, in view of the sustained fertility declines in a majority of countries, including demographic giants such as China and India, there have been speculations in recent years about the likelihood of eventual "population implosion" (Eberstadt, 1997).

Two thousand years ago, the population of the world stood at around 300 million. At the end of this first millennium, world population size had changed little. Natural disasters, epidemics, and wars did not allow the population to grow. However, due to progress in medicine and improved life standards, mortality declined—true of infant mortality in particular—and the population exploded during the second millennium. By the year 2000, the world's population had surpassed the 6 billion mark, and is expected to continue to grow for several more decades. Over the past 50 years, the world population grew at an average rate of about 1.7 percent per year. Over the next 50 years, according to the medium variant projection of the United Nations (2004), the world population is expected to grow at a rate of about 0.8 percent per year. Thus, the world population could potentially grow to as many as 9 billion people by 2050. However, the United Nations' projections also indicate that in a number of countries and regions in more developed parts of the world, populations are likely to experience negative rather than positive growth rates.

In this chapter, evidence is presented to suggest that recent fertility declines have either already brought or will bring in the future large-scale changes in the ways of thinking and behaviour of people, countries, and governments. Some examples of such changes are: the introduction of pronatalist policies, the ease in the immigration of working-age foreign nationals, the modification in intergenerational support systems, and potential changes in the ethnic equilibrium of various nation-states. These changes are affected by both levels and age patterns of fertility. These dimensions influence social change through several mechanisms, including reductions in population growth and modifications in age structure.

GLOBAL FERTILITY DECLINE AND CONVERGENCE

During the past half-century, especially during the latter part, most countries of the world have experienced a fertility decline. The world total fertility rate has dropped from about 5.0 births per woman in the early 1950s to 4.5 in the early 1970s and about 2.7 in 2000. Except for a few countries in Africa, fertility has been declining in every part of the world, depicting a convergence between world regions (Figure 2.1).

The world average conceals large differences across countries and regions. While some countries have been experiencing below-replacement level fertility for many years, others observed large reductions rather quickly. There is yet another group of countries where fertility levels are high, but have been declining at a moderate pace in recent years. Only in a few countries (mostly in Africa) are fertility rates much above replacement level (more than three times) and the decline did not begin until very recently.

At present, almost all industrialized countries have a fertility level at or below replacement. A number of countries (e.g., Austria, Belgium, Denmark, France, Germany, Greece, Luxembourg, Netherlands, Russian Federation, Sweden, Switzerland, Ukraine, and the U.K.) have been experiencing below-replacement fertility for at least three decades. France, Sweden, and Germany were front-runners, with long histories of low fertility. Italy, Spain, Greece, and Portugal entered the transition rather late, but experienced fertility declines at a very fast pace, surpassing all others and exhibiting total fertility rates below 1.5 today. Japan is the only country outside of Europe, North America, and Australia that experienced an early fertility transition. The fertility decline in Japan began during the 1930s, but plunged to a spectacularly low level within less than a decade, reaching 2.0 by the end of the 1950s (Kono, 1994). During the following 15 years (1960–1975), the total fertility rate stabilized around two children, but then declined further to a level significantly below replacement (1.39 in 2000–2005).

Several other Asian countries, most notably Singapore, Hong Kong, Taiwan, and the Republic of Korea (South Korea), were latecomers but joined the low-fertility group rather quickly (Figure 2.2). Their fertility levels started to decline in the late 1950s or 1960s but were reduced by more than half within less than two decades. Fertility levels of these

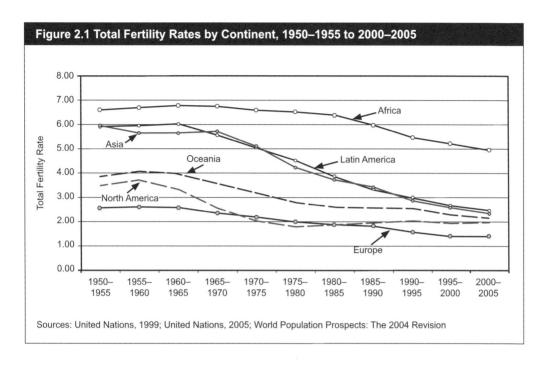

Figure 2.1 Total Fertility Rates by Continent, 1950–1955 to 2000–2005

Sources: United Nations, 1999; United Nations, 2005; World Population Prospects: The 2004 Revision

countries have converged with the levels of the "pioneer countries," which have been experiencing low fertility for quite some time. The experiences of Indonesia, Sri Lanka, and Thailand, which have already reached total fertility levels below 3.0, are somewhat similar. China's experience is especially noteworthy. Up to 1970, its fertility had been high, fluctuating around six births per woman, except during crisis periods. During the 1970s, China experienced an unprecedented fertility decline, and within a brief interval of just 10 years, its total fertility rate was reduced to less than half, reaching 2.3 in 1980. With the announcement of the one-child policy in 1979, China's fertility level was further reduced to 1.75 by 2000. It is important to note that China's case is not typical of other less industrialized countries because its fertility decline is primarily an outcome of the governmental effort to direct its population growth.

In India—another demographic giant—which is a subcontinent in itself and represents much of the diversity of South Asia, fertility decline has been rather slow despite its decades' old national family-planning program. However, levels in some of its provinces (e.g., Goa, Kerala, and Tamil Nadu) have already reached below the replacement level. In Bangladesh, despite its low economic development, the fertility rate was halved within less than 20 years from 6.7 in 1975–1980 to 3.25 in 2000–2005.

For a long time, Latin America and the Caribbean in general fell into the high-fertility zone. Over recent decades, fertility rates in some smaller countries (e.g., Cuba, Barbados, Trinidad and Tobago, Puerto Rico) have reached replacement level, whereas in some larger ones (e.g., Brazil, Mexico, Argentina, Venezuela, and Colombia), declines have been marked. Africa as a whole still belongs to the group where fertility has been declining slowly. Prominent among those with little fertility decline (with a total fertility rate of six or more) include Angola, Burundi, Chad, Congo, Ethiopia, Guinea-Bissau, Cameroon, Mali, Niger, Somalia, Uganda, and Sierra Leone. However, recently, major fertility declines have occurred in countries such as Botswana, Ghana, Kenya, South Africa, Swaziland, and Zimbabwe. Although both the desired number of children and actual fertility have been reduced substantially in some countries, it is likely that high infant mortality and lack of education, especially among women, stand as major obstacles to further fertility decline.

The effect of the high prevalence of HIV/AIDS on African fertility is not clear. It is generally known that sub-Saharan Africa has the highest adult prevalence of HIV in the world (8.8 percent in 2000), with Botswana (36 percent), Zimbabwe (25 percent), Swaziland (25 percent), Lesotho (24 percent), Zambia (20 percent) and South Africa (20 percent) as the worst-affected countries (Ntozi, 2002). The impact of HIV/AIDS on fertility could be serious, since it is the women in reproductive age groups who are affected most. A review of the literature prepared by Ntozi (2002) suggests that HIV infection induces sterility, increases fetal mortality, decreases frequency of intercourse, and consequently reduces the pregnancy rate and raises levels of induced abortion.

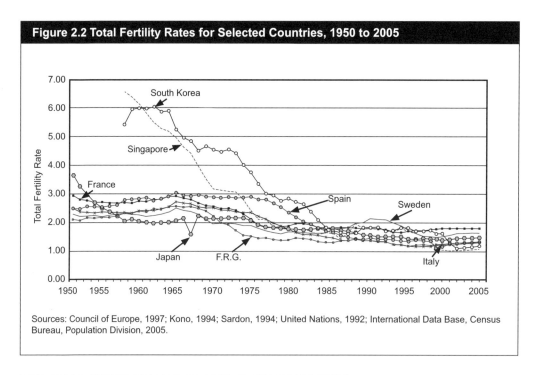

Figure 2.2 Total Fertility Rates for Selected Countries, 1950 to 2005

Sources: Council of Europe, 1997; Kono, 1994; Sardon, 1994; United Nations, 1992; International Data Base, Census Bureau, Population Division, 2005.

DELAYED CHILD-BEARING AND CHILDLESSNESS

In recent years, increasing proportions of women in industrialized countries are not only having a smaller number of children but they are having them—especially the first ones—later in life. In most countries, the age of motherhood has been rising since the 1970s, although the largest increase has taken place in recent years (Table 2.1). Studies show that the first-order birth rate, which is generally a demographic phenomenon of women in their twenties, has been increasing among women over the age of 30 since the early 1970s (Morgan, 1996; Ram, 2000). Delayed child-bearing is largely a function of delayed marriage patterns, although many people who delay getting married—at least in the West—may be living common-law, and therefore, they are not necessarily less exposed to sexual unions. However, studies show that people living in common-law unions are more likely to delay having children and not produce as many children as legally married couples because they are not as certain about their conjugal status.

Substantial delays in the initiation of motherhood have often been linked with ultimate childlessness (Morgan, 1991, 1996). Postponing child-bearing until the mid-thirties can have an adverse effect on the physiological potential of women to conceive. It is also likely that the longer a woman remains childless, the less inclined she will be to have a child. Either she gets involved in activities that are not compatible with having children or she gets used to living alone. Yet while in most industrialized countries the average age at first birth has increased markedly, the incidence of childlessness has increased only modestly (Morgan, 1996). Japan is a classic example where women start child-bearing at a much later age, but fewer remain permanently childless. In Canada, the United States, and Germany, which were all at the forefront of an increased acceptance of childlessness, the proportions of married women who never have any children by the near-end of their

Table 2.1 Mean Age of Women at Birth of First Child, Selected Countries: 1965 to 2001

Country	1965	1970	1975	1980	1985	1990	1992	1993	1994	1995	1996	2001
France	24.3	23.8	24.2	24.9	25.9	27.0	27.4	27.6	27.9			28.7
West Germany	24.9	24.3	24.8	25.2	26.2	26.9	27.3	27.6	27.9			28.0
Sweden			24.5	25.5	26.1	26.3	26.7	27.0	27.2	27.3	27.4	27.9
Norway		23.6	24.2	25.2	26.1	25.5	25.9	26.0	26.3	26.5	26.7	27.5
Denmark		23.7	24.0	24.6	25.5	26.4	26.9	27.2	27.3	27.5	27.5	27.1
United Kingdom	24.2	23.5	24.1	24.5	24.8	25.5	26.0	26.2	26.5	26.7	28.8	27.1
Switzerland		25.1	25.7	26.4	27.0	27.6	28.0	28.1	28.3	28.1	28.2	28.7
Italy	25.4	25.1	24.7	25.1	25.9	26.9	27.4	27.4	27.5	27.5	28.1	
Greece	25.4	24.0	23.6	23.3	23.7	24.7	25.4	25.9	26.1	26.4	26.4	27.3
Spain			25.4	24.6	25.4	26.5	27.2	27.8	28.1	28.4	28.5	29.0
Portugal		24.4	24.0	23.6	23.8	24.7	25.0	25.2	25.4	25.6	25.8	26.5
Czech Rep		22.5	22.5	22.4	22.4	22.5	22.5	22.6	22.9	23.3	23.6	25.3
Canada	23.0	23.1	23.8	24.6	25.5	26.3	26.6	26.7	26.8	26.9	27.1	29.9

Note: For France, West Germany, and Italy, figures shown for 1995 refer to 1994.

Sources: United Nations, 1992, 1998; Council of Europe, 1997; UNECE.ORG, 2005: Economic Commission for Europe: Demographic Database of the Population Activities Unit, Geneva, Switzerland.

reproductive lives is only slightly higher than for women of earlier cohorts. In Europe, the proportion of women who regard childlessness as ideal has basically remained unchanged over recent decades.

In less industrialized countries, the extent of voluntary childlessness is even smaller. World fertility surveys and demographic and health surveys indicate that almost all women in less developed countries would like to have a child. The proportions of women who had never had any children by the end of their reproductive lives have either remained unchanged or have declined in most countries (United Nations, 1998:68). The incidence of childlessness was usually less than 5 percent, which could well be the level of natural sterility in a population. Also, unlike in the West, there does not seem to be any rise in the proportions of couples who prefer to have only one child (United Nations, 1998).

FUTURE PROSPECTS

What then is to be expected in the future? In view of the sustained fertility declines, with levels as low as 1.5 children per woman in almost half of the countries in Europe, a continuation of below-replacement fertility is not an unrealistic situation. According to the low scenario of the most recent projections from the United Nations (2004), during the next 50 years the total fertility level could vary between 1.4 and 1.5 for more developed regions and as low as 1.2 to 1.3 for eastern and southern Europe. It is important to note, however, that predicting births beyond 25 to 30 years involves a high level of uncertainty. Having witnessed the post-World War II turnaround in fertility (i.e., the well-known baby boom that virtually no one forecasted), any projection of future fertility is somewhat risky as nobody can know for certain as to whether or not low fertility is to continue indefinitely into the future.

Having reached a very low level, fertility in a number of countries has already been showing some potential for rebounding in recent years. Between the early 1980s and the early 1990s, the total fertility rate rose from 1.61 to 2.13 in Sweden before falling back down to about 1.66 in the early 2000s. Over this same period, fertility rose from about 1.38 to 1.75 in Denmark, from 1.66 to 1.79 in Norway, from 1.63 to 1.79 in Finland, and from 1.42 to 1.79 in Luxembourg.

Predicting future fertility levels in less industrialized countries is even more presumptuous. High-fertility norms are rational responses to conditions of high mortality and kinship systems in predominantly agricultural economies. This is even more so the case in highly patriarchal societies (such as India, China, and South Korea) where the preference for a son is strong and couples will continue to have children until they have at least a few male offspring.

REDUCTIONS IN POPULATION GROWTH: PROSPECTS FOR POPULATION DECLINE

The most obvious result of fertility decline is the decrease in population growth, which could eventually lead to population decline. Currently most (but not all) populations in low-fertility countries are still growing. However, declines can be expected within the next few years, according to population projections prepared by the United Nations (2004).

The population of Europe, which was growing by about 1 percent annually during the mid-20th century, was growing at about .5 percent per annum during the last two decades of this century, and has reached very close to 0 percent population growth early into the 21st century. Over the next few decades, Europe's population is expected to witness negative growth. In contrast, the population of North America is expected to continue to grow at a rate about 0.80 percent between 2000 and 2025, and about 0.45 between 2025 and 2050. A large factor in explaining the continued growth in North America are higher rates of immigration, which currently makes up almost half of the United States' growth and over two-thirds of Canada's.

The prospect of population decline could be more serious for certain sub-national groups. The case of French Canada is worth mentioning in this context. The prospect for population decline in the province of Quebec, which is largely inhabited by a francophone population, has given rise to political resurgence in the province. Quebec's fertility level used to be the highest in Canada, but since the mid-1950s and especially after its so-called Quiet Revolution in the 1960s, fertility plummeted (Lachapelle, 1990). In spite of a number of pronatalist measures introduced by provincial governments, its fertility has remained low, hovering around 1.5–1.6 births per woman for about two decades. Many demographers and politicians fear that if the low fertility is sustained in the future, its population will start declining by 2016, which means a threat of survival to a culture unique in North America (McNeill, 1998:335; Teitelbaum and Winter, 1998:176).

DILEMMA OF IMMIGRATION SOLUTION

With sustained fertility decline in industrialized countries, the relative importance of natural increase (births – deaths) and immigration as components of population growth have shown a dramatic shift in recent years. Europe presents a classic example of this scenario, where international migration accounted for 27 percent of the total population increase during 1985–1990, and virtually all growth by 1995–2000 (United Nations, 2004). Italy shifted from a country of high fertility and emigration to a country of low fertility and a total reliance on immigration to maintain growth (primarily return migration). In the Federal Republic of Germany, natural increase and international migration each accounted for about half of the total population increase in 1960; by 1990, international migration accounted for virtually all of it. Canada, which in the industrialized world stands only next to Australia in terms of percentage born abroad (18 percent in 2001), registered a similar trend. In spite of its volatile economic conditions and sometimes unfavourable public opinion, Canada has been receiving a substantial number of immigrants to maintain its population growth at about 1 percent annually. Between 1961–1966, international migration accounted for just 15 percent of the population growth; the share quickly rose to 30 percent in 1966–1971 and to 38 percent in 1971–1976. In recent years, the contribution of immigration has risen to about 70 percent of the population growth.

Although from time to time many countries have introduced pronatalist policies to increase population growth, they have not been successful in the long run. The experiences of European countries suggest that pronatalist measures such as family allowance, financially compensated maternity leaves, shorter and flexible working hours for women with young children, and the like have a small but only temporary effect on fertility (McIntosh, 1981; United Nations, 1992:72–73). Studies show that these incentives are either not enough to cover the additional cost of a child, or they are ineffective in stimulating fertility (Keyfitz, 1986).

Increased immigration has often been suggested as a viable means of offsetting the tendency for a low-fertility population to shrink (Espenshade, 1986:259), although intellectuals and popular opinion have not always favoured this option. According to a most recent compilation of global population policies by the United Nations (1999), lower population growth does not seem to be a grave concern to many governments; most view their current levels of population growth to be satisfactory and do not see a need for intervention to modify growth. Also, most governments want to maintain immigration, while others, including Denmark, the U.K., Austria, France, Germany, Switzerland, Greece, and Portugal, want to reduce immigration. Only a few governments see the need of increased immigration as a means of achieving their demographic stability.

The findings of Prinz and Lutz's (1993) simulation for 20 large member states of the Council of Europe are highly suggestive of the increased need of immigration for stabilizing population growth. They showed that with a total fertility rate of 1.3 births per woman (to be reached by 2015), a low rise in life expectancy, and no immigration, Europe's total population size could be reduced from 450 million in 1990 to only 340 million in 2050. As shown in Table 2.2, under this extreme scenario, the population size of countries such as Austria, Belgium, Bulgaria, Germany, Italy, and Hungary would be reduced by about 30 percent over a 60-year period. Interestingly, even if fertility was to remain at 1.7 births per woman and net immigration was to be constant at half a million, the population of a number of countries would either decline or would barely increase.

Statistics Canada has also produced similar population projections for Canada. Four scenarios are presented in Table 2.3. The first scenario assumes a constant total fertility rate at 1.5 births per woman throughout the projection period (1998–2051), an immigration of 210,000 per year during that period, and a slightly rising volume of emigration from 64,000 in 1998 to 75,000 in 2051. The remaining three scenarios assume the net international migration to be absent during the projection period, while assuming varied fertility rates. In one case, the total fertility is assumed to remain constant at 1.5, whereas in the other it is assumed to increase linearly to 1.8 in 2051; in the last scenario the fertility rate is assumed to decline linearly to 1.3 in 2051. In all these four scenarios, between 1998 and 2051 the life expectancy at birth is assumed to increase from 76 years in 1998 to 80 years in 2051 for males and from 81 years to 84 years for females.

As indicated in Table 2.3, unless Canada receives a substantial amount of immigration, its population will ultimately decline. If the total fertility rate remained constant at 1.5 births per woman during the projection period, and there was a net annual international migration in the tune of about 150,000, the population is likely to rise from 30.3 million today to 36.6 million in 2041 and start declining thereafter. However, if Canada had to experience a zero net migration, its population could start declining as early as 2031, and could be reduced to just 25.8 million by 2051. According to the extreme scenario with declining fertility and zero net migration, the population could be reduced further to

Table 2.2 Population Size (in Millions) for Twenty European Countries, 1990 and 2050

Country	Population in 1990	Projected Population in 2050		Percentage Change	
		Scenario 0	Scenario 1	Scenario 0	Scenario 1
All Countries	448.9	467.7	342.1	4.2	-23.8
Austria	7.6	7.6	5.4	0.0	-28.9
Belgium	9.9	9.7	7.1	-2.0	-28.3
Bulgaria	9.0	8.0	6.3	-11.1	-30.0
Czechoslovakia	15.7	15.8	12.5	0.6	-20.4
Denmark	5.1	5.1	3.7	0.0	-27.5
Finland	5.0	5.1	3.8	2.0	-24.0
France	56.7	65.2	47.6	15.0	-16.0
Germany	78.0	78.8	53.8	1.0	-31.0
Greece	10.2	10.5	7.5	2.9	-26.5
Hungary	10.6	9.0	7.0	-15.1	-34.0
Iceland	3.7	5.2	4.0	40.5	8.1
Italy	57.7	55.9	40.4	-3.1	-30.0
Netherlands	14.9	16.4	11.7	10.1	-21.5
Norway	4.2	4.8	3.5	14.3	-16.7
Poland	38.4	41.3	32.8	7.6	-14.6
Portugal	9.9	11.6	8.4	17.2	-15.2
Spain	39.3	39.4	29.6	0.3	-24.7
Sweden	8.5	9.4	6.7	10.6	-21.2
Switzerland	6.6	7.4	4.9	12.1	-25.8
U.K.	57.3	61.3	45.4	7.0	-20.8

Note: Scenario '0' assumes a total fertility rate of 1.7 to be reached in year 2015; an increase in the life expectancy by 2 years per decade until it reaches 83.5 years for males and 89.0 years for females; and 0.5 million immigrants annually to be reached in year 2000. Scenario '1' assumes a total fertility rate of 1.3 to be reached in year 2015; an increase in the life expectancy by 2 years per decade until it reaches 77.0 years for males and 83.0 years for females; and zero immigration.

Source: Prinz and Lutz (1993).

24.2 million in 2051. During this period, even if the total fertility rate were to rise to 1.8, the population in 2031 could be lower than what it is today, and by 2051 could be as low as 28.7 million.

Generally, large-scale immigration is not viewed "as a politically viable response to declining population" in many industrialized countries (Teitelbaum and Winter, 1985:150). One of the major reasons for this is the fact that most immigrants in these countries originate from high-fertility countries, located primarily in non-Western regions. European countries are less likely to contribute to migration because they themselves are experiencing

Table 2.3 Projected Population (in Millions) for Canada Under Four Alternate Scenarios, 1998–2051

	1998	2001	2011	2021	2031	2041	2051
1. Medium Fertility and Net International Migration (TFR = 1.5; Immigrants = 210,000; Emigrants = 75,000)							
	30.28	31.03	33.27	35.14	36.31	36.65	36.53
2. Medium Fertility (TFR in 2051 = 1.5; Zero net international migration)							
	30.28	30.56	30.97	30.85	29.92	28.08	25.82
3. High Fertility (TFR in 2051 = 1.8; Zero net international migration)							
	30.28	30.59	31.32	31.66	31.27	30.12	28.65
4. Low Fertility (TFR in 2051 = 1.3; Zero net international migration)							
	30.28	30.56	30.81	30.40	29.14	26.92	24.22

Source: Author's calculations using Statistics Canada's 1998-based Population Projections.

low fertility and declining population growth. Italy presents a classic example; it used to be a high-emigration country, but it is facing its own population stagnation because of sustained low fertility. Canada, the United States, and Australia, which are largely inhabited by immigrant populations born in Europe, have been experiencing a decline in the European share of new admissions in recent years, whereas the share of immigrants originating from developing regions, particularly from Asia, has substantially increased. Between 1975–1979 and 1990–1994, for instance, the proportion of immigrant admissions of Asian origin rose from 38 percent to 42 percent in the United States, from 32 percent to 55 percent in Canada, and from 33 percent to 51 percent in Australia. Since the latter 1990s, the proportion of immigrants of Asian origin has declined slightly in Canada, down to 48.6 percent in 2004 (Citizenship and Immigration Canada, 2005).

In many receiving countries, there has been some anxiety and hostility toward immigrants of non-European origin, especially because they bring with them a culture alien to the native population. According to the Leger Marketing Survey conducted in 2002, 54 percent of Canadians believed that Canada accepted too many immigrants. In Germany, there is a fear that if ethnic differentials in fertility were to remain unchanged, with German fertility far below replacement and Turkish fertility far above, the country would become predominantly Turkish in the not too distant future (McNeill, 1998:332). Japan, which faces a possible population decline within the next decade, remains xenophobic (Martin 1991:528) with negligible immigration. In Singapore, one of the lowest fertility countries in the East, the government has been enthusiastic about increasing immigration, but that has caused concerns among Malays and Indians, who form a minority. In the late 1980s, Singapore's decision to grant permanent residency status to some 100,000 people from Hong Kong within a short duration was interpreted as a move to increase the Chinese majority (Martin, 1991).

Anxiety and hostility toward immigration from non-Western countries is also associated with a high degree of residential concentration of ethnic minorities. Due to various historical, cultural, and economic factors, members of certain ethnic and immigrant groups, despite economic pushes at the places where they initially settled and economic pulls from other areas, tend to congregate in a few large metropolitan areas that are heavily populated by their ethnic predecessors. In most receiving countries, there have been, from time to time, hostile expressions and outbreaks of violence against these communities. Some well-known examples of such hostility include those against Turks in Germany, Algerians in France, Pakistanis and West Indians in Great Britain, and (East) Indians and Somalis in Canada.

CHANGES IN AGE STRUCTURE

Changes in fertility patterns are clearly reflected in the age distribution of populations. The impact of current fertility declines will have an impact on the number of new admissions in primary schools about five years from now, on new entrants to the labour force about 18 to 20 years later, and so on. In 1950, about 27.0 percent of the population in the industrialized world was below age 15; this was reduced to 18.2 percent in 2000. As a consequence of sustained fertility declines, this proportion could be reduced to just 15.2 percent in 2050. The corresponding percentage in Europe has already reached this level. Low-fertility countries will also see marked reductions in the working-age population. Europe's population between the age group 15 to 64, for instance, could decline from 67.8 percent now to 58.0 percent in 2050. These trends imply that populations in low-fertility countries are aging, which is bound to exert large effects not only on the working-age population, but on society overall.

GREYING OF THE INDUSTRIALIZED WORLD

It is well established that in its initial stages, population aging results primarily from fertility decline, although at later stages, mortality reduction at older ages can also be important. Aging is not a new phenomenon in countries where fertility has been below replacement for some time. According to certain observers, it has reached an alarming stage, especially due to the extension of life expectancy among the elderly. As Peterson (1999) predicts, global aging will likely become the transcendental political and economic issue of the 21st century, which will call for a global solution.

All major regions of the world except Africa are growing older. Between 1965 and 2005, the median age of the world's population increased by 5.6 years, from 22.5 years to 28.1 years. In North America, the increase was 8.2 years, from 28.1 to 36.3 years, while in Europe, the median age rose even further, from 31.1 to 39.0. There is a clear relationship between low fertility and the intensity of aging; in countries that are among the world's "oldest," fertility rates have been significantly below replacement for quite some time. In Germany, for instance, the median age rose from 34.4 years in 1965 to 42.1 years in 2005; in France, from 32.7 to 39.3 years; and in Sweden, from 36.2 to 40.1 years.

The aging process has been accelerated in countries that experienced large fertility declines in a much shorter time span. Thus, between 1965 and 2005, the median age rose from 27.3 to 42.9 years in Japan, from 30.7 to 39.7 years in Greece, and from 30.1 to 38.6 years in Spain. It is important to note, however, that even if fertility were to increase moderately, the aging process is not likely to be modified significantly (Martin, 1989). A simulation performed on Canadian data revealed that fertility would have to increase from less than two births to four or five births per woman over the next 25 years in order to cancel out the aging of population (George, Nault, and Romaniuc, 1991). In view of the increasing proportions of the elderly in the industrialized world living into their eighties and nineties, the process of aging is expected to intensify in the future. The extremes are expected to occur in several European countries, with Italy, Greece, and Spain taking the lead position, where within the next 50 years, the median age could rise beyond 50 years and about a third of the population could be 65 years and over.

Following rapid fertility declines, many less industrialized countries are also aging rapidly. The most dramatic changes have occurred in eastern Asia, especially Singapore and Hong Kong, where the median age jumped from less than 20 years in 1965 to well beyond 35 years in 2005. China, Thailand, North Korea, South Korea, and Sri Lanka are also fast approaching these countries, although because their fertility declines are so recent, their aging process is still at a very early stage. This acceleration of the aging process in these countries could "require qualitatively different responses from those observed in Western countries" (Jones, 1993:275).

These trends are bound to profoundly influence the social fabrics of the industrialized world, although much depends on the socio-economic conditions of the elderly themselves. For example, it is not certain what social security provisions are going to be available to them, how financially well-off they are going to be, how much further life expectancy of older people may rise, and how much of it will be in a healthy and active state. Equally uncertain are the impacts of medical and technological advances in the areas of genetics, cancer vaccines, and the like (Wilmoth, 1998).

INTERGENERATIONAL SUPPORT

Longer life expectancy has increased multigenerational ties, which by implication means that potential supporters (i.e., those in their forties and fifties) are "sandwiched" between the responsibilities for their own late-born (although fewer) children and those of their elderly parents and perhaps grandparents. In 1950, for every elderly person aged 65–79, there were 2.18 people aged 45–54 (potential supporters) at the world level. This so-called "generational support ratio" declined to 1.63 by the year 1990. By 2050, this ratio could dwindle down to as low as 1.0 (or even lower to the extent that future fertility rates decline). This pattern is likely to be most pronounced in regions that have experienced large declines in fertility and old-age mortality. In Europe, for instance, where the generational support ratio has been hovering around 1.20 over the past three decades, this ratio is very likely to drop well below 1.0 over the next 50 years.

Many older people in industrialized countries are financially well-off due to both their own independent savings as well as social security provisions available to them from the state. However, the traditional emotional and day-to-day support that older people receive from family members, children, grandchildren, and other relatives may be missing. Moreover, people who provide support to the elderly are getting old themselves. As the aforementioned generational support ratio declines further, Western societies will have to face the challenge of the increased loneliness of the oldest-old, most of whom will be elderly widows.

In many low-fertility countries in non-Western regions, the situation is quite different, especially in light of the fact that fertility decline and population aging have been more recent. In many agricultural societies, throughout Asia in particular, the family is the main source of economic and social support to the elderly, who generally live and work with their children. In South Korea, which has experienced large fertility declines in recent years, more than two-thirds of the elderly population are dependent on family members for most of their living costs, while less than one-fifth earn incomes through their work (Lee and Palloni, 1992). Even in Japan, the proportion of older persons co-residing with their children is still higher (65 percent compared to 4 percent in Denmark), and a substantial majority want to be cared for by family members and find it best for older and younger generations to live together (Martin, 1989; UN, 1994: 3–4). This is clearly a very different situation from North America and throughout most of Europe.

CONCLUSION

Over the past several decades, fertility has declined almost everywhere in the world except in a few African countries. However, there are marked variations between countries in terms of the pace of decline, while some low-fertility countries have been showing signs of stabilization. Two dominant themes emerge from the analysis of this global transition.

First, parenthood remains an essential element in the lives of most people, although increasing proportions of them desire and are having much smaller families. It is highly likely that on average, fertility will not be reduced below one child per couple in most industrialized societies, whereas it may very well be reduced to around the replacement level in less industrialized societies over the next half century. Secondly, as a result of this shift to low fertility, many nations currently face rapid population aging and the prospect of declining growth (and even negative growth rates).

A future of low fertility or possibly further fertility decline implies that there will be an increased need in industrialized societies for workers from high-fertility countries, originating primarily from non-Western cultures. Industrialized countries will be competing among themselves to attract immigrants who could easily assimilate and integrate into the society and economy of the host country. In this context, many immigrant groups may face hostility, suggesting that a major policy challenge facing low-fertility countries will be how to stabilize their populations through immigration while successfully integrating newcomers without social and ethnic conflict.

● ●

CRITICAL THINKING QUESTIONS

1. UN projections suggest that the world's population could very well reach 8–9 billion people before stabilizing sometime in the 21st century. Do you consider this problematic?
2. While we can anticipate continued population growth on a global scale, many of the most affluent industrialized nations face the prospect of population implosion. Why has this occurred, and what do you think are some of the longer-term implications of this?
3. The fact that Canada has below-replacement fertility has important consequences. What are some of these consequences, and do you think that there is anything that governments can do (or should do) about this situation?

● ●

CHAPTER 3

THE NORTHERN AMERICA FERTILITY DIVIDE

Barbara Boyle Torrey and Nicholas Eberstadt

● ●

CANADA AND THE U.S. ARE MORE SIMILAR TO EACH OTHER than any two other large countries on the planet today. We share a language, a continent, and a colonial history. Our two affluent and resource-rich countries, moreover, have forged the largest trading bond in the modern world. Since the implementation of NAFTA in 1993, of course, the volume of U.S.–Canadian trade has steadily increased; this economic integration is drawing the two economies ever closer.

Yet for all their similarities—and the unfolding forces pressing for still greater homogenization—Canada and the United States are remarkably distinct from one another. In recent years, government policies in these two similar countries have diverged recurrently and conspicuously on a number of issues: Think of Iraq, missile defence, lumber, gay marriage, and marijuana. And these highly visible differences may not be the biggest ones. A quiet and as yet largely unrecognized divergence may be even more fundamental. Its indicators are found in the relatively new but steadily increasing differentiation of demographic trends in North America.

Twenty-five years ago, the population profiles of Canada and the United States were similar. Both were younger than their European allies, and their societies were more heterogeneous. In 1980, their populations had almost the same median age, fertility rates, and immigration rates. In the years since then, small changes in demographic variables have accumulated, ultimately creating two very different countries in North America by the end of the 20th century.

Canadians now have half a child fewer than Americans during their lifetimes—their fertility level is roughly 25 percent lower than that of their neighbours south of the border—and they are living two years longer. Both populations are growing at about the same rate, but the components of growth have diverged. Immigration is relatively more important in Canada's growth rate, and fertility is more important in the United States'.

Canadians marry later and less often than Americans. They enter common-law unions more often and their children are increasingly likely to be born out of wedlock. Canadians and Americans have similar labour force participation rates, but Americans work more hours per year. They have higher incomes but less leisure. And even though Canada's birth rate is now substantially lower than America's, the Canadian government provides more child services and benefits than the U.S. government.

Changes in patterns of marriage and fertility are the accumulated outcomes of millions of personal decisions by men and women. When couples, one at a time, make decisions that differ in aggregate from the couples in a neighbouring country, it is a reflection of deliberate agency rather than mere chance. That's why the still-widening demographic gap that has opened up between Canada and the U.S. says even more about the two societies and their futures than public or policy differences on any single issue. It also demonstrates that macroeconomic integration since NAFTA may not have had a homogenizing effect at a household level. This exploration should make Canadians who fear becoming too much like the U.S. a bit less fearful.

WHY FERTILITY MAY CHANGE

One of the most important and interesting debates in demography today centres on the decline in fertility in developed countries. When the decline in total fertility rates begins and when it stops is of importance not only to demographers but also to societies. Age structure changes that are caused by declining fertility have far-reaching ripple effects: They touch on all age-specific activities and programs throughout society.

Over the past generation, child-bearing patterns in nearly all developed countries have changed significantly, falling to levels that (if continued indefinitely in the absence of immigration) would presage a steady shrinking of successive generations. This shift to markedly sub-replacement fertility patterns (and the accompanying changes in marital patterns) has been dubbed "the second demographic transition" by demographers (Lesthaeghe, 1991). This "transition," however, constitutes a set of facts in search of a theory—the reasons for this dramatic demographic shift remain to be explained.

There are competing explanations in the fertility debates. The Family Economics hypothesis focuses on the changing value of women's time due to their labour force participation (Butz and Ward, 1979). It suggests that the opportunity cost of having children increases directly with women's education and income. According to this theory, fertility will be likely to fall as women become better educated and more employable, at least up to the point at which women's incomes become larger than their partners'. Beyond that point, the theory predicts, further increases in women's economic opportunity would become positively related to fertility.

The Relative Income hypothesis suggests that large birth cohorts will have more trouble reaching their expected income goals than smaller cohorts (Easterlin, 1978). For relatively large birth cohorts, the theory conjectures that female labour force participation rates would rise and fertility rates would fall as women try to reach their income goals. A modification of this hypothesis suggests that women's participation in the labour force depends on how close males' wages are to their joint expectations: Females' wages would have either a net positive income effect on their future fertility or a net negative opportunity cost effect depending on their role in fulfilling the couple's income expectations (Macunovich, 2002).

The Role Incomparability hypothesis posits that the ability of women to combine childbirth and work is a strong determinant of how many children they will eventually have (Brewster and Rindfruss, 2000). Government policies, such as child-care provisions, child-friendly labour practices, and child benefits, are important in explaining fertility trends in specific countries. In addition to the hypotheses above, some researchers believe that a significant factor in fertility rates may be cultural values, such as religion.

The various hypotheses about why total fertility rates change are not necessarily incompatible. All of the factors they suggest may be important, and their importance may vary over the life cycle of an individual or cohort. Family formation is a complex social phenomenon that has no single determinant or simple explanation. Comparing the fertility in two societies increases the complexity of the analysis. But following the question of why fertility differs between neighbours can be revealing of fundamental differences that may be unacknowledged and of erstwhile similarities that have been forgotten.

CANADIAN AND U.S. FERTILITY DIVERGENCE

Canadians have 25 percent fewer children than Americans today, though historically they have had more children. In 1945 Canadian women had a half child more than American women (a total fertility rate of 3.0 vs. 2.5). And the fertility rate in Quebec was even higher than the Canadian average. Each country had a major baby boom after World War II, but Canada's boom was louder. Both booms peaked in 1959 and then declined. By 1966 the total fertility rates in both countries were equal (2.7), and they declined together to about 1.8 children in 1978. In the late 1970s, the fertility rates began to diverge, with the Canadian rate sinking slowly to 1.49 in 2002 and the U.S. fertility rate increasing back up toward the replacement rate; it has remained slightly above 2.0 for almost a decade and a half (see Figure 3.1).

This slow but inexorable divergence over the past quarter-century can be accounted for by a number of factors (which are not additive; some categories overlap):

Americans have their babies earlier than Canadians. American teenagers have 1.5 times as many births as Canadian teenagers (52 per 1,000 vs. 20). This represents about one-third of the difference in fertility between the U.S. and Canada. Two-thirds of the difference is caused by earlier American births to women in their twenties. Minorities in the U.S. have higher fertility rates than the non-Hispanic White population, especially in the younger age groups. If all American women had the fertility rates of non-Hispanic White women, it would reduce the fertility divergence with Canada by 0.2 children. Geography also matters in heterogeneous countries. If the non-Hispanic White fertility rates in American border states and neighbouring Canadian provinces are compared, the divergence in the national fertility rates is reduced from 0.5 children per woman to 0.4 (0.38) children. That can explain about 20 percent of the difference in fertility, leaving 80 percent unexplained.

The important point to underscore in these disaggregations is not what they can explain about current differences in Canadian–U.S. fertility differences, but rather what they cannot. The closest "apples to apples" comparison across the Canadian–U.S. borders would be for the ethnic majority populations of the two nations. In the United States today, period

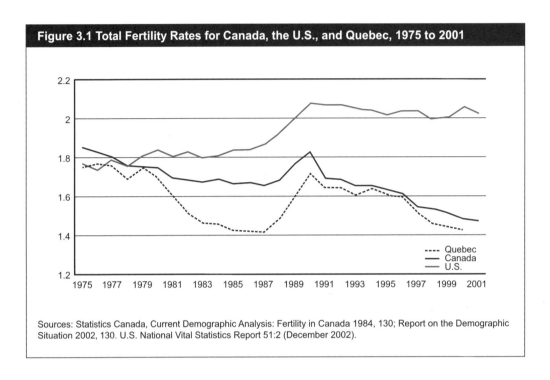

Figure 3.1 Total Fertility Rates for Canada, the U.S., and Quebec, 1975 to 2001

Sources: Statistics Canada, Current Demographic Analysis: Fertility in Canada 1984, 130; Report on the Demographic Situation 2002, 130. U.S. National Vital Statistics Report 51:2 (December 2002).

total fertility rates for the non-Hispanic White population are substantially higher than for their counterparts in Canada. That gap has steadily increased over the past generation, and by all indications it is continuing to increase. Disaggregating trends can't tell us why the differences among ages, ethnic groups, and geography exist, but they can point to subsequent questions to ask. In this case, the differences in the timing of births lead to follow-up questions about patterns of marriage, divorce, and other forms of unions.

MARRIAGE, DIVORCE, COMMON-LAW UNIONS

In 1975, both Canadians and Americans had relatively high rates of marriage. The Canadian rate of nine per 1,000 was 90 percent of the U.S. rate of 10 per 1,000. Crude marriage rates in Canada have declined 40 percent since 1975, while the U.S. rate has declined 15 percent. Consequently the Canadian marriage rate in 1999 is only 60 percent of the U.S. rate.

Historically, Canadians have married at older ages than Americans, and that difference has increased recently. The 3.9-year increase in age at first marriage for Canadian women since 1980 is higher than the 3.1-year increase for U.S. women. Not only do Canadian women get married later on average than American women, but they also wait longer to have their first child. In 1999, the age of a Canadian mother at her first birth was three years (2.9) older than the American mother. The increases in Canadian ages at first marriage and first births relative to the U.S. are consistent with a relative decrease in Canadian fertility. The U.S. increases in ages at first marriage and first birth seem at odds with the absolute increases in U.S. fertility since 1980.

Although Canadians enter marriage later than Americans, they have longer marriages because they divorce less often. The Canadian Divorce Act of 1968 for the first time provided "no-fault" divorce after a formal separation of three years. Two decades later, in 1986, the Divorce Act was amended to reduce the time of formal separation to a year. It also made divorce generally available in Quebec for the first time. Despite these changes in the divorce laws, Canadians still use this option only half as often as Americans. Of course, Americans, who marry earlier and divorce more often, have more time to have multiple marriages and divorces. This marital optimism of Americans tends to increase their rates of marriage and divorce.

One of the reasons that the marriage rate is declining and age of first marriage increasing in both countries is because of the increase in common-law unions, which grew from 6 percent of all couples in Canada in 1981 to 14 percent in 2001 (see Figure 3.2). Increases in common-law unions, however, are not compensating for the decreases in marriage among Canadians aged 20–29. The equivalent estimates of cohabitation for the United States are 3 percent and 9 percent. The majority of first unions in Canada are now common-law unions, as they are in the United States (in 1990–1994, 57 percent and 54 percent, respectively). "Common-law union" is an imprecise term and an imperfect statistic. In some surveys, it includes a union of either opposite-sex or same-sex partners; in other areas, it refers only to opposite-sex partners. In both Canadian and American censuses,

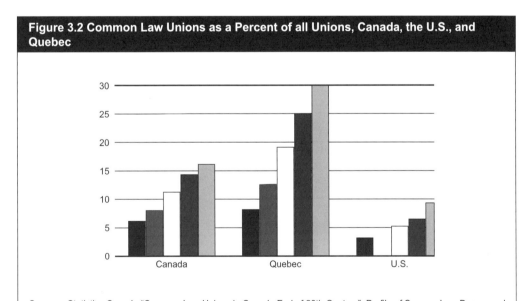

Figure 3.2 Common Law Unions as a Percent of all Unions, Canada, the U.S., and Quebec

Sources: Statistics Canada "Common Law Unions in Canada End of 20th Century"; Profile of Source: Jean Dumas and Alain Bélanger, "Common-Law Unions in Canada at the End of the 20th Century," Report on the Demographic Situation in Canada 1996, (Statistics Canada, March 1997). Larry Bumpass and Hsien-Hen Lu, "Trends in Cohabitation and Implications for Children's Family Contexts in the United States," Population Studies 54:1 (March 2000). Stephanie Ventura and Christine Bachrach, "Nonmarital Childbearing in the United States, 1940–99," National Vital Statistics Reports 48:16 (Centers for Disease Control and Prevention, October 18, 2000) Jason Fields and Lynne M. Casper, "America's Families and Living Arrangements: March 2000," Current Population Reports P-20-537 (U.S. Census Bureau, 2001).

common-law unions or cohabitation is self-defined (Bumpass and Raley, 1995). Because the definition of cohabitation or common-law marriages is still a term of art and a state of mind, international comparisons should be made with caution.

The kinds of women entering common-law unions are quite different in Canada and the U.S. In 1995, Canadian women whose first union was common-law were more likely to have been to university than to have dropped out of high school, although the differences were not statistically significant (Dumas and Bélanger, 1997). In the United States in 1995, American women who had ever cohabited were more likely not to have graduated from high school than to have had some college education. And the American women were as likely to be White as Black (45 percent); in Canada they were most likely to be francophone Québécois.

Among Canadians in the same age groups, common-law unions are almost twice as likely to dissolve as marriages (Le Bourdais et al., 2000). This may be one of the reasons that the fertility rate of women in common-law unions is much lower than in marriages. In the 1985–1994 period, the total fertility rate of Canadian women in common-law unions for their entire fertile years was 1.44, whereas it was over two children for those who were married.

One reason common-law unions may be more prevalent in Canada than in the U.S. is because they are legally recognized more explicitly there. The Income Tax Act of Canada treats a common-law union as a marriage if the parties have a child together or have lived

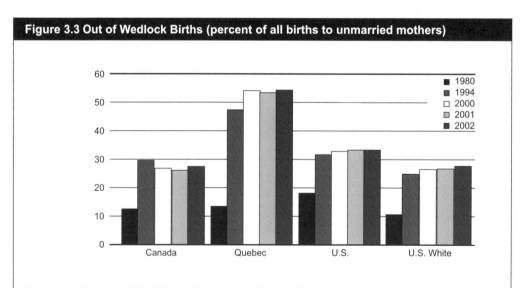

Figure 3.3 Out of Wedlock Births (percent of all births to unmarried mothers)

Sources: Jean Dumas and Alain Bélanger, "Common-Law Unions in Canada at the End of the 20th Century," Report on the Demographic Situation in Canada 1996, (Statistics Canada, March 1997). Larry Bumpass and Hsien-Hen Lu, "Trends in Cohabitation and Implications for Children's Family Contexts in the United States," *Population Studies* 54:1 (March 2000). Stephanie Ventura and Christine Bachrach, "Nonmarital Childbearing in the United States, 1940-99," *National Vital Statistics Reports* 48:16 (Centers for Disease Control and Prevention, October 18, 2000) Jason Fields and Lynne M. Casper, "America's Families and Living Arrangements: March 2000," *Current Population Reports* P-20-537 (U.S. Census Bureau, 2001). CANSIM2 Statcan.ca/cgi-win/Table102-4506.

together for at least one year. Canadian Pension Plan benefits pass on to the partner at death, though partners cannot share property unless it is jointly owned. In contrast, most U.S. states have abolished common-law marriage by statute. Ten states continue to have varying forms of recognition; five recognize such unions only if they began prior to a certain date. New Hampshire recognizes common-law unions for inheritance only.

Out-of-wedlock births, including those in common-law unions, have increased in both countries—i.e., the drop in total marital fertility rates has been offset to a degree by the total non-marital fertility rates. In Canada, the percentage of children born out of wedlock has grown from 13 in 1980 to 28 in 2002. The equivalent numbers for the United States are 18 and 34 (see Figure 3.3). In both countries, the increase since 1980 in out-of-wedlock births is largely because of the increasing number of births of common-law unions. And nearly all of that increase in the U.S. was among non-Hispanic White women. In Canada, however, the increase in out-of-wedlock births has not offset the decrease in births in wedlock.

OTHER FACTORS INFLUENCING FERTILITY
Research suggests several other possible influences that may help suggest why Canada and U.S. fertility rates have diverged: income and labour force trends, government programs and policies, and values and the role of religion.

INCOME AND LABOUR FORCE INFLUENCES
In both the New Family Economics and the Relative Income hypotheses, fertility is affected by income and women's labour force participation rate. At a macro level, gross national income in both countries has increased substantially since 1975. However, the national fertility rates went in opposite directions. Canada's national fertility rate declined as gross national income (GNI) grew and the U.S.'s national fertility rate increased (see Figures 3.4 and 3.5). This suggests that growth in national income will not be a discriminating factor in explaining the opposite fertility trends.

Women's labour force participation rates are also very similar in each country. Since 1980, women's civilian employment rates (16 years and older) in Canada and the United States started at just below 50 percent and climbed to 56–57 percent in 2001. Canadian women aged 15–24 were employed at slightly higher ratios than in the U.S. in 1990, but the U.S. rate was higher in 2000. The ratio of women's employment to the population 25–54 years old has been almost the same in both countries since 1983. The labour force participation rates for women with no children, one child, and two or more are also very similar to each other, differing by no more than three percentage points over the period. The number of women 16 and over who work part-time has also not changed much in either country as they remain within one percentage point.

Although the part-time labour force participation rates are similar between Canada and the United States for all ages, they differ for women in their child-bearing and child-caring years. Part-time employment is much more prevalent in Canada for women 25–54, and the percentage increases with the number of children they have (as it does in the U.S.). The increased prevalence of part-time work in Canada for women 25–54 might make it easier to juggle the roles of parent and worker.

Although labour force participation rates between the two countries are similar, since 1980, the economic uncertainties have not been. Canadian unemployment rates have been 50 percent to 75 percent higher than in the United States as officially reported and as adjusted for comparability (Sorrentino, 2000). Over the period 1973–1990, the adjusted

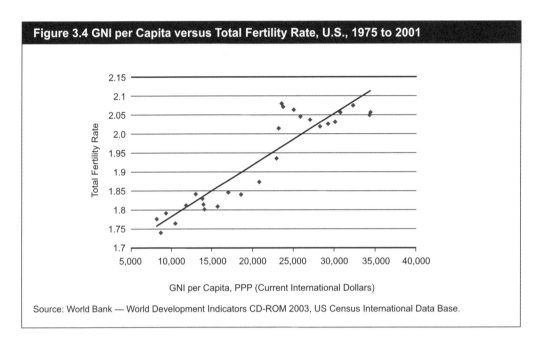

Figure 3.4 GNI per Capita versus Total Fertility Rate, U.S., 1975 to 2001

GNI per Capita, PPP (Current International Dollars)

Source: World Bank — World Development Indicators CD-ROM 2003, US Census International Data Base.

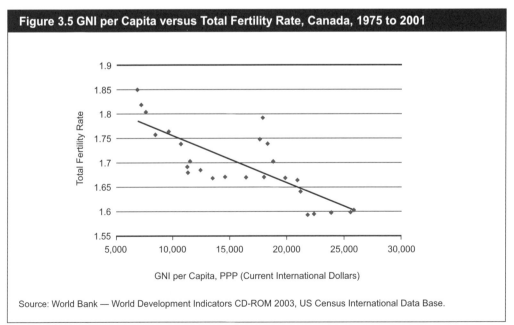

Figure 3.5 GNI per Capita versus Total Fertility Rate, Canada, 1975 to 2001

GNI per Capita, PPP (Current International Dollars)

Source: World Bank — World Development Indicators CD-ROM 2003, US Census International Data Base.

Canadian unemployment rates averaged 8.1 percent, while the rate was 6.9 percent in the U.S. Between 1990 and 2000, the average rates increased to 8.6 percent and 5.6 percent respectively. On the other hand, Canadian job stability (four-year retention rate) increased slightly between 1987 and 1995, while U.S. stability declined slightly (Heisz, 2002).

American women work more hours than Canadian women, partly because Canada has higher unemployment rates and higher part-time work rates. The difference in hours worked has increased from two weeks in 1979 to three weeks in 2000. In 2001, employed Americans, both men and women, worked 10 percent more hours than employed Canadians, and they were 10 percent more productive. Part of the reason Americans were more productive was because Canadians took twice as much vacation leave as Americans. The result of these and other factors was that Americans had 17 percent more real income per capita than Canadians in 2001 (Fortin, 2003).

The lower incomes of Canadians may have a positive effect on female labour force participation rates; it may also make Canadian women feel that they can't afford to have children as early as American women with higher household incomes. On the other hand, American women are working more hours than Canadians, which would make bearing and raising children in the U.S. more difficult, according to the Role Incompatibility hypothesis.

Another way that unmet income expectations could affect fertility is if they resulted in a lack of affordable housing for young people. The homeownership rates (including co-operative housing) by age of household head are slightly higher before 50 years of age in Canada than in the U.S; American homeownership rates of older household heads are higher than Canada's (Chiuri and Jappelli, 2000). The down payment ratio average from 1970 to 1995 was higher in Canada (23.3 percent) than in the U.S. (17 percent), and the Canadians cannot deduct their mortgage interest from their income tax as the U.S. homeowner can. (However, the U.S. tax deduction makes the owning of a U.S. home cheaper, and therefore may tend to bid up the price of U.S. homes, which at least partly offsets the tax benefit.) Homeownership rates in Canada and the U.S. are not different enough to appear to be a cause of the differences in their fertility.

Homeownership costs in Canada also do not seem to explain the variance in its total fertility rates. The Royal Bank of Canada's Housing Affordability Index is the percentage of pretax household income taken up by homeownership costs. The index for the last quarter of 2003 ranges from 26.8 percent in the Atlantic provinces to 42.9 percent in British Columbia. The provinces had the same fertility rate in 2001 (1.4). Housing affordability and fertility are uncorrelated both in 1990 and 2003, suggesting that homeownership costs are unrelated to the patterns of fertility within Canada as well as between Canada and the United States.

GOVERNMENT POLICIES ON CHILDREN

The lower household incomes in Canada compared with the United States could be partly offset by government policies. Public policies, such as cash benefits, services, or tax policy, may change income incentives for having children if they reduce the cost of raising them. In terms of the percentage of gross domestic product (GDP), the U.S. spent about

0.23 percent on family cash benefits in 1999. It had been twice that level in 1980, but had slowly declined to the 0.2 percent range by 1986 and had stayed there. It also provided another 0.28 percent of GDP in family services in 1999. The two forms of U.S. government programs combined were 0.51 percent of GDP. The equivalent numbers for Canada were 0.74 percent of GDP, provided in family cash benefits. (The last year of OECD data on Canadian family services was 1990, and it was then only 0.08 percent.) These data suggest that the Canadian government spends about 50 percent more of their GDP for their family benefits than the U.S. provides for benefits and services combined.

The Canadian government also provides a much more generous parental leave policy. Maternity leave of 15 weeks began in 1971; in 1990, 10 more weeks were added for either parent to claim. In 2000, parent leave benefits were increased again to 35 weeks of paid leave (up to 55 percent of prior weekly insurable earnings up to a maximum of $413 a week). The percentage of mothers taking between nine and 12 months of leave went from 8 percent in 2000 to 47 percent in 2001. Ten percent of fathers participated in parental leave in 2001, up from 3 percent the year before (Statistics Canada, 2003).

The generosity of the Canadian parental leave system stands in contrast to the American system. The U.S. 1993 Family Medical and Leave Act allows employees to take up to 12 weeks of unpaid leave a year for family or medical reasons. Canadian public policies are more generous in both cash benefits and in parental leave benefits than the U.S. system, which should make having children easier and encourage higher Canadian fertility. But larger Canadian government programs are not enough incentive to offset the decrease in total fertility rates, nor are the smaller U.S. government programs a disincentive to offset U.S increases in fertility.

VALUES AND RELIGION

The role of values in explaining social trends such as fertility is harder to quantify than personal income or government services. But changing values may still hold insights that the better-quantified variables cannot. A number of studies have documented differences in some core values between Canada and the United States. And other studies have shown how some values may be related to birth rates (Simmons, 1995).

One value that is correlated with fertility is the role of the man in the family. A recent survey asked people in Canada and the U.S. whether they agreed that "The father of the family must be master in his own house." The percentage of people agreeing with that statement was highly correlated with total fertility rates across Canadian provinces and U.S. regions in 2000. The lowest agreements were in the Canadian provinces, with the lowest being in Quebec, at 15 percent, and the highest being in Alberta, which was only six percentage points higher. All of the U.S. regions were higher than any of the Canadian provinces (Adams, 2003), and the variance among the U.S. regions was much higher than in Canada. The percentage of households surveyed in the South agreed with the statement more than twice as much as in New England.

Another value that is both measurable and germane to fertility is the importance of religion. People who are actively religious tend to marry more and stay together longer (Bélanger and Ouellet, 2002). To the extent that time spent married during reproductive years increases fertility, then religion would be a positive factor in fertility rates. For example, in Canada, women who had weekly religious attendance were 46 percent more likely to have a third child than women who did not (Bélanger and Oikawa, 1999).

Over time, several different nationally representative surveys have asked about church attendance in both Canada and the U.S. The World Value Survey, taken periodically in both countries, found that in 1981, 62 percent of Americans and 45 percent of Canadians attended church monthly. A decade later, American attendance had decreased by 6 percent, but Canadian attendance had fallen by 16 percent. Moreover, the number of people who rated the "importance of God in their lives" as 10 out of 10 was 48 percent for Americans and only 28 percent for Canadians. An index of religiosity based on the European Value Survey showed that the U.S. was considerably more religious than Canada in 1981, and by 1990, Canadian religiosity had decreased and the U.S. had increased. This happened at the same time that the number of people not attending church at all increased in both countries. Despite the drop in church attendance, women of child-bearing age were much more likely to have attended church weekly in the U.S. (34 percent) than in Canada (18 percent) in 1995. (And in Canada's three largest metropolitan areas, the foreign-born were much more likely to have attended religious services at least once a month than the Canadian-born.)

Religiosity, as defined by importance of God and church attendance, is also significant for fertility because it is the most powerful predictor of attitudes toward abortions. In 1980, the World Value Survey found 42 percent of Americans and 38 percent of Canadians responding that abortion "can never be justified." Ten years later, that percentage had dropped to 33 and 21 respectively. This represented a 20 percent drop in the U.S., but a 46 percent drop in Canada. The larger value change in the acceptance of abortion in Canada has been correlated with a significant increase in Canadian abortions since 1980, at a time when the U.S. abortions were declining (see Figure 3.6).

The change with respect to abortions arises partly from the change in the legal climates of the U.S. and Canada. Abortions were outlawed in both countries for most of the 20th century. In 1969, Canada passed a law making therapeutic abortions possible if approved by a committee of doctors; similar conditions prevailed in the U.S. In 1973, abortions for any purpose were legalized in the U.S. In 1988, the Canadian law that allowed abortions only for therapeutic reasons was declared unconstitutional. Therefore, Canadian and American women had the same legal protection for abortions by the late 1980s, but they responded differently. The Canadian abortion rate began to rise and the American rate, which had always been higher than Canada's, and had been at 0.8 abortions per woman for 20 years, began to fall.

The total abortion rate is an estimate of how many abortions a woman is likely to have over her reproductive life. It is, in concept and in calculation, consistent with the total fertility rate. In both cases, the event (either a birth or an abortion) is calculated for each five-year age group of reproductive-age women, and aggregated for a particular year to estimate how many "events" a woman would have over her reproductive life if she followed the age-specific patterns of current cohorts. Because the concepts and the estimate of the total fertility rate and the total abortion rate are consistent, it is possible

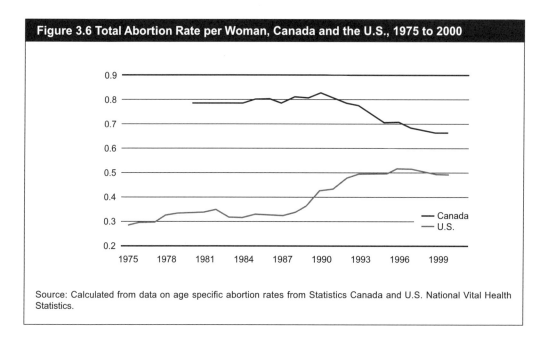

Figure 3.6 Total Abortion Rate per Woman, Canada and the U.S., 1975 to 2000

Source: Calculated from data on age specific abortion rates from Statistics Canada and U.S. National Vital Health Statistics.

to estimate how much the total abortion rates per woman are affecting the total fertility rate per woman.

Since 1975, abortions per Canadian woman have increased from 0.3 to 0.5. This was at the same time that abortions per American woman decreased from 0.8 to 0.7. Therefore the trend in abortions is converging while the total fertility rate trend is diverging. If the total abortion rates per woman in both countries had not changed, the divergence in fertility would be 60 percent lower than it was in 2000 (see Figure 3.7). The rise in the Canadian total abortion rate would explain 35 percent of the divergence by itself. The drop in the U.S. total abortion rate per woman is not unambiguously related to the increase in American fertility over that time, as the reduction may have been because of fewer unwanted pregnancies. (U.S. pregnancy rates dropped 7 percent over the same time.) However, the increase in the Canadian total abortion rate *is* unambiguously related to the decline in total fertility rate.

These data cannot indicate whether the increase in Canadian abortions is the result of changes in values or other conditions, such as the legal or economic context. What it does suggest, however, is that the change in the total abortion rate per woman and the change in values it may represent are important in explaining between 35 and 60 percent of the divergence in the total fertility rate between Canada and the United States.

IMPLICATIONS OF DIVERGING FERTILITY

In summary, there are clues to why there is such a divergence in fertility between Canada and the U.S., but there are no definitive answers. The levels of Canadian and American long-term trends in age of first marriage, first births, and common-law unions are consistent with the divergence in total fertility rates in the two countries, but the

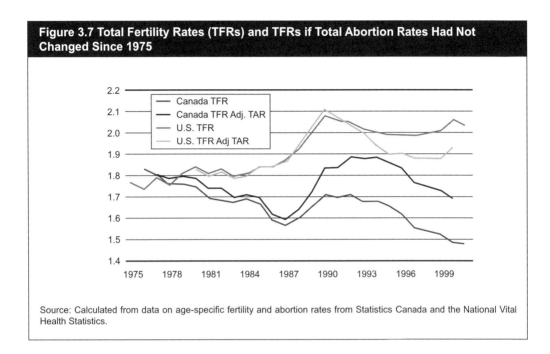

Figure 3.7 Total Fertility Rates (TFRs) and TFRs if Total Abortion Rates Had Not Changed Since 1975

Source: Calculated from data on age-specific fertility and abortion rates from Statistics Canada and the National Vital Health Statistics.

divergence in none of these proximate variables is large enough to explain the much larger divergence in fertility. Higher unemployment rates and lower incomes in Canada may also be consistent with lower fertility rates in Canada than in the U.S. But the more generous cash and maternity benefits in Canada would tend to offset some of the U.S. economic advantage. And the longer working hours in the U.S. for women are inconsistent with their increase in fertility since 1980, according to the role incompatibility hypothesis.

Finally, changing values in the U.S. and Canada may be contributing to the fertility divergence. The stronger notional role of men in U.S. families and the greater religiosity of Americans are positively associated with fertility, and the latter is also a strong predictor of negative attitudes toward abortion. Increased total abortion rates per woman in Canada may be the result of changes in values, which are also reflected in the changes in the Canadian legal context. An increase in Canadian abortions can explain 35 percent of the fertility divergence with the U.S. The decline in the U.S. abortion rate combined with the Canadian increase would explain more.

The divergence in fertility may continue to increase in the near future. But once the delay in age of fertility in both countries stops, as it inevitably will, then there may be a slight increase in fertility, at least in Canada, because of what is described as the tempo effect (Bongaarts and Feeney, 1998). This is because the calculation of the total fertility rate does not accurately reflect the outcomes of delays in births, and therefore underestimates fertility while the transition to births at later ages is in process.

What declining fertility does do in societies such as Canada's is make them age more rapidly. Canada is becoming an older country than the U.S. because Canadians have fewer children and live two years longer. In 2000, the median age in Canada was 36.9; in the

U.S. it was 35.2. But in 25 years, the difference will be larger, at 43.5 vs. 39.0 (U.S. Census Bureau, 2005). That means that Canada will have an older labour force and relatively more people 65 and over. In 2000, 12 percent of the Canadian and American populations were 65 years old or older (12.7 vs. 12.4). But in 25 years, there will be an increasing divergence (22.9 percent vs. 19.6 percent in 2030). The aged dependency burdens will be higher, but the total dependency burdens will not. The aging population will put more pressure on the Canadian health care system than on the U.S. system. But the higher fertility rates in the U.S. will put continuing pressure on school systems, especially since school-age children are becoming increasingly diverse ethnically.

As countries age at different rates, the financial flows between them may be affected (Canton et al., 2004). An aging society is likely to save more, both privately and through pension funds, and therefore have more to invest. Younger countries with lower savings rates may offer better rates of return. But there is no evidence of this kind of movement yet in developed countries. And between Canada and the U.S. there is already so much cross-investment that the aging differential may have only a marginal effect.

Ultimately, the differences in fertility rates between Canada and the United States may say less about the future than they say about the present. The societies of these two countries are becoming different at the same time as their economies integrate and become more interdependent. The basic rhythms of private lives are diverging as women in Canada enter common-law unions more often, wait longer than American women to marry, and have children later and less often. Abortion is the one demographic trend that is converging, but this accentuates the underlying difference in fertility rather than reducing it.

Many people worry that as the world becomes more economically integrated, it will produce a homogenized culture with similar values and social behaviour. This concern is even greater in North America, where the U.S. economy and population are much larger than those of Canada. The divergence in fertility, however, suggests an alternative. It raises the possibility that economic integration in North America may not necessarily result in a homogenized culture with similar values and behaviour. Fertility is a leading indicator of other changes taking place in society. If the North American fertility divergence continues, it may become an example of how countries can converge at the macroeconomic level while diverging at the micro level of individuals and families.

● ●

CRITICAL THINKING QUESTIONS

1. How does the demographic behaviour of Americans and Canadians differ, particularly in terms of their fertility and family life?
2. Of the various hypotheses mentioned by Torrey and Eberstadt in explaining the North American fertility divide, which holds greatest weight, in your opinion, in explanation?
3. It has been argued that as the world becomes more economically integrated, a homogenized culture with similar values and behaviour is the result. Do you feel that this argument applies well in explaining family life and fertility behaviour in the North American context? Why or why not?

● ●

CHAPTER 4

WOMEN, PRIESTS, AND PHYSICIANS:
FAMILY LIMITATION IN QUEBEC, 1940–1970

Diane Gervais and Danielle Gauvreau

● ●

IN THE PROVINCE OF QUEBEC, the fertility transition occurred relatively late and at a much slower pace than in most industrialized countries. Only after 1920 did marital fertility reach levels usually associated with widespread contraception. This is not to say that contraception was not practised earlier, it is just that it was limited to a small portion of the population using relatively ineffective methods. The cohort data in Table 4.1 shows a slow decline in family size, beginning with women born in the last quarter of the 19th century. This trend became more pronounced for women born in the early 1900s, with a decline in fertility during the 1920s and 1930s. The Great Depression had an additional downward effect on fertility, whereas World War II and the economic expansion of the postwar period helped to maintain higher marital fertility. Nevertheless, even as the baby boom was occurring across many industrialized countries, married women in Quebec were having fewer children than their mothers or grandmothers. While fertility was still high compared with other Canadian provinces, this was about to change dramatically (Beaujot, 2000; McInnis, 2000).

FOCUS OF THE STUDY

To enable a better understanding of these trends, this study uses qualitative methodologies to investigate the context of fertility decisions in Quebec between 1940 and 1970. This follows in the footsteps of several other studies that have attempted to link people's narratives with their observed behaviour. The period ends (1970) when the contraceptive pill became more widely accepted and available, immediately after the Catholic Church had taken a position against its use. In Quebec, this event helped to create a definitive rift between the population and its religious elites.

In the current paper, we summarize the many interviews conducted with a sample of Catholic priests and physicians who practised during the 1940s, 1950s, and early 1960s. In other words, we derive information influencing fertility decisions in the years prior to Quebec's Quiet Revolution. Forty-five individuals were interviewed, for a total of 135 hours of material.

Table 4.1 Number of Children per Married Woman by Birth Cohort, Quebec

Born	Number
Prior to 1876	6.4
1876–1886	6.2
1886–1896	5.7
1896–1906	4.6
1906–1916	3.9
1916–1926	3.8
1926–1931	3.6
1931–1936	3.2
1936–1941	2.7
1941–1946	2.2

Sources: Jacques Heniprin, *Tendances et facteurs de la fécondité au Canada* (Ottawa, 1968); Statistics Canada, Nuptiality and Fertility, 1981 Census of Population, Catalog 92-906 (Ottawa, 1983); Statistics Canada, Fertility, 1991 Census of Population, Catalog 93-321 (Ottawa, 1993).

The interviews with retired priests were arranged through the Archdiocese of Montreal. Of our 17 informants—all trained in the Grand Séminaire de Montréal—seven had performed their ministry in the parishes; the others had worked as hospital chaplains, family-planning counsellors, moral educators, or teachers. Two had left their holy orders in the late 1960s.

The names of retired physicians came from the Collège des médecins (Quebec College of Physicians). Just under a third of those contacted agreed to be interviewed, most of whom were obstetricians and general practitioners. Unfortunately, few wished to participate. Four of the 20 interviewees in this group had been on the front lines during the second half of the 1960s when the first family-planning clinics or similar institutions emerged. The oldest informants had started their professional practice in the early 1940s; the youngest had begun their careers in the mid-1960s.

The priests were questioned on the principles that had guided them, and the physicians on the medical practices that had been associated with a growing interest in contraception. But the physicians, like the priests, gave evidence of a value system not specifically medical. Filtering informants' responses to the interview questions was minimal. The interviewer intervened only to bring the discussion back to the main topics—confession, faith in Church doctrine, reaction to the encyclical *Humanae Vitae*, etc. Half of the interviews were recorded on tape. The rest were reconstructed from notes and then revised, corrected, and completed in a second interview. All of the interviewees were French Catholics, and all worked in the Montreal area. Indications are that the problems regarding contraception encountered there were similar to those in other French Catholic circles in Quebec, although they were probably more acute in a large urban centre such as Montreal.

Two other series of interviews, involving elderly women and men, completed in August 2002, will eventually supplement the existing information. The testimony of men, which is rare on the subject of contraception, is particularly important, especially since the professionals generally worked only with women in giving moral advice about contraception or medical care during pregnancy. If spouses did not agree about contraception, they may have had to undergo a delicate phase of "negotiation." Moreover, the contraceptive methods available until the 1960s required considerable co-operation on the part of the husband. Other occasional sources also helped to complete the information obtained from the interviews and to determine its relevance to other groups of women, including the records of Seréna—the first birth-control service established in Montreal (especially 145 letters that this organization received during the 1960s from distraught women living in various parts of Quebec)—and various journals and magazines published at the time, several of them medical or religious (for further details, see Gervais, 2002).

WOMEN, PRIESTS, AND MORALITY

In 1930, the doctrine of the Catholic Church was set out in an official document, the encyclical *Casti connubii*, which condemned contraceptive practices as contrary to the natural order. The encyclical had been issued in response to a resolution adopted a few months earlier by Anglican bishops at the Lambeth Conference to the effect that birth-control methods were permissible when there was a clear moral obligation to limit or prevent conception and a morally sound reason not to practise total abstinence. For the Anglican Church, contraceptive methods were morally neutral; only the motivations behind the actions were important. For the Catholic Church, periodic abstinence alone was finally considered an acceptable means of controlling births, but only so long as serious reasons for limiting family size of the family existed. This doctrinal opposition is at the root of the different contraceptive behaviours adopted by Catholics and Protestants (Sevegrand, 1995).

When the encyclical came out, the Ogino-Knauss (or calendar) method of periodic abstinence had just become known. Even though some members of the Church regarded the emergence of this method as providential, they felt compelled to be discreet about recommending it to the faithful. In 1934, Mayrand, a Dominican, published, at his own expense, in France a pamphlet explaining the method; the Dominican Fathers in Quebec were the first, even before the medical profession, to disclose the technique (Mayrand, 1934). The method subsequently became known mainly through the Catholic Action movement (in the context of classes given by the *Services de préparation au mariage* [marriage preparation services] and the *Services d'orientation des foyers* [services offering moral and spiritual guidance to families]). A lot of books popularized this method, but not everyone understood them fully (Dumas and Chaput, 1935; Forest, 1934; Hudon, 1936). According to some of the interviewees, even medical practitioners did not know much about the method. One of the problems with it, however, is that it was not suited to women with irregular menstrual cycles, especially when their goal was to stop having children altogether rather than to increase the birth interval between them. Whatever the reasons, it caused a great many failures.

Eventually, another rhythm method came to the fore—the sympto-thermal, or temperature method, the underlying theory of which was hardly novel, though not until the early 1950s did it find application in family planning. In Quebec, the new method became known through the efforts of Father Georges Matte, a young curate, and Gilles and Rita Breault, a working-class couple from Lachine, who introduced it to parishes in 1956 despite the lack of enthusiasm of the episcopal authorities. The couple's teachings were soon widely publicized, enabling them to launch the Seréna service. After an article was published in a woman's magazine, and they appeared on a television show, they received roughly 1,000 letters from distraught couples. Notre-Dame hospital offered them the use of an auditorium, where they began to hold public conferences that attracted large audiences. Francophone Catholic couples in Quebec developed a keen interest in this method, discussion of which soon spread like wildfire among the working classes. A book entitled *La régulation des naissances. Précis de la méthode sympto-thermique,* published in 1963, became a bestseller; 65,000 copies were sold in Quebec within the decade (Baillargeon and Pelletier-Barllargeon, 1963).

By the time the sympto-thermal method appeared, the Ogino-Knauss method had lost much credibility. In its favour, the new technique looked to be far more effective if used correctly. Nonetheless, surveys conducted in the late 1960s show that relatively few couples adopted it—hardly to the surprise of even those who publicized it. Clearly, it was not for everyone. The method requires a highly regulated lifestyle and a fastidious attention to the temperature graph, as well as a prolonged abstinence from sexual relations, since only the last 12 days of the woman's cycle are completely safe.

This method proved to be a lifesaver for the priesthood, although the ecclesiastical authorities only endorsed it with prudence. Interviews show that beginning in 1960, this method helped to alleviate many of the priests' anguish about how to resolve couples' problems. Based on a superficial understanding, which amounted to the belief that women were likely to be fertile only for a few days in the middle of their cycle, some priests saw the technique as a godsend. Periodic abstinence had become safe. Knowing a woman's cycle and practising abstinence at the appropriate time was all that was necessary to preserve the principle of conjugal morality centred on control of the sexual instinct. Other priests, however, fully cognizant of how demanding the method was, rebelled against the clergy's lack of compassion. Physicians remained guarded in their opinions. Many saw the new method as arduous and unsafe. Others viewed it as a major breakthrough, occasionally referring their patients to Seréna. In all circumstances, they had to respect their patients' moral principles.

In general, the problem of birth control in the 1950s and 1960s involved considerable moral, sexual, and social suffering, as evidenced by the many letters received by Seréna. French-Canadian Catholic spouses found themselves in a moral dilemma, torn between the physical desire that they felt for one another, their desire to limit the size of their families, and their desire to live in a proper Christian way. Over time, nervous overexcitement, grievance, and conflict often reached a boiling point, and marriages began to break up.

As reported by Breault (1975), one secularized priest expressed resentment about the Church's lack of understanding of Catholic couples' problems with sexual issues:

Women were extremely distraught ... I heard a priest say [to one woman], ... [that] when her husband takes her, she only has to say her prayers and she won't feel pleasure. I never saw any compassion for women. "All they have to do is abstain!" ... The repression [that] they experienced led to all kinds of perversions.... Some people were smart enough to promise not to fall into the same sin again. They had learned that this is what they were expected to say.... The most free-thinking of them said to themselves: I'll make my peace with the Good Lord on the other side.

To some couples, a platonic relationship seemed to be the only solution, especially when the woman's cycle was too irregular for the Ogino-Knauss method. According to a Montreal teacher who heroically opted for complete abstinence for two years, however, the price could be mental imbalance, terror, or marital breakdown. Those who defied the prohibitions experienced an enormous degree of guilt. Particularly troubling was the inability to receive absolution. People found themselves marginalized and deprived of the soothing relief of the sacraments. Many turned to Seréna with hopes of returning to the fold. Others trusted in God's mercy, bypassing the clergy entirely. This approach severely undermined the power of the Church in Quebec. Ultimately, freedom of conscience won out.

Before the pill and the intrauterine device (IUD) appeared on the scene, coitus interruptus also seems to have been popular; it was the least expensive, most direct, and easiest method to use (Gauvreau and Gossage, 1997). As one interviewee confided, "I didn't have any means of contraception, but my husband would say, 'I'll be careful.'" Condemned by the most conservative in Quebec, forbidden as it was by the Church in principle, this method was viewed by others less strict with a fickle and capricious tolerance. Women were generally forgiven, provided that they did not take pleasure in and consented to relations only after unsuccessfully trying to convince their husbands about the merits of abstinence. Men could be forgiven, too. Georges Méthot, a well-known preacher at Catholic retreats, reasoned that making love and withdrawing at the appropriate moment was not a sin because the intention had not been to make love completely, even if withdrawal occurred too late to prevent ejaculation. Méthot's words left people with the idea that coitus interruptus was not a serious sin and that they could take communion.

A first reading of the priests' interviews shows considerable uniformity, testifying to the strength of the ideology that inspired them. All of the priests spoke about controlling sexual urges, God's mercy, life's burdens, and the grace of the sacraments that gives believers the strength to abstain. None claimed to have denied anyone absolution; only one priest maintained that such refusals still happen today. All of the priests had placed great hope in the Vatican Council that began in 1962, believing that the pill would be accepted, only to be shocked by Pope Paul VI's 1968 encyclical, *Humanae Vitae*, which completely rejected it. Few priests, however, express disagreement with the encyclical. They admire its beautiful descriptions of human love and its ability to help couples to reach their religious goals.

The priests who criticized the encyclical did so in a restrained way on the grounds of form rather than content: The Pope's phrasing might have been better. Most shocking was the reiteration of Pius XI's condemnation of contraception as "intrinsically evil." But this disagreement was more sensed than heard. The topic is the focus of muffled controversy even today. The interviewed priests generally respected the hierarchy, submitted willingly to doctrine, and showed genuine affection for the current Pope, as well as for his predecessors. They tended to view the popes as human beings with merits and faults, not simply as the personification of supreme authority.

Nevertheless, several of the priests doubted the Church's doctrine on birth control, and, beyond the considerable uniformity in their discourse, differences in their practice emerged. One priest, though well aware of the discrepancy between Church doctrine and the realities of married life, began his ministry with complete confidence in the official position on birth control. After the Vatican Council, however, he became far less certain. This man, who had consistently given sharp and clear answers, ended his interview with a question widely debated in the 1960s: "How does one reconcile doctrine and life?", as though he was still unsure of the answer.

Another priest admitted to discomfort when he had to counsel women about birth control. Although he "believed in God's mercy to forgive women's weaknesses" and "was filled with pity for the women who brought their problems to [him]," he also "wanted to be loyal to the Church." This interviewee always had doubts about the moral issues, but he, too, was torn between his loyalty to the Church and his desire to relieve women's suffering.

A third priest described how his reputation for open-mindedness spread throughout the parish where he was first sent to practise his ministry. Eventually, people began to avoid the priest with whom he worked, "who refused to give absolution to anyone who in any way tried to limit the size of their family," and found ways to confess to him instead. He became so upset about his collusion with them that he ended up "in hospital with stomach ulcers." Despite his reservations about the Church's attitude toward conjugal relations, he was still a prisoner of the prevailing ideological system, wondering whether his ill-considered absolutions were leading people to hell. He had no more inner peace than the other two priests. He finally left his religious order.

These brief accounts demonstrate that, regardless of their position on Church doctrine, these priests found themselves in an untenable moral predicament. Church doctrine and married life were irreconcilable. The Church was forcing couples into a corner, making them choose God over love or love over God, as one priest wrote in 1966. Before the Vatican II Council, confessors simply refused absolution to penitents who did not promise to stop sinning, whereas, during the Council, the Church was riven with conflict about the doctrine. Even the Pope admitted uncertainty. Many in the Church changed their views at that point, although some, who had always been doubtful, had adopted a conciliatory attitude, based on the Gospel much earlier (Charbonneau, 1966).

WOMEN AND PHYSICIANS

Contraception did not become a medical issue for some time, partly because it did not fall under the heading of illness and partly because physicians—generally men—were sexual beings and, for the most part, practising Catholics before they were physicians.

The opposition to contraception that they expressed was clearly shared by society as a whole, but it is especially interesting to find it in the social group most capable of offering a neutral and scientific judgment (Gagnieux, 1975).

In the publication *Relations*, d'Anjou (1964:227), a Jesuit, spelled out a main principle to guide physicians that, to him, left no room for ambiguity: "To act morally means to treat an illness or remedy a disorder (whether physical or mental) through the use of effective medication. One is not acting morally when one disrupts a healthy function for the sole purpose of obtaining pleasure and avoiding the responsibilities associated with the exercise of this function." During the 1950s, students at the Université de Montréal's Faculty of Medicine studied a text by Paquin (1960), another Jesuit, *Morale et médecine*, which followed pontifical teachings in all aspects. Students were taught, as a "serious obligation of conscience," that they not recommend any contraceptive method. However, physicians could advise couples to use the rhythm methods whenever a new pregnancy might prove to be dangerous. All other methods were considered immoral.

In 1960, when the third edition of Paquin's text appeared, the birth-control pill was about to make its appearance on Canadian markets. In this new edition, still following the teachings of Pius XII, Paquin specified that use of the pill was prohibited as a contraceptive but not as a menstrual-cycle regulator. In this regard, Paquin quoted a recent declaration by Pius XII, based on the old moral principle that the justification of an act with both a good and bad effect depended on intention. Physicians recognized the pernicious, and even hypocritical, nature of this principle, as did some of the priests who taught it.

The double-effect principle was used, for example, to judge the morality of hysterectomies, which resulted in permanent sterility. If a hysterectomy was a medical necessity, it was allowed despite its sterilizing effect because the primary intention was therapeutic. Tubal ligation, on the other hand, was totally forbidden because the practice could not be justified by any organic illness. Its sole purpose was sterilization. Not even the prevention of a conception likely to lead to a difficult birth or to result in the death of either the mother or the child was permissible on moral grounds. Hence, tubal ligation, a far less physically invasive practice for women than hysterectomy, was not performed in hospitals until the 1970s when women were receiving hysterectomies for contraceptive purposes. The principle was also used when the birth-control pill came out.

In the words of one physician, "Before the pill, we had nothing!" Another interviewee clearly expressed the limited degree of latitude that physicians had in the area of family planning: "In the 1950s and 1960s, there weren't many methods available to us. So we didn't talk about it and patients didn't talk to us about it. Priests hearing confessions were privy to far more secrets in this area and had to make many more decisions than we did.... Doctors at that time were the last to arrive on the scene, for a miscarriage, an abortion, or a birth."

Most physicians loathed the idea of abortion. They encountered it mainly through its disastrous consequences when performed with makeshift devices; illegal abortions were apparently common at that time. Physicians were forbidden to finish illegal abortions themselves, but they were expected to do what they could to save a patient—that is, call an ambulance or write a diagnosis that would enable the patient to receive the appropriate care as quickly as possible. Until the 1950s, their involvement in family planning often amounted to little more than remedying the harm done by others.

For reasons as yet unexplained, French Canadians, with the exception of a few well-informed women from the upper class, seemed unwilling to use diaphragms. Moreover, physicians and the general public considered the use of condoms only with reluctance, if not repugnance. Physicians seldom recommended condoms to their patients, morally opposed as they were to such "wasting of the semen." Most of the interviewees stated, almost dismissively, that condoms were just for soldiers during war, for anglophones (who took a more pragmatic approach toward contraception), or for men with prostitutes or mistresses, but not with their wives. Their view of coitus interruptus was equally disparaging. They considered French Canadians to be incapable of controlling their sexual urges. Some of them were not adequately informed about the rhythm methods, even though these were the only methods that they generally advocated, and they tended to scorn all others. Many simply advised women to "be careful," usually a discreet reference to withdrawal. Coitus interruptus, however, was probably more popular than they thought, especially as a complement to the rhythm methods.

One general practitioner, a Catholic who began his practice in a working-class village near Montreal in 1948, reported that he never felt authorized to advise a method of contraception forbidden by the Church, even when further pregnancy was likely to prove dangerous for a patient. But, curiously enough, the moral problem seemed to disappear for him with the advent of the pill. In the words of another physician, "the pill removed the moral obstacles." Why? The answer is simple: Because it was a "medication." The pill forced physicians to become involved in the area of family planning.

All of the physicians interviewed agreed that the pill was less of a moral impediment than other contraceptives, although they were not entirely at ease with it. As one said, "I started to prescribe the pill with a certain degree of reluctance. At that time I found myself in something of a moral conflict. At first, the pill was presented to us as a means of controlling irregular menstrual cycles. It was not a method of contraception.... It had a contraceptive effect, but contraception was not the intention." A 1965 survey of young physicians, published in the weekly newspaper *Photo Journal*, confirms the testimony of the interviewees, revealing how their argument was able to soothe a troubled conscience: "It is clear that women asking for the pill are asking for a contraceptive and not a medical treatment. If the woman does have an irregular cycle, I prescribe the pill, not as a contraceptive, but as a treatment. It comes to the same thing in terms of the results, but the moral principle is upheld" (Laberge, 1965).

Because the first contraceptive pill had harmful side effects, physicians were cautious about prescribing it. But physicians reluctant to do so on moral grounds could use its medical contraindications to avoid the moral issue entirely. One middle-class Catholic practitioner, who began his medical career in 1954, about 10 years before the pill's arrival, working in a modest working-class neighbourhood, is representative in this regard: "Women might come into our office without any explanation whatsoever and say, 'I want the pill!' ... I didn't say, 'What about your husband, what about the religious issues, etc.' I said, 'What about the high blood pressure, cardiac insufficiency, varicose veins, etc.?' ... [W]hen people asked for the pill, it was at least appropriate to perform a physical examination, a Pap test. But, at first, people refused. We had to be careful because then we would be characterized in a certain way. That's why doctors had to be married." Women could find themselves confronted with an ambivalence for which they might be ill prepared.

This interviewee was visibly upset by the incursion of the birth-control pill into his medical practice. At no time during the interview did he state that suggesting the pill was his idea. He seemed to have been offended by the change in patients' behaviour from seeking help with ailments to demanding prescriptions. In the beginning, women did not dare to ask directly for a contraceptive; they alluded to it "with symptoms" until eventually physicians were able to ascertain the real problem. When women were no longer too shy or ashamed to bring up the subject, physicians might have been able to regain the upper hand only by emphasizing the medical concerns. Reinforcing this impression is the fact that at several points during the interview, instead of referring to "the birth-control pill" or "contraceptives," this interviewee used the term "medication" to keep the discussion on a medical or technical level. However, he also lamented that birth control had evolved from a moral issue involving husbands to a women's decision exclusively and thus a source of concern for husbands.

Nonetheless, since the pill was a medication that clearly presented risks, especially due to its high levels of estrogen prior to 1975, this physician, like most of the others, was right to exercise caution in prescribing it and to require a thorough physical examination before doing so. The new breed of determined women, however, saw the pill as a miracle solution to their problem regardless of any dangers. The conclusion to a 1978 report issued by Health and Welfare Canada noted the risks associated with the use of oral contraceptives, citing an editorial in *The Lancet*, a leading medical journal: "Those who have even more difficult judgments to form are the doctors who must decide whether or not to prescribe the pill for a particular patient and also the women to whom they must explain the risks. (There is little that) is going to dismay the many women who regard oral contraceptives as a blessing which carries a minute risk of premature death" (Health and Welfare Canada 1978:747–748).

Notwithstanding the sound professional judgment of our informant, his technical language does not entirely hide the uneasiness that circumscribed the need for a gynecological examination, even though he had done a great deal of obstetrical work and had assisted with nearly 100 births a year. What triggered the uneasiness between a woman and her physician was the underlying subtext of the woman as not so much a future mother or a person in pain as an object of desire and a seeker of pleasure. This erotic component turned the doctor-patient relationship into a delicate situation. The reason why a physician had to be married was a husband's possible jealousy about a gynecological examination, especially since the examination was not, strictly speaking, medical.

DISCUSSION

The interviews with the priests and physicians working in the Montreal area between 1940 and 1970 elicit several important issues confronting Catholic couples who were trying to have smaller families. They received little solace from the Church, which left almost no latitude for believers, and physicians, whose religious morality often overrode their scientific knowledge. Their sole recourse was the use of demanding methods that were often less effective than those used by English Quebecers (rhythm and withdrawal methods).

In an attempt to circumvent these extremely demanding birth-control techniques, some women "shopped around" for a confessor who would not refuse them absolution, and physicians often consulted theologians. One of the important findings to come out of this qualitative survey is the variability of the stances and practices among the clergy, even before the arrival of the pill. Morality sometimes became "situational," thus perhaps shaking the foundations of Catholic morality. But the fact that the sympto-thermal method became a virtual craze testifies to the sense of powerlessness that many people felt with regard to the birth-control issue, and indicates the profound influence that religious belief had on a large proportion of the population. Although this method helped many couples, in a sense it represented the last gasp of a religious ideology that emphasized a high level of self-control.

A number of factors were involved in radically changing these conditions during the 1960s, among them the high level of frustration and distress experienced by affected couples (which we hope to highlight further through interviews with a number of elderly women and men) and the uncertainty that prevailed between the beginning of the Council in 1962 and the publication of the encyclical in 1968. As dramatically shown by the data from the 1960s and 1970s, civil society after that point was able to free itself from the religious authority that had dominated the sphere of responsible parenthood. A shift in the distribution of roles was already underway. Women and doctors would move to the forefront of the scene, and priests would be relegated to a relatively minor role. The radical nature of the changes that were to come was in equal opposition to the extent of the repression that had been caused by so many constraints and prohibitions. Today, Quebec currently has one of the highest proportions of cohabiting couples and of births within such unions in the world. The reversal occurred within a relatively brief period of time.

Apart from the information that they provide about the initial focus of this study, the interviews raise other related matters that call for further analysis: the subject of sexuality, which involves, for example, the notion that women's sexual pleasure is non-existent, and the likelihood that the various methods of contraception are linked to particular sexual practices, suggesting that certain groups or countries have specific sexual cultures.

● ●

CRITICAL THINKING QUESTIONS

1. What generalizations can we make on the relevance of religion to fertility behaviour in Quebec?
2. The use of qualitative interviews to draw inferences on social change is increasingly popular among sociologists and social demographers. Discuss the utility of this approach, including possible shortcomings.
3. Interviews with Catholic clergy and family physicians suggest near uniformity in opinion as to the role of birth control in limiting fertility in the 1940s and 1950s in Quebec. Why do you think this was the case, and why do you think there has been such a dramatic change in Quebec, beginning with the Quiet Revolution in the 1960s?

● ●

CHAPTER 5

THE FERTILITY OF IMMIGRANT WOMEN AND THEIR CANADIAN-BORN DAUGHTERS

Alain Bélanger and Stéphane Gilbert

● ●

INTRODUCTION

Historically, immigration has played an important role in the settlement of Canada. Except for a few quite limited periods, such as the years following the Crash of 1929 or the war years, Canada has always welcomed immigrants in large numbers.

While immigration has almost always accounted for a sizable proportion of Canada's population growth, its proportional importance has recently tended to increase. Since the mid-1990s, migratory increase has been responsible for more than half the total growth. The low fertility of Canadian women and the inevitable aging of the population are causing the rate of natural increase to decline. Between 1981 and 2001, it went from 8.1 per 1,000 to 3.3 per 1,000, a decrease of nearly 60 percent. Another 20 years and, according to the medium scenario in the most recent projections, the number of deaths should exceed the number of births (Statistics Canada, 2001).

Partly in response to this decline in natural increase, the Canadian government has, since the late 1980s, been favourable to an increase in the number of immigrants admitted to Canada. In 2001, Canada received more than 250,000 immigrants, and nearly 70 percent of Canada's population growth resulted from positive net migration. The resulting immigration rate of 8.1 per 1,000 is approaching the government's long-term objective of 1 percent (Citizenship and Immigration Canada, 2001).

The contribution of immigration to the growth of the Canadian population is not limited to its direct effects on the population count for the year. The newcomers are often young, and once they have settled in Canada, many of them start a family and have Canadian-born children.

The fertility of foreign-born Canadian women was formerly lower than that of women born in Canada (Balakrishnan et al., 1979; Henripin, 1972; Kalbach, 1970), but is estimated to have overtaken it since the early 1980s (Dumas and Bélanger, 1994; Ram and George, 1990; Ng and Nault, 1997). This is because the changes in Canadian immigration are not only quantitative. Whereas before, almost all immigrants came from Europe, most now come from Asia. In the past, immigrants tended to come from countries where until the baby bust, fertility was lower than in Canada. Today's immigrants tend to come from countries with higher fertility, and they seem to retain, at least for a time, some of the fertility behaviour of their country of origin. But for how long? And what about the fertility of the daughters of immigrants? Is it more similar to that of women of Canadian origin (i.e., women born in Canada of Canadian-born parents), or to that of their immigrant mothers?

Fertility analysis is an important component of studies that look at the integration of newcomers into their host society (Massey, 1981). From a purely demographic standpoint, a better knowledge of different groups' fertility behaviour can also be used to develop scenarios for the future course of fertility in laying the groundwork for population projections. The higher fertility of recently arrived immigrant women is one of the few factors that could support a possible rise in Canadian fertility in the short run (Bélanger, 2000).

The objective of this article is to take stock of how the fertility of immigrant women evolved between 1976–1981 and 1996–2001. Using measures of the phenomenon by country of birth and period of immigration, we will observe whether or not the fertility behaviour of immigrant women is tending to converge with that of Canadian-born women and, if so, how rapidly this is occurring for different immigrant groups. Second, drawing on the question on parents' place of birth asked in the 2001 Census for the first time since 1971, we estimate the fertility of second-generation Canadian women (i.e., the children of immigrants actually born in Canada) and compare it with that of first-generation immigrant women (born elsewhere) and women of Canadian origin (third generation or higher).

This essentially comparative analysis fits into different theoretical frameworks proposed in the sociological literature relevant to the integration of new immigrants: the theory of assimilation (which originated in the 1920s and would today instead be described as the theory of immigrant integration), the segmented integration perspective, and the success-oriented immigrant model, developed more recently (Boyd and Grieco, 1998).

According to the theory of integration, it is expected that the longer immigrants reside in the host country, the more they will resemble its population. Like the other theories, the theory of integration has most often been used to describe and explain divergences in the level of social mobility of the different waves of immigrants and their descendants. When transposed to the study of differential fertility, it could translate into the following series of statements:

1. The fertility behaviour of women born abroad should fall somewhere between that of the women of their region of origin and that which prevails in Canada.
2. The longer immigrant women live in Canada, the more their fertility should approach that of native-born Canadian women.
3. The fertility of the children of immigrant women (second generation) should lie between that of Canadian women whose parents were born in Canada (third generation) and that of immigrant women (first generation).

According to the segmented integration perspective, again as it might be applied to differential fertility, the fertility of immigrant women and their female descendants should, according to the theory, generally converge toward that of third-generation Canadian women, but it should do so at different speeds for different groups, and for some groups it may actually tend to diverge.

Lastly, according to the success-oriented approach, the children of immigrants, pushed by the success orientation of their immigrant family, are more motivated than others to invest in their human capital and to have higher aspirations with respect to their participation in the labour market than others. In particular, this would be reflected by a stronger tendency to pursue education for a prolonged period. The prolongation of education and the participation of women in the labour market are among the variables usually put forward to explain the drop in fertility in Canada as elsewhere in the world. At the individual level, the prolongation of education almost always entails postponing the first child, and this often means having fewer children than the number initially desired. Thus, the fertility of children of immigrants may not lie between that of their parents, who are first-generation Canadians, and that of people of Canadian origin, as postulated by the theory of integration. Instead, it may be lower than that of the latter group.

MEASURING THE FERTILITY OF IMMIGRANT WOMEN AND THEIR DAUGHTERS

The mother's place of birth is one of the variables available in vital statistics, but, unfortunately, the number of records showing a missing value for this variable is sizable, and it varies from year to year. Some provinces have not always reported the parents' place of birth on birth records, with the result that before 1990, the database often has more than 40 percent missing values. Since 1996, an effort has been made to improve the collection of this information, and the percentage of missing values remains under 2 percent.

It is difficult to make hypotheses concerning the distribution of these missing data. It may be assumed that the probability that the country of birth will be reported is higher for mothers who are born in Canada, but it is impossible to determine that probability or estimate what proportion of incomplete records are for mothers born in Canada and what proportion are for mothers born abroad. In any case, vital statistics do not register the grandparents' place of birth, which would be needed in order to determine second-generation status. Therefore, such data do not lend themselves to an in-depth analysis of differential fertility according to the mother's place of birth, let alone to a comparative analysis based on generational status.

However, there is an indirect method of estimating fertility based on census data alone. Known as the "own children method," it draws on the fact that the vast majority of young children are living with their mother at the time of the census. Since the date of birth of both mother and children is known, it is easy to calculate age-specific fertility rates and thus obtain an estimate of the total fertility rate. An approximate correction can be made to take account of infant mortality and the proportion of children not living with their mother at the time of the census. Table 5.1 compares estimates of fertility rates by age group and the total fertility rate obtained using the own children method (census) and vital statistics.

The total rate obtained using the own children method (1.54 children per woman) is slightly higher than the estimate obtained using the traditional method based on vital statistics (1.52 children per woman). The difference between the two estimates represents approximately 1 percent of the total period rate. For women born in Canada, the estimate obtained using the own children method is 2 percent higher than that obtained using vital statistics, whereas conversely, the estimate for women born abroad is nearly 3 percent lower.

Table 5.1 Comparison of Fertility Rates by Age Group and the Total Fertility Rate, Estimated According to the Own Children Method (Census) and Vital Statistics, Women Born in Canada and Abroad, Canada, 1996–2001

Age Group	Women Born Abroad				Women Born in Canada	Total
	Europe	Asia	Others	Total		
	Vital Statistics Estimates					
15–19	0.049	0.044	0.154	0.070	0.097	0.095
20–24	0.251	0.357	0.537	0.364	0.299	0.308
25–29	0.484	0.646	0.754	0.603	0.481	0.503
30–34	0.454	0.569	0.693	0.537	0.396	0.425
35–39	0.182	0.279	0.341	0.248	0.145	0.166
40–44	0.029	0.056	0.079	0.048	0.022	0.027
45–49	0.001	0.003	0.004	0.002	0.001	0.001
TFR	1.45	1.95	2.56	1.87	1.44	1.52
	Census Estimates					
15–19	0.005	0.006	0.022	0.010	0.015	0.014
20–24	0.124	0.155	0.285	0.174	0.172	0.172
25–29	0.402	0.502	0.630	0.492	0.408	0.420
30–34	0.546	0.639	0.732	0.607	0.515	0.533
35–39	0.323	0.420	0.509	0.390	0.279	0.301
40–44	0.089	0.144	0.186	0.128	0.073	0.084
45–49	0.012	0.023	0.031	0.019	0.009	0.011
TFR	1.50	1.89	2.40	1.82	1.47	1.54

Source: Statistics Canada, 2001 Census of Canada and Health Statistics Division.

Table 5.1 also shows that while the differences between the two estimation methods are not very sizable with respect to the total fertility rate, the gaps are greater for some age groups. The relative gap between the two estimates is minimal between ages 25 and 34, but it increases in one direction or the other at either end of the fertility period.

Among younger women, the estimate based on vital statistics indicates higher fertility rates than the estimate based on the census alone. Beyond age 30, on the other hand, the estimate based on the census is higher. This is because of a well-documented bias in the own children method (Cho et al., 1986; Desplanques, 1993), which probably results from a greater propensity among children with young mothers to live in another family (or in a non-family setting), among other factors. However, this bias in age-specific rates generally does not result in any major divergence for the total fertility rate.

RESULTS

In the 2001 Census, nearly 5.5 million people born outside Canada were enumerated, representing 18 percent of the total population. This proportion is one of the highest in the world. For many people, American immigration has an almost mythical quality, yet the proportion of people in the United States who were born abroad (11 percent) is barely half that in Canada, a fact that underlines how important a role immigration plays in Canadian population growth.

The proportion of children under five years of age born in Canada whose mother was born abroad is even larger than the proportion of the population that has immigrated, which gives us a first indication of the greater fertility of those mothers. Already in 1981, the approximately 300,000 children whose mother had immigrated to Canada accounted for 18 percent of all enumerated children under five. By the time of the 2001 Census, this

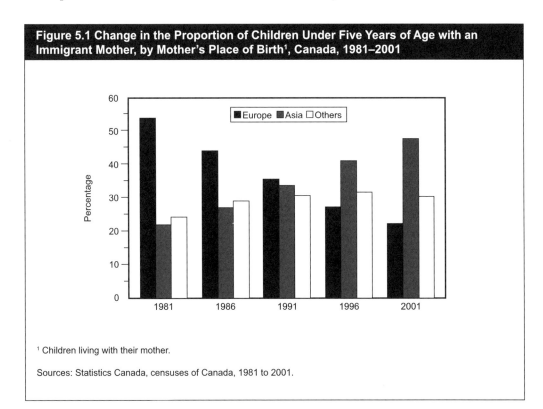

Figure 5.1 Change in the Proportion of Children Under Five Years of Age with an Immigrant Mother, by Mother's Place of Birth[1], Canada, 1981–2001

[1] Children living with their mother.

Sources: Statistics Canada, censuses of Canada, 1981 to 2001.

proportion had risen to more than 22 percent. Major changes may also be observed in the composition of the group of children with an immigrant mother. In 1981, children with a mother born in Europe accounted for 54 percent of all children with a foreign-born mother, whereas those whose mother was born in Asia accounted for only 22 percent of the whole (Figure 5.1). In the 2001 Census, children whose mother was born in Europe accounted for only 22 percent of all children whose mother was born abroad, whereas those whose mother was of Asian origin accounted for nearly half (48 percent).

FERTILITY OF IMMIGRANT AND NATIVE-BORN CANADIAN WOMEN

Table 5.2 shows the change in the total fertility rate of native-born Canadian women and immigrant women between 1976–1981 and 1996–2001. During this quarter century, the fertility of immigrant women was consistently higher than that of Canadian-born women, exceeding it by 20 percent to 25 percent depending on the period.

Both for women born abroad and Canadian-born women, the fertility trend was downward during the study period. The downward change is fairly similar for the two groups. At most, it may be noted that during the 1980s, when immigration was lower, the fertility differences between the two populations narrowed slightly. This is perhaps because the proportion of newly arrived immigrant women was smaller and these women, as we will see, have a higher fertility level than immigrant women who have lived in Canada longer.

Over the study period as a whole, the rate for Canadian-born women went from 1.64 children per woman for the period 1976–1981 to 1.47 children per woman for the period 1996–2001, representing a decrease of 10 percent. During the same period, the rate for women born abroad also fell by 10 percent, going from 2.03 children per woman to 1.82 children per woman.

But the immigrant population is a heterogeneous group whose composition changed substantially over the study period. During the last decade of the 20th century, nearly three immigrants in five (59 percent) were from Asia, with most of them coming from east Asia (China, Hong Kong, and Taiwan), south Asia (India, Pakistan, and Sri Lanka), and, to a lesser extent, southeast Asia (the Philippines). This preponderance of Asian countries as a source is relatively recent in the history of Canadian immigration. In the mid-1960s, the vast majority of immigrant women were still coming from Europe. Indeed, at that time, two European countries dominated Canadian immigration to a much greater extent than China, Hong Kong, and India do today. Between 1964 and 1968, for example, one immigrant in four came from the United Kingdom (25 percent) and one in six from Italy (16 percent).

The composition of the population of women of child-bearing age born abroad has changed considerably. In the 1981 Census, 62 percent of foreign-born women aged 15 to 54 were from Europe, with the remaining 38 percent divided nearly equally between Asia and the rest of the world (Figure 5.2). By the time of the 2001 Census, the proportion of foreign-born women of child-bearing age who were from Europe was only 33 percent and, for the first time, the proportion who were from Asia (45 percent) exceeded the proportion from Europe.

| Table 5.2 Total Fertility Rate of Canadian-born Women and Canadian Women Born Abroad by Region of Birth, Canada, 1976–1981 to 1996–2001 |

Birth Region	1976–1981	1981–1986	1986–1991	1991–1996	1996–2001
Total Canada	1.70	1.61	1.61	1.66	1.54
Born in Canada	1.64	1.56	1.56	1.60	1.47
Born Outside Canada	2.03	1.87	1.88	1.99	1.82
Total Europe	1.90	1.68	1.66	1.66	1.50
United Kingdom	1.66	1.64	1.64	1.58	1.46
Northern Western Europe	1.76	1.74	1.68	1.76	1.67
Eastern Europe	1.68	1.63	1.68	1.75	1.34
Southern Europe	2.17	1.71	1.72	1.68	1.62
Total Asia	2.54	2.15	2.07	2.13	1.89
Middle East and Middle West Asia	2.74	2.46	2.36	2.56	2.17
Eastern Asia	2.09	1.85	1.66	1.51	1.32
Southeast Asia	2.48	2.03	1.98	1.99	1.76
Southern Asia	3.04	2.50	2.51	2.88	2.51
Rest of the World	2.06	2.02	2.04	2.18	2.02
United States	2.05	2.11	2.07	2.15	1.99
Central and South America	2.27	2.13	2.24	2.25	1.99
Caribbean and Bermuda	1.96	1.86	1.86	2.02	1.73
Africa	1.95	1.94	1.91	2.39	2.38
Oceania and Others	2.19	2.11	2.21	2.02	1.97

Sources: Statistics Canada, censuses of Canada, 1981 to 2001.

The different groups formed by grouping countries of birth exhibit major differences with respect to their fertility level. The fertility of European women is quite different from that of Asian women, both when they are in their country of origin and once they are settled in Canada. Furthermore, even within the major groups of countries in Table 5.2, there are sizable variations in fertility. While fertility has evolved along similar lines among native-born Canadian women and immigrant women, this overlooks contrasts between the different groups defined by country of birth. For example, throughout the study period, women born in Europe—especially those born in the United Kingdom—exhibit a fertility level similar to that of native-born Canadian women, although it is slightly lower. By contrast, women from south Asia have a much higher fertility level, which drops off less rapidly than that of other groups. And the total rate for women from Africa actually increased substantially (25 percent) during the 1990s.

According to the estimates shown in Table 5.2, only women in three groups of countries of birth—east Asia, the United Kingdom, and eastern Europe—exhibit a lower fertility

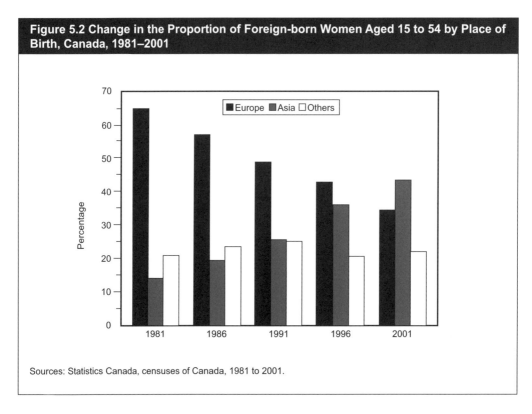

Figure 5.2 Change in the Proportion of Foreign-born Women Aged 15 to 54 by Place of Birth, Canada, 1981–2001

Sources: Statistics Canada, censuses of Canada, 1981 to 2001.

level than native-born Canadian women during the period 1996–2001. Two of these three groups of countries are European.

Women from southern Europe are among those who saw their fertility decline the most rapidly during the quarter-century studied, with their total fertility rate going from 2.17 children per woman to 1.62 children per woman, a 25 percent drop. It is interesting to note that Spain, Italy, and Greece are today among the countries with the lowest period fertility rates in the world, whereas 25 years ago, the fertility of countries in southern Europe was higher than that of the rest of the continent. It appears that the fertility of the women who came from these countries and settled in Canada has evolved along similar lines as that of the women who remained in their country of origin.

While it has fallen substantially, the fertility of Asian women is still, according to the 2001 Census, much higher than that of native-born Canadian women. During the first censual period, the fertility of Asian-born women was much higher than that of Canadian- or European-born women. The total fertility rate for these women went from 2.54 children per woman for the period 1976–1981 to 1.89 children per woman for the most recent period, 1996–2001. While the fertility of these women remains considerably higher than that of Canadian-born women (29 percent higher), it has nevertheless fallen more rapidly, and therefore some convergence is observed.

The fertility of women from east Asia in particular fell the most dramatically during the period. Whereas the rate for women from this region exceeded two children per woman in

1976–1981, in the most recent censual period it was the lowest for any group of countries of birth, at 1.32 children per woman.

While the fertility of women from east Asia has fallen sharply, this is not the case with women from other regions of Asia. The fertility of women from south Asia in particular has remained at high levels compared with that of all other groups. With a total rate of 2.5 children per woman during the period 1996–2001, these women have reached a fertility level comparable to that last posted by Canadian women in 1967, at the end of the baby boom.

Women from the Middle East and western Asia have also tended to maintain a relatively high fertility level after coming to Canada (2.2 children per woman in 1996–2001). The increased proportion of immigrant women who originate from these regions, combined with the maintenance of a relatively high level of fertility, means that the proportion of children born to women from these two regions has increased substantially. In 1981, children born in Canada to women from South Asia and the Middle East represented less than 10 percent of all children whose mother was born abroad, whereas in 2001, they represented one-quarter.

During the period 1996–2001, the fertility of women from Europe was only 2 percent higher than that of Canadian-born women, while the fertility of Asian women was 29 percent higher. On the other hand, women from the rest of the world (Africa, Latin America, and the Caribbean) maintained a high and nearly stable fertility approaching the replacement level throughout the study period. For the period 1996–2001, their fertility exceeded that of Canadian-born women by 37 percent. Table 5.2 also shows that during the study period, the total fertility rate fell for almost all groups of countries of birth. Only the rate for women from Africa rose.

CHANGES BY IMMIGRATION PERIOD

Various studies have found that the fertility of immigrant women varied according to length of residence in the host country (Goldstein and Goldstein, 1981; Hervitz, 1985). According to these studies, the fertility of the newcomers declined in the years following their arrival. This decrease, they find, results from the disruption caused by migration, with immigrant couples limiting their fertility during the period surrounding their emigration. Subsequently, their fertility rises, but the increase is only temporary. After this rebound, the fertility of immigrant women declines the longer they live in the host country. This pattern has been observed in Canada by Ram and George (1990) and Beaujot (1991).

Some authors (Ng and Nault, 1997) find that this pattern results primarily from a decrease in fertility prior to emigration when the future immigrants are still in their country of origin, rather than from a decrease in their fertility once they arrive in the host country. They come to this conclusion focusing solely on children under one year of age rather than children aged zero to four, arguing that many of the older children of women who had immigrated in the five years preceding the Census could have been born abroad, since on average, these women would have spent half of those five years in their country of origin. However, in the latter study, the authors did not look at the child's place of birth (i.e., in Canada or outside Canada).

Figure 5.3 presents an estimate of the total fertility rate of women born abroad according to the length of time since their immigration to Canada. These estimates, obtained using the own children method (for children aged zero to four), cover only children born in Canada. The denominators of the rates are also corrected to take account of the years lived abroad by women who immigrated during the period preceding each census. These are therefore estimates of the fertility of immigrant women once they have settled in Canada.

For each of the five censuses considered, the pattern supporting the hypothesis of a disruption of fertility is not apparent. The fertility of immigrant women is very high during the period immediately following their arrival in Canada. It falls substantially during the following period, after which it declines more slowly. According to the estimate obtained by applying the method to data from the 2001 Census, for example, the fertility of immigrant women, once they have arrived in Canada, is 3.1 children per woman for those who arrived in the previous five-year period. It declines to 2.0 children per woman for those whose length of residence in Canada is five to nine years. Subsequently it reaches just over 1.5 children per woman for those admitted 10 to 14 years earlier and 1.4 children per woman for those who received their immigrant status 15 to 19 years before the census (Figure 5.3).

As suggested by Ng and Nault (1997), the disruptive effect that immigration can have on fertility does indeed appear to result in a decrease in the fertility of women who are future immigrants while they are still in their country of origin. The Census collects the child's place of birth and allows us to compute the number of person-years lived in Canada or

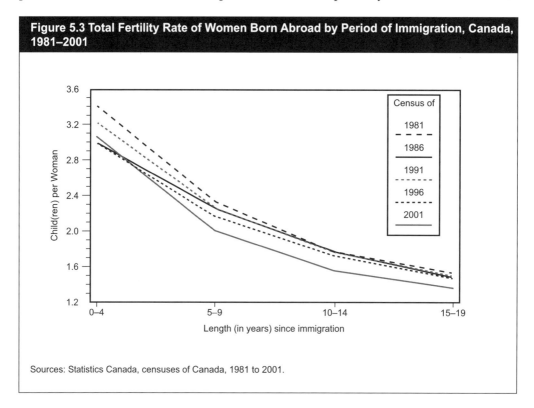

Figure 5.3 Total Fertility Rate of Women Born Abroad by Period of Immigration, Canada, 1981–2001

Sources: Statistics Canada, censuses of Canada, 1981 to 2001.

abroad by women included in the most recent immigrant cohort, and therefore it enables us to estimate the fertility of these women according to whether the birth occurred before or after immigration. The results of such a calculation are shown in Table 5.3.

Clearly, the newcomers' fertility is much greater after their arrival in Canada than prior to it: it is at least three times higher, but generally four to five times higher. It is possible

Table 5.3 Total Fertility Rate of Immigrant Women Admitted During the Five Years Preceding the Census According to Whether the Child was Born in Canada or Abroad, Canada, 1981 to 2001

Census Place of Birth	Place of Birth of Child			
	Born Abroad (1)	Born in Canada (2)	Total (3)	Ratio (2)/(1)
1981				
Europe	0.97	4.05	2.20	4.2
Asia	0.85	4.22	2.28	5.0
Other	0.70	3.20	2.08	4.6
Total	0.84	3.78	2.19	4.5
1986				
Europe	0.75	3.23	1.86	4.3
Asia	0.65	3.14	2.00	4.8
Other	0.77	3.39	2.20	4.4
Total	0.71	3.22	2.01	4.5
1991				
Europe	0.91	3.88	1.70	4.3
Asia	0.69	3.63	1.72	5.3
Other	0.82	3.79	2.16	4.6
Total	0.76	3.71	1.83	4.9
1996				
Europe	0.85	3.63	1.72	4.3
Asia	0.50	3.62	1.86	7.2
Other	0.59	4.24	2.30	7.2
Total	0.57	3.75	1.93	6.6
2001				
Europe	0.99	3.09	1.54	3.1
Asia	0.76	4.15	1.85	5.5
Other	0.72	5.96	2.36	8.3
Total	0.77	4.24	1.89	5.5

Sources: Statistics Canada, censuses of Canada, 1981 to 2001.

that some children were born in Canada while their parents had not yet received their landed immigrant status, inflating those ratios, but probably not enough to change this conclusion. This disruptive effect of immigration on fertility appears to be greater among non-European women than among Europeans; the ratio between the rate calculated for the period following immigration and that for the period prior to immigration is higher for the former group in all censuses.

With some exceptions—and here we are thinking in particular of the case of refugees who must sometimes flee their country of origin precipitously—the decision to migrate is made long before the event occurs, if only because of the lag between when the person applies to immigrate and when the application is accepted. In such circumstances, it is not surprising that immigrants plan the birth of a child and their immigration concurrently, and they often prefer to postpone the child's arrival. On the other hand, once settled in Canada, they seem to be in a hurry to end the wait. In a sense, this may be an indication of their desire to put down roots in their new country.

As Figure 5.4 shows, this pattern is observed for immigrant women from all regions of origin, although each group's fertility level differs, as noted above. In fact, it appears that compared to women from Europe, the higher fertility of women from Asia and those born in the rest of the world is primarily due to greater fertility in the years following their arrival in Canada. The fertility gaps between immigrant women from Europe and those from Asia or the rest of the world are greater in the first 10 years after the year in

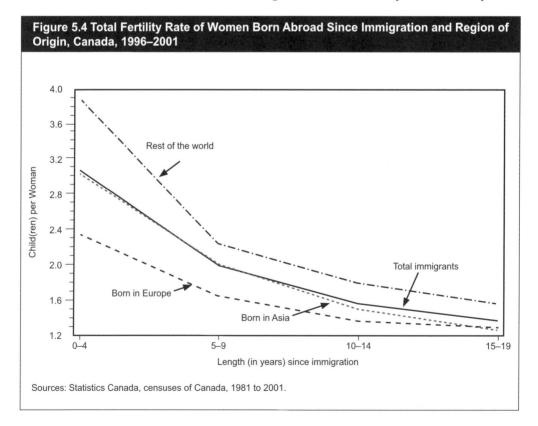

Figure 5.4 Total Fertility Rate of Women Born Abroad Since Immigration and Region of Origin, Canada, 1996–2001

Sources: Statistics Canada, censuses of Canada, 1981 to 2001.

which they received their immigrant status. The fertility of Asian women in particular is similar to that of European women 10 years after their arrival in Canada. For Asian women, the fertility rate is 1.5 children per woman, while for European women, it is roughly 1.4 children per woman. It appears that economic and social factors in Canada influence the fertility level of Canadian women as well as the fertility of major groups of female immigrants, and that after a relatively short period, these immigrants adopt fertility behaviours similar to those of Canadian women.

Figure 5.5 compares age-specific fertility rates of immigrant women from different periods of immigration with those of native-born women as estimated from the 2001 Census. It shows that the greater fertility of immigrant women admitted five to nine years before the Census is primarily due to a relatively high fertility level after age 25, whereas the greater fertility of immigrant women whose length of residence is shorter is more apparent among those who are younger, although it is observable for all ages.

Immigrant women admitted to Canada between 10 and 14 years prior to the Census have a fertility level similar to that of native-born Canadian women, but they have a somewhat slower tempo than the latter: their fertility is lower before age 30 and higher thereafter. While the youngest of these women were born abroad, they arrived in Canada at a very young age. For example, those between 20 and 24 years of age who received their immigrant status between 10 and 14 years ago were between five and 14 years of age at that time. They therefore attended Canadian schools and were probably socialized

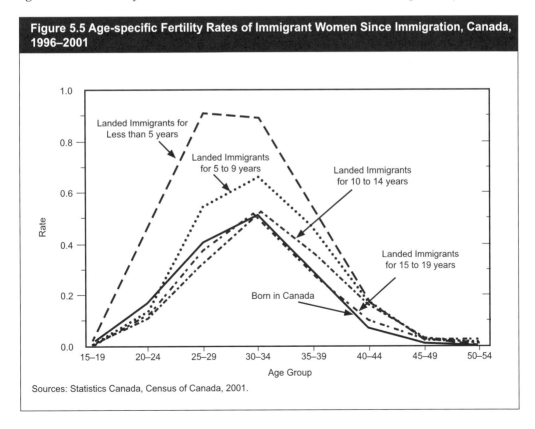

Figure 5.5 Age-specific Fertility Rates of Immigrant Women Since Immigration, Canada, 1996–2001

Sources: Statistics Canada, Census of Canada, 2001.

differently from those arriving later in their life. Their fertility behaviour is not entirely comparable either to that of other immigrant women or to that of native-born Canadian women. Thus the question that arises is, what about the fertility of the daughters of immigrant women—that is, second-generation Canadian women?

THE FERTILITY OF SECOND-GENERATION CANADIAN WOMEN

The 2001 Census allows us, for the first time in 30 years, to estimate the fertility of the daughters of immigrant women and therefore answer this question. According to the estimate obtained using the own children method (Table 5.4), the total fertility rate for second-generation women is 1.4 children per woman and is thus lower than that of first-generation women (1.8 children per woman) and third-generation women (1.5 children per woman).

It is important to note that second-generation Canadian women as identified by answers to the question on parents' place of birth in the 2001 Census are mostly the children of European immigrants. It should therefore be kept clearly in mind that the ethnic origin of the women who are first-generation Canadians is much different from that of second-generation Canadian mothers. For example, some 30 percent of women aged 15 to 54 in the 2001 Census who immigrated to Canada (first generation) have parents born in Europe, whereas the corresponding proportion of women of the same age group belonging to the second generation is approximately 70 percent. Also, whereas nearly 60 percent of women aged 15 to 24 in the first generation report having visible minority status, only 23 percent of those of the second generation do so. If we control for some of these characteristics, the fertility differences between these generational groups obviously become significantly smaller (Bélanger and Gilbert, 2003).

Table 5.4 Age-specific Fertility Rate and Total Fertility Rate by Generation, Canada, 1996–2001

Age Group	Generations				Total
	Women Born Abroad	Women Born in Canada with Both Parents Born Abroad	Women Born in Canada with One of the Parents Born Abroad	Women Born in Canada with Both Parents Born in Canada	
15–19	0.010	0.014	0.015	0.023	0.026
20–24	0.174	0.078	0.121	0.193	0.168
25–29	0.492	0.242	0.323	0.447	0.407
30–34	0.607	0.538	0.518	0.523	0.523
35–39	0.390	0.376	0.324	0.269	0.300
40–44	0.128	0.116	0.092	0.068	0.085
45–49	0.019	0.017	0.012	0.009	0.012
TFR	1.82	1.38	1.41	1.53	1.52

Source: Statistics Canada, Census of Canada, 2001.

CONCLUSION

Through an analysis of the fertility of immigrant women over the past 25 years, we have been able to measure differences in fertility between Canadian women born in Canada and those born abroad. Our analysis has also shown that the differences are mainly observable among newcomers, i.e., those who have resided in Canada for less than 10 years. The fertility of foreign-born women tends to start declining relatively soon after their arrival. The longer the time elapsed since they immigrated, the more fertility declines, tending to reach the level observed for Canadian-born women. This is true for the entire study period and for all major groups of countries of origin.

Thus, measurement of the fertility behaviours of newly immigrated women by means of demographic methods tends to support the hypothesis of the integration of these women into Canadian society insofar as fertility is an indicator of integration, since their fertility tends increasingly to resemble that of Canadian-born women the longer they reside in Canada. This tendency for the fertility of newcomers to converge with that of native-born Canadian women is especially notable where immigration has occurred at a younger age. In particular, women born abroad who immigrated to Canada before the age of 15 and who therefore received part of their education in Canada tend, once they reach child-bearing age, to exhibit fertility rates very similar to those of native-born Canadian women. The fertility behaviours of newly arrived immigrant women appear to tend to converge with that of native-born Canadian women. A similar convergence has also been noted in Australia (Abbasi-Shavazi and McDonald, 2000), another country that encourages newcomers to maintain their cultural differences.

On the other hand, this integration would seem not to be as rapid for all immigrant women, with some groups even maintaining high fertility in all censuses. This supports the idea of a segmented process. While the fertility of immigrant women is higher than that of native-born Canadian women, this is mainly because of the greater fertility of women originating from a few groups of countries of birth. The fertility of women from south Asia, central-western Asia, and the Middle East, along with the fertility of women from Africa in the last two censuses, largely exceeds the level of two children per women. The fertility of women born in Central or South America or the United States also approaches or exceeds this level, while the total fertility rate for women born in the various regions of Europe or east Asia is much lower.

Lastly, when we control for age only, as is done with the total fertility rate, we observe differences between the generational groups in the probability that a woman is living with a young child at the time of the Census. It appears that immigrant women are 9 percent more likely to live with a young child than women of Canadian origin, whereas second-generation Canadian women would seem to be between 7 percent and 17 percent less likely, depending on whether both their parents or only one are foreign-born. However, the differences between the generational groups as measured by means of the total fertility rate are at least partially due to differences in the composition of each group—the ethnic origins of women who are first generation is much different from that of second-generation women, as is also true of women of third generation or higher.

● ●

CRITICAL THINKING QUESTIONS

1. In general terms, what is the likely effect of immigration on overall fertility rates in Canada?
2. Is region/country of origin relevant in explaining the fertility of immigrants?
3. Several different theoretical frameworks have been proposed in the sociological literature on new immigrants. This includes the theory of immigrant integration, the segmented integration perspective, and the success-oriented immigrant model. Which of these theoretical orientations holds the most relevance in explaining the fertility patterns of new Canadians over recent years?

● ●

SECTION 2
MORTALITY

• •

IN CHARTING THE LAST 100 YEARS OF POPULATION HEALTH, Crompton's chapter highlights the rather dramatic reduction in mortality that has characterized Canada as, for example, life expectancy increased by almost 30 years over the course of the 20th century. In explanation, Crompton emphasizes the impact of advances in public health, including improvements in terms of sanitation, pharmaceuticals, vaccines, and medical technology. For a wide assortment of reasons, each successive generation of Canadians has been found to be somewhat healthier than its predecessor, with consistent gains made in terms of reducing the risk of premature death. With industrialization, Canadians also witnessed a dramatic improvement in their standard of living, nutritional standards, levels of literacy, among other factors known to be associated with good health.

This "epidemiological transition" from high to low mortality involved a gradual evolution in the causes of death from an era whereby contagious and parasitic diseases were responsible for a large portion of all deaths to the present, whereby chronic and degenerative diseases are predominant. This transition is described in some detail by Bourbeau and Smuga in their chapter on mortality decline in Quebec. In working with several standard benchmarks on mortality, this paper highlights how Quebec's mortality transition was similar to other parts of Canada, albeit somewhat delayed during the first half of the 20th century. As Bourbeau and Smuga document, Quebec witnessed an important shift in the timing of deaths as infant mortality dropped precipitously, the risk of premature death declined, and a growing proportion of Quebecers survived through to advanced ages.

As a result, both Quebec and Canada are now in an enviable position by international standards, as few countries in the world currently have lower mortality. With the risk of premature mortality at unprecedented low levels, the UN consistently ranks Canada as among the world leaders in terms of population health. Relative to the United States, mortality is significantly lower as, for example, the average Canadian now lives about two years longer than the average American. While half a century ago, Americans and Canadians had almost the same longevity and mortality, chances of survival have since improved at a more rapid pace in Canada than south of the border. Torrey and Haub's contribution to the current volume is specifically concerned with explaining this differential, an issue that has surprisingly drawn relatively little attention by both American and Canadian demographers.

Torrey and Haub enact a standardization exercise that suggests that if Americans were to experience the same sorts of age/sex specific mortality rates as Canadians, there would be more than 250,000 fewer deaths in the United States per annum. To put this into perspective, about 16,000 Americans were murdered in the United States in 2004, which compares to only 620 people in Canada. In explanation, this chapter draws comparisons across the two countries in terms of several risk factors, including differentials in terms of smoking, hypertension, and obesity (with the latter risk factor estimated to be of particular importance in this context). In addition, Torrey and Haub point out that Canada has universal health care coverage, whereas fully one-quarter of all non-elderly Americans have no health insurance whatsoever. Furthermore, social inequality is significantly higher in the United States than in Canada, as a larger proportion of Americans experience economic hardship and poverty—with direct implications for quality of life and state of health.

Beyond these differences as observed across societies, Trovato's chapter considers the substantial differential in life expectancy by sex. To provide some indication as to the magnitude of this differential for Canada, in the early 1980s, the difference in life expectancy was in the order of seven years to the advantage of women. While this differential has since narrowed to about five years in 2000, it is not obvious as to why it persists. Demographers have emphasized a wide range of factors from biological and genetic differences to structural and sociological causes. The emphasis in Trovato's paper is decidedly "sociological," with an emphasis on lifestyle and personal habits (and past smoking behaviour in particular). Both male and female life expectancy at birth continues to climb in Canada, albeit over recent years, the gains observed for men have slightly outpaced those as observed for women.

FURTHER READINGS

Murphy, Christopher, and Alan Lopez (eds.). (1996). *The Global Burden of Disease: A Comprehensive Assessment of Mortality and Disability from Diseases, Injuries, and Risk Factors in 1990 and Projected to 2020.* Cambridge: Harvard University Press. This volume brings forth a wealth of information on international disease patterns, summarizing information available from the World Health Organization.

Péron, Yves, and Claude Strohmenger. (1985). *Demographic and Health Indicators.* Ottawa: Statistics Canada. Cat. no. 82–543. This publication includes a systematic collection of demographic health indicators, along with comments on levels and trends regarding given indicators.

Raphael, Dennis. (2004). *Social Determinants of Health: Canadian Perspectives.* Toronto: Canadian Scholars' Press, Inc. This edited collection provides an extensive portrait of the state of various social (societal) determinants of health in Canada.

Royal Commission on the Future of Health Care in Canada. (2002). *Building on Values: The Future of Health Care in Canada, Final Report.* Commissioner Roy Romanow. Ottawa: Canadian Government Publishing. This report summarizes the findings from the highly publicized Royal Commission on Health Care in Canada, which argues for giving high priority to health in government social expenditures.

Statistics Canada. (2002). *Comparable Health Indicators: Canada, Provinces and Territories.* Ottawa: Statistics Canada. Cat. no. 82-401-XIE. This electronic publication provides detailed information on a series of indicators that address health status, outcomes of health services, and quality of health services.

Wilkins, Kathryn. (2006). "Predictors of Death in Seniors." *Health reports* 16 (supplement). Ottawa: Statistics Canada. Cat. no. 82-003. This paper updates information on the leading causes of death for Canadians aged 65 or older, and examines factors associated with death among seniors over an eight-year period.

Wilkins, Russell, Jean-Marie Berthelot, and Edward Ng. (2002). "Trends in Mortality by Neighbourhood Income in Urban Canada from 1971 to 1996." *Health Reports* 13 (supplement). Ottawa: Statistics Canada. This analysis of data at the aggregate level shows slight declines in socio-economic differentials over time.

RELATED WEB SITES

Canadian Institute for Health Information
<http://secure.cihi.ca>

The Canadian Institute for Health Information (CIHI) is a not-for-profit organization with the mandate to provide health information to Canadians. Its research informs health policy and supports the effective delivery of health services.

Northwestern Mutual Life Insurance
<http://www.nmfn.com/tn/learnctr--lifeevents--longevity>

This site developed by actuaries working for Northwestern Mutual Life Insurance allows you to forecast your life expectancy, given your current age, gender, and lifestyle.

Public Health Agency of Canada
<http://www.phac-aspc.gc.ca>

This Web site summarizes the services provided by the Public Health Agency of Canada. This federal agency promotes activities that focus on preventing chronic diseases, like cancer and heart disease, preventing injuries, and responding to public health emergencies and infectious disease outbreaks.

Statistics Canada
<http://www.statcan.ca>

Statistics Canada regularly updates its health statistics on both the state of population health and the state of Canada's health care system.

World Health Organization
<http://www.who.int>

The World Health Organization is the United Nations' specialized agency for health. It regularly compiles detailed international data on mortality.

CHAPTER 6

100 YEARS OF HEALTH

Susan Crompton

● ●

IF HEALTH IS TO BE PRIZED MORE THAN WEALTH, then the rise in Canadians' overall material standards during the 20th century is nothing compared to the vast improvements in their health status. In the 19th century, infectious and communicable diseases like typhoid, cholera, diphtheria, scarlet fever, and many others devastated Canada's farming communities, towns, and cities. Deaths from infection of wounds and septicemia due to unhygienic practices and conditions were common, and puerperal fever following childbirth killed thousands of women.

Infectious and communicable diseases arrived in Canada by ship from Europe and Asia and travelled up river systems from New York and New Orleans. There were four major outbreaks of cholera between 1832 and 1854. Diphtheria epidemics occurred fairly regularly in the later 19th and early 20th century. Measles epidemics, which generally attacked children between three and seven years old, were common (for example, in 1846 in the Red River district). In the late 19th century, over 3,000 Montrealers died in a smallpox epidemic, even though a vaccine was available. Authorities instituted a mandatory vaccination program against smallpox, but Montrealers rioted in protest. Resistance subsided only with the mounting death toll (Briggs and Briggs, 1998). The last outbreak of smallpox was recorded in Windsor, Ontario, in 1924.

The development of the science of bacteriology in the last half of the 1800s transformed the relationship between humans and disease. Armed with the knowledge that microbes transmit disease, physicians learned that they could control disease by preventing such transmission. Largely because of the control and prevention of infectious diseases by public health programs, Canadians' life expectancy has changed dramatically in the past 100 years. Between the 1920s and the 1990s, life expectancy for a Canadian newborn rose from 59 to 78 years.

Women recorded an additional 20 years, from 61 to 81 years; and men, 16 more years, from age 59 to 75. This article looks briefly at changes in health over the last 100 years, with special focus on the current concerns of Canadians in childhood, mid-life, and old age.

MOST LEADING CAUSES OF DEATH ARE NOW VERY DIFFERENT

In the early 1920s, the biggest killers of Canadians were heart and kidney diseases (Leacy, 1983). With an annual mortality rate of 222 per 100,000 population, they were the leading causes of death. The next most common cause was influenza, bronchitis, and pneumonia (141 per 100,000), followed by diseases of early infancy. Tuberculosis (TB) took more lives than cancer. Intestinal illnesses like gastritis, enteritis, and colitis, and communicable diseases such as diphtheria, measles, whooping cough, and scarlet fever were also among the leading causes of death.

Table 6.1 Leading Causes of Death, Canada, 1921–25 and 1996–97

1921–25	Rate per 100,000
All causes	1,030.0
Cardiovascular and renal disease	221.9
Influenza, bronchitis, and pneumonia	141.1
Diseases of early infancy	111.0
Tuberculosis	85.1
Cancer	75.9
Gastritis, duodenitis, enteritis, and colitis	72.2
Accidents	51.5
Communicable diseases	47.1
1996–97	**Rate per 100,000**
All causes	654.4
Cardiovascular diseases (heart disease and stroke)	240.2
Cancer	184.8
Chronic obstructive pulmonary diseases	28.4
Unintentional injuries	27.7
Pneumonia and influenza	22.1
Diabetes mellitus	16.7
Hereditary and degenerative diseases of the central nervous system	14.7
Diseases of arteries, arterioles, and capillaries	14.3

Note: Disease categories not identical over time. Rates in 1996–97 are age-standardized.

Sources: Statistics Canada, Catalogue nos. 11-516 and 84-214.

The large-scale introduction of vaccines and antibiotics completed much of the work begun by public health programs. Vaccines against diphtheria, tetanus, typhoid, and cholera had been developed in the late 19th and early 20th centuries; penicillin became available in the 1940s, offering a cure for tuberculosis, septicemia, pneumonia, and typhoid, among other illnesses (Briggs and Briggs, 1998; Porter, 1997). By 1950, the number of people diagnosed with diphtheria and typhoid had plummeted to less than five per 100,000; by the 1970s, the incidence of diseases like measles, whooping cough, and scarlet fever were so low that these illnesses were considered mainly nuisances. This may be why cases of measles and whooping cough became more common in the first half of the 1990s, suggesting that vaccinations against these diseases were being abandoned as parents forgot they could be killers. By the late 1990s, however, incidence rates for both diseases had fallen again.

Since 1987, the rate of new active cases of tuberculosis has remained fairly stable at about six per 100,000. However, TB is an opportunistic disease, attacking those whose resistance to infection is already compromised by malnutrition or poor living conditions; the incidence rate of TB in the Aboriginal population, for example, is four times as high as that in the general population (Health Canada, Statistics Canada, and Canadian Institute for Health Information, 1999).

At the close of the 20th century, cardiovascular disease (heart disease and stroke) remains the leading cause of death among Canadians as it had been when the century began. Nevertheless, it has declined dramatically in the last 50 years, probably reflecting changes in lifestyle (not smoking, eating a low-fat diet, exercise) and improvements in treatment (new pharmaceutical, medical, and surgical techniques). In contrast, the rate for cancer has grown to become the second leading cause of death in Canada, compared to fifth in 1921.

However, the mortality rates for different age groups show very clearly that these two diseases are the biggest killers of older people. Cardiovascular disease is the primary cause of death among Canadians aged 75 and over, while cancer is the leading cause of death among Canadians aged 40 to 69. Unlike 100 years ago, when the principal victims of many diseases were children, Canadians now die mainly of diseases related to growing old.

For example, the increasing age of the population has had a substantial effect on the growing incidence of cancer in Canada. It is estimated that, in 1995, aging of the population alone accounted for one-third of over 30,000 cancer deaths among men and more than one-quarter of over 25,000 deaths among women (assuming that mortality rates prevailing in 1971 remained constant (National Cancer Institute of Canada, 2000).

PUBLIC HEALTH: CLEANING UP CITIES CLEANS OUT MAJOR DISEASES

Epidemics were almost commonplace in 19th-century Europe's industrial cities. Overcrowded, with overflowing cesspits, garbage piled underfoot in the streets and yards of residential and commercial buildings, and unsafe drinking water, the impoverished working-class tenements of British, German, and American cities bred typhoid, scarlet fever, whooping cough, diphtheria, and many other diseases. The biggest killer was tuberculosis; the most frightening was cholera.

When breakthroughs in bacteriology showed that many of the worst diseases were spread by bacteria and viruses in water, air, and food, authorities were able to deal much more effectively with epidemics. Public health medicine prescribed clean water, sewage disposal, garbage removal, and the sanitary handling of food to prevent epidemics.

Cities that provided clean filtered drinking water, proper sewage disposal, and garbage removal from the streets recorded dramatic and steady declines in outbreaks of infectious and communicable diseases. In hospitals, using simple antiseptics such as carbolic acid and iodine to treat wounds, and demanding that physicians wash their hands between patients, greatly reduced deaths from infection.

Public health councils were introduced to regulate and enforce "sanitary control" in England beginning in the 1850s and 1860s; in the United States, procedures were adopted somewhat piecemeal starting in the 1870s. In Canada, the provinces started establishing boards of health in the 1880s to administer and enforce public health regulations. These provincial and municipal boards could, for instance, investigate the origins of outbreak of disease, enforce quarantines, and impose compulsory vaccinations. As their duties and responsibilities grew, boards became more professional, employing specialists in public health and medicine to develop and administer programs. By the late 19th and early 20th century, most of the epidemic killers of European and North American urban populations were under control and mortality rates were down substantially (Briggs and Briggs, 1998; Dominion Bureau of Statistics, 1967; Porter, 1997).

NEW HEALTH PROBLEMS EMERGE IN CHILDHOOD

In 1921, the mortality rate for children under one year old was 102 per 1,000 live births; effectively, 10 percent of children did not live to their first birthday, 4 percent for less than one month. Within 25 years, the rate had been almost halved to 48 per 1,000 in 1946, and by 1996, it had dropped below 6 per 1,000 live births. Lower neonatal infant mortality is associated with better prenatal care, including better nutrition during pregnancy, improved hygiene, and technological advances in caring for the fetus before, during, and after delivery. Immaturity and congenital abnormalities—problems that are now routinely handled in neonatal units—accounted for the majority of infant deaths in the early 1930s; the other principal killers (diarrhea and enteritis, bronchitis and pneumonia, and communicable diseases) are now largely preventable with standard hygiene practices and vaccines or are curable with antibiotics.

Chronic problems rather than acute illness now comprise the principal health difficulties of Canadian children. Partly because of improved medical intervention, including neonatal technology and increased multiple births, there appears to be a growing trend toward pre-term births (less than 37 weeks) and low birth-weight babies (under 2,500 grams). The two conditions are often linked; in 1996, 53 percent of premature babies were low birth weight. Small babies not only have higher mortality rates than babies of normal weight, they also have more health problems that may last into adulthood. A 1999 study of Canadian children under age three showed that being a pre-term low birth-weight baby, and having a mother who was in poor health, were both significantly associated with a child being in poor health (Chen and Millar, 1999).

The rapid growth in the incidence of asthma also alarms health professionals. The percentage of Canadian children under 15 diagnosed with asthma increased from less than 3 percent in 1978–1979 to over 11 percent in 1994–1995. Asthma is more often reported among boys than girls (13 percent versus 9 percent), among school-age children than preschoolers (13 percent versus 7 percent), and among children in either low- or higher-income homes. Having a history of bronchitis or allergies, and having a parent or parents who also have a history of asthma, are significantly associated with asthma in children. Quality of life for asthmatic children can be significantly impeded: Compared with other children, those with asthma are seven times as likely to be in only fair or poor health (7 percent versus 1 percent) and four times as likely to have activity limitations (13 percent versus 3 percent) (Millar and Hill, 1998).

HEALTH STATUS IMPROVING IN YOUNG AND MIDDLE ADULTHOOD

Accidents (mainly motor vehicle accidents, falls, suicides, and homicides) were the single largest cause of death among young adults aged 25 to 39. The mortality rate ranged from 37 to 40 per 100,000 in 1997, with car accidents the main cause of accidental deaths. Dying from cancer is notable only by its rare occurrence: The mortality rate for cancer ranged between seven and 24 per 100,000. In fact, the National Cancer Institute of Canada estimates there is only a one in 90 probability that a 30-year-old woman will develop cancer by the time she is 40, and a one in 143 probability that a man the same age will do so.

On the other hand, cancer is the principal killer of Canadians in their forties and fifties. Mortality rates remain comparatively low, though: In 1997, less than 100 per 100,000 for adults in their forties, and between 160 and 300 for those in their fifties. Lung, breast, and colon cancers are the three biggest killers.

Probably of greater day-to-day worry to adults in later mid-life are the creaks and aches that herald advancing age. On the whole, though, Canadians are healthier now than they were 20 years ago by a number of measures. A recent analysis of adults in three different age cohorts found that, after controlling for the effect of age, the odds of having heart disease, high blood pressure, arthritis, and activity limitations were significantly lower for both men and women today than in the late 1970s (Chen and Millar, 2000).

Improved treatment of disease has contributed to the better health of Canadian adults, as have health education efforts aimed at disease prevention. Asked in 1996–1997 if they had done anything in the previous year to improve their health, almost half (48 percent) of 45- to 64-year-olds said they had. Most often, this health-conscious group of Canadians had increased the amount of exercise they did, although many said they had lost weight or improved their eating habits.

Another factor to which researchers attribute improved health is the lower prevalence of smoking. The National Cancer Institute of Canada cites smoking as the cause of one-quarter of all deaths among 35- to 84-year-olds. The substantial drop in smoking rates among mid-life adults is associated with declining rates of heart disease and stability in the incidence rates for certain types of cancers.

MOST SENIORS STILL GROW OLD AT HOME

Cardiovascular disease is the major cause of illness, disability, and death in Canada, and one of the major causes of hospitalization in this country (Heart and Stroke Foundation of Canada, 1999). It is the leading cause of death among Canadians over the age of 75. Mortality rates in 1997 rose from 1,735 per 100,000 for people aged 75 to 79 to almost 11,000 for seniors 90 or older.

Since the 1980s, mortality rates for both categories of heart disease (heart attack and ischaemic heart disease) have been falling, while those for stroke have remained fairly constant. However, with an increasingly large elderly population, death rates from ischaemic heart disease and stroke are expected to rise throughout the first decade or more of the 21st century.

Cardiovascular disease and many other long-term health conditions common to later years, including dementia, can result in chronic pain, disability, and activity limitation. In 1996–1997, 25 percent of seniors lived with chronic pain and 28 percent had some kind of activity limitation because of a long-term health problem. Senior women had a greater chance of having a chronic condition than men of the same age group. The most common chronic ailment was arthritis (42 percent); others included high blood pressure (33 percent), food and other allergies (22 percent), back problems (17 percent), and diabetes (16 percent). Many seniors had more than one chronic condition. On the whole, though, most seniors (78 percent) reported themselves to be in good to excellent health.

Nevertheless, one of many seniors' greatest fears is that their declining health will lead to their eventual committal to a health care institution. In fact, very few seniors actually live in long-term health care facilities; in 1995, only 5 percent of the senior population aged 65 or older (and 18 percent of those aged 80 or older) were in an institution. Of course, health status is a key predictor of institutionalization. The odds of living in a health care institution are higher for seniors who need personal care (bathing, dressing, etc.), have chronic health problems (particularly Alzheimer's), experience urinary incontinence, or suffer the effects of stroke. Socio-demographic factors also play a role: Being over age 80, being unmarried, having less than Grade 9 education, and having a lower income, also increase the odds of living in a health care institution (Trottier et al., 2000).

Getting help at home can prevent or delay the need for a senior in poor health to enter a health care facility. In 1996, about 22 percent of seniors in private households (over 750,000) were receiving some care at home because they had a long-term health problem. The majority of this caregiving was being provided by family and friends, but some seniors also received additional care provided by professional or volunteer organizations, or from a caregiver hired by the senior. As for publicly funded home care, in 1998–1999, about 8 percent of seniors aged 65 to 79 and 28 percent of those aged 80 or older were receiving it.

LOW INCOME AND POOR HEALTH

The principal reason for introducing universal health care in Canada was to ensure that no one could be denied access to health care because they were unable to pay. But almost 40 years after its introduction, people with low incomes are more likely to be afflicted by a variety of diseases, to be in poor health, and to have lower life expectancy than people with high incomes. This disparity exists despite the fact that low-income Canadians use health care services more frequently than those with higher incomes; in 1998–1999, people with low income were more likely to visit their doctors frequently, to go to emergency departments for care, and to be admitted to hospital. They were also more likely to be using more than one medication (Statistics Canada, 1999).

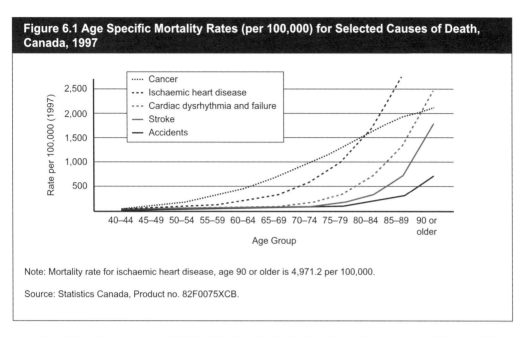

Figure 6.1 Age Specific Mortality Rates (per 100,000) for Selected Causes of Death, Canada, 1997

Note: Mortality rate for ischaemic heart disease, age 90 or older is 4,971.2 per 100,000.

Source: Statistics Canada, Product no. 82F0075XCB.

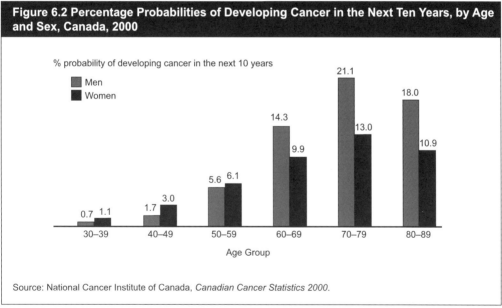

Figure 6.2 Percentage Probabilities of Developing Cancer in the Next Ten Years, by Age and Sex, Canada, 2000

Source: National Cancer Institute of Canada, Canadian Cancer Statistics 2000.

Certainly, risk behaviours and health status are closely related to educational level (and education and income are highly correlated). People with more education are less likely to smoke, drink heavily, or be overweight; they tend to be more physically active and to have a positive outlook on life and good mental health. More people with a university degree also had better health care coverage for dental care, vision care, and prescription drugs, probably provided as an employment benefit (Statistics Canada, 1999).

Research findings like these suggest that social, environmental, and genetic factors play key roles in determining an individual's health status. Thus, it seems possible that health education and making disease prevention the primary goal of health care could ultimately produce improvements in the health status of low-income Canadians.

TODAY'S NIGHTMARE DISEASES

In 2000, an estimated 132,100 new cases of cancer will be identified in Canada, most commonly prostate cancer for men and breast cancer for women. But after rising for many years, incidence rates for prostate cancer began to fall in 1994, while those for breast cancer have grown steadily for 30 years. In 2000, a projected 65,000 Canadians will die of cancer, most commonly of lung cancer, which accounts for one-third of male and one-quarter of female cancer deaths. Overall cancer mortality rates have been declining for men since 1988, and for women since the 1970s (except for lung cancer).

Table 6.2 Incidents of Selected Health Problems by Age and Sex, Canada, 1978–79 and 1996–97

	Age 32–49		Age 50–67		Age 68–85	
	1978–79	1996–97	1978–79	1996–97	1978–79	1996–97
			%			
Men						
Heart disease	1.4	1.1	10.5	8.1	20.4	19.8
High blood pressure	9.7	5.0	21.7	18.6	32.2	26.0
Diabetes	1.1	1.7	4.5	7.2	4.6	12.1
Arthritis	6.1	5.3	23.6	17.3	32.3	30.9
Activity limitation	8.5	8.7	23.5	16.9	35.6	25.2
Daily smoker	47.6	31.8	42.6	24.7	29.6	13.9
Overweight	32.8	36.0	43.8	42.3	32.0	31.6
Women						
Heart disease	1.7	1.2	8.1	5.1	19.7	15.7
High blood pressure	8.9	4.4	30.0	21.6	46.3	37.2
Diabetes	1.1	1.9	5.0	5.4	8.6	9.4
Arthritis	13.2	9.3	36.3	30.5	50.9	47.2
Activity limitation	10.5	10.6	22.5	17.4	35.3	27.0
Daily smoker	39.5	26.4	31.2	19.2	14.7	9.7
Overweight	27.5	22.0	47.0	34.7	38.9	30.8

Source: Statistics Canada, Catalogue no. 82-003, 11, 4 (Spring 2000).

The probability of developing cancer is fairly high over a person's entire lifetime—one in 2.5 for men and one in 2.8 for women. Nevertheless, cancer is most often diagnosed in older Canadians: 70 percent of new cases and 82 percent of deaths are reported for people age 60 or older.

HIV INFECTION/AIDS

Between 1985 and the end of 1999, a total of 45,534 Canadians had tested positive for HIV infection. The main victims of HIV infection have changed in recent years. Over the period 1985–1994, 75 percent of HIV diagnoses were among men who have sex with men; in 1999, the proportion was 37 percent. In contrast, infection is increasing among intravenous drug users, from 9 percent in 1985–1994 to 28 percent in 1999. HIV is also more frequently diagnosed among women now: 24 percent of new cases in 1999 compared with less than 10 percent over the 1985–1994 period. There has also been an increase in HIV exposure via heterosexual sexual contact, from about 6 percent of positive tests in 1984–1995 to over 19 percent in 1999.

From 1985 to 1999, a cumulative total of 16,913 Canadians had been diagnosed with AIDS; about 70 percent had also died of AIDS over this period. But mortality has dropped substantially in recent years. In 1994 and 1995, AIDS deaths reached highs of over 1,400 per year, but less than five years later (1998 and 1999), the numbers had fallen to only 249 and 106, respectively (Health Canada, 2000).

SUMMARY

Advances in public health measures and sanitary control, pharmaceuticals and medical technology in the 20th century have had a dramatic effect on the overall level of health in Canada. Diseases that caused deadly epidemics in the 19th century—cholera, typhoid, tuberculosis, measles, whooping cough, and many others—have been virtually eliminated; death from infection has become rare in an era when cleanliness is standard practice and antibiotics are available. Life expectancy has increased by almost 20 years and the general overall level of health seems to be improving for each successive generation.

However, the World Health Organization (WHO) has warned that a number of infectious diseases, including tuberculosis and pneumonia, are becoming increasingly resistant to antimicrobial drugs. The emergence of drug-resistant TB is of particular concern because it appears to be closely associated with HIV infection. At the same time, WHO's 1998 annual report identifies Canada as part of the trend toward a population that will be longer lived, with a life expectancy of 81 years by 2025. It further forecasts that Canadians will enjoy good health throughout most of that extended lifespan, as disability due to heart disease and some cancers continues to decline.

● ●

CRITICAL THINKING QUESTIONS

1. One hundred years ago, Canadians were far more likely to die in infancy or at a relatively young age. Today, the overwhelming majority survive through to an old age. What are some of the most salient factors responsible for this shift in the age distribution of mortality?
2. Throughout the 20th century, each successive generation of Canadians has been found to be somewhat healthier than its predecessor, with consistent gains made in terms of reducing the risk of premature death. Do you expect this trend to continue (i.e., will infants being born today be healthier than their parents)? Why or why not?
3. Crompton compared life expectancy at the beginning and end of the 20th century. What life expectancy would you envisage for Canada at the end of the 21st century? Defend your prediction.

● ●

CHAPTER 7

DECLINING MORTALITY AND IMPROVED HEALTH STATUS IN 20TH-CENTURY QUEBEC: THE BENEFITS OF MEDICINE AND SOCIO-ECONOMIC DEVELOPMENT

Robert Bourbeau and Mélanie Smuga

● ●

INTRODUCTION

The 20th century was a major turning point in the evolution of the demographic and epidemiological condition of most industrialized countries. Quebec was no exception. Like a number of other countries, Quebec completed its demographic transition (decline in mortality, followed by a decline in fertility) and reached a state of below-replacement fertility during the last quarter of the 20th century. As part of this demographic transition, Quebec's epidemiological transition witnessed a move from being a high-mortality society, with high infant mortality, to one with relatively low mortality, and whose situation is enviable in many respects. We would not have seen such a transition had it not been for medical advances in the broad sense (public health) and for social and economic development.

Our purpose in this chapter is to show the spectacular advances made by Quebec in the control of mortality and in its efforts to eradicate the inequalities that contributed to mortality. These advances are described with the aid of basic demographic indicators that provide the reader with clear benchmarks on mortality decline. This is followed by an examination of changes over time in the causes of death in Quebec that assists us in considering whether declining mortality was more so due to medical developments or socio-economic development. In conclusion, we shall take some time to look at a few of the challenges facing us in the 21st century in terms of emerging trends in mortality and public health.

A CENTURY OF REMARKABLE PROGRESS

DECLINE IN MORTALITY

The annual number of deaths in Quebec rose steadily throughout much of the 20th century. Between 1921 and 1999, the annual number of deaths among men rose from 17,510 to 28,303, and among women, from 15,923 to 26,290 (Figure 7.1). This increase in the number of deaths of about 62 percent for men and 65 percent for women was the result of both population growth and changes in the age distribution. In this connection, we note that during this same period, the total population in Quebec more than tripled, increasing from about 1.2 to 3.7 million for each sex. In addition, by the end of the 20th century, men and women aged 65 and older were much more numerous than in 1926, up by over sevenfold among men and by a multiple of 10 among women. In fact, when we take into account both demographic growth and population aging, we actually observe a real drop in the relative risk of death over the course of the 20th century despite a climb in deaths overall.

The crude death rate (obtained as the total number of deaths relative to total population size) roughly embodies this evolution. The rate declined substantially from 1921 up to the beginning of the 1960s. After that, the crude death rate stagnated at around eight deaths per 1,000 for men and six per 1,000 for women. The recent increase in this crude rate for women is essentially linked to population aging, as the female population has aged to a greater extent than the male. The absolute number of deaths and crude death rates are strongly influenced by variations in both total population size and age structure, which has not remained constant over time. For this reason, we can rely on additional indicators

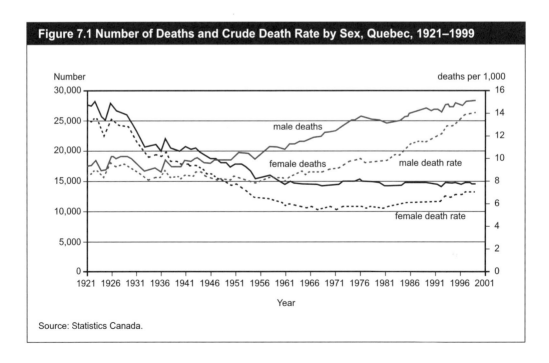

Figure 7.1 Number of Deaths and Crude Death Rate by Sex, Quebec, 1921–1999

Source: Statistics Canada.

in order to get a better grasp of the evolution of mortality independent of population growth and shifts in the age distribution.

EXTENDED LIFE EXPECTANCY

Life expectancy at age x corresponds to the average number of years a person can expect to live from that age x assuming a continuation of age specific mortality rates observed for a specific year. Life expectancy at birth, like infant mortality, is one of the most revealing indicators of both population health and a society's level of socio-economic development.

During the 20th century, life expectancy at birth in Quebec increased dramatically. Male life expectancy rose from about 45 years in 1901 to 75.3 years in 1999 (Figure 7.2), a gain of about 30 years (or an increase of 67 percent). The increase achieved by women is even more astonishing, as female life expectancy at birth rose from 47.7 years in 1901 to 81.4 years by the end of the century. The lives of women have thus been extended by 33.7 years for an increase of 71 percent. From the 1940s onward, the inequality between female and male life expectancies became quite accentuated, reaching a peak in 1979 with a gap of 7.7 years. Since this point in time, this gap in life expectancy has lessened somewhat to about six years, i.e., to levels observed sometime during the mid-1960s. This narrowing was the result of differences in the rate of mortality decline, which was more pronounced among men as of late than women—true of the last 20 years of the 20th century. Yet even with these gains, the 1999 life expectancy among males at birth was merely comparable to what was observed for women in the early 1970s, fully 30 years earlier.

The 65th birthday has frequently been used in a wide variety of contexts to define the threshold of old age or, somewhat arbitrarily, the age of retirement. Yet in 1999, men

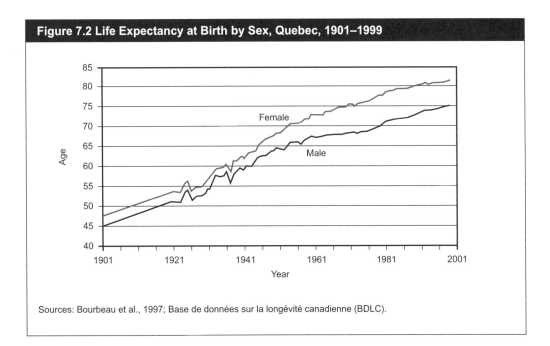

Figure 7.2 Life Expectancy at Birth by Sex, Quebec, 1901–1999

Sources: Bourbeau et al., 1997; Base de données sur la longévité canadienne (BDLC).

at the age of 65 could expect to live an additional 15.9 years on average, which is fully five years longer than those who reached this same age at the start of the century. For women, progress has been much more marked, as life expectancy at age 65 is fully 20 years, an increase of 8.2 years relative to older women in 1901. Yet at the beginning of the 20th century, only about 35 percent of male births and 41 percent of female births could actually expect to make it to the age of 65. In contrast, by 1999, over 82 percent of male births and about 90 percent of females reached their 65th birthday. There has thus been a considerable increase over the years in the number of people surviving until the age of 65; better yet, these people can expect to live much longer than their counterparts once reaching this age relative to the situation earlier. Even at 65, there continues to be a difference in life expectancy by sex, albeit we have continued to witness somewhat of a narrowing in this gap in life expectancy since the end of the 1980s.

In drawing comparisons with Canada overall, the 20th century for Quebec was marked by excess mortality, particularly during the earlier part of this century. At the beginning of the century, life expectancy for Quebecers was in the order of two years less than elsewhere in Canada, whereas currently the difference is about a year for men and non-existent for women. While Quebec men continue to experience slightly higher mortality, Quebec women reached parity with other Canadian women over 20 years ago. Quebec nevertheless finds itself in a good position in comparison with a number of other developed countries. In 1999, male life expectancy at birth was 75.3 years, 1.3 years more than in the U.S. and 0.2 years more than in France. On the other hand, life expectancy is higher in Iceland (77.8 years), Japan (77.4), Sweden (77.1), and Switzerland (76.8) (Institut National d'Études Démographiques, 2002). Quebec women put up a better show, with a life expectancy of 81.4 years in 1999, which is among the highest in the world, yet lower than among Japanese (83.9), Swiss (82.5), Spanish (82.5), French (82.4), and Swedes (81.9).

SPECTACULAR DROP IN INFANT MORTALITY

In 1926, almost one Quebec child in seven died before the age of one. Over seven decades later, that ratio is now no more than about one child in 200. The 20th century has thus brought a considerable decline in infant mortality, i.e., deaths of infants in their first year of life. Between 1926 and 1999, the rate of male infant mortality was divided by 30, going from 157.2 to 5.1 per 1,000, while for girls it was divided by 25, going from 125.7 to 4.6 per 1,000 (Figure 7.3). This decline, true of the whole period, was more rapid during the second half of the century, particularly from 1961 to 1982. More recently, the infant mortality rate has fallen far more slowly, especially during the 1990s. By 1996, infant mortality rates in Quebec had fallen to an unprecedented low of 5.0 deaths per 1,000 for boys and 4.2 per 1,000 for girls. The male excess mortality observed among newborns has varied continually for many years, at an average of about 21 percent. The higher mortality among males is an observable phenomenon from the first year of life, suggestive that "male excess mortality at younger ages is largely of biological origin, as there is no reason to believe that conditions of life differ according to the sex of the child" (Duchesne, 2000:27).

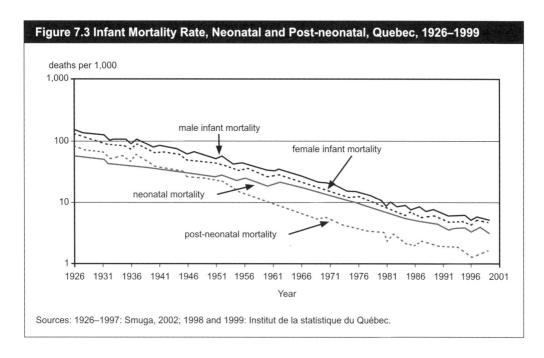

Figure 7.3 Infant Mortality Rate, Neonatal and Post-neonatal, Quebec, 1926–1999

deaths per 1,000

male infant mortality

female infant mortality

neonatal mortality

post-neonatal mortality

Year

Sources: 1926–1997: Smuga, 2002; 1998 and 1999: Institut de la statistique du Québec.

This mortality in the first year of life can be further subdivided into neonatal mortality (deaths occurring during the first 28 days of life), and post-neonatal (deaths occurring after 28 days yet prior to the infant's first birthday). Throughout the 20th century, both these components contributed to a drop in infant mortality, but in different ways at different times. From 1926 to 1960, post-neonatal mortality dropped far more than neonatal mortality, mainly due to improved social and health conditions as well as the use of vaccines and antibiotics. During this period post-neonatal mortality declined by 87 percent, falling from 83.3 to 11.2 per 1,000, while the neonatal mortality rate fell by 69 percent, from 58.7 to 18.2 per 1,000. Between 1961 and 1999, neonatal mortality dropped at a faster rate and achieved a reduction of 84 percent, falling from 20.4 to 3.2 deaths per 1,000. The increasing medicalization of pregnancy and childbirth and the increased proportion of births taking place in hospitals made it possible for further reductions in neonatal mortality. During this same period, post-neonatal mortality still showed a noticeable drop (by 85 percent) as the number of deaths fell from 10.5 per 1,000 live births in 1961 to 1.6 in 1999. Although post-neonatal was formerly almost one and a half times higher than neonatal mortality, today it is only at about half the level of neonatal mortality.

During much of the 20th century, infant mortality in Quebec was notable when contrasting its level with the situation observed in other Canadian provinces. For a long time, from 1926 until the end of the 1960s, Quebec suffered from a rather high excess infant mortality. A major reversal was observed from the 1970s onward, linked among other things, with Quebec's expansion of health care services for young mothers and infants. By the end of the century, infant mortality in Quebec was actually lower than in most other Canadian provinces, although it is worth noting that differences in infant mortality rates between the provinces have greatly diminished over time and are now rather minor. By international standards, Quebec has a very favourable situation at the end of the century, as only Japan and the Scandinavian countries have lower infant mortality rates, reaching levels never before recorded, at about four deaths per 1,000 births or even less (Institut National d'Études Démographiques, 2002).

AGE GROUPS AND LIFE EXPECTANCY: AN APPRECIABLE CHANGE

When we break down gains in mortality over the 1921 to 1999 period across broad age groups, we can measure the relative contribution of each age group's decline in mortality and to overall gains in life expectancy (Table 7.1). For example, it is noteworthy in this context that reduced infant mortality between 1921 and 1999 was responsible for fully 43.7 percent of the gains made in terms of extending life expectancy. Furthermore, the decline in mortality among children and adolescents (ages one to 14) was responsible for an additional 18.1 percent of the overall gains, as reduced mortality among the young played a principal role in explaining the changes observed in life expectancy during the 20th century. The contribution of reduced mortality among people 65 and over was relatively modest, at least initially as, for example, it was responsible for 9.2 percent of overall gains in life expectancy for the 1921–1999 interval. This is not to deny an important transition in the profile of the age distribution of mortality in explaining the evolution of life expectancy in Quebec. Until the beginning of the 1960s, almost half the gains in life expectancy (48.4 percent) were due to reduced infant mortality, and more than 70 percent due to reduced mortality among infants and children under the age of 15. While reduced mortality among the very old had a modest effect initially on the evolution of life expectancy (responsible for only 3.2 percent of the decline over the 1921–1964 period),

Table 7.1 Contribution (in %) by Age Groups to Gains in Life Expectancy at Birth, Both Sexes, Quebec, 1921–24 and 1995–99

Age Interval	Period					
	1921–1924 to 1960–1964		1960–1964 to 1995–1999		1921–1924 to 1995–1999	
	Gain	%	Gain	%	Gain	%
0–1 years	8.35	48.4	1.93	24.4	10.99	43.7
1–14 years	3.77	21.9	0.54	6.8	4.56	18.1
15–34 years	2.53	14.7	0.37	4.7	3.12	12.4
35–64 years	2.03	11.8	2.51	31.8	4.17	16.6
65–84 years	0.54	3.1	2.28	28.8	2.13	8.5
85 years and over	0.01	0.1	0.28	3.5	0.17	0.7
Total	17.23	100.0	7.91	100.0	25.14	100.0

Source: Base de données sur la longévité canadienne (BDLC).

things were quite different from the 1960s onward. Gains in reducing mortality among those aged 65 years and over has been responsible for almost one-third (32.3 percent) of the overall gains made in life expectancy since 1960, growing in importance in terms of overall impact on life expectancy.

THE COMPRESSION OF MORTALITY AND THE RECTANGULARIZATION OF SURVIVAL CURVES

The compression of mortality and the rectangularization of the survival curve are two phenomena that characterize the 20th-century evolution of mortality. The compression of mortality can be seen by examining the distribution of deaths by age for a few different periods. There is a compression of mortality when a climbing proportion of all deaths occur within a more and more restricted age range as the years go by. Figure 7.4 demonstrates this compression by including the distribution of deaths by age for three distinct periods, each separated by an interval of 40 years. For men, the modal age at death in 1921–1924 was about 78 with about 2.4 percent of deaths according at this age; in 1955–1959, the mode was 76 years with 3.0 percent of all deaths; finally, in 1995–1999, the modal age was 81 with 3.6 percent of all deaths. In the case of females, in 1921–1924, 1955–1959, and 1995–1999, the modal ages for women were 78, 79, and 87 years, respectively, with 2.4 percent, 3.6 percent, and 4.0 percent of all deaths. We note that in general, the further one advances in time, the more deaths become progressively concentrated around the same ages and the older the age at which the compression occurs. In addition, this compression of mortality is clearly occurring at a later age for women relative to men, whereas its intensity is also greater.

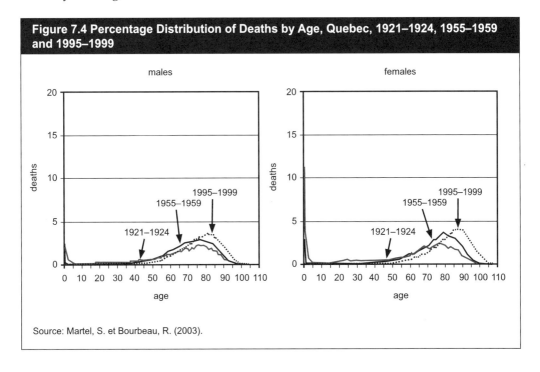

Figure 7.4 Percentage Distribution of Deaths by Age, Quebec, 1921–1924, 1955–1959 and 1995–1999

Source: Martel, S. et Bourbeau, R. (2003).

The survival curve demonstrates the progressive decline in the proportion of individuals born to a specific birth cohort to survive through to different ages, assuming a continuation of age-specific mortality rates over an extended period. As mortality and the risk of premature death decline, the survival curve becomes more and more rectangular. This rectangularization of the survival curve can be observed in Figure 7.5, which provides the corresponding survival curves from several different life tables, for men and women separately. For 1921–1924, the proportion of survivors, male and female, falls sharply during the first years of life because of the high infant and child mortality; only 80 percent of the initial births are still alive by the age of 10 years for boys, and about 20 for girls. Upon reaching this age, the survival curve levels off somewhat, and thus declines much more slowly until about 60 years of age, prior to dropping off rapidly into advanced old age. By 1955–1959, we already observe progress in reducing mortality among young children: More than 90 percent of births are still alive in their twenties and even thirties. The survival curve drops gradually until about 65, after which the proportion of survivors falls rapidly.

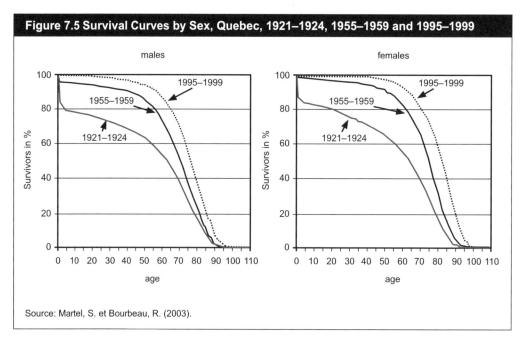

Figure 7.5 Survival Curves by Sex, Quebec, 1921–1924, 1955–1959 and 1995–1999

Source: Martel, S. et Bourbeau, R. (2003).

The evolution of the survival curve through to 1995–1999 is much more of the same, except that the curve becomes even more convex in moving in the direction of almost a right angle, hence the expression "rectangularization" (Vallin and Meslé, 2001). In 1921–1924, half of deaths occurred after the age of 63 for men and 65 for women. In 1955–1959, half the male survivors were dead by 71 as compared with 76 for females. At the turn of the century, half of deaths were occurring after 77 years of age for men and 84 years for women. This again bears witness to the fact that the Quebec population is surviving to more and more advanced ages.

CHANGES IN THE CAUSES OF DEATH: THE EPIDEMIOLOGICAL TRANSITION

The decline in mortality observed throughout the 20th century is described as an "epidemiological transition" or "mortality transition." The epidemiological transition, as proposed by Omran (1971), corresponds to changes in the structure of the causes of death that accompanied declining mortality (Robine, 2001). This drop in mortality was largely driven by the improvement in social and economic conditions, health status, public hygiene, nutrition, and the organization of health services. These changes brought with them a transformation in the causes of death. Contagious diseases that, in the old days, were responsible for a large portion of deaths gradually disappeared and were replaced by chronic and degenerative diseases and, to a lesser extent, accidental death. Here we will demonstrate that in the course of the last century, Quebec went through an evolution in the causes of death that conforms with the epidemiological transition. For the sake of simplicity, 10 broad groups of causes of death will be retained for our purposes.

EVOLUTION OF PRINCIPAL CAUSES OF DEATH

Figure 7.6 shows that in 1926, the principal causes of death included respiratory diseases (15.6 percent), diseases of the digestive system (15.3 percent), infectious and parasitic diseases (15.2 percent), and congenital anomalies and perinatal diseases (13.5 percent). These causes alone represented three-fifths of all deaths. A major proportion of all deaths were the result of illnesses that are now largely preventable and curable. Illnesses that today pose few problems were particularly serious at the beginning of the century, such as diarrhea and enteritis (responsible for 9.2 percent of all deaths), tuberculosis (8.8 percent), influenza (5.6 percent), broncho-pneumonia (3.6 percent), and pneumonia (3.5 percent), which in combination were responsible for almost one-third of all deaths. Contagions and parasites were difficult to control as the sanitary environment in which people lived was often very difficult. Improvements in people's social and health conditions, especially as a result of vaccination campaigns, were decisive in reducing the impact of many of these diseases.

Through to the 1960s, several causes of death that were considered particularly threatening earlier on in the century saw their relative importance decline in a remarkable fashion. The percentage of all deaths due to infectious and parasitic diseases declined by fully 88 percent over this period, as their share dropped from 15.2 percent in 1926 to only 1.8 percent in 1961. Diseases of the digestive system also declined considerably by fully 73.5 percent, and diseases of the respiratory system by 69.0 percent. On the other hand, cardiovascular disease and cancer increased significantly over this period. From 1926 to 1961, the share of deaths from diseases of the cardiovascular system increased from 12.4 percent of all deaths to 44.6 percent. Deaths from cancer and malignant tumours similarly increased from 5.2 percent to 17.8 percent. Injuries and poisonings, almost half of which consisted of motor vehicle accidents, also increased as a share of all deaths, doubling in percentage during that period.

From the beginning of the 1960s to the end of the 20th century, the most appreciable gains were made in reducing the percentage of all deaths due to congenital anomalies and

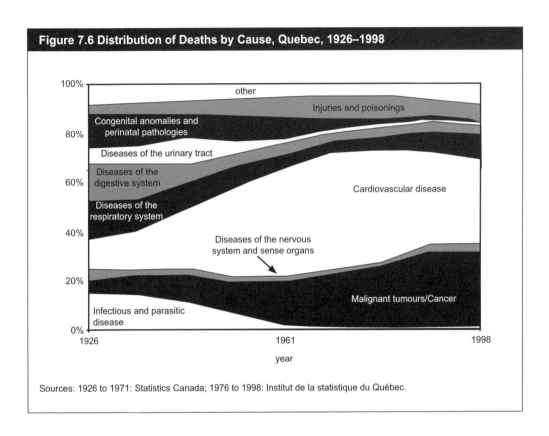

Figure 7.6 Distribution of Deaths by Cause, Quebec, 1926–1998

Sources: 1926 to 1971: Statistics Canada; 1976 to 1998: Institut de la statistique du Québec.

perinatal pathologies. Their percentage relative to all deaths declined eleven fold, from 9.0 percent to only 0.8 percent. As for infectious and parasitic diseases, their percentage continued to decline, although a slight rise was observed due to the advent of AIDS during the 1980s. The percentage dying from cardiovascular disease first increased, yet more recently has declined, with a far from linear trend over time. Of all causes of death, cardiovascular diseases caused the most damage during the 1970s, alone causing almost half of all deaths in 1971 (47.3 percent). In other words, this was the highest percentage ever recorded for any single cause of death throughout the 20th century. Respiratory disease and diseases of the nervous system doubled in relative terms between 1961 and 1998, from 4.8 percent to 10.0 percent and 1.7 percent to 3.3 percent, respectively. Deaths caused by cancer went up from 17.8 percent to 30.7 percent, an increase of fully 73 percent.

In the space of seven decades, we have seen a huge shift in the causes of death, a change that occurred largely in the first half of this period. In 1926, the distribution of causes of death was much more heterogeneous than at the end of the century. Some causes of death increased considerably between 1926 and 1998: The percentage of deaths due to cancer grew by a multiple of six, increasing from 5.2 percent to 30.7 percent. The percentage of all deaths due to cardiovascular diseases almost tripled, moving from 12.4 percent to 34.2 percent. At the end of the century, cardiovascular diseases and cancer alone make up nearly two-thirds of all deaths combined. In 1926, they constituted only a little over one-sixth. We must also mention a 71 percent increase in the percentage of all deaths due to injuries and poisonings between 1926 and 1998, while other causes of death generally declined in relative importance.

Taking everything into account, Quebec went through the three different phases of the epidemiological transition over the last century, consistent with Omran's (1971) conceptualization of this transition. More specifically, Omran coined the first phase as "the age of pestilence and famine," the second as "the age of receding pandemics," and the third as "the age of degenerative and man-made diseases." In the Quebec context, the early 20th century was noted as (1) a period of predominantly infectious and parasitic disease; followed by (2) a period of receding infectious disease and the appearance of degenerative disease; and, more recently, (3) a period of degenerative disease as shaped by lifestyle choices (or so called "man-made" diseases). For Omran, this third phase of the epidemiological transition was expected to correspond with a halt in mortality decline, a situation that has yet to occur. Olshansky and Ault (1986) have proposed a fourth phase to this transition, namely "an era of delayed degenerative diseases." This phase is characterized by a continued decline in overall mortality due to the deferral of chronic and degenerative diseases through to older and older ages. At the dawn of the 21st century, Quebec has entered this fourth phase of the epidemiological transition, but we will have to wait a few more years to see what develops in terms of the distribution of deaths by cause.

RECENT TRENDS IN MORTALITY DUE TO CERTAIN CAUSES

Crude death rates are not comparable over time and space, since they are strongly influenced by change in age structure. To allow an appropriate comparison of mortality by sex and for some causes of death, it is sometimes useful to use standardized rates that control for changes in age distribution over time. For current purposes, we take as our reference population the age distribution for Quebec in 1996 (both sexes combined) and calculate what mortality rates would have looked like if Quebec's age distribution remained unchanged from this reference population. These standardized rates are free of the effect of change in age distribution and make it possible to properly examine the evolution of the different causes of death. The data presented cover the last two decades and thus portray a relatively recent picture of how mortality has evolved.

Between 1977 and 1998, the standardized mortality rate for all causes of death dropped by 27 percent for men and 25 percent for women. Among males, this rate declined from 1,273.5 deaths per 100,000 to 927.9 per 100,000. For females, this rate declined from 730.7 to 548.9 deaths per 100,000. In spite of a slightly larger drop among men than among women, these rates clearly bear witness to the fact that men continue to suffer excess mortality. In moving on to consider these standardized rates, yet for specific causes of death, it is noted that the evolution of mortality rates over the last two decades differ greatly from one cause of death to the next. The mortality from certain selected causes have clearly declined while others have actually climbed over time. For both sexes, the largest increases and decreases in mortality were observed for the same causes of death, but in a different order of magnitude according to sex.

The largest gains in reducing mortality for men were from motor vehicle accidents, as the corresponding standardized mortality rate in 1998 (12.5 deaths per 100,000) was almost three times lower than in 1977 (34.3 deaths per 100,000). Next in line in terms of reducing mortality are the rates as associated with cerebrovascular disease and for ischemic cardiomyopathy, which have diminished by 59 percent and 52 percent respectively over this same period. For females, progress in reducing mortality was a little less than for their male counterparts, although both sexes made considerable gains. Among women, we still observe a reduction by one half in the mortality rate from motor vehicle accidents, cerebrovascular disease, and ischemic cardiomyopathy. It is not surprising to see such drops in these death rates, as great efforts were made to reduce deaths due to these types of causes. For example, in 1976, it became obligatory for front-seat passengers in motor vehicles to wear a seat belt, and by 1990, the law made it obligatory for all passengers to buckle up. The Société de l'assurance automobile du Québec (SAAQ)—the auto insurance board of Quebec—subsequently launched promotions and educational campaigns on such themes as drunk driving and speeding, which certainly had an impact on safe driving. Also, as mentioned above, the 1970s stand out because of a high proportion of deaths from cardiovascular diseases, which has led to the promotion of healthy lifestyle choices among people faced with this health risk. The reduction in the amount of fat in the diet, more physical exercise, a reduction in the number of smokers, and improvements in treatment of high blood pressure have all contributed to the reduction of heart disease.

Although there have been gains in terms of reducing overall mortality, there have nevertheless been clear increases in the death rates for certain causes of death. Malignant tumours of the trachea, the bronchi, and the lungs, respiratory diseases, and suicide are the causes of death that have increased in Quebec over recent years. However, there are strong variations according to sex as, for example, deaths due to malignant tumours of the trachea, bronchi, and lungs have tripled in women, while for men, the increase has been far less dramatic, up from 88.7 deaths to 102.7 deaths per 100,000. While improvements for men have been slowing since the end of the 1980s, the level of mortality from lung cancer remains far higher than for women. Deaths caused by respiratory diseases have also increased in the last two decades, namely by 12 percent for men and 31 percent for women. This increase is explained by deaths from chronic obstructive lung disease, the majority of these linked to tobacco use (Ministère de la Santé et des Services sociaux, 2001). The other rising cause of mortality in the last few years is suicide. The mortality rate from suicide has increased from 22.6 to 29.1 deaths per 100,000 for men and from 7.9 to 8.4 deaths for women, increases of 29 percent and 6 percent, respectively. Compared with the other Canadian provinces, it is Quebec that has the highest suicide rate across provinces both for men and for women (Statistics Canada, 2002).

As we have noted, the 20th century has been characterized by an important change in the distribution of causes of death, which can be described as the "three revolutions in mortality" (Nizard, 1997). This, in turn, has been related to the three phases of the epidemiological transition. The first revolution involved major reductions in infectious and parasitic diseases, as well as congenital anomalies and perinatal diseases, made possible by vaccination and antibiotics that safeguarded the lives of infants in particular.

Most of the progress began in the early 1940s and lost impetus during the 1960s. The second revolution was that of the cardiovascular therapies, which have prolonged the lives of old people, including the introduction of numerous preventive measures during the 1970s and 1980s. Finally, the third revolution in mortality, which started at the very beginning of the 1990s, emphasizes a reduction in the so called "man-made" diseases, which is reducing mortality further through the successful treatment and avoidance of cancers, particularly of the trachea, bronchi, and lungs, and also suicide. Even if chronic and degenerative diseases are predominant today, there is still hope of reducing mortality further in the future, as many predominant causes of premature death continue to be principally connected with individual behaviour and lifestyle.

CONCLUSION: WHAT IS AT STAKE IN THE 21ST CENTURY?

Quebec has experienced a considerable decline in mortality over the course of the 20th century. Life expectancy at birth has risen by 30.3 years for men and 33.7 years for women. This was largely due to the rather spectacular drop in infant mortality, especially in the earlier part of the century. After that, the reduction in mortality associated with cardiovascular disease and accidental injuries made it possible for further reductions through to the end of the century. More recently, progress has been made in reducing mortality at older ages, which further contributed to increased life expectancy and puts forth the promise of a lengthening of the human lifespan.

On the other hand, some causes of death, such as lung cancer among women and suicide among men, have shown worrying trends since the 1980s. In the former, we appear to be observing the effects of past smoking patterns and how they have differed by sex over the last several decades, and in the latter, the combined effects of many social and economic variables. We can, however, be optimistic as these deaths are historically dependent on factors linked with behaviour and lifestyle, and action can be taken to prevent them, such as, for example, the reduction in the number of women smokers since 1998.

In the Canadian context, Quebec is in a favourable position after having long suffered from considerable excess mortality, particularly with regard to infant mortality. However, Montreal still lags behind other large Canadian cities due to excess mortality for certain causes of death. In the international context, Quebec occupies a middle-of-the-pack position in terms of mortality among the most developed countries (Choinière, 2003).

What does the 21st century have in store on questions of health and mortality? First, let us acknowledge that it would be foolhardy to predict future developments for a very long period. Who, at the beginning of the 20th century, could have foreseen the enormous progress made in health and longevity? When it comes to forecasting mortality decline, typically demographers have been overly pessimistic, as virtually all the forecasts made in the past predicted fewer gains than what happened in reality (Oeppen and Vaupel, 2002). Nevertheless, let us take a look at what recent trends in Quebec mortality seem to suggest for the future.

It is more than likely that we will witness a continuation of the decline in mortality. Initially we have reason to expect that Quebec will surely attain a level already reached in the lowest mortality countries like Japan, where a life expectancy at birth is already over 85 years for women and over 77 for men. This eventuality is all the more probable in that mortality at advanced ages in Canada and Quebec is already among the lowest in the industrialized world (Bourbeau and Lebel, 2000). Furthermore, the mid-range projections of the Institut de la statistique du Québec and Statistics Canada support the expectation that we will easily reach these levels by 2040. Far more optimistic forecasts might suggest a life expectancy of much as 100 for infants born at the beginning of the 21st century, i.e., half of all of the births occurring recently may very well reach the age of 100. Becoming a supercentenarian (i.e., reaching the age of 110) could become almost commonplace instead of being quite exceptional as it is now. To attain mortality levels like these, the limits of human lifespan would have to be pushed back (to ages like 125, 130, or even 135), which are currently not yet accessible (Bourbeau et al., 2002).

In the quest for ever longer lifespans, a fundamental issue surfaces that has begun to attract some attention at the end of the 20th century, i.e., while we may be living longer lives, in what state of health are we doing so? Should we favour quantity at the expense of quality of life? We know that improvements in life expectancy in the last two decades have also meant more years lived in a state of good health without serious disability or chronic disease. But this progress is uncertain and we will have to keep a close watch on health indicators to make sure that our gains also mean a greater number of years lived without disability. This is surely one of the challenges of the 21st century.

To reach these objectives, we must pay attention to those causes of death that are on the rise, such as respiratory diseases among women and suicide among men. Further prevention strategies are required as the health care system must allow us to offer appropriate care—remedial and supportive care, rehabilitation, and special care and attention (home and extended care). In the context of Quebec, whose population will age considerably in the next 25 years, the question of health care costs and funding will inevitably arise. As a matter of intergenerational equity, we should discuss the possibility of providing ourselves with a health fund (a capitalization system) to supplement the pay-as-you-go method currently in place, which is less suitable for an aging population (Légaré et al., 2003).

The fact that the population is aging also means that a large number of people will need health care. For example, mortality from cancer has been in decline since 1988, but we are seeing an increase in new cases because the population is aging. Thus, according to Health Canada, more than 18,000 Quebecers are going to die of cancer in 2003, and there will be 36,000 new cases. It has been estimated that 80 percent of cancers are environmental. However, we must realize that in matters of cost, the aging of the population has a greater effect on the cost of extended care services and home care than on extended hospital care since the latter is concentrated in the last few years or even last few months of life.

Another important issue is the possible reappearance of easily transmissible infectious diseases. We already know the extent of the AIDS epidemic; at present, the incidence of HIV is not falling, and the reduction in mortality due to AIDS has brought an increase in the population living with the virus. Other transmissible infectious diseases have recently appeared; mad cow disease, avian influenza, the West Nile virus, and atypical pneumonia, otherwise known as severe acute respiratory syndrome (SARS). Viruses seem to be more and more resistant and the search for new vaccines may take some time. In a world where people travel rapidly from one continent to another, no country is safe from new epidemics; the 14th century had the Black Death, the 16th syphilis, and the 20th cholera and Spanish influenza; the 21st will probably not escape its turn.

The other key issue in the 21st century is the pursuit of health for all as an objective. Quebec will need to equip itself with a health policy that aims to reduce social inequalities as they affect death, those inequalities being still too great at the end of the 20th century. Montreal, in fact, remains Canada's capital of social inequality. The first strategy to pursue in order to compensate in part for social inequality is to preserve the universality of the health care system. Health services must continue to be accessible to all. Efforts should be made to prevent disease by promoting a better lifestyle (campaigns against sedentarism and being overweight or obese) and by keeping a watchful eye on the quality of our environment. We must also improve our health care system and social support, given the aging of our population, and plan for large investment in long-term care for support, rehabilitation, and supportive care and attention for the aged.

● ●

CRITICAL THINKING QUESTIONS

1. Male life expectancy rose from about 45 years in 1901 to about 75 years in 1999, a gain of about 30 years. The increase achieved by women is even more astonishing, as female life expectancy at birth rose from about 48 years in 1901 to 81.4 years for an increase of 33.4 years. If we witness comparable gains throughout the 21st century, can we anticipate a male life expectancy of about 105 by 2100 and a female life expectancy of over 110? Do you think this is possible or likely?

2. When we break down gains in mortality over the 1921 to 1999 period across broad age groups, we can measure the relative contribution of each age group's decline in mortality and to overall gains in life expectancy. Where have the gains been greatest in explaining the aforementioned improvement in overall life expectancy at birth?

3. What is meant by the idea that there has been "a compression in mortality" and "the rectangularizaton in the survival curve"? Is this a positive advancement from the point of view of population health?

● ●

CHAPTER 8

A Comparison of U.S. and Canadian Mortality in 1998

Barbara Boyle Torrey and Carl Haub

● ●

HALF A CENTURY AGO, IN 1955, Americans and Canadians had almost the same life expectancy at birth: 69.5 years in the United States and 69.9 years in Canada, as calculated for the two sexes combined. In the next 43 years, chances of survival improved in both countries, but improved faster in Canada. In 1998, life expectancy was 76.7 years in the United States and 78.8 years in its northern neighbour. Thus, the difference in life expectancy between the two countries, to the disadvantage of the U.S., rose from 0.4 years to 2.1 years. This was a notable divergence, especially since it occurred at a time when life expectancy among high-income countries was tending to converge (White, 2002).

What are the implications of Americans dying 2.1 years earlier, on average, than Canadians? What are the causes of death that account for this difference? Using basic mortality data for the two countries for 1998 (the most recent year for which cause-of-death statistics are directly comparable), we calculate the numbers of deaths by age and sex that would have occurred in the United States on the assumption that Canadian mortality rates prevailed in the 1998 U.S. population. The difference between the resulting hypothetical numbers and the actual numbers of U.S. deaths recorded in that year provides an estimate of the excess U.S. deaths, by age and sex, in comparison to Canada. We also present the analogous calculation for the White U.S. population only. We then briefly discuss the causes of deaths that resulted in the observed excess and the underlying risk factors that help explain U.S.–Canadian differences in death rates.

DATA AND METHODS

Deaths in Canada and the United States are recorded, respectively, by Statistics Canada and by the U.S. National Center for Health Statistics (NCHS), from provincial and state vital statistics registers. In 1998 both Canada and the United States were using the International Classification of Diseases (ICD)-9th Revision (National Center for Health Statistics, 2002; Statistics Canada, 2001). In 1999, the U.S. moved to ICD-10, which increased the number of detailed categories of causes of death from 5,000 to 8,000 and created some discontinuities between the old and new categories (Anderson et al., 2001).

Race is an important variable in mortality differentials between the United States and Canada. Classification of race is treated differently in the two countries. NCHS defines "White" as including Hispanics who have identified themselves as White. In 1998, the non-White population so defined amounted to 17 percent of the total. In Canada's 2001 census, 13.4 percent of the population was classified as "visible minorities." Canadian mortality rates, however, are not disaggregated by ethnic or racial groups. Thus, in this analysis we compare death rates for the total Canadian population with American White and non-White death rates.

Using a familiar method of standardization, we applied Canadian age- and sex-specific death rates to the 1998 U.S. population, subdivided into five-year age groups. Age zero to four is further subdivided into those aged zero and aged one to four, and those aged 85 and older are treated as constituting a single group. The resulting numbers of deaths by age and sex are compared with the corresponding actual numbers: The differences indicate the number of excess U.S. deaths by age and sex in 1998. The details of the calculation are shown in Table 8.1. Using the same procedure, we show the excess number of deaths in the U.S. White population in Table 8.2. Finally, by applying Canadian age- and sex-specific death rates by cause of death to the 1998 U.S. population, we calculate the number of excess U.S. deaths in that year by cause and by age and sex. The results of this calculation are presented for three broad age groups and for seven broad categories of causes in Table 8.3.

DEMOGRAPHIC CHARACTERISTICS OF EXCESS U.S. DEATHS

As Table 8.1 indicates, the number of excess American deaths in 1998 was 253,237. This is equivalent to some 11 percent of all U.S. deaths in that year. Of that figure, the number of excess deaths among White Americans in the same year, as shown in Table 8.2, was 164,756. Using an age-sex distribution other than that of the 1998 U.S. population (but broadly similar to it, for example, the age-sex distribution of the Canadian population) as the standard would change these precise numerical results, but not their general magnitude.

Turning to the causes of these excess deaths relative to Canadian deaths, we find that they occur in five of the seven categories of the causes we investigated (Table 8.3 and Figure 8.1). In one category, suicides, the hypothetical and the actual numbers were roughly the same, while in another category, neoplasms, U.S. deaths showed a shortfall compared to the number that would have been obtained had Canadian cause-specific death rates prevailed in the U.S. population. Circulatory diseases are the most important cause of death in both Canada and the United States; these diseases accounted for 68 percent of all American excess deaths. Circulatory diseases were the cause of 95 percent of the excess deaths of all U.S. women over age 65; among men, the excess in this category was greater than for all causes combined, compensated by shortfalls from other causes, notably among deaths caused by neoplasms and injuries. Circulatory diseases were also the largest single category of deaths among men and women under age 65.

Circulatory diseases include 34 distinct conditions such as ischemic heart, cerebrovascular, and hypertensive diseases and congestive heart failure. These diseases

Table 8.1 Excess U.S. Deaths Relative to Canada by Age and Sex, 1998

Age	U.S. midyear population		U.S. actual deaths		U.S. death rates per 100,000		Canadian death rates per 100,000		U.S. deaths with Canadian death rates		Excess U.S. deaths relative to Canada		
	Males	Females	Males	Females	Males	Females	Males	Females	Males	Females	Males	Females	Total
0	1,929,312	1,847,077	15,786	12,584	818	681	572	484	11,030	8,940	4,756	3,644	8,400
1–4	7,766,906	7,422,843	2,920	2,331	38	31	28	23	2,144	1,700	777	631	1,408
5–9	10,195,027	9,725,835	2,039	1,488	20	15	15	13	1,488	1,264	551	224	774
10–14	9,854,788	9,387,020	2,651	1,615	27	17	20	14	1,991	1,286	660	329	989
15–19	10,045,566	9,493,761	9,915	3,873	99	41	69	31	6,972	2,953	2,943	921	3,864
20–24	8,996,110	8,678,024	12,801	4,035	142	47	97	31	8,744	2,699	4,057	1,336	5,394
25–29	9,246,888	9,341,226	12,890	5,259	139	56	93	33	8,581	3,101	4,309	2,158	6,467
30–34	10,006,893	10,179,403	16,321	8,042	163	79	108	48	10,827	4,845	5,494	3,196	8,690
35–39	11,256,018	11,369,766	24,032	13,200	214	116	139	74	15,635	8,391	8,397	4,809	13,206
40–44	10,844,698	11,049,377	33,109	18,530	305	168	193	118	20,952	13,082	12,157	5,447	17,604
45–49	9,252,354	9,607,011	41,710	23,700	451	247	284	185	26,314	17,735	15,396	5,966	21,362
50–54	7,647,607	8,077,912	50,023	31,051	654	384	452	294	34,544	23,765	15,479	7,286	22,765
55–59	5,956,213	6,450,696	60,896	39,749	1,022	616	776	473	46,202	30,492	14,694	9,257	23,951
60–64	4,849,497	5,419,564	79,241	53,838	1,634	993	1,275	753	61,817	40,782	17,424	13,056	30,480
65–69	4,392,568	5,200,929	110,192	79,585	2,509	1,530	2,195	1,206	96,417	62,697	13,775	16,887	30,663
70–74	3,857,005	4,944,791	149,150	120,050	3,867	2,428	3,555	1,984	137,109	98,085	12,042	21,965	34,006
75–79	2,997,107	4,220,900	171,426	158,039	5,720	3,744	5,743	3,308	172,127	139,606	–701	18,433	17,731
80–84	1,764,311	2,969,871	162,786	189,415	9,227	6,378	9,590	5,861	169,199	174,070	–6,431	15,345	8,932
85+	1,187,459	2,866,191	199,057	413,517	16,763	14,427	17,930	14,064	212,914	403,110	–13,856	10,407	–3,449
Total	132,046,327	138,252,197	1,156,945	1,179,902	876	853	754	688	1,045,006	1,038,604	111,939	141,298	253,237

Sources: U.S. 1998 midyear population: U.S. Census Bureau, unpublished file NESTV 98; U.S. deaths 1998 generated by applying death rates from NCHS to the 1998 population from U.S. Census Bureau, unpublished file NESTV 98; U.S. death rates 1998: National Center for Health Statistics, "Death rates for 282 selected causes by 5 year age groups, race and sex: Unites States 1979–1998", Canadian death rates 1998: Statistics Canada, Mortality—1998 Shelf Tables.

Table 8.2 Excess U.S. White Deaths Relative to Canada by Age and Sex, 1998

Age	U.S. midyear white population		U.S. actual white deaths		U.S. white death rates per 100,000		Canadian death rates per 100,000		U.S. white deaths with Canadian death rates		Excess U.S. white deaths relative to Canada		
	Males	Females	Males	Females	Males	Females	Males	Females	Males	Females	Males	Females	Total
0	1,532,601	1,460,840	10,327	8,233	674	564	572	484	8,762	7,070	1,565	1,163	2,728
1–4	6,179,436	5,879,264	2,008	1,617	33	28	28	23	1,706	1,346	303	270	573
5–9	8,038,436	7,648,803	1,423	1,033	18	14	15	13	1,174	994	249	38	287
10–14	7,799,351	7,402,657	1,926	1,229	25	17	20	14	1,575	1,014	351	215	566
15–19	7,991,575	7,500,658	7,248	3,075	91	41	69	31	5,546	2,333	1,702	743	2,445
20–24	7,224,785	6,868,796	9,132	2,837	126	41	97	31	7,022	2,136	2,110	701	2,810
25–29	7,473,057	7,394,657	9,080	3,579	122	48	93	33	6,935	2,455	2,145	1,124	3,269
30–34	8,201,666	8,145,421	11,909	5,514	145	68	108	48	8,874	3,877	3,035	1,637	4,672
35–39	9,364,283	9,261,994	18,026	9,281	193	100	139	74	13,007	6,835	5,019	2,445	7,464
40–44	9,098,379	9,079,303	24,939	13,101	274	144	193	118	17,578	10,750	7,361	2,352	9,712
45–49	7,858,712	7,972,031	31,545	17,188	401	216	284	185	22,350	14,716	9,195	2,471	11,666
50–54	6,624,094	6,849,723	39,367	24,063	594	351	452	294	29,921	20,152	9,446	3,911	13,357
55–59	5,180,801	5,491,752	49,140	31,413	949	572	776	473	40,187	25,960	8,952	5,453	14,406
60–64	4,231,745	4,621,563	65,270	43,489	1,542	941	1,275	753	53,942	34,777	11,328	8,712	20,040
65–69	3,857,225	4,483,704	94,344	66,408	2,446	1,481	2,195	1,206	84,666	54,051	9,678	12,357	22,035
70–74	3,452,264	4,369,679	130,958	102,954	3,793	2,356	3,555	1,984	122,721	86,677	8,237	16,277	24,514
75–79	2,705,650	3,781,930	153,164	139,599	5,661	3,691	5,743	3,308	155,388	125,087	-2,224	14,511	12,287
80–84	1,609,889	2,698,506	148,429	170,991	9,220	6,337	9,590	5,861	154,390	158,165	-5,961	12,826	6,865
85+	1,065,773	2,600,068	181,696	380,140	17,048	14,620	17,930	14,064	191,095	365,681	-9,399	14,459	5,060
Total	109,489,380	113,511,349	989,931	1,025,743	904	904	754	688	926,841	924,078	63,091	101,665	164,756

Sources: U.S. 1998 midyear population: U.S. Census Bureau, unpublished file NESTV 98; U.S. deaths 1998 generated by applying death rates from NCHS to the 1998 population from U.S. Census Bureau, unpublished file NESTV 98; U.S. death rates 1998: National Center for Health Statistics, "Death rates for 282 selected causes by 5 year age groups, race and sex: Unites States 1979–1998"; Canadian death rates 1998: Statistics Canada, *Mortality—1998 Shelf Tables*.

Table 8.3 Excess U.S. Deaths Relative to Canada by Broad Age Groups, Sex, and Cause of Death, Whites and Non-whites, 1998

Cause of death[a]	Males			Females			Both sexes		
	All races	Whites	Non-whites	All races	Whites	Non-whites	All races	Whites	Non-whites
All causes									
Total	111,939	63,091	48,848	141,298	101,665	39,633	253,237	164,756	88,481
0–29	18,053	8,424	9,629	9,243	4,253	4,990	27,296	12,677	14,619
30–64	89,041	54,336	34,705	49,018	26,981	22,037	138,059	81,317	56,742
65+	4,846	330	4,516	83,037	70,430	12,607	87,883	70,760	17,123
Neoplasms (140–239)									
Total	−11,435	−16,670	5,235	−6,780	−8,021	1,241	−18,215	−24,691	6,476
0–29	208	173	35	144	75	69	352	248	104
30–64	6,873	2,223	4,650	−363	−2,205	1,842	6,510	18	6,492
65+	−18,516	−19,066	550	−6,561	−5,890	−671	−25,077	−24,956	−121
Diabetes mellitus (250)									
Total	2,979	508	2,471	6,956	2,283	4,673	9,935	2,790	7,145
0–29	55	−1	56	112	52	60	167	51	116
30–64	3,671	2,149	1,522	3,792	2,137	1,655	7,463	4,286	3,177
65+	−746	−1,640	894	3,053	94	2,959	2,307	−1,546	3,853
Circulatory diseases (390–459)									
Total	68,889	51,604	17,285	102,557	80,746	21,811	171,446	132,350	39,096
0–29	1,440	800	640	991	518	473	2,431	1,318	1,113
30–64	37,576	25,037	12,539	22,579	12,852	9,727	60,155	37,889	22,266
65+	29,873	25,767	4,106	78,988	67,375	11,613	108,861	93,142	15,719
Respiratory diseases (460–519)									
Total	5,832	5,103	729	17,803	18,004	−201	23,365	23,107	258
0–29	628	254	374	450	164	286	1,078	418	660
30–64	6,835	4,964	1,871	5,726	4,474	1,252	12,561	9,438	3,123
65+	−1,631	−115	−1,516	11,627	13,367	−1,740	9,996	13,252	−3,256
Injuries (800–949)									
Total	14,469	10,967	3,502	2,291	1,453	838	16,759	12,420	4,339
0–29	5,571	4,602	1,149	2,642	2,133	509	8,393	6,735	1,658
30–64	9,296	6,916	2,380	4,155	3,189	966	13,451	10,105	3,346
65+	−579	−550	−29	−4,506	−3,869	−637	−5,085	−4,419	−666
Suicides (950–959)									
Total	−538	1,102	−1,640	−812	−198	−614	−1,350	904	−2,254
0–29	−719	−400	−319	−518	−366	−152	−1,237	−766	−471
30–64	−1,510	−313	−1,197	−231	168	−399	−1,741	−145	−1,596
65+	1,681	1,815	−124	−63	−1	−62	1,628	1,814	−186
Homicides (960–978)									
Total	11,270	4,419	6,851	2,859	1,384	1,475	14,129	5,803	8,326
0–29	6,418	2,224	4,194	1,230	510	720	7,648	2,734	4,914
30–64	4,601	2,062	2,539	1,359	672	687	5,960	2,734	3,226
65+	252	133	119	270	203	67	522	336	186
All other									
Total	20,473	6,058	14,415	16,424	6,014	10,410	37,168	12,073	25,095
0–29	4,272	772	3,500	4,192	1,167	3,025	8,464	1,939	6,525
30–64	21,699	11,298	10,401	12,001	5,694	6,307	33,700	16,992	16,708
65+	−5,498	−6,014	516	229	−849	1,078	−5,269	−6,863	1,594

[a] ICD-9 numbers shown in parentheses.
Sources: Calculated from sources given in Table 8.1.

have multiple causes and varied outcomes. Both the United States and Canada have reported decreases in deaths from circulatory diseases since 1980 (Manuel and Yang, 2002). Canadians, however, have made more progress than Americans.

In absolute terms, excess American deaths relative to Canadian deaths were most prominent among middle-aged men and among older women. In proportionate terms, 35 percent of all excess U.S. deaths occurred to non-Whites, a percentage twice as high as the share of non-Whites in the U.S. population in 1998. The major cause of excess deaths among non-White Americans compared with Canadians of all races was death from circulatory diseases, just as it was for White Americans.

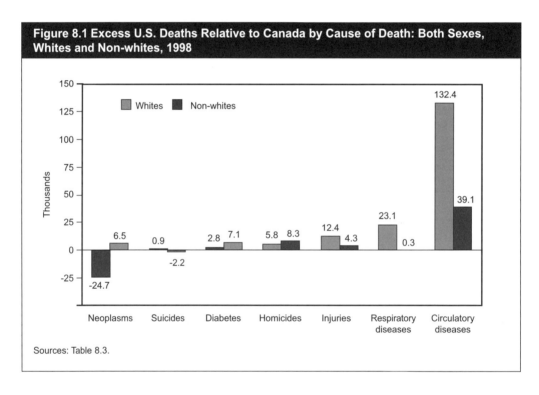

Figure 8.1 Excess U.S. Deaths Relative to Canada by Cause of Death: Both Sexes, Whites and Non-whites, 1998

Sources: Table 8.3.

Fifty-six percent of excess U.S. deaths occurred among females, indicating a somewhat higher relative disadvantage of American females compared to Canadians than was the case among American males. Among women, some 59 percent of all excess deaths occurred at age 65 and older; among men, this figure was only 4 percent. The relative Canadian advantage is most notable among the young (Figure 8.2). This pronounced relative disadvantage of Americans in younger ages in comparison to Canadians is, of course, also evident in comparing the relative magnitudes of U.S. and Canadian age- and sex-specific death rates shown in Tables 8.1 and 8.2.

BEHAVIOURAL RISK FACTORS ASSOCIATED WITH THE LEADING CAUSES OF EXCESS AMERICAN DEATHS

Mortality statistics lack much of the information we would like to have for a deeper analysis. We have no data concerning the risk behaviours of the deceased; we do not know their socio-economic status; and we do not know whether they had health insurance and were under medical care at the time of death. Information of that sort would require longitudinal studies, permitting us to link specific behaviours with causes of death. A number of cross-sectional surveys of risk behaviours are helpful, nevertheless, in providing clues for future research on the demography and etiology of excess U.S. deaths.

As noted above, the major cause of excess U.S. deaths in 1998 was cardiovascular diseases. Three important known risk factors for cardiovascular diseases are smoking, hypertension, and obesity (McGinnis and Foege, 1993). Several national surveys of prevalence of these risk behaviours in Canada and the United States exist, so at least some cautious national comparisons can be made.

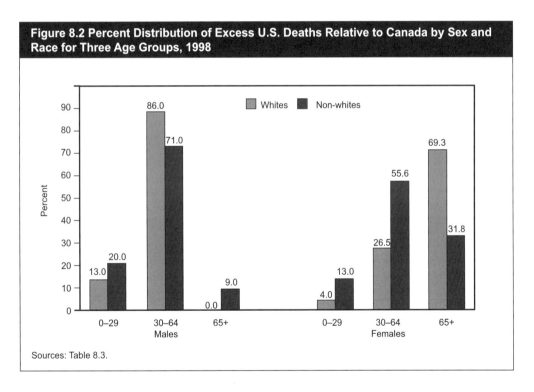

Figure 8.2 Percent Distribution of Excess U.S. Deaths Relative to Canada by Sex and Race for Three Age Groups, 1998

Sources: Table 8.3.

Data on the prevalence of smoking in Canada and the U.S. have been collected for years in the Canadian National Population Health Survey and its predecessors, and in the U.S. National Health Interview Survey (National Center for Health Statistics, 2002: Table 61; Tanguay et al., 2003:2–3). The national surveys asked about daily smoking and also identified people who smoke on "some days" in the U.S. and were "occasional smokers" in Canada. The Canadian data include all individuals aged 12 years and older, whereas the U.S. data include those aged 18 and older. In 1985 more Canadians smoked compared to Americans (35 percent vs. 30 percent) and this was true at every education level (Schoenborn, 1993:15–21). Surveys in 1998–1999 found that smoking had decreased in both countries, but Canadians still smoked more than Americans (28 percent vs. 23 percent). Adding an estimate of smokers aged 12–17 to the American total would not change the relative results. Since Canadians smoked more than Americans before 1998, smoking behaviour is not likely to be a factor in accounting for the excess U.S. deaths from circulatory and other diseases for that year.

Data on the prevalence of hypertension are collected in both the U.S. National Health and Nutrition Examination Survey (NHANES III) and the Canadian Heart Health surveys. A recent study using these data reported that the prevalence of hypertension in the Canadian population aged 18 years and older was 21.1 percent compared with 20.1 percent in the United States (Joffres et al., 2001). The percentage of Canadian men with isolated systolic hypertension (140 mmHg or above) who were not treated was higher than among American men (7.5 percent vs. 5.7 percent). The percentage of hypertensive women in both countries who were untreated was about the same (5.6 percent vs. 5.4 percent). Canadians had a lower percentage of individuals whose hypertension was under control and a lower percentage with blood pressure in the optimal range. These findings were consistent with another multinational study that examined some of the same issues for 35–64-year-olds in the two countries (Wolf-Maier et al., 2003). The scientific consensus about measurement and treatment of hypertension continues to evolve as new research is completed. But until more is known on this subject, the differences described above in prevalence of hypertension are not large enough nor in the right direction to make hypertension a major suspect in causing the excess American deaths from circulatory diseases.

Data on the prevalence of being overweight and obese are collected in both countries: in the Canadian National Population Health Survey and through NHANES (Gilmore, 1999; Flegal et al., 2002; National Center for Health Statistics, 2002:Table 70). Overweight is defined as a body mass index (BMI) of 25 or greater and obesity as a BMI of 30 or greater. Canada collects data for individuals aged 15 and older whereas the U.S. data cover individuals aged 20–74 in older surveys and ages 20 and older in more recent surveys. The U.S. data are based on actual measurement of survey participants; Canadian data are based on self-reports, which may be biased downward by about 10 percent (Cairney and Wade, 1998).

The percentage of overweight individuals has increased in both countries since the 1970s. According to the 1998–1999 Canadian survey and the 1999–2000 U.S. survey, the percentage of Canadian males with a BMI between 25.0 and 29.9 was higher than that among U.S. males (44 percent vs. 40 percent). The percentage of Canadian women with a BMI between 25.0 and 29.9 was slightly lower than among American women (24 percent vs. 28 percent). But the comparisons of obesity told a sharply different story. Obesity among American men was twice as high as among Canadian men (28 percent vs. 13 percent), and the proportion of obese among American women was three times as high as among Canadian women (34 percent vs. 11 percent). Recent estimates of remaining life expectancy for people who are overweight and obese suggest that the consequences of being overweight and obese are substantial.

A 40-year follow-up to the Framingham, Massachusetts, community study recently reported on how life expectancy at age 40 was reduced because of excess weight (Peeters et al., 2003). People at age 40 with a BMI between 25.0 and 29.9 who were non-smokers without hypertension or diabetes had their remaining life expectancy reduced by about three years (among men by 2.63 years and among women by 3.08 years). People at age 40 who were obese (BMI equal to or greater than 30) but also non-smokers and without hypertension or diabetes had their remaining life expectancy from all causes reduced by about seven years (by 6.85 years among men and 7.01 years among women).

Presumably, if Americans had Canadian BMIs, excess deaths caused by obesity would be reduced. The Framingham study's estimates of lost life expectancy at age 40 for the overweight and obese can account for much of the 1.5-year difference between 42.6 and 41.1, the life expectancy of Canadian and American women, respectively, at age 40 in 1998, and for more than half of the 1.4-year difference between 37.8 and 36.4, the life expectancy of Canadian and American men at the same age and date. Obesity is also a known risk factor for disease categories other than circulatory diseases (Calle et al., 2003), and circulatory diseases have causes other than obesity. But the estimated effect of obesity alone among Americans on life expectancy at age 40, based on the Framingham study, is substantial.

NEEDED RESEARCH

A number of other factors should also be considered in future investigations of U.S. patterns of mortality relative to Canada. A recent Statistics Canada study compared income inequality and mortality in Canadian provinces and U.S. states as well as in American and Canadian metropolitan areas in 1990–1991 (Ross et al., 2000). It found that the positive relationship between income inequality and mortality was statistically significant in the United States for both States and metropolitan areas. The relationship was strongest for 25–64-year-olds, both for men and women, but was not significant after age 65. The relationship between income inequality and mortality in Canada at all ages was not statistically significant.

The effect of differences in health care coverage in Canada and the United States on their comparative patterns of mortality should also be examined. About one-quarter of non-elderly Americans were not covered by health insurance some time in 1998 (Congressional Budget Office, 2003). Ninety-six percent of excess male deaths in the United States occur among non-elderly males. Slightly more men than women are without insurance; more non-Whites than Whites are not covered (14 percent among Whites, 21 percent among Blacks, and 33 percent among Hispanics). As noted above, the mortality data used in this analysis contain no record of whether the decedent was covered by health insurance before death. Therefore, longitudinal survey data will be needed to determine whether there is a relationship between health care coverage and the pattern of excess U.S. deaths shown in the above analysis.

The comparisons of data on mortality and risk factors in Canada and the U.S. reinforce the validity of the now widely expressed concerns over obesity in the United States. The causes and consequences of the differences in the prevalence of obesity in Canada and the United States need to be further explored. If these are the differences that are causing some of the excess mortality in the United States, it may give a sinister new meaning to the nautical term "deadweight."

● ●

CRITICAL THINKING QUESTIONS

1.   Relative to the United States, mortality is significantly lower in Canada as, for example, the average Canadian now lives about two years longer than the average American. What do you think are some of the more important factors in explaining this situation?
2.   It is possible to demonstrate through standardization how many fewer deaths Americans would experience on an annual basis if they experienced Canadian mortality levels. What is meant by standardization, and what is Torrey and Haub's estimate of annual deaths?
3.   Canada has universal health care coverage, whereas fully one-quarter of all non-elderly Americans have no health insurance whatsoever. To what extent do you feel this is relevant in explaining this differential in mortality across the two societies?

● ●

CHAPTER 9

NARROWING SEX DIFFERENTIAL
IN LIFE EXPECTANCY IN CANADA

Frank Trovato

● ●

INTRODUCTION

During the 20th century, mortality in the Western world declined to an unprecedented level (Coale, 2003; Preston, 1976; Riley, 2001; Tuljapurkar, Li, and Boe 2000). In this generalized context of improved survival, gains in female life expectancy surpassed those of males (Riley, 2001; Rogers, Hummer, and Nam, 2000; Smith, 1993). At present, life expectancy at birth across industrialized countries ranges from the mid to upper seventies for men and from the upper seventies into the lower eighties for women (Population Reference Bureau, 2004). The purpose of the current paper is to examine recent trends in terms of this differential in life expectancy by sex, with a specific emphasis on Canada.

Figure 9.1 illustrates the long-term trends in life expectancy at birth by sex for Canada from 1830 to 2000. Early in the 20th century the differential in longevity was about three to four years. By 1950, it had widened to about 4.5 years. By 1970, this differential had expanded to fully seven years, to the clear advantage of women. More recently, this sex differential in life expectancy has narrowed somewhat, down to about five years by the turn of the century. The purpose of this chapter is to explain this evolution by taking a careful look at the causes of death by sex and by examining how recent trends have differed for men and women.

Table 9.1 looks at selected high-income countries for the period between the early 1970s and the late 1990s (in two cases, 2000 and 2001). As is observed across these countries, the sex differential in life expectancy continues to be to the advantage of females, although this differential appears to be narrowing. England and Wales led the way in terms of this narrowing differential, followed by most of the other countries listed, to a greater or lesser extent. As shown in the table, what happened first in Britain was to later spread to other countries. The exceptional case is Japan, where the sex gap has continued to expand in favour of women (and is worthy of a separate investigation).

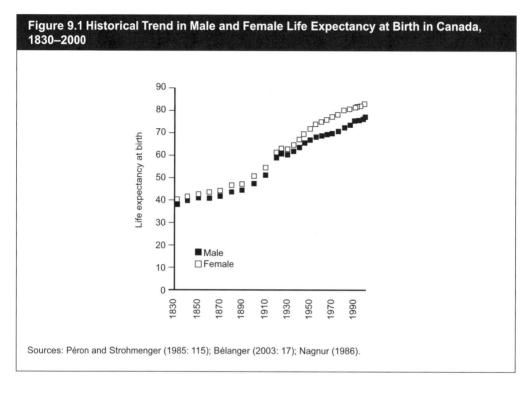

Figure 9.1 Historical Trend in Male and Female Life Expectancy at Birth in Canada, 1830–2000

Sources: Péron and Strohmenger (1985: 115); Bélanger (2003: 17); Nagnur (1986).

STUDY OBJECTIVES

This investigation expands on recently published works in this area of mortality analysis (Nathanson, 1995; Pampel, 2002, 2003; Trovato and Lalu, 1996a, 1996b, 1998; Waldron, 1993). However, rather than examining an aggregate of countries, I look specifically at Canada. The period of observation is roughly three decades, between 1970 and 2001. Observed sex differences in life expectancy are decomposed into the relative contribution of 10 major cause-of-death components. I situate the analysis in the context of epidemiological transition theory and explanations pertaining to gender role change and mortality in post-industrial societies.

THEORETICAL FRAMEWORK

Sex Differences in Life Expectancy and Epidemiological Transition

Notwithstanding the exceptional case of Japan, the tendency for a growing number of high-income nations to experience reduced sex differences in life expectancy over the past two decades can be viewed as a new feature of the epidemiological profile of post-industrial societies. The epidemiological transition theory explains the historical shift in mortality as countries experience modernization from a period in history when infectious and parasitic diseases dominate as the leading killers to a stage where chronic and degenerative ailments become the predominant causes of death (Omran 1971). All societies in the Western world have passed through three stages, described by Omran

Table 9.1 Sex Differentials of Life Expectancy at Birth in Selected High-income Countries; Early 1970s to Late 1990s/Early 2000s

Country	Early 1970s			Early 1980s			Early 1990s			Late 1990s/early 2000s			Change between periods		
	Male	Female	D1	Male	Female	D2	Male	Female	D3	Male	Female	D4	D2–D1	D3–D2	D4–D3
Canada	69.48	76.65	7.17	71.92	79.24	7.33	74.44	81.00	6.56	76.87	82.22	5.35	0.16	-0.77	-1.21
Austria	66.73	73.80	7.07	69.23	76.46	7.23	72.75	79.36	6.60	76.06	81.88	5.82	0.11	-1.12	-0.24
USA	67.23	74.73	7.50	70.30	78.00	7.70	71.91	78.97	7.07	74.08	79.47	5.39	0.20	-0.64	-1.68
England/Wales	69.30	75.60	6.30	71.18	77.18	6.00	73.52	79.18	5.66	75.92	80.68	4.76	-0.31	-0.34	-0.90
West Germany	67.60	74.04	6.45	70.28	77.03	6.75	73.02	79.50	6.48	---	---	---	0.31	-0.28	---
Germany	---	---	---	---	---	---	72.06	78.60	6.55	74.89	81.01	6.11	---	---	-0.43
Italy	68.82	75.05	6.22	71.58	78.24	6.66	73.73	80.47	6.74	76.27	82.58	6.31	0.44	0.08	-0.43
France	69.14	76.85	7.72	71.03	79.27	8.25	73.58	81.99	8.41	75.10	82.75	7.64	0.53	0.17	-0.77
Sweden	72.18	77.58	5.40	73.16	79.33	6.16	75.14	80.82	5.68	77.08	82.01	4.92	0.76	-0.48	-0.76
Japan	70.22	75.66	5.45	74.08	79.64	5.56	76.28	82.17	6.43	77.20	84.08	6.88	0.11	0.87	0.46

Note: D1, D2, D3, D4 represent period-specific differences in life expectancy at birth (female – male). The last three columns express the change (second order differences) of these differences across sequential periods. The actual time points for the countries are as follows: Canada (1971, 1981, 1991, 2000); Austria (1970, 1980, 1990, 2001); USA (1970, 1980, 1990, 1999); England and Wales (1971, 1980, 1991, 2000); West Germany (1970, 1980, 1991); Germany (1990, 1999); Italy (1970, 1980, 1990, 1999); France (1970, 1980, 1990, 1999); Japan (1970, 1981, 1990, 1999); Sweden (1970, 1980, 1990, 1999). East and West Germany were reunited in 1990; therefore after this date, the World Health Organization reports mortality data for Germany as a whole. --- means data not available.

Source: Author's computations based on data from the World Health Organization, www.who.org.

(1971) as "the age of pestilence and famine," "the age of receding pandemics," and "the age of man-made and degenerative diseases."

An important proposition in this theory states that with modernization, populations experience widening sex differences in mortality, resulting in faster life expectancy gains for females. The larger improvements in survivorship for females that occur with the recession of pandemics (stage II) are especially beneficial to infants and children of both sexes, and to females in the adolescent and reproductive age periods. During the transition from infectious to degenerative disease predominance (stage III) "women switch from a level of mortality in the reproductive years higher than that of men to a level more advantageous" (Omran, 1971:525). Omran's theory remains an important framework for the study of disease and mortality change. However, this formulation is silent with specific reference to the phenomenon of interest to this investigation. It does not anticipate that after a prolonged period of widening sex differences in life expectancy, nations would experience a pattern of reduced differences in this measure.

Extensions of Omran's theory (Olshansky and Ault, 1986; Rogers and Hackenberg, 1987; Salomon and Murray, 2002) point to the continued predominance of chronic and degenerative diseases in the most advanced countries. A fourth stage has been proposed, the "age of delayed degenerative diseases" (Olshansky and Ault, 1986). In these populations, a large proportion of deaths annually are caused by chronic and degenerative ailments, and consequently most deaths are concentrated in the older ages. The segment of the population that experiences the most pronounced improvements in survival probabilities are the elderly as mortality in the younger ages and in infancy has reached historic low levels (Olshansky and Ault, 1986). Taken together, these features of advanced societies imply that sex differences in life expectancy obtain principally from sex differences in mortality among older adults, and that chronic and degenerative diseases would account for most of the discrepancy in life expectancy between men and women.

Rogers and Hackenberg (1987) add that risky behaviours and lifestyle underlie a large proportion of deaths in contemporary high-income countries. For instance, in Canada, during 1995 about 15,000 people lost their lives to lung cancer, a disease connected to tobacco use. In the United States, the number of such cases exceeded 149,000 (World Health Organization, 1998). It is also true that a large number of accidental deaths are linked to alcohol and other substances, and that suicide and homicide continue to be significant causes of premature death among young and middle-aged adults (Stack, 2000a, 2000b). These prevailing epidemiological trends in the advanced societies suggest the existence of a "hubristic" configuration of factors whereby chronic diseases associated with aging and conditions related to poor lifestyle and personal habits are mainly responsible for premature mortality (Rogers and Hackenberg, 1987).

In tandem with these epidemiological features, advanced societies during the postwar years have also experienced major social demographic changes. The view has been expressed that such countries are actually in the midst of a "second demographic transition" (Lesthaeghe and Surkyn, 1988; Van de Kaa, 1987, 1999, 2004), characterized by a pluralization of living arrangements among young adults and a pervasive tendency to postpone marriage, a large percentage of couples living in cohabiting unions, declining marriage rates, increased divorce probabilities, very high contraceptive prevalence levels, sub-replacement fertility rates, increased proportion of couples remaining childless, and an increasing tendency among couples for child-bearing outside of traditional marriage. As part of this configuration of change, gender roles in these societies have become more egalitarian (Davis, 1984; McDonald, 2000). It is precisely in this context that we have witnessed a convergence in the sex differential on mortality and life expectancy in a context whereby gender roles have become less traditional and more egalitarian.

Explanations for the sex differential in mortality emphasize a wide range of factors from biological and genetic differences between the sexes to structural and sociological causes underlying differential behaviours of men and women. A review of this vast literature is avoided here due to space limitations. For more extensive reviews, see Luy (2003), Waldron (1976, 1995, 2000), Perls and Fretts (1998), and Owen (2002). In countries where the sex difference in life expectancy has narrowed, change in mortality from heart disease and lung cancer have contributed significantly to this (Trovato and Lalu 1996a, 1996b, 1998). These causes of death are known to be strongly associated with prolonged tobacco use (Bartecchi et al., 1994; Doll and Peto, 1981; McGinnis and Foege, 1993; Mokdad et al., 2004; Peto et al., 1992, 2000; Ravenholt, 1990; Waldron, 1976, 1986, 2000). It is estimated that smoking caused approximately 440,000 deaths in the United States during 2004 (Bombard et al., 2004). In the European Union, the number of male deaths from lung cancer in 2000 was close to 140,000 (Boyle et al., 2003).

The negative health effects of tobacco in a population are typically felt decades after the onset of widespread smoking (Hegmann et al., 1993; Lopez, 1995; Nathanson, 1995). Support has been found for the proposition that past patterns of smoking behaviour have had their impact on mortality, particularly given that there has been somewhat of a convergence in smoking behaviour by sex over the course of the latter part of the 20th century. As the incidence of smoking among Canadian women actually increased throughout the 1950s and 1960s before stabilizing and then gradually declining from the 1970s onward, past patterns have been associated with lagged increases in female lung cancer and other smoking-related mortality in the 1970s and thereafter. This has contributed to the recently observed narrowing of the sex difference in mortality. Pampel (2002) observes that a significant proportion of the observed narrowing in the sex gap in mortality between 1975 and 1995 across many industrialized countries may have resulted from a convergence in smoking prevalence between men and women: "The results …do not suggest that cigarette smoking fully accounts for the sex differential in mortality between males and females; rather, smoking fully explains the recent narrowing of the sex differential" (p. 96). Thus, according to Pampel (2002), the female relative advantage in life expectancy has fallen recently because of the adoption of smoking by women in the 1950s and 1960s, which had consequent lagged effects on their survival probabilities. In addition, the reductions in smoking among men have been more pronounced than among women since the 1970s with consequent improvements in male mortality rates.

It should be noted, however, that in addition to smoking-related diseases in the industrialized countries, accidents, violence, suicide, and cirrhosis of the liver also account for a large number of deaths annually (Mokdad et al., 2004; Pampel, 2001; Peto et al., 1992).

These causes of premature mortality have little direct association with smoking, and tend to be heavily concentrated among young adults, with death rates being considerably greater in men (Owens, 2002). For instance, death rates from accidents and adverse effects exceed female rates by a ratio of 3 to 1 or greater (Nathanson, 1984; Perls and Frets, 1998; Verbrugge, 1976; Waldron, 1976, 1986, 1993; Wingard, 1984). Change in sex differences in mortality due to these causes may also account for narrowing sex differences in life expectancy.

DECOMPOSITION OF SEX DIFFERENCES IN LIFE EXPECTANCY

The following two statements follow from the above discussion of epidemiological transition theory and its connection with sex differences in life expectancy.

1. Being in the most advanced stage of epidemiological transition, patterns of morbidity and mortality in Canada are such that chronic/degenerative diseases are the dominant causes of death. Therefore, change in heart disease and cancer mortality should account for a large part of narrowing sex differences in life expectancy. In examining these trends, it is assumed that past sex differences in smoking prevalence underlie many of these changes as observed in mortality over recent decades.
2. In accordance with the notion that social pathologies also account for a significant number of deaths on annual basis in the industrialized countries (McGinnis and Foege, 1993; Mokdad et al., 2004; Rogers and Hackenberg, 1987), it is anticipated that change in external causes of death—namely suicide, accidents, violence, and cirrhosis of the liver—would also account for part of the decline in the sex gap in life expectancy.

Support for both of these statements can be obtained via a decomposition methodology, which takes the observed difference in the female-male life expectancy at birth and breaks it down into the contribution of sex differences in mortality with respect to 10 cause-of-death components (for further detail, see the note at the end of this paper). A cause component can have a positive or negative contribution. The sum of cause contributions adds up to the observed sex difference in life expectancy. Mortality and population data for this part of the analysis were taken from the World Health Organization's electronic database (www.who.org). This source provides detailed mortality information for a large number of countries by cause of death, age, and sex and corresponding populations for the computation of death rates. Deaths were classified into 10 cause components: (1) heart disease, (2) other diseases of the circulatory system, (3) lung cancer, (4) breast cancer, (5) prostate cancer, (6) all other cancers, (7) cirrhosis of the liver, (8) accidents and violence excluding suicide, (9) suicide, (10) all other causes of death (see Appendix A). Four discrete time points are examined (1971, 1981, 1991, and 2000).

Table 9.2 displays this decomposition, with sex-specific life expectancies at birth across four discrete periods, the corresponding female-male differences, the change in the sex gaps across sequential periods, and the cause of death contributions to these

Table 9.2 Decomposition of the Female-Male Differential in Life Expectancy at Birth by Period and its Change due to Ten Cause-of-Death Components

	Period				Change across sequential periods		
	(1) 1971	(2) 1981	(3) 1991	(4) 2000	(5) 1971– 1981	(6) 1981– 1991	(7) 1991– 2000
Female e0	76.649	79.244	80.999	82.126	2.595	1.755	1.217
Male e0	69.649	71.915	74.438	76.869	2.436	2.523	2.431
Female e0 – Male e0	7.170	7.329	6.561	5.347	0.159	-0.768	-1.214
Decomposition (years of life expectancy)							
Heart disease	2.956	2.800	2.067	1.468	-0.156	-0.733	-0.599
Other circulatory	0.394	0.403	0.352	0.302	0.009	-0.051	-0.050
Lung cancer	0.681	0.885	0.838	0.527	0.204	-0.047	-0.311
Breast cancer	-0.493	-0.535	-0.596	-0.511	-0.042	-0.061	0.085
Prostate cancer	0.228	0.286	0.394	0.364	0.058	0.108	-0.030
Other cancers	0.344	0.591	0.742	0.838	0.247	0.151	0.096
Cirrhosis of the liver	0.145	0.188	0.140	0.120	0.043	-0.048	-0.020
Accidents/violence (-suicide)	1.415	1.131	0.770	0.615	-0.284	-0.361	-0.155
Suicide	0.272	0.394	0.432	0.364	0.122	0.038	-0.068
Other causes of death	1.228	1.186	1.422	1.260	-0.042	0.236	-0.162
Total	7.170	7.329	6.561	5.347	0.159	-0.768	-1.214
Decomposition (in percentage terms)							
Heart disease	41.23	38.21	31.50	27.45	-3.02	-6.71	-4.05
Other circulatory	5.50	5.50	5.37	5.65	0.00	-0.13	0.28
Lung cancer	9.50	12.08	12.77	9.86	2.58	0.69	-2.92
Breast cancer	-6.88	-7.30	-9.09	-9.56	-0.42	-1.79	-0.47
Prostate cancer	3.18	3.90	6.00	6.81	0.72	2.10	0.80
Other cancers	4.80	8.07	11.31	15.67	3.27	3.24	4.36
Cirrhosis of the liver	2.02	2.56	2.13	2.24	0.54	-0.43	0.11
Accidents/violence (-suicide)	19.73	15.43	11.73	11.50	-4.30	-3.70	-0.23
Suicide	3.80	5.38	6.59	6.81	1.58	1.21	0.22
Other causes of death	17.12	16.17	21.69	23.56	-0.95	5.52	1.89
Total	100.00	100.00	100.00	100.00	0	0	0

Source: Author's computations based on data from the World Health Organization, www.who.org.

associated changes. These results are shown in terms of actual years of life expectancy and also in terms of their percentage distributions. The use of percentages is to help in the interpretation of relative importance of given causes of death, recognizing that reliance on percentages in this case can be problematic because theoretically it is possible for one cause of death to contribute more than the actual difference being decomposed when the other causes contribute negatively. The first four columns in the tables list the contribution of given cause components to observed sex gaps in life expectancy within periods, whereas columns 5, 6, and 7 reflect change in cause contribution between sequential periods to either widen or narrow the sex differential.

DECOMPOSITION BY CAUSE OF DEATH

As noted in Table 9.2, Canada saw its sex gap reduce from just over seven years in the early 1970s to 5.35 years in Canada in 2000. Between the early 1980s and the early 1990s, the difference narrowed by 0.77 of a year, and in the final decade, by 1.21 of a year. Within both periods examined, sex differences in heart disease mortality (i.e., higher male than female death rates) account for a large portion of the differentials in life expectancy. Given the dominance of this cause of death in the industrialized countries, this is not unexpected.

Male death rates are generally higher than female death rates from major causes of death such as heart disease, lung cancer, most other cancers, accidents and violence, and suicide. Therefore, reduced contributions of a given cause component to the sex gap in life expectancy over time in the decomposition analysis would reflect varying degrees of convergence in male and female death rates from a given cause. In the context of Canada, for the periods examined this obtains from greater male gains in survival relative to women under the condition where both sexes improve their survival probabilities over time. Breast and prostate cancers are unique in that they are sex-specific (breast cancer afflicts predominantly women; prostate cancer is strictly a male disease). Improvement in survival probabilities from breast cancer would, all other things being equal, serve to widen the sex gap in life expectancy in favour of women, whereas reductions in prostate cancer mortality, all other things being equal, would help narrow the female-male differential in life expectancy.

Depending upon period, differences in mortality due to heart disease explains between 27 to 41 per cent of the observed sex gaps in Canadian life expectancy. In actual years of life expectancy, these translated into a contribution of 2.96 years in 1971 and about 1.5 years in 2000. Thus, the impact of heart disease as a factor in the sex difference in life expectation has declined with time, most notably since the early 1980s. In substantive terms, this indicates the occurrence of substantial reductions in the sex differential in mortality from this disease during this time interval, and therefore constitutes an important reason underlying the occurrence of reduced sex gaps in the average length of life.

Sex differences in mortality from accidents and violence (excluding suicide) also explain a substantial portion of the sex differences in life expectancy. In Canada, this cause of death contributed between roughly 11 and 20 percent across periods (or approximately between 1.42 years of life expectancy in 1970, and 0.62 of a year in 2000). As is the case with heart disease, this trend for differential mortality due to accidents and violence (excluding suicide) indicates that Canadian men in recent years have managed to close some of their risk disadvantage in relation to women with respect to this cause of premature death.

With reference to lung cancer, its pattern of change in contribution across time periods also underlies the occurrence of reduced sex gaps in mortality. This is especially evident since the early 1980s (see columns 6 and 7 of Table 9.2). The contribution of declining sex differences in lung cancer mortality relates to the stage of the lung cancer epidemic for men and women. By the early 1980s, the pace of change in lung cancer mortality rates in Canadian men had slowed while that of women had gained momentum.

As would be expected, given their sex specificity, the contribution of breast cancer mortality to the life expectancy differential is consistently negative within periods, whereas that of prostate cancer is consistently positive. However, the change in the contribution of these two components across time periods can be either positive or negative in terms of their effects on the sex gap in life expectancy. As indicated in Table 9.2 (columns 5, 6, and 7), breast cancer contributed to a narrowing of the difference in longevity between 1970–1971 and 1990–1991, but widened this difference between 1990–1991 and 2000–2001. This indicates that during this most recent period, there have been some declines in breast cancer mortality among women. In the case of prostate cancer, its change over time has been to widen the sex differential in life expectancy in favour of women (though during the most recent interval, there is evidence of a negative contribution). It should be mentioned that notwithstanding these effects, the contributions of these two cause components are generally small. As far as "other cancers" are concerned, sex differences in death rates from this cause category have been diverging to expand the female advantage in life expectancy in relation to men, though at a diminishing degree of change across time. In other words, men continue to experience higher mortality rates from "other" cancers than do women, but over time, the male excess mortality in relation to women has been getting smaller, though not sufficiently so to produce a negative contribution to the sex difference in overall life expectancy.

The effect of sex differences in mortality from cirrhosis of the liver in the 1990s has been to diminish the gap in expectation of life. Concerning suicide, its contribution has ranged between roughly 0.27 and 0.36 of a year (in 1971 and 2000, respectively). As reflected in these figures, some convergence in suicide risk has occurred over time between men and women in these two populations, translating into small contributions toward closing some of the discrepancy in life expectancy between men and women, particularly between 1991 and 2000. Finally, with reference to "other" causes of death (residual), the effect has been irregular, although in the latest interval of observation the influence of this component has been to narrow the sex difference by 0.16 of a year.

Table 9.3 looks at the contributions of cause components to the change in the longevity gap between 1980–1981 and 2000–2001. This interval covers the change in the differential from the approximate point at which it had reached a maximum to the most recent period of observation for which data are available. During this time span, the sex gap narrowed by almost two years (1.98). Most of this reduction in the female-male difference in longevity is attributable to declines in sex differences in heart disease mortality (i.e., by 1.33 years of life expectancy—a 67 percent contribution), and to a lesser degree, to reduced sex differences in mortality from accidents and violence (26 percent contribution), lung cancer (18 percent contribution), "other" circulatory conditions (5 percent contribution), cirrhosis of the liver (3 percent contribution), suicide (1.5 percent contribution), and "other" causes (3.7 percent contribution). The three remaining cause components show positive contributions to widen the gap in favour of females. For the most part, however, these effects tend to be relatively minor (with the exception of "other" cancers, whose impact is about 12 percent).

Table 9.3 Change in the Contribution of Ten Cause-of-Death Components to the Change in Female-Male Difference in Life Expectancy at Birth between the Peak Period of the Differential and the Latest Time Point of Observation, Canada, 1980–2000

Cause component	Contribution to the change in F-M gap in life expectancy between 1981 and 2000 (years of life expectancy)	%
Heart disease	-1.332	-67.2
Other circulatory	-0.101	-5.1
Lung cancer	-0.358	-18.1
Breast cancer	0.024	1.2
Prostate cancer	0.078	3.9
Other cancers	0.247	12.5
Cirrhosis of the liver	-0.066	-3.4
Accidents/violence (-suicide)	-0.516	-26.0
Suicide	-0.030	-1.5
Other causes of death	-0.074	-3.7
Total change	-1.982	100.0

Note: A negative value for a cause component denotes that the effect of change over time in sex differences in mortality due to the cause of death served to narrow the sex gap in life expectancy; a positive sign implies the opposite effect.

Source: Author's computations based on data from the World Health Organization, www.who.org.

AGE DECOMPOSITION OF THE SEX DIFFERENTIAL IN LIFE EXPECTANCY

Period shifts in life expectation at birth are usually not equally attributable to change in all age groups in the life table (Arriaga, 1984; Fries, 1980; Kannisto et al., 1994; Manton, 1982; Murthy, 2005; Vaupel and Canudas Romo, 2003). Therefore, a further aspect of the decomposition analysis considers the contribution of mortality differences within age categories to the sex difference in life expectation at birth. Whereas the earlier decomposition focused on the contribution of causes of death, the factor of interest here is age. Specifically, the female-male difference in life expectancy at birth is decomposed into the contribution of five age vector factors: (1) age 0–14, (2) age 15–34, (3) age 35–54, (4) age 55–74, and (5) age 75+. Through this approach one is able to address the question: How much of the observed female-male difference in life expectancy at birth within a given time period is attributable to sex difference in mortality in given age categories? A related question is: How much of the observed change between periods (i.e., narrowing) in life expectancy at birth is attributable to change in sex differences in mortality in given age categories?

Age decompositions for Canada for the interval between 1981 and 2000 are shown in Table 9.4. The female advantage in average length of life rises with age, though declining somewhat at age 75+. The largest contribution to the differential is due to age 55–74. About 52 percent of the change in the life expectancy difference between females and males is due to reduced sex differences in mortality in this age class. The next largest contributions are associated with the age categories of 35–54 (about 23 percent) and 15–34 (about 20 percent). The youngest age group (<15) shows a relatively small effect (9 percent). It is interesting to note that mortality differences in the oldest age group (75+) serve to expand the female advantage in life expectancy over males by about 5 percent.

Table 9.4 Age Decomposition of the Female-Male Difference in Life Expectancy (the Contribution of Mortality Differences within a Given Group to the F-M Difference in Life Expectancy at Birth and its Change between Specified Periods

Age group	Contribution (years of life expectancy) 1981	Contribution (years of life expectancy) 2000	Change 1981–2000	%
<15	0.310	0.128	-0.182	-9.2
15–34	0.902	0.499	-0.403	-20.3
35–54	1.091	0.639	-0.452	-22.8
55–74	3.210	2.172	-1.038	-52.4
75+	1.816	1.909	0.093	4.7
Total	7.329	5.347	-1.982	100.0

Source: Author's computations based on data from the World Health Organization, www.who.org.

$$[e0_{females} - e0_{males}] = F(a, b) - F(A, B) =$$
$$[F(a, b) - F(A, b) + F(a, B) - F(A, B)] / 2 \text{ (cause 1)} + [F(a, b) - F(a, B) + F(A, b) - F(A, B)] / 2 \text{ (cause 2)}$$

DISCUSSION

In high-income countries in the West, the sex differential in life expectancy widened during most of the 20th century. However, in many countries this long-established differential peaked around 1980 and has since followed a declining trend. The present investigation looked at the continuation of this phenomenon into the early years of the new millennium in Canada. It was hypothesized that being in the fourth stage of epidemiological transition, changes in the sex gap in longevity in Canada would be explained mostly by changes in chronic diseases among older adults. The decomposition analysis executed here revealed that a large portion of the change in the sex gap in Canada was accounted for by change in sex differences in heart disease mortality, which, along with cancer, is a leading cause of premature death. Convergence in lung cancer death rates between men and women has played an important role as well, though to a lesser degree than heart disease. Notwithstanding men's generally higher death rates as compared to women, men in Canada have managed, over recent years, to close some of their relative disadvantage from these major causes of death. As anticipated, a large portion of the observed change in the sex differential between women and men is specific to the contribution of mortality differences among older adults. Another hypothesis emphasized the relevance of external types of mortality (i.e., social pathologies). The decomposition results are consistent with the proposition that accidents and violence constitute an additional important factor in the explanation of sex differences in life expectancy and their change over time.

Some of the literature in this area of inquiry has focused on how change in the position of women relates to change in the sex differential in mortality. The analysis in the present study indicated that a significant part of the reductions in the sex differential in life expectancy in recent years has obtained from larger-than-expected mortality improvements in men as compared to women. This suggests that greater attention should be directed to how the male role in society may be changing and how this may relate to improvements in their survival probabilities. An important question in this regard pertains to change in men's mortality risk from not only lung cancer (mostly attributable to smoking), but also accidents and violence.

On the question of whether convergence in smoking-related mortality fully underlies convergence in life expectancy between men and women, this analysis suggests that smoking differences are undoubtedly important in this respect. It would seem that in the adult ages between 40 and 65, mortality associated with prolonged tobacco consumption is a principal causal source of the sex differential in mortality. Thus, change in smoking behaviour among men and women must explain a large portion of the observed change in the sex differential in life expectancy. However, as shown in the decomposition analysis, smoking could not account for all of the observed narrowing of the gap in life expectancy. Beside the contributions of chronic conditions, of which many such diseases are linked to smoking, a sizable part of the reductions in the sex gap is also attributable to the combined contributions of convergence in male and female mortality from accidents and violence and cirrhosis of the liver, which bear no or limited direct relationship to cigarette smoking.

Lastly, one may speculate on the possible future course of the sex differential in longevity. Will the recent narrowing trend continue, or will the differential revert to its past form and widen? One thing that is clear is that future trends in mortality and life expectancy among men and women are dependent not only on smoking differentials but also to a significant degree on change in sex differences in other lifestyle habits and behaviours that impact health in the long term (Waldron, 1995). To the extent that sex differences in cancer and heart disease mortality are dependent on additional factors beside prolonged tobacco use, improved health habits in men should translate into further male gains in survival, even in a context of widespread reductions in the prevalence of smoking among females. And given the importance of accidents, violence, and suicide as causes of premature death in men, further improvements in risk from these would also enhance male life expectancy and thus engender further reductions in the difference in life expectation between men and women.

APPENDIX: STANDARDIZATION METHODOLOGY

To elaborate a bit further on this methodology, consider the hypothetical case where only two causes of death wholly determine life expectancy in the population, and thus the expectation of life at birth is a function of two cause-specific vector factors for ages zero through to the last age in the life table. The expectations of life at birth for males and females can be expressed as, $e0_{males} = F(A, B)$, and $e0_{females} = F(a, b)$, were, A is the vector of age-specific probabilities of death from cause 1 for males, B is the vector of age-specific probabilities of death from cause 2 for males, a is the vector of age-specific probabilities of death from cause 1 for females, and b is the vector of age-specific probabilities of death from cause 2 for females. These vectors can be rearranged algebraically in the context of cause-eliminated life tables to decompose the difference in expectation of life into the contribution of the two cause-of-death components (Das Gupta, 1993).

$[e0_{females} - e0_{males}] = F(a, b) - F(A, B) =$

$[F(a, b) - F(A, b) + F(a, B) - F(A, B)] / 2$ (cause 1) $+ [F(a, b) - F(a, B) + F(A, b) - F(A, B)] / 2$ (cause 2)

Appendix A1: Causes of Death and Corresponding ICD Codes (abbreviated lists)

Cause of Death Category	ICD-8	ICD-9	ICD-10
1. Heart Disease	A81-A84	B25-B28	I20, I21, I22, I23-I25
2. Other Circulatory Diseases	A85-A88	B29-B30	I26-I51, I60-I69, I70, I71-I78, I80-I82, I83-I99
3. Lung Diseases	A51	B101	C33-C34
4. Breast Cancer	A54	B113	C50
5. Prostate Cancer	A57	B124	C61
6. Other Cancers (-benign type)	A45-A48, A50, A52, A53, A55, A56, A58-A61	B08, B09, B100, B109, B110-B112, B114-B119, B120-B123, B125-B129, B13-B17	C00-C32, C37-C49, C51-C60, C62-C95, C97, D00-D48
7. Cirrhosis of the Liver	A102	B347	K70, K73-K74, K76
8. Accidents/Violence (excluding suicide)	AE138-AE146, AE148-AE150	BE47-BE53, BE55, BE56	V01-X59, X85-Y09, Y10-Y36, Y40-Y89
9. Suicide	AE147	BE54	X60-X84
10. Other causes of death	All else	All else	All else

Note: For the four periods examined in this study, ICD-8 pertains to 1970 and 1971; ICD-9 to 1980 and 1981; ICD-10 to 2000 and 2001.

● ●

CRITICAL THINKING QUESTIONS

1. Following from Omran's theory of the epidemiological transition, why would we anticipate a widening in the sex differential in life expectancy with modernization? Has this largely occurred across societies?
2. What has occurred over the last 20 years in Canada with regard to this difference in life expectancy by sex, and what might be some possible explanations for this?
3. Do you expect the current difference of about five years in life expectancy at birth between males and females to widen or narrow into the future? Why?

● ●

Section 3
International Migration, Domestic Migration, and Population Distribution

• •

IN TERMS OF POPULATION POLICY, the most explicit attempts to influence demographic trends in Canada have occurred in the area of international migration. Immigration policy has always been fundamental to Canada's demographic situation, as governments since Confederation have relied upon immigration in stimulating settlement in its vast territory. The chapter by Boyd and Vickers demonstrates this fact quite plainly by broadly sketching the impact of immigration on Canada, from 1900 through to 2000. For example, at the beginning of the 20th century, there was considerable need to stimulate development and establish effective sovereignty over the Canadian West, such that an unprecedented number of immigrants were admitted to populate the western provinces. By the end of the century, a whole series of additional factors have come to influence immigration policy, from declining rates of natural increase through to a dramatic growth in communications, transportation, and economic networks linking people from around the world.

As events within Canada most obviously shape and influence immigration policy, so too do events external to Canada. This is precisely the emphasis in Simmons's contribution, which endeavours to draw a formal theoretical link between globalization and international migration patterns. As argued, Canadian immigration can be better understood in terms of this wider context of globalization with its corresponding economic, cultural, and political transformations. The process of globalization has had its impact on the scale of international migration, the expanding web of source-destination country connections, the scale of worldwide refugee flows, and the extent to which societies are transformed by the human capital and national identities of their migrants. As Simmons points out, these changes are all occurring in the post-9/11 era, such that public anxieties about possible links between migrants, refugees, and terrorist attacks have had their impact on sentiments toward refugees and immigrants and, in turn, on immigration policy.

Few countries in the world are as strongly influenced by immigration as is Canada, and for this reason, there is an obvious need to expand the Canadian research agenda on immigration. Green's essay demonstrates some of the most fundamental insights that demographers can bring to public debates on immigration policy. In addressing merely a few of the more important issues, Green considers the impact of immigration on population growth, population aging, on potential skill shortages, as well as population distribution and regional economic development. As immigration is shown to be far from a panacea for many of these fundamental economic and demographic challenges, Green asks the essential question: "What type of society do we wish to build in Canada, and what is the role of immigration in achieving this?" Even further, he raises an issue that is typically neglected in narrowly conceived policy debates surrounding immigration policy, i.e., "What is the role of social and humanitarian issues in this context?"

Regardless of academic debates on public policy, several consecutive governments in Canada have explicitly introduced immigration policies working with the idea that immigration can act as a catalyst for economic growth. This has led to more selective immigration policies or, more specifically, efforts to attract better-educated and skilled immigrants (beginning with the introduction of the point system in the 1960s). While this remains central to Canada's current immigration policy, the remaining two chapters of this section provide direct evidence to suggest that not all is well in this regard. Many immigrants encounter major hurdles in establishing a foothold in Canada's knowledge-based economy. Both the chapters by Picot and Sweetman as well as Hiebert provide evidence to indicate somewhat of a deterioration in the economic welfare of new Canadians. While newly arrived immigrants have always had lower earnings than comparable non-immigrant workers (with the gap narrowing as they adjust to the labour market of the receiving society), this disparity in earnings has widened most recently, an observation that is largely true regardless of the higher educational credentials of new Canadians.

Both chapters review a variety of factors in explanation, from changes in the language skills and cultural origins of immigrants (and the possibility of increased discrimination) through to difficulties in the recognition of foreign educational credentials and labour market experience. New immigrants face a very competitive labour market as the educational qualifications of Canadians are relatively high and have continued to improve over recent decades. Hiebert is particularly interested in the relationship between cultural diversity (as driven by immigration), new settlement and residential patterns, as well as the issue of social equity in Canada. As immigration and new patterns of settlement continue to modify the social geography of our cities, the potential for "ghettoization" and economic marginalization for newcomers remains a fundamental challenge. This is particularly true since immigration will inevitably increase in relative importance in maintaining population growth and meeting skill shortages in the labour force.

RECOMMENDED READINGS

Beach, Charles, Alan Green, and Jeffrey Reitz (eds.). (2003). *Canadian Immigration Policy for the 21st Century*. John Deutsch Institute for the Study of Economic Policy, Queen's University. Montreal and Kingston: McGill-Queen's University Press. This comprehensive volume covers a wide assortment of topics, from the role of immigration in meeting Canada's demographic and labour force needs through to research on the social exclusion of immigrants and visible minorities.

Castles, Stephen, and Mark Miller. (1998). *The Age of Migration: International Population Movements in the Modern World.* Houndmills: Macmillan. This very readable text takes the longer-term perspective by demonstrating how the current situation in terms of international migration is quite distinct in terms of both the level and diversity.

Fong, Eric (ed.). (2006). *Inside the Mosaic.* Toronto: University of Toronto Press. This edited collection summarizes Canadian research on immigration and its impact on one of the world's most ethnically diverse cities, Toronto.

Massey, Douglas, Joaquin Arango, Graeme Hugo, Ali Kouaouci, Adela Pellegrino, and J. Edward Taylor. (1993). "Theories of International Migration: A Review and Appraisal." *Population and Development Review* 19:431–466. This paper provides a critical review of the more important theoretical perspectives in the study of international migration.

Statistics Canada. *Annual Demographic Statistics.* Ottawa: Statistics Canada. Cat. no. 91-213-XPB. Statistics Canada carefully charts on an annual basis all international migration influencing Canada (immigration, emigration, and change in the number of non-permanent residents). This publication also has a CD-ROM that includes time series data on all relevant components that enter into population growth in Canada, both national migration and migration between provinces and territories.

RELATED WEB SITES

Citizenship and Immigration Canada
<http://www.cic.gc.ca/>

On this site of Citizenship and Immigration Canada you can find useful information on Canada's immigration policy as well as information on the characteristics of Canada's immigrants, and research on the effect of immigration on Canadian life.

Forum for Comparative Research and Public Policy Development
http://canada.metropolis.net

This site contains a forum for comparative research and public policy development about population migration, cultural diversity, and the challenges of immigrant integration in Canada and around the world.

Statistics Canada
<http://www.statcan.ca>

With each Census, Statistics Canada produces a series of community profiles, providing Census information on population distribution for thousands of municipalities spread across the country.

United Nations Refuge Agency
<http://www.unhcr.ca>

This Web site corresponds to the Canadian branch of the United Nations Refuge Agency. This agency seeks to contribute to informed decision making and public debate by providing accurate, relevant and up-to-date information on refugees, asylum seekers, returned refugees, internally displaced and stateless people in more than 150 countries.

University of California, Davis
<http://migration.ucdavis.edu>

This site, maintained by the University of California, Davis, provides timely information and analysis of issues relating to international migration.

CHAPTER 10

100 YEARS OF IMMIGRATION IN CANADA

Monica Boyd and Michael Vickers

● ●

RECORD NUMBERS OF IMMIGRANTS came to Canada in the early 1900s. During World War I and the Depression years, numbers declined, but by the close of the 20th century, they had again approached those recorded almost 100 years earlier. Despite the superficial similarities at the beginning and the end of a century of immigration, the characteristics of immigrants are quite different. This change reflects many factors: developments and modifications in Canada's immigration polices; the displacement of peoples by wars and political upheaval; the cycle of economic "booms and busts" in Canada and other countries; Canada's membership in the Commonwealth; the growth of communication, transportation, and economic networks linking people around the world.

These forces have operated throughout the 20th century to alter the basic characteristics of Canada's immigrant population in five fundamental ways. First, the numbers of immigrants arriving each year have waxed and waned, meaning that the importance of immigration for Canada's population growth has fluctuated. Second, immigrants increasingly chose to live in Canada's largest cities. Third, the predominance of men among adult immigrants declined as family migration grew and women came to represent slightly over half of immigrants. Fourth, the marked transformation in the countries in which immigrants had been born enhanced the ethnic diversity of Canadian society. Fifth, alongside Canada's transition from an agricultural to a knowledge-based economy, immigrants were increasingly employed in the manufacturing and service sectors of the economy. This chapter provides an overview of these important changes over the last 100 years.

THE EARLY YEARS: 1900–1915

The 20th century opened with the arrival of nearly 42,000 immigrants in 1900. Numbers quickly escalated to a record high of over 400,000 in 1913. Canada's economy was growing rapidly during these years, and immigrants were drawn by the promise of good job prospects. The building of the transcontinental railway, the settlement of the Prairies, and expanding industrial production intensified demand for labour. Aggressive recruitment campaigns by the Canadian government to boost immigration and attract workers also increased arrivals: Between 1900 and 1914, more than 2.9 million people entered Canada, nearly four times as many as had arrived in the previous 14-year period.

Such volumes of immigrants quickly enlarged Canada's population. Between 1901 and 1911, net migration (the excess of those arriving over those leaving) accounted for 44 percent of population growth, a level not reached again for another 75 years. The share of the overall population born outside Canada also increased in consequence, so that while immigrants accounted for 13 percent of the population in 1901, by 1911 they made up 22 percent.

Most of the foreign-born population lived in Ontario at the start of the century, but many later immigrants headed west. By 1911, 41 percent of Canada's immigrant population lived in the Prairies, up from 20 percent recorded in the 1901 Census. This influx had a profound effect on the populations of the western provinces. By 1911, immigrants represented 41 percent of people living in Manitoba, 50 percent in Saskatchewan, and 57 percent of those in Alberta and British Columbia. In contrast, they made up less than 10 percent of the population in the Atlantic provinces and Quebec, and only 20 percent in Ontario.

Men greatly outnumbered women among people settling in Canada in the first two decades of the 20th century (Urquhart and Buckley, 1965). The 1911 Census recorded 158 immigrant males for every 100 females, compared with 103 Canadian-born males for 100 females. These unbalanced gender ratios are not uncommon in the history of settlement countries such as Canada, Australia, and the United States. They often reflect labour recruitment efforts targeted at men rather than women, as well as the behaviour of immigrants themselves. In migration flows, particularly those motivated by economic reasons, men frequently precede women, either because the move is viewed as temporary and there is no need to uproot family members, or because the man intends to become economically established before being joined by his family. By the time of the 1921 Census, the gender ratio for immigrants had become less skewed, standing at 125 immigrant males for every 100 immigrant females. It continued to decline throughout the century, reaching 94 per 100 in 1996.

Of course, women also immigrated for economic reasons in the early decades of the century. There was strong demand for female domestic workers, with women in England, Scotland, and Wales being most often targeted for recruitment. Between 1904 and 1914, "domestic" was by far the most common occupation reported by adult women immigrants (almost 30 percent) arriving from overseas (Urquhart and Buckley, 1965). Men immigrating from overseas during that period were more likely to be unskilled and semi-skilled labourers (36 percent) or to have a farming occupation (32 percent). Historians observe that, contrary to the image of immigrants being farmers and homesteaders, immigrants at the turn of the century were also factory and construction workers. And although many did settle in the western provinces, many also worked in building railroads or moved into the large cities, fuelling the growth of industrial centres.

Immigration from outside Britain and the U.S. began to grow in the 1910s. At the start of the century, the majority of immigrants to Canada had originated in the United States or the United Kingdom. However, during the 1910s and 1920s, the number born in other European countries began to grow, slowly at first, and then rising to its highest levels in 1961 and 1971.

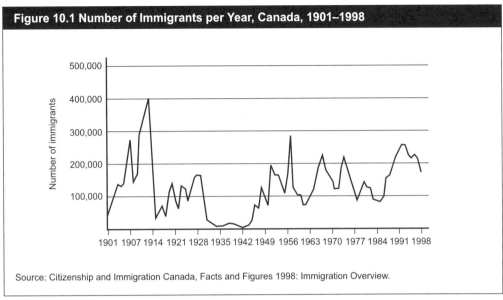

Figure 10.1 Number of Immigrants per Year, Canada, 1901–1998

Source: Citizenship and Immigration Canada, Facts and Figures 1998: Immigration Overview.

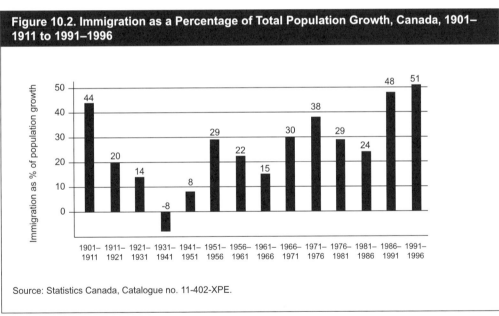

Figure 10.2. Immigration as a Percentage of Total Population Growth, Canada, 1901–1911 to 1991–1996

Source: Statistics Canada, Catalogue no. 11-402-XPE.

This change in countries of origin had begun in the closing decades of the 19th century, when many new groups began to arrive in Canada—Doukhobors and Jewish refugees from Russia, Hungarians, Mormons from the U.S., Italians, and Ukrainians. This flow continued up until World War I. It generated public debate about who should be admitted to Canada: For some writers and politicians, recruiting labour was the key issue, not the changing origins of immigrants; for others, British and American immigrants were to be preferred to those from southern or eastern European countries.

By comparison, immigration from Asia was very low at this time, in dramatic contrast to the situation at the end of the 20th century. Government policies regulating immigration had been rudimentary during the late 1800s, but when legislation was enacted in the early 1900s, it focused primarily on preventing immigration on the grounds of poverty, mental incompetence, or on the basis of non-European origins. Even though Chinese immigrant workers had helped to build the transcontinental railroad in 1885, the first piece of legislation regulating future Chinese immigration required every person of Chinese origin to pay a tax of $50 upon entering Canada. At the time, this was a very large sum. The "head tax" was increased to $100 in 1900, and to $500 in 1903. This fee meant that many Chinese men could not afford to bring brides or wives to Canada. As evidence of this fact, the 1911 Census recorded 2,790 Chinese males for every 100 Chinese females, a figure far in excess of the overall ratio of 158 immigrant males for every 100 immigrant females.

The Act of 1906 prohibited the landing of people defined as "feebleminded," having "loathsome or contagious diseases," "paupers," people "likely to become public charges," criminals, and "those of undesirable morality." In 1908, the Act was amended to prohibit the landing of those who did not come to Canada directly from their country of origin. This provision effectively excluded the immigration of people from India, who had to book passage on ships sailing from countries outside India because there were no direct sailings between Calcutta and Vancouver. Also in the early 1900s, the Canadian government entered into a series of agreements with Japan that restricted Japanese migration. It should be noted that although Asians were the most severely targeted by efforts to reduce immigration by non-Europeans, other ethnic groups such as Blacks from the United States and the Caribbean also were singled out (Calliste, 1993; Kelley and Trebilcock, 1998; Troper, 1972).

THE WARS AND THE GREAT DEPRESSION: 1915–1946

With the outbreak of World War I, immigration quickly came to a near standstill. From a record high of over 400,000 in 1913, arrivals dropped sharply to less than 34,000 by 1915. Although numbers rebounded after the war, they never again reached the levels attained before 1914. As a result, net immigration accounted for about 20 percent of Canada's population growth between 1911 and 1921, less than half the contribution made in the previous decade. However, the influence of earlier foreign-born arrivals continued, reinforced by the more modest levels of wartime and postwar immigration: at the time of the 1921 Census, immigrants still comprised 22 percent of the population.

The number of immigrants coming to Canada rose during the 1920s, with well above 150,000 per year entering in the last three years of the decade. But the Great Depression and World War II severely curtailed arrivals during the 1930s and early 1940s—numbers fluctuated between 7,600 and 27,500. Furthermore, there was actually a net migration loss of 92,000 as more people left Canada than entered between 1931 and 1941. The 1930s is the only decade in the 20th century in which this occurred. By the time of the 1941 Census, the percentage of the total population that was foreign-born had fallen to just under 18 percent.

While more men than women had immigrated to Canada in the first three decades of the century, the situation was reversed when immigration declined in the 1930s and 1940s. During this period, women outnumbered men, accounting for 60 percent of all adult arrivals between 1931 and 1940, and for 66 percent between 1941 and 1945 (Urquhart and Buckley, 1965). As a result of these changes, the overall gender ratio of the immigrant population declined slightly.

While lower numbers and the predominance of women among adult immigrants represent shifts in previous immigration patterns, other trends were more stable. The majority of immigrants continued to settle in Ontario, Manitoba, Saskatchewan, Alberta, and British Columbia. Increasingly, though, they gravitated to urban areas, foreshadowing the pattern of recent immigration concentration in large cities that became so evident in the last years of the century.

Britain was still the leading source of immigrants, but the arrival of people from other parts of the globe also continued. During the 1920s, the aftershocks of World War I and the Russian Revolution stimulated migration from Germany, Russia, the Ukraine, and eastern European countries, including Poland and Hungary (Kelley and Trebilcock, 1998). During the Depression, the majority of immigrants came from Great Britain, Germany, Austria, and the Ukraine. Fewer than 6 percent were of non-European origin.

Public debate over whom to admit and the development of immigration policy to regulate admissions was far from over. Regulations passed in 1919 provided new grounds for deportation and denied entry to enemy aliens; to those who were enemy aliens during the war; and to Doukhobors, Mennonites, and Hutterites (Kalbach, 1970). The 1923 Chinese Immigration Act restricted Chinese immigration still further (Avery, 2000). Responding to labour market pressures following the Crash of 1929 and the collapse of the prairie

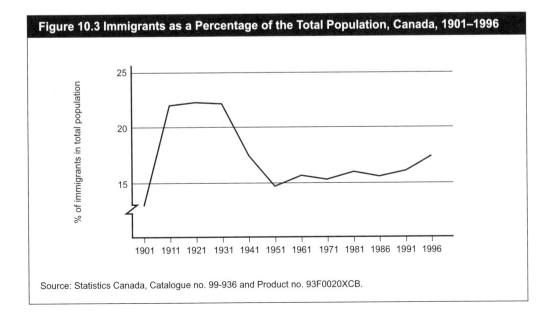

Figure 10.3 Immigrants as a Percentage of the Total Population, Canada, 1901–1996

Source: Statistics Canada, Catalogue no. 99-936 and Product no. 93F0020XCB.

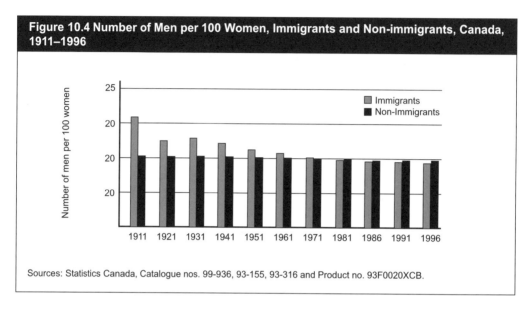

Figure 10.4 Number of Men per 100 Women, Immigrants and Non-immigrants, Canada, 1911–1996

Sources: Statistics Canada, Catalogue nos. 99-936, 93-155, 93-316 and Product no. 93F0020XCB.

economy, farm workers, domestics, and several other occupational groups, as well as relatives of landed immigrants, were struck from the list of admissible classes. Asian immigration was also cut back again (Kalbach, 1970; Statistics Canada, 1990).

Then, with the declaration of war on Germany on September 10, 1939, new regulations were passed that prohibited the entry or landing of nationals of countries with which Canada was at war. In the absence of a refugee policy that distinguished between immigrants and refugees, the restrictions imposed in the interwar years raised barriers to those fleeing the chaos and devastation of World War II. Many of those turned away at this time were Jewish refugees attempting to leave Europe (Abella and Troper, 1982; Kelley and Trebilcock, 1998; Knowles, 1997). War-related measures also included the forced relocation—often to detention camps—of Japanese-Canadians living within a 100-mile area along the British Columbia coastline. It was argued that they might assist a Japanese invasion.

THE BOOM YEARS: 1946–1970

The war in Europe ended with Germany's surrender on May 6, 1945; in the Pacific, Japan surrendered on August 14. With the return of peace, both Canada's economy and immigration boomed. Between 1946 and 1950, over 430,000 immigrants arrived, exceeding the total number admitted in the previous 15 years.

The immediate postwar immigration boom included the dependants of Canadian servicemen who had married abroad, refugees, and people seeking economic opportunities in Canada. Beginning in July 1946, and continuing throughout the late 1940s, orders-in-council paved the way for the admission of people who had been displaced from their homelands by the war and for whom return was not possible (Kalbach, 1970; Knowles, 1997). The ruination of the European economy and the unprecedented boom in Canada also favoured high immigration levels.

Numbers continued to grow throughout most of the 1950s, peaking at over 282,000 admissions in 1957. By 1958, immigration levels were beginning to fall, partly because economic conditions were improving in Europe, and partly because, with the Canadian economy slowing, the government introduced administrative policies designed to reduce the rate of immigration. By 1962, however, the economy had recovered and arrivals increased for six successive years. Although admissions never reached the record highs observed in the early part of the century, the total number of immigrants entering Canada in the 1950s and 1960s far exceeded the levels observed in the preceding three decades.

During this time, net migration was higher than it had been in almost 50 years, but it accounted for no more than 30 percent of total population growth between 1951 and 1971. The population effect of the large number of foreign-born arrivals was muted by the magnitude of natural growth caused by the unprecedented birth rates recorded during the baby boom from 1946 to 1965.

Many of the new immigrants settled in cities, so that by 1961, 81 percent of foreign-born Canadians lived in an urban area, compared with 68 percent of Canadian-born. The proportion of the immigrant population living in Ontario continued to grow, accelerating a trend that had begun earlier in the century; in contrast, the proportion living in the prairie provinces declined.

Such shifts in residential location went hand in hand with Canada's transformation from a rural-agricultural and resource-based economy in the early years of the century to an urban-manufacturing and service-based economy in the later years. Postwar immigrants were important sources of labour for this emerging economy, especially in the early 1950s. Compared to those arriving at the turn of the century, the postwar immigrants were more likely to be professional or skilled workers and they accounted for over half of the growth in these occupations between 1951 and 1961.

Although the largest number of immigrants arriving after World War II were from the United Kingdom, people from other European countries were an increasingly predominant part of the mix. During the late 1940s and 1950s, substantial numbers also arrived from Germany, the Netherlands, Italy, Poland, and the U.S.S.R. Following the 1956 Soviet invasion of Hungary, Canada also admitted over 37,000 Hungarians, while the Suez Crisis of the same year saw the arrival of almost 109,000 British immigrants (Avery, 2000; Hawkins, 1972; Kalbach, 1970; Kelley and Trebilcock, 1998). During the 1960s, the trend increased. By the time of the 1971 Census, less than one-third of the foreign-born population had been born in the United Kingdom; half came from other European countries, many from Italy.

NEW POLICIES HELP DIRECT POSTWAR IMMIGRATION TRENDS

Much of the postwar immigration to Canada was stimulated by people displaced by war or political upheaval, as well as by the weakness of the European economies. However, Canada's postwar immigration policies also were an important factor. Because they were statements of who would be admitted and under what conditions, these policies influenced the numbers of arrivals, the types of immigrants, and the country of origin of new arrivals.

Within two years of the war ending, on May 1, 1947, Prime Minister Mackenzie King reaffirmed that immigration was vital for Canada's growth, but he also indicated that the numbers and country of origin of immigrants would be regulated. Five years later, the Immigration Act of 1952 consolidated many postwar changes to immigration regulations that had been enacted since the previous Act of 1927. Subsequent regulations that spelled out the possible grounds for limiting admissions included national origin; on this basis, admissible people were defined to be those with birth or citizenship in the United States, the United Kingdom, Australia, New Zealand, the Union of South Africa, and selected European countries.

In 1962, however, new regulations effectively removed national origins as a criterion of admission. Further regulations enacted in 1967 confirmed this principle and instead introduced a system that assigned points based on the age, education, language skills, and economic characteristics of applicants. These policy changes made it much easier for people born outside Europe and the United States to immigrate to Canada.

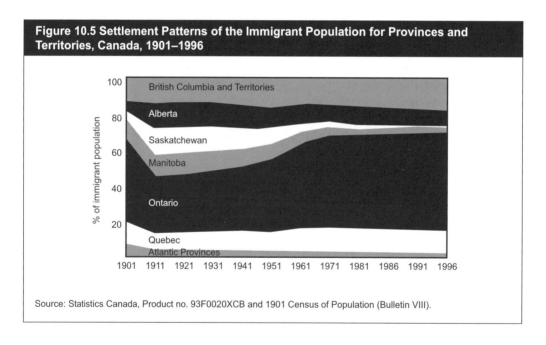

Figure 10.5 Settlement Patterns of the Immigrant Population for Provinces and Territories, Canada, 1901–1996

Source: Statistics Canada, Product no. 93F0020XCB and 1901 Census of Population (Bulletin VIII).

The 1967 regulations also reaffirmed the right, first extended in the 1950s, of immigrants to sponsor relatives to enter Canada. Family-based immigration had always co-existed alongside economically motivated immigration, but now it was clearly defined. As wives, mothers, aunts, and sisters, women participated in these family reunification endeavours: Women accounted for almost half of all adult immigrants entering Canada during the 1950s and 1960s. As a result of this gender parity in immigration flows, gender ratios declined over time for the foreign-born population.

GROWTH AND DIVERSITY: 1970–1996

In the 1960s, changes in immigration policy were made by altering the regulations that governed implementation of the Immigration Act of 1952. But in 1978, a new Immigration Act came into effect. This Act upheld the principles of admissions laid out in the regulations of the 1960s: family reunification and economic contributions. For the first time in Canada's history, the new Act also incorporated the principle of admissions based on humanitarian grounds. Previously, refugee admissions had been handled through special procedures and regulations. The Act also required the minister responsible for the immigration portfolio to set annual immigration targets in consultation with the provinces.

From the 1970s through the 1990s, immigration numbers fluctuated. The overall impact, however, continued to be a significant contribution to Canada's total population growth that increased as the century drew to a close. During the early- and mid-1970s, net migration represented nearly 38 percent of the total increase in the population; with consistently high levels of arrivals between 1986 and 1996, it accounted for about half of the population growth. These percentages exceeded those recorded in the 1910s and the 1920s. The cumulative effect of net migration from the 1970s onward was a gradual increase in the percentage of foreign-born Canadians. By the time of the 1996 Census, immigrants comprised just over 17 percent of the population, the largest proportion in more than 50 years.

Having an immigration policy based on principles of family reunification and labour market contribution also recast the composition of the immigrant population. It meant that people from all nations could be admitted if they met the criteria as described in the immigration regulations. The inclusion of humanitarian-based admissions also permitted the entry of refugees from countries outside Europe. As a result, the immigrants who entered Canada from 1966 onward came from many different countries and possessed more diverse cultural backgrounds than earlier immigrants. Each successive Census recorded declining percentages of the immigrant population that had been born in European countries, the United Kingdom, and the United States.

Meanwhile, the proportion of immigrants born in Asian countries and other regions of the world began to rise slowly at first and then more quickly through the 1980s. By 1996, 27 percent of the immigrant population in Canada had been born in Asia and another 21 percent came from places other than the United States, the United Kingdom, or Europe. The top five countries of birth for immigrants arriving between 1991 and 1996 were Hong Kong, the People's Republic of China, India, the Philippines, and Sri Lanka. Together, these five countries accounted for more than one-third of all immigrants who arrived in those five years.

IMMIGRATION: THE LARGEST CONTRIBUTOR TO GROWTH OF VISIBLE MINORITY POPULATION

The visible minority population has grown dramatically in the last two decades. In 1996, 11.2 percent of Canada's population—3.2 million people—identified themselves as members of a visible minority group, up from under 5 percent in 1981. Immigration has been a big contributor to this growth: about seven in 10 visible minorities are immigrants, almost half of whom have arrived since 1981.

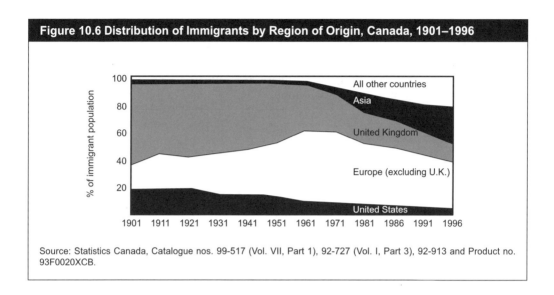

Figure 10.6 Distribution of Immigrants by Region of Origin, Canada, 1901–1996

Source: Statistics Canada, Catalogue nos. 99-517 (Vol. VII, Part 1), 92-727 (Vol. I, Part 3), 92-913 and Product no. 93F0020XCB.

Most immigrants live in Canada's big cities, with the largest numbers concentrated in the Census metropolitan areas (CMAs) of Toronto, Montreal, and Vancouver. This continues the trend established earlier in the century. Proportionally more immigrants than Canadian-born have preferred to settle in urban areas, attracted by economic opportunities and by the presence of other immigrants from the same countries or regions of the world. In 1996, 85 percent of all immigrants lived in a CMA, compared with just 57 percent of the Canadian-born population. As a result, the largest CMAs have a higher concentration of immigrants than the national average of just over 17 percent. In 1996, 42 percent of Toronto's population, 35 percent of Vancouver's, and 18 percent of Montreal's were foreign-born.

The attraction to urban centres helps to explain the provincial distribution of immigrants. Since the 1940s, a disproportionate share has lived in Ontario and the percentage has continued to rise over time. By 1996, 55 percent of all immigrants lived in Ontario, compared with 18 percent in British Columbia and 13 percent in Quebec.

RECENT IMMIGRANTS' ADJUSTMENT TO LABOUR FORCE CAN BE DIFFICULT

Just as immigrants have contributed to the growth in Canada's population, to its diversity, and to its cities, so too have they contributed to its economy. During the last few decades, most employment opportunities have shifted from manufacturing to service industries, and immigrants are an important source of labour for some of these industries. However, compared with non-immigrants, they are more likely to be employed in the personal services industries, manufacturing, and construction. Moreover, the likelihood of being employed in one industry rather than another often differs depending on the immigrant's sex, age at arrival, education, knowledge of English and/or French, and length of time in Canada.

Living in a new society generally entails a period of adjustment, particularly when a person must look for work, learn a new language, or deal with an educational system, medical services, government agencies, and laws that may differ significantly from those in his or her country of origin. The difficulty of transition may be seen in the labour market profile of recent immigrants: Compared with longer-established immigrants and with those born in Canada, many may experience higher unemployment rates, hold jobs that do not reflect their level of training and education, and earn lower incomes.

In 1996, immigrants aged 25 to 44 who had arrived in the previous five years had lower labour force participation rates and lower employment rates than the Canadian-born, even though they were generally better educated and more than 90 percent could speak at least one official language (Badets and Howatson-Leo, 1999). Both male and female immigrants who were recent arrivals were more likely than the Canadian-born to be employed in sales and services occupations and in processing, manufacturing, and utilities jobs. However, the proportion of immigrant men in many professional occupations was similar to that of Canadian-born men; in contrast, recent immigrant women were considerably less likely than Canadian-born women to be employed in occupations in business, finance, administration, health, social sciences, education, and government services. Recent immigrants also earned less on average than the Canadian-born (Picot and Heisz, 2000).

In the past, the disparities between recent immigrants and the Canadian-born have often disappeared over time, indicating that initial labour market difficulties reflect the adjustment process. The differences in the 1990s may also result from the diminished employment opportunities available during the recession, also a period of difficulty for the Canadian-born who were new entrants to the job market. Nevertheless, the gaps in employment rates and earnings widened between recent immigrants and the Canadian-born during the 1980s and 1990s, suggesting that newcomers were having an increasingly difficult time in the initial stages of labour market adjustment.

NON-PERMANENT RESIDENTS

One category of newcomers to Canada that has grown considerably in recent years is that of non-permanent residents. Although they accounted for less than 1 percent of the total national population (or 167,000 people) at the time of the 1996 Census, the importance of these people, particularly to the labour force, is growing.

Non-permanent residents comprise a diverse group: They include highly skilled managers and technicians, semi-skilled agricultural and domestic workers, refugee claimants, and foreign students. They differ from landed immigrants in that they are more likely to be of prime working age (20 to 49 years old) and men significantly outnumber women. They do, however, resemble recent immigrants in that they have congregated primarily in Canada's largest urban areas: Nearly three-quarters of them live in the CMAs of Toronto, Vancouver, and Montreal.

Temporary residents probably congregate in the cities because that is where the work is (for temporary workers) and where the major educational institutions are located (for foreign students). Refugee claimants also tend to settle in larger cities, partly because they represent the principal entry points to the country, and partly because work and support services are more likely to be available.

The largest group of non-permanent residents is that of people admitted for temporary employment. Since the early 1980s, the number of temporary workers has exceeded the number of working-age immigrants (15 to 64 years), sometimes by a ratio of more than two to one. Although foreign managers and business people have historically resided in Canada to direct the operations of foreign-owned enterprises, the image of temporary workers also includes people from developing countries working in low-skilled jobs. However, in the wake of the FTA and NAFTA agreements, and with the growing demand for labour from information technology industries, this image of the temporary worker is quickly being replaced by one of highly skilled managerial or technical employees.

Another significant group of non-permanent residents is composed of people waiting for rulings on their refugee claims. Indeed, one of the largest single increases in the number of non-permanent residents occurred in 1989. Almost 100,000 refugee claimants and out-of-status foreigners were given the opportunity to apply for permanent residence from inside Canada, under a special Backlog Clearance Program and were given the right to work without having to apply for Employment Authorization (for more information, see McKie, 1994; Michalowski, 1996).

SUMMARY

Few would quarrel with the statement that the 20th century in Canada was an era of enormous change. Every area of life, ranging from the economy to family to law, was altered over the course of 100 years. Immigration was not immune to these transformative forces. The size and character of immigration flows were influenced by economic booms and busts, by world wars and national immigration policies, and indirectly by expanding communication, transportation, and economic links around the world.

The ebb and flow of immigration has presented the most volatile changes over the last 100 years. The century began with the greatest number of immigrant arrivals ever recorded. Thereafter, levels fluctuated, often with dramatic swings from one decade to the next. The lowest levels were recorded in the 1930s during the Depression. By the close of the century, though, the number of immigrants arriving annually were again sufficiently large that net migration accounted for over half of Canada's population growth.

Other changes in immigration are better described as trends, for they followed a course that was cumulative rather than reversible. The high ratio of men to women immigrants dropped steadily throughout the century. There were two main reasons for this decline. First, the number of men immigrating fell during the two wars and the Depression; and second, the number of women immigrants increased in the last half of the century as a result of family reunification after World War II and of family migration, in which women, men, and their children immigrated together.

Even in the 1900s and 1910s, the foreign-born were more likely to live in urban areas. After the initial settlement of the Prairies in the early 1900s, the trend toward urban settlement accelerated. By the 1990s, the vast majority of recent immigrants were residing in Census metropolitan areas, mainly those of Toronto, Vancouver, and Montréal.

Government policies regulating who would be admitted and under what conditions also evolved. Much of the effort during the first 50 years of the century focused on restricting immigration from regions of the world other than the U.S., Britain, and Europe. This position changed in the 1960s when national origin was removed as a criterion for entry. The policies enacted thereafter entrenched the basic principles guiding admissions, such as family reunification, economic contributions, and humanitarian concerns. With these changes, the source countries of immigrants to Canada substantially altered. By 1996, close to half of the foreign-born in Canada were from countries other than the U.K., the U.S., and Europe.

As a result of these changes, Canada at the close of the 20th century contrasted sharply with Canada 100 years before. Immigrants had increased the population; they had diversified the ethnic and linguistic composition of the country; and they had laboured in both the agrarian economy of old and in the new industrial and service-based economy of the future.

• •

CRITICAL THINKING QUESTIONS

1. It has been said that in terms of population policy, the most explicit attempts to influence demographic trends in Canada have occurred in the area of international migration. Discuss while providing examples.
2. The character of Canada's immigration policy shifted dramatically in the 1960s when new regulations effectively removed national origins as a criterion of admission. In the decades to follow, a whole series of additional factors came to influence immigration policy. Elaborate on some of these changes, and on your opinion as to their relative success.
3. If you were responsible for immigration policy, what would you recommend to Parliament regarding the level and composition of immigration for the next several years? Why?

• •

CHAPTER 11

GLOBALIZATION, UNDOCUMENTED MIGRATION, AND UNWANTED REFUGEES: TRENDS, EXPLANATIONS, AND SOLUTIONS

Alan B. Simmons

● ●

INTRODUCTION

Interest in research, theory, and policy frameworks for better understanding international migration and refugee flows is high and continues to grow around the world. In the post-September 11 period, public anxiety in Western nations about possible links between migrants, refugees, and terrorist attacks has tended to reinforce sentiment against migrants and refugees, particularly those from less-developed non-Western nations. In this process, human rights values that support the admission of asylum seekers are undermined. Increasing numbers of people who flee violence remain as displaced people in their home countries.

The poorest nations also reveal contradictory pressures with respect to international migration. Economic conditions lead many people in very poor nations to think about possible advantages of moving to a wealthier country, but they often lack the occupational skills, knowledge, and money that it takes to gain legal admission in more developed nations. Migration is therefore often undocumented and "underground." The migrant workers involved are vulnerable to exploitation by their employers and to being viewed as criminals by the police. Refugees who cannot gain legal status in countries of asylum are the most prone to victimization.

It is widely recognized that the above trends in international migration and immigration policy are linked to a process of worldwide economic, cultural, and political transformation generally referred to as "globalization." The present paper begins by briefly commenting on the way in which globalization has been understood and analyzed in the research literature on international migration. It then reviews some important trends in international migration and refugee flows as they reflect contradictory processes of globalization.

THE RECENT LITERATURE

A range of theoretical models have been proposed to explain international migration and refugee movements. Explanatory models of international migration are rather fragmented into different disciplinary and analytic perspectives (Brettell and Hollifield, 2000; Massey et al., 1998). Within the broader migration research literature, refugee flows are under-theorized. Refugees are often viewed as special cases of international migration in which "push" factors (especially violence and human rights abuses in the home country) dominate over "pull" factors (such as jobs and other opportunities in receiving countries); at the same time, political models and political-economic models that focus particularly on refugee movements have proven to be particularly useful even when they point to a great deal of overlap between refugee movements narrowly conceived and international emigration from underdeveloped countries (Zolberg et al., 1989).

A significant part of contemporary research and theory on international migration and refugee flows does not explicitly incorporate globalization as a concept. Many recent theoretical models view globalization as irrelevant or somehow outside the frame of the issues they wish to examine. This lack of attention to globalization might be considered reasonable if the focus of research were ahistorical—that is, abstracted from wider social and economic transformations. Thus, for example, a theory of migrant decision making may be based on a model of expected outcomes of migration that could be applied in any historical or social situation. Yet ignoring globalization seems much more surprising when the research seeks to provide a macro-level systemic framework for assessing contemporary migration trends and related national policy issues, intended to account for a particular historical period.

The very well known and useful review of diverse theoretical approaches on migration by Massey et al. (1998) gives some attention to globalization, but only as a sub-component of one of the many perspectives reviewed. This widely cited review of theories of migration includes a brief assessment of globalization as a component of the world systems and global cities approaches to economic and social transformation. Considered in this way, the globalization approach is credited with advancing hypotheses largely on questions of the links between the "new" international division of labour, racial, ethnic, and gender stratification in migrant-receiving societies and international migration. Yet this partial view of globalization can be criticized for not explicitly considering the role of contemporary international travel and communications patterns on expanding transnational cultural linkages and their impact on future migration and refugee flows. Similarly, it seems to largely ignore important issues surrounding refugee production, population displacement, and national policy—that is, the conflict between forces that increasingly seek to retain the displaced within their country or region of origin and those that are favourable to providing asylum.

Peter Stalker's (2000) *Workers without Frontiers: The Impact of Globalization on International Migration* is largely about the globalization of trade and economic production. International migration is addressed in terms of the relative trade-offs of moving workers to production sites in other countries versus moving the production facilities to the countries where they live. Stalker treats cultural and political dimensions of globalization and its links to international migration only very briefly in several introductory paragraphs on "global consciousness" and later in a section on "political disruption" associated with the impact of open trade and fast-moving capital shifts on job loss and labour force adjustment. Refugee flows are treated only marginally as extreme cases of violence and political-economic dislocation in poor countries faced with adjustments to new global conditions.

An overlapping approach to globalization with somewhat different emphases may be found in Stephen Castles and Mark J. Miller's (1998) *The Age of Migration: International Population Movements in the Modern World*. In this work (with its emphasis on contemporary migration patterns and new minorities), particular attention is given to the link between globalized migration (all parts of the world are more linked through the movement of people) and the parallel globalization of culture and trade. In drawing more attention to culture, this work also draws more attention to issues of racism, ethnocentrism, and unequal migrant incorporation in receiving societies. Future scenarios for international migration therefore focus particularly on the kinds of ethnic stratification and international order that current trends imply.

Globalization has entered into the vocabulary of research and theory on international migration, but this entry is recent and relies on somewhat different and generally incomplete conceptualizations of globalization. Typical of such an approach, Castles (2003:293) uses a globalization framework and uses the term repeatedly in his work, but devotes only a sentence to defining it as "a proliferation of cross-border flows and transnational networks." In the following sections of the chapter, I turn to an examination of some United Nations data on empirical trends in international migration and refugee flows over the past several decades—the so-called "era of contemporary globalization." These data cover the period from the 1960s to the 1990s.

GLOBAL EMPIRICAL TRENDS

Frameworks on globalization and international migration are grappling with a shifting picture of major trends in international migration. What are the global empirical trends that such models are particularly concerned with? The following points address the empirical evidence on selected points.

1. INCREASED FLOWS?

It has been assumed that globalization will tend to lead to ever larger movements of people between countries. However, such a one-sided perspective ignores the fact that globalization also creates cultural, political, and economic (fear of job loss, etc.) insecurities in migrant-receiving nations leading them to tighten their borders. The world is therefore characterized by an increasingly intense contradiction: Pressures to move may be rising, but border controls and rejection of foreigners may reduce actual flows. These opposing trends may both be accentuated by different aspects of the same globalization process.

The available data on overall world trend in international migrant flows indicate that only a very small percentage of the world's population moves to another country and that this percentage appears to have remained constant at around 2.3 percent over the period from 1965 to 1990 (see Table 11.1). In other words, the perception that international migration is increasing with globalization is wrong when assessed in terms of worldwide trends. That does not mean, as will be noted below, that the worldwide trend is reflected in the experience of every country.

A few countries have in fact experienced increased inflows of international migrants. Perhaps more importantly, a number of wealthy nations would not have experienced significant increases in international migration if they had sought to impose new, more restrictive controls on migrant entry. Equally important is the fact that the source countries of migration into wealthy destination nations have been changing. Migrants to Europe and to countries where people of European ancestry predominate are increasingly from non-European origins—Africa, Asia, the Caribbean, and Latin America. This leads to a perception in many of these receiving countries that immigration is increasing when in fact what is changing is the visibility of the cultures and ethnic backgrounds of immigrants from non-European sources.

Table 11.1 Migrant Origins by Region, 1965 to 1990

Region	Immigrant population in millions		Immigrants as a percent of population	
	1965	1990	1965	1990
Total (world)	75,214	119,761	2.3	2.3
Developed nations	30,401	54,231	3.1	4.5
Underdeveloped nations	44,813	65,530	1.9	1.6
Africa	7,952	15,631	2.5	2.5
Asia	31,429	43,018	1.7	1.4
Latin America	5,907	7,475	2.4	1.7
North America	12,695	23,895	6.0	8.6
Western Europe	11,753	22,853	3.6	6.1
Oceania	2,020	4,675	14.4	17.8

Source: Zlotnik, 1999, tableau 1a.

2. Expanding Web of Source-Destination Country Connections?

A fundamental assumption is that globalization of trade and culture in conjunction with expanding communications and travel should over time bring all countries into international migration networks, either as migrant-sending countries and/or as migrant-receiving nations (many countries are both migrant sending and migrant receiving). This predicted pattern is supported by the available evidence. However, some qualifications need to be added. Some receiving countries, such as Canada and the United States, were already highly connected to a worldwide range of immigrant source countries as early as 1965–1969 and have experienced a further diversification of immigrant sources since then. Over the same period, other countries moved from a situation in which their immigrants came from few countries, often ones to which they had common cultural and historical links, to a situation characterized by a great diversity of immigrant origins, near the level of that of Canada, for example. The greatest component of this diversification of source countries is international migration from developing countries in Africa, Asia, the Caribbean, and Latin America. Some of the diversification comes from the post-1989 emergence of states in the former U.S.S.R. as major source countries, and in the mid-1990s, the emergence of developing countries in the war torn Balkans as major source countries. Figures 11.1 and 11.2 show the impact of the above trends on the diversification of migrant source countries for a few major receiving nations.

3. RISING REFUGEE FLOWS?

Globalization is understood to have many potential impacts on worldwide refugee flows. It has been argued that rapid shifts in exports, production, and work opportunities associated with changing global investments and trade can spark or exacerbate political unrest, social conflict, and repression of dissent in poor countries (Simmons, 1989). The spread of international communication and travel links also suggests that asylum seekers, like other international migrants, are more likely to know about alternative countries of residence and find ways to move to them. On the other hand, the spread of global trade and economic interdependence has been viewed by many as a trend that should over time reduce conflicts between nations and between regions within nations. The World Bank and other leading financial institutions not only actively promote "export-oriented" economic growth policies, but also promote democracy, "good governance," and related social development policies as part of their overall programs. When countries adopt the full range of recommended policies, it is generally assumed that they no longer produce

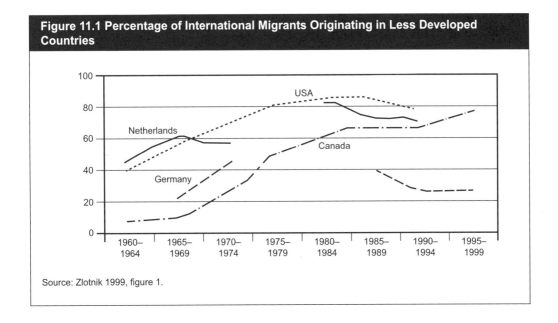

Figure 11.1 Percentage of International Migrants Originating in Less Developed Countries

Source: Zlotnik 1999, figure 1.

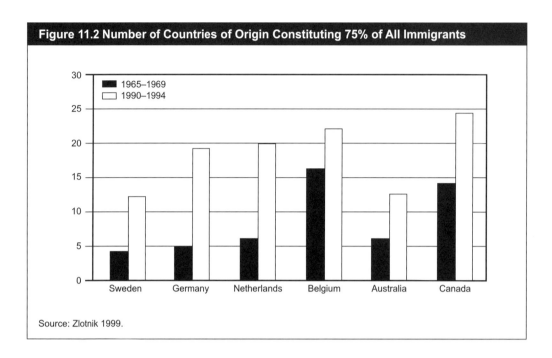

Figure 11.2 Number of Countries of Origin Constituting 75% of All Immigrants

Source: Zlotnik 1999.

refugees. People who leave such countries claiming refugee status may find it difficult to obtain asylum abroad. In sum, globalization seemingly creates contradictory trends in the flow of refugees.

A UN convention refugee is a person residing outside his or her country of nationality and unable to return due to "a well-founded fear of persecution by reason of his race, religion, nationality, membership in of a particular social group or political opinion" (United Nations 1967 protocol). Are the numbers of such people rising in the world over the global era? The answer is unclear. The rise and fall of ethnic conflicts and authoritarian states are driven primarily by local historical and regional dynamics. How globalization might affect refugee movements and flows of asylum seekers is therefore a complex question. The available evidence from the United Nations High Commissioner for Refugees (UNHCR) indicates that refugee flows rose during the period from the late 1980s to the early 1990s, corresponding to a wave of ethnic conflicts and civil wars during that period. Many of these conflicts were exacerbated by cold war politics between superpowers; others were sparked by the end of the cold war and the collapse of the former U.S.S.R. and Eastern-bloc countries such as the former Yugoslavia. From the mid-1990s, as the cold war and immediate post-cold war conflicts subsided, refugee flows related to them and hence refugee flows worldwide have declined, even though they remain enormous and deeply troubling in certain regions (such as Africa). Figure 11.3 provides some details on these trends.

Possible explanations for the fact that worldwide total refugee populations have declined somewhat over the late 1990s and the early 2000s include: (a) the end of the cold war in 1989; and (b) the fact that, as noted above, refugee-receiving countries have

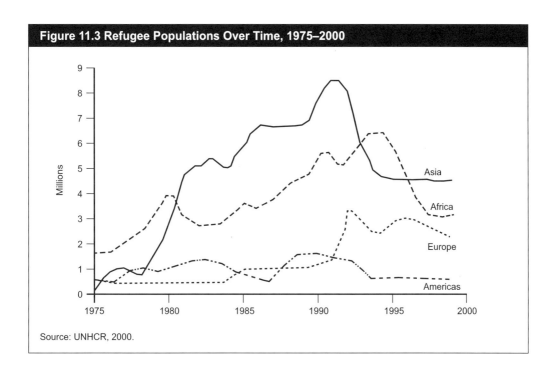

Figure 11.3 Refugee Populations Over Time, 1975–2000

Source: UNHCR, 2000.

made it more difficult for asylum seekers to enter their territories. The symptom of the latter is the rising number of "displaced persons" worldwide. These are individuals who remain inside their own national territory after having been displaced by civil war, violence, and insecurity of the kind that might have led them to leave their nation. The growth of populations of displaced people around the world has been fast and the size of such population is so great that the United Nations High Commissioner for Refugees (UNHCR) has expanded its mandate and now monitors and seeks to resolve problems of population displacement. Displaced people are in effect viewed as equivalent to refugees; they are potential refugees; the conditions that they face are similar in many respects to convention refugees except that they remain within their own national borders, unable to return to their hometowns and regions because of "a well-founded fear" of what would happen to them if they did. Estimates of the worldwide population of displaced persons are shown in Table 11.2.

4. A GREATER FOCUS ON "HUMAN CAPITAL" AND LABOUR DEMAND IN SELECTING IMMIGRANTS?

All "countries of immigration" (i.e., those with proactive immigration targets and admission policies) select at least a portion of immigrants on the basis of work skills (other immigrants are admitted through family reunification, refugee criteria, or other channels). The United States, Canada, Australia, and New Zealand all have significant provisions for admitting desired workers. In some cases, these work skill and labour market-based immigration policies have long histories, predating contemporary globalization.

Table 11.2 Populations in Need of UNHCR Assistance (January 1, 2001)

	Refugees	Displaced Persons	Displaced as a percentage of Refugees
Africa	3,604,315	1,112,028	30.9
Middle East	211,191	0	0.0
Asia	4,950,742	1,465,139	29.6
Europe	2,715,167	2,163,168	79.7[a]
Americas	666,602	525,000	78.8[b]
Total	12,148,017	5,265,335	43.3

[a] Displaced persons in Europe are nearly all in Eastern Europe.
[b] Displaced persons in the Americas are nearly all in South America.

Source: UNHRC, Global Appeal 2002 (www.unhrc.org).

The main impact of globalization has been to increase the level of education and work skills that receiving countries look for in prospective immigrants. A secondary impact has been to increase the number of countries entering into competition with one another for particularly sought-after categories of skilled immigrants. With respect to policy trends, one can cite the case of Canada, where policy shifts since the early 1990s in particular have sought to increase the proportion of all immigrants that are selected on social-adaptability criteria (ones that emphasize education, training, and occupational skills) and to increase the skill level of those entering in this category (Simmons, 1999).

Countries that have never considered themselves as "countries of immigration" are also now starting to generate policies that would attract and admit more highly skilled workers and retain them for longer periods of time. The increased demand for highly skilled migrants not only in the traditional countries of immigration discussed above, but also increasingly in newly industrializing countries (such as Singapore and Malaysia) as well as in countries such as Germany, which have historically viewed themselves as *not* being countries of immigration, raises the question of whether there are enough desirable immigrants in source countries to meet the demands for them worldwide. Such a question is difficult to answer given that demand for such workers is increasingly defined in global terms somewhat independent of location. The work of the sought-after skilled professionals and technicians can often be done in their home countries and distributed elsewhere as part of the global trade in high-technology services. In consequence, the demand for sought-after workers in wealthier nations is now both increased and moderated by a demand for them in their home countries (often on contracts from wealthy nations).

While it is not known how this competition between nations for high-skilled workers will evolve, the pattern that is emerging suggests that there is a hierarchy of desirable destinations for highly skilled workers who wish to relocate internationally. The United States is at the top of the hierarchy, drawing in skilled migrants from parts of the world.

Countries like Canada and Australia gain highly skilled immigrants from certain other regions, such as south Asia, but then subsequently lose many of their own highly trained workers and some highly trained immigrants through emigration to the United States. Smaller countries with restricted labour markets for high-technology workers are able to attract some highly skilled immigrants from Asia, but the number who come are few given competition from nearby Australia as well as from the United States and Canada.

Wealthy nations seem to "hedging their bets" (that is, pursuing alternative strategies to ensure that at least one strategy will succeed even if others fail) with regard to skilled labour. Educational standards and levels are a key focus of both public and private concern in developed countries. One of the consequences of this is that levels of post-secondary schooling have been rising quickly in the most developed countries and in the newly industrializing countries of Asia. On the other hand, in Latin America and Africa, levels of post-secondary schooling have been rising, but at much slower levels, such that the education gap between them and developed nations has been increasing. For example, the proportion of the population aged 20–24 attending college or university in Latin America increased slightly from 14 percent to 15 percent between 1980 and 1993. Over the same period in the industrially developed nations this proportion rose from 35 percent to 56 percent (World Bank, 1997). The industrially developed nations are not only responding to global competition by investing in the education of their own future labour force at home, but they are increasingly orienting their immigration policy to admission of the most highly educated from the poor countries.

5. Increasing Competition between Skilled Immigrants and Skilled Native-Born Workers?

Successful migrant incorporation in a receiving nation is a function of their "human capital" in significant part. Those immigrants with higher levels of schooling and more occupational skills and experience tend to move more quickly to better jobs and incomes after migration. This said, there is evidence in both the United States and Canada that more recent immigrants are taking longer in finding the better jobs and incomes than did earlier immigrants. The reasons for this are complex and still being studied. Explanations for the Canadian case include the following:

Peter Li (2000) points to the fact that recent immigrants are more likely to be from non-European backgrounds and therefore may be assumed to face disadvantages arising from prejudice similar to the native-born of non-European ethnicity. Wanner (1998) argues that the recent immigrants come from countries with low levels of development and may therefore have lower skills (arising from weaker educational institutions, particularly at the post-secondary level) than their degree status would imply.

Jeffrey Reitz (2001) argues that the rapidly rising educational levels of young Canadians mean that newly arriving immigrants face tougher competition for jobs than they did in the past. This is true even for those immigrants with high levels of training. Ironically, many of these young Canadians with high levels of training are children of the previous wave of immigrants who were not only relatively successful themselves (at a time when immigrants with relatively high skills did well in the Canadian labour market) but who then encouraged their children to achieve even higher education standards in Canadian schools.

6. Is There a Trend toward New or Stronger Transnational Identities and Dual Citizenship?

Trends in transnational identity and citizenship are key issues for a globalization approach to international migration. They are also very poorly understood since research on them is partial and recent. The general assumption is that societies around the world, even those that consider themselves monocultural, are increasingly challenged by the emergence of multicultural communities, transnational social linkages and solidarities, and real or de-facto dual citizenships. Yet it also seems clear that nation-states remain the dominant actor in controlling migration flows and establishing economic and cultural policy, even as new global trade, economic co-operation agreements, as well as expanding travel and cultural bridges tend to make national borders less sovereign than they once were.

There are many other questions on worldwide trends in immigration flows and policies in relation to globalization that can only be answered in part based on existing evidence. For example, expanding trade links between countries may lead to or arise from higher levels of international migration between these countries, but the effect may vary from one receiving/sending country to another. In addition, there is no doubt that receiving countries are becoming very deeply concerned about "security" issues related to migrant smuggling and terrorism. Yet, there is no evidence to suggest that migrant smuggling has increased (Salt, 2001). Nor is there evidence to suggest that terrorism is particularly related to migration when acts of terrorism worldwide are typically generated by groups within the nation and/or by travellers and visitors who do not intend to settle.

Arguments on the links between migration, trade, and security issues draw attention to the very blurred distinction between certain kinds of travellers, visitors, and international migrants. Formal definitions based in law or international agreement may clarify these terms for day-to-day border control, but they do not resolve the underlying conceptual blurring when one examines the association of these often overlapping kinds of mobility for trade and security, transnationality, dual citizenship, and the impact of global mobility patterns on home and destination countries.

DISCUSSION AND CONCLUSIONS

The problems of "illegal" migrants and of "unwanted" refugees are generated in the world system by the contradictory forces of globalization. The process includes various dimensions. At the core of the process is a political and economic competition between nations for "highly skilled immigrants" and a rejection of "unskilled migrants and refugees" that come from poor countries where human skills have not been developed. Contributing to this core process is an international system that promotes the rapid "adjustment" of politically and economically underdeveloped nations to new global trade patterns without providing sufficient support to their concomitant political and economic development. The expansion of communications and travel in the world facilitates the legal movement of skilled migrants and the illegal or undocumented movement of migrants who are both welcomed abroad (by employers seeking cheap workers) and rejected in the same countries (by segments of the population who fear their presence, and by states who do not want them).

Solutions to the problems of undocumented migrants, unwanted refugees, and large numbers of displaced people must be systemic and global if they are to really make a difference. Paradoxically, the solution may be more advanced globalization in which expanding trade is linked to the promotion of global human and labour rights. This may not lead to the end to all violence, war, and human rights abuses, but it could systemically reduce their incidence. Humanitarian programs that provide immediate support to trafficked migrants, food and shelter to refugees, and national reconstruction for displaced people will still be necessary, but hopefully fewer in incidence and easier to address.

● ●

CRITICAL THINKING QUESTIONS

1. Globalization involves a dramatic growth in communications, transportation, and economic networks linking people from around the world. In this context of dramatic economic and social change, has the scale of international migration and international refugee flows increased or declined? Why do you think this is the case?

2. One clear impact of globalization on Canada's immigration policy is that it has led to an expanding web of source-country connections, such that the immigrants now coming to Canada are more culturally diverse than ever before. How else has globalization had an impact on Canadian immigration policy?

3. What sort of effect do you think the events of 9/11 might have had (if any) on Canada's immigration policy?

● ●

CHAPTER 12

WHAT IS THE ROLE OF IMMIGRATION IN CANADA'S FUTURE?

Alan G. Green

●●●●●●●●●●●●●●●●●●●●●●●●●●●●

INTRODUCTION

We are at a critical juncture in the history of immigration policy in this country. The voices of those opposed to current levels of immigration are being raised against those who see great benefits in maintaining, or even raising, the present levels of admission. The debate over the number of immigrants to be admitted is not unique to Canada. European countries are in even greater turmoil. For many, immigration is a whole new experience, since for almost two centuries, most have been sending, not receiving, countries. With sharply declining birth rates, they find it imperative to import workers rather than send excess population overseas. The ascendancy of Le Pen in France and the rise of other extreme right-wing political parties is only the most recent manifestation of this problem over the admission of strangers. In Canada, there has been a spate of recent publications recommending a reduction in the level of inflow for both economic and security reasons (see Collacott, 2002; Francis, 2002; and Stoffman, 2002).

The United States is no exception to this debate. After almost two decades of admitting about 1 million documented immigrants a year, questions are being raised about the economic benefits of running at this level of admission. For example, George Borjas (1999), in his most recent book, *Heaven's Door*, suggests that this inflow be cut in half. His reasoning is straightforward. Research suggests that the average "quality" of immigrants admitted to the United States over the last three decades is lower than it was for those entering during the 1950s and 1960s. As a result, current immigration levels threaten to lower the pace of economic growth.

The current minister of immigration in Ottawa has taken a very different view toward immigration. In a recent policy statement, Denis Coderre has pledged to admit over a million immigrants in the next decade. Indeed, the targeted number is equivalent to 1 percent of the population or a gross immigration of about 300,000 a year. Furthermore, this proposal has been made within the context of admitting this number annually, regardless of the state of the current labour market in Canada. It is clear that this government, and the one that preceded it, have both adopted a strong pro-immigration position. Both Canada and the United States, therefore, have witnessed an upward trend in the level of admissions over the last 20 years.

GOALS OF CANADIAN IMMIGRATION POLICY

It is here, with the parallel trends in admissions that the similarity between Canada and the United States ends. Canada sees immigration as the solution to a wide range of current economic problems facing the country, while the United States focuses more on family reunification as the central goal of its immigration policy. Canadian goals are more demographic and economic. They include:

- The aging of the population; that is, an attempt to ease, through immigration, the fiscal burden associated with a rising share of non-working to working population.
- Responding, through immigration, to the need for additional skills (human capital) associated with the expansion of the knowledge economy.
- Promoting economic growth especially, at present, regional growth, by dispersing immigrants to small centres across Canada.

The question that arises, then, since the Canadian position on immigration seems to be out of step with other receiving countries (old and new), is "Can immigration solve these problems?" Or even more pointedly if the answer to this question is "no": "Do we need immigration at all?" These questions are not meant to downplay the contribution that immigration has played in shaping economic and social developments in this country in the past. They are raised to help us focus on just what role immigration might be expected to play over the next century. An attempt to answer such questions might also help us define more precisely what level of inflow would be viable in the future.

THE AGING POPULATION

The problem of an aging population first emerged in the early 1980s, as the long-term consequences of the "Bust" in *Boom, Bust, and Echo* (Foot, 2000) made its presence known. The newly elected Conservative government of the day was anxious to revive immigration levels after close to a decade of inflows that had fallen to levels not seen since the Great Depression. The taste for high levels of immigration had waned during the 1970s with the advent of stagflation and its accompanying high levels of unemployment and slow growth. The decade from 1974 to 1984 had been a sharp break from the quarter-century of rapid growth and high levels of immigration that Canada had enjoyed from the end of the war until the mid-1970s.

By the mid-1980s, the full consequences of a steadily declining birth rate that had begun a decade or so earlier were finally being seen. Two effects of this decline in fertility were now evident. First, there was about to be a slowdown in the level of new domestic labour force entrants—a potential repeat of what had happened in the 1950s as a result of a similar drop in birth rates during the 1930s. Second, with declining youth dependency ratios, plus the fall in new domestic labour force entrants, older (i.e., over 65) dependency ratios were expected to rise in the years ahead. How, then, were the costs associated with this aging population to be covered and who was going to pay the bill? The answer given then, and repeated often since, was to lower the average of the population by accelerating the rate of immigration.

Another demographic problem was occurring at the same time. Quebec's rate of population growth was falling. Birth rates in the province that, in the 1950s, had been the highest in Canada, had, by the 1980s, fallen to among the lowest in the country. Indeed these rates were well below replacement levels. The threat here was not just with the consequences of an aging population as bad as that may have been, but with maintaining the political and cultural viability of the province itself. The answer was similar to that for the aging problem—accelerate the rate of immigration into Quebec and, if possible, focus this inflow from French-speaking countries. This goal was furthered by Quebec taking greater control over immigration destined to reside in the province. One way this was accomplished was to establish overseas offices to help attract immigrants to the province.

In an earlier conference volume *The Role of Immigration in Canada's Future* (Beach and Green, 1988), the noted French-Canadian demographer Jacques Henripin (1988) examined the consequences of such a plan; that is, to build up the population of Quebec through high levels of immigration. His conclusion was simple. The plan would not work! His reasoning was straightforward. At the level of immigration necessary to restore population growth to past rates, the effect would be to change the composition of that which its proposers sought to protect. By the early decades of the 21st century, he predicted that at these levels of inflow the foreign-born arrivals would dominate the population. For example, at levels of inflow that would eliminate the fertility deficit, the population of Montreal Island by mid-21st century would be 60 percent foreign-born. It was his contention that such inflows would have a profound effect on the cultural or ethnic or language composition of the host region/country. The newcomers, he suggests, may well not have the same attachment to such questions as independence as do many native-born Quebecers. Hence a low-fertility/high immigration strategy raises, at the very least, some disturbing questions about how the native-born population in Quebec (and for that matter in all of Canada) would respond to such an approach. One might recall the intemperate outburst of Jacques Parizeau on that fateful November night in 1995.

What about immigration as a solution to that other problem—the aging of the population? David Green and I (1999), drawing on research findings that, at politically acceptable levels, immigration has only a marginal effect on the host country's population age structure at least for modern economies. For example, at annual levels of inflow of 200,000 the ratio of those out of the labour force to those in the labour force is about 24 percent. When the annual inflow is increased to 500,000 a year, this ratio falls by only two percentage points to 22 percent. One of the reasons for this small decline in the ratio is that many immigrants, although in their twenties and thirties themselves, often sponsor older relatives (Green and Green, 1999).

In a study of Canada's demographic future (Health and Welfare Canada, 1994), the authors come to similar conclusions. Under conditions of an annual inflow of 200,000 the study found that 22 percent of the population would be over the age of 65 by 2036. If the inflow was raised to 600,000 a year, the share of the population over 65 in 2036 would have fallen to 17 percent. This five-percentage point drop is not insignificant, but again it could only be achieved at levels of inflow that are clearly beyond a politically achievable level. Tom Kent (former deputy minister of manpower and immigration in the 1960s) suggested at the 1988 policy forum on immigration that future immigration policies be directed toward young immigrants. The latter would include orphans from the Third World, families with a number of young children, single mothers with children, etc. (Kent, 1988:10). Even this approach, apparently, does not make a great difference to the age structure of the population. For example, recent work (the *Demographic Review 1994*) has found that, if one assumed 50 percent of the inflow entering the country was under 15 years of age, the drop in the percentage over 65 by 2036 would still only be five percentage points; that is, from 22 to 17 percent. However, although such a youth-oriented policy as advocated by Tom Kent would have only a limited impact on the age structure of the population, it would accelerate the growth of the labour force and hence aggregate savings rates (see Wilson, 2003). In addition, a greater percentage of the immigrants entering the Canadian workforce would have been trained in this country and thus would integrate faster than migrants trained in their home countries.

HUMAN CAPITAL EXPANSION

One of the most highly publicized goals of immigration policy during the last three decades has been its role in adding to the stock of human capital; that is, augmenting the supply of skills available to employers. One of the main benefits of such a goal was seen as fostering intensive economic growth. Does it work this way? Not really. Over much of the 20th century, Canadian and American growth rates have, in the main, been very similar. In fact, for much of the last century Canadian growth rates have exceeded those of the United States (Green, 2000:196), while the stock of human capital has grown much faster in the latter. Hence, simply expanding the growth of the labour force through immigration is not a sufficient condition to insure strong economic growth.

Whether or not one is seeking to maximize the rate of growth of human capital, there are important consequences in how this is accomplished. The import of highly skilled workers must be seen in the context of building the stock of human capital in the host country (see Green and Green, 1999:442). Clearly immigration of such workers constitutes a substitute for the education of domestic workers. Thus, large inflows of skilled workers will have the effect of lowering the skill premia; that is, reducing the gap between the wages of skilled and unskilled workers. The lowering of this gap has important consequences for the decision-making process of Canadians interested in extending their education. In an imperfect world (i.e., one where innate ability is not evenly distributed) and where financing for advanced education is not equally available, the impact of lowering the skill premia is likely to discourage Canadians from seeking to acquire these skills. If the world were perfect (the reverse of the above conditions), this might not matter since the skill mix would remain unaltered even with immigration.

There are times, however, when immigration of skilled workers plays a critical role in the development of the economy. One of these times was in the 1960s. At that time the Canadian government was engaged in attempting to transform the economy from resource-based to an urban industrial-based economy. The government recognized that there was a desperate shortage of skilled workers and a shortfall in the whole educational structure, especially at the post-secondary level. The government was anxious to shift the focus of immigration from unskilled resource-directed workers to skilled workers. Immigrants were to be used as shock troops to fill occupational gaps in the labour force. Recent research (D. Green, 1999; Green and Green, 1998) has shown that this has worked; migrants tended to move toward expanding sectors faster than did native-born workers and out of declining sectors faster as well. To effect this change, immigration policy, first in 1962 and then with the introduction of the point system in 1967, changed the orientation from a country-of-origin-based policy to a universal admission approach based not on where the prospect immigrant was born but on the migrant's skill in relation to the demand for such skills within Canada.

This change toward a skill-based policy was driven by the realization, beginning in the late 1950s, that the Canadian economy was being driven more from the secondary manufacturing and service sectors than from the traditional resource industries. This structural shift required, therefore, a more sophisticated (i.e., better trained) labour force. Unfortunately, the Canadian labour was not adequately equipped to handle these new demands. This problem was carefully presented in a Senate report on manpower and employment released in 1961.

An important conclusion to the study states:

we emphasize[d] the structural changes that have taken place in the economy (since the end of the war); shifts between industries, the effects of evolving technology, the changing nature and rising level of skill demanded of workers, and above all the need for rapid adjustment which these changes have imposed on the labour force. (Canada, 1961:57)

It was probably not an accident that a year after this report was published, Canada shifted to a universal skills-based immigration policy. The interesting question is whether this shift toward focusing on skills was meant to be a temporary policy (i.e., until Canada got "on its feet" in terms of an educational infrastructure) or a permanent orientation in this direction. In essence, was this new policy meant to follow the old prescription of alternating large inflows targeted at specific economic goals followed by periods of virtual shutdown in the face of domestic labour market conditions (Green and Green, 1999:426) where the shutdown would occur when the domestic educational infrastructure was finally in place?

Therefore, the question today is whether immigration is still the most economically efficient means to fill skill gaps in the labour force. Clearly, we can all think of situations where the answer to this question is "yes"; for example, a shortage of welders in the Alberta oil fields or a shortage of computer programmers in Kanata. On a broader level of skill acquisition, the case is less clear. Besides the problem of credentialization, there is the question of the morality of transferring the best and the brightest from developing countries to meet our needs in Canada.

Three other problems are inherent in relying on imported skilled workers. First, it takes time for new entrants to adjust to the competitive conditions in the labour markets of a modern urban economy (see studies on the assimilation problem, e.g., Abbott and Beach, 1993). Second, it takes time to identify a skill shortage and to find someone qualified to fill the need—move the prospective immigrant to Canada. The search and moving time, including all the paperwork necessary prior to getting an entry visa, may well exceed the time needed to train a domestic worker to do the job, especially if the training time is less than two years; that is, about the average time to train students in a college of technology. One example of this approach, although over a longer training time, is the initiative of the Ontario government to expand the number of students taking computer science courses. The government provided funds to allow participating universities to double their output of such students. Finally, it may not always be the case that the stated occupation of the new migrant is the occupation actually followed. Hence, the gap goes unfilled. Recall our earlier statement that large inflows of skilled immigrants may well distort the decision-making process of prospective labour force entrants; for example, dissuade them from seeking advanced training. This suggests that immigration policy cannot be treated in isolation.

REGIONAL NEEDS

One of the contributions of immigration is to spur economic growth. There is evidence that this was the case during the opening years of the last century (Green and Sparks, 1999). One way it has this effect is by increasing the size of the market, generating economies of large-scale production. The effect of the latter is to increase real per capita income. This type of response has regional as well as national consequences. However, recent studies can find little direct link between population growth and an increase in the standard of living in mature economies (Economic Council of Canada, 1991)

It seems surprising, on the surface at least, that the current minister of immigration is proposing to disperse immigrants to the smaller centres across Canada. The policy implies that one or both of the following conditions hold. First, that the marginal cost (increased congestion on the highways, greater levels of pollution, access to public goods, etc.) of adding an additional person to the main urban receiving centres is rising faster than the marginal benefits (e.g., economies of scale, benefits of diversity, etc.) from a larger population, and so immigrants should be dispersed to the smaller centres and diverted from the major cities. Second, that the smaller centres lack the range of human skills necessary to promote growth in these areas, and immigration is the answer to this problem. The questions that need answering are whether immigration adds to the first problem; that is, marginal costs of increased population are rising faster than the marginal benefits, and second, can we close the income gap between the poor regions/smaller communities and the larger cities by dispersing immigrants to the former?

We have a natural experiment within the country to examine the success of attempting to steer immigrants to a new region. In 1925, the government passed the Railways Act. This

Act allowed the two major railway companies (CN and CP) to search for and transport to Canadian farm workers and prospective farmers from central and eastern Europe who were willing to settle on the Prairies. By the late 1920s, over 70 percent of those admitted declared that their intended destination was the Prairies and their intended occupation was farming. In a recent study by Byron Lew (2000) on the implications of this policy, he found that by 1931, few of the immigrants from these regions in Europe still resided in the West. The majority had drifted south, moved to the cities, or gone home. Indeed, the defection from the western farms was so great that inspectors had to be sent to the farms to check if the immigrants were still in residence. This does not mean that the policy was a complete failure. There were several short-term benefits from having additional workers available during at the harvest season. However, there were apparently few long-term benefits to emerge from this policy.

What about the current proposal to steer immigrants to smaller centres and lower income regions? First, most migration is from low- to high-income regions. Hence, deliberately sending immigrants in the reverse direction will clearly meet with some resistance. As in the case of the 1925 Railways Act, the stay in such regions will not last long as the new immigrants follow their native-born counterparts to the big cities. Second, the attempt, as has been suggested, to require new migrants to remain in these rural communities for three to five years (and if they don't, to deport them) would seem to run against the basic tenets of freedom of movement guaranteed to all Canadian citizens, including landed immigrants. Hence, the government will be forced to enter into a contract with prospective immigrants that they will indeed stay in the centres to which they are directed. The question, then, is: Who is likely to sign such a contract? Clearly, only those migrants who are marginal to the review process for landed immigrant status. Immigrants with sufficient points to enter directly will not sign up for direction to rural areas. Hence, the plan will send low-skilled marginal migrants to the periphery and the best and the brightest will head for the cities. It is difficult to see how this arrangement will narrow the income gap between the lower income regions and the cities. Using immigration policy to solve congestion in the major cities and skill deficiencies in the smaller communities seems doomed to failure. History provides some interesting lessons in attempting to institute a plan to steer immigrants in non-market-determined directions.

We do not need to dip into deep history to see this point. The topic of dispersing immigrants away from the larger cities was examined almost three decades ago as part of the general review of immigration policy. In presenting a summary of this study on February 3, 1975, before the House, Robert Andras, then minister of immigration and manpower, said that:

> few means exist at present to steer immigrants against prevailing population currents, and these are limited in their effectiveness. It would be an exercise in futility to attempt to direct people towards destinations where adequate employment opportunities and their accompanying social amenities were lacking. Canadian immigration policy has generally avoided measures to compel immigrants to settle and remain in any particular place ... however imaginatively the current techniques to induce more broadly distributed settlement are applied, it must be

frankly recognized that the apparent irresistible attraction of major cities for migrants ... will persist in the years immediately ahead (Andras, 1975:6).

What was true then would seem to be true today. Directed or steered immigration is not the solution to eliminating regional income inequality.

CONCLUSION

The central conclusion of this paper, then, is that the goal of immigration policy in the 21st century is likely to be very different from what it was in the last century. For much of the 21st century immigration was an important element of economic policy. Immigrants filled the West at the turn of the last century, filled the demographic gaps of the 1950s, and, in the 1960s, helped the country adjust quickly to a more sophisticated economy. These economic rationales, I would suggest, have largely disappeared. We have no empty lands, the major structural changes have taken place, and we now have an educational infrastructure in place that can meet our needs for skilled workers. The rationale for admitting immigrants in the future will be more social and humanitarian than economic. This does not mean that immigration will not continue to have an impact on the economy, only that in framing future immigration policy, economic determinants are likely to play a much smaller role. In fact these are the same type of considerations that have dominated U.S. immigration policy since the early 1920s. Family reunification and refugee policy have dominated immigration policy debates in the United States for the last 80 years.

As we enter the 21st century, then, the question we should be asking ourselves is "What type of society do we wish to build in Canada?" One of the great gifts brought to us by the new immigrants is diversity in our way of life. We need to address the question as to the extent of diversity we desire and the speed with which we wish to achieve this goal. One thing is certain: We have come a long way from the goals of immigration policy set out by Mackenzie King in his famous statement before the House in 1947. King put economic and demographic concerns at the core of immigration policy for the postwar period, and he put out of consideration any de-Europeanization of the population with his statement that "[the] people of Canada did not wish, as a result of mass immigration, to make a fundamental alteration in the character of our population" (quoted in Green and Green, 1999:430). We have come a long way since then.

What does this shift in emphasis in policy direction suggest about the levels of immigration (we take as given the concept of a universal policy of admission based on an individual's personal characteristics, not on the prospective immigrant's place of birth)? The first thing it suggests is that setting the level of immigration at 1 percent of the population or any other arbitrary level to satisfy presumed economic needs is out of step with the reality of the current role of immigration. As we outlined above, immigration, at any politically acceptable level, will not solve problems like the aging of the population or regional inequality. It is also the case that we now have the educational facilities to meet our domestic needs for skilled workers in all but extreme circumstances. Immigration is not the panacea for all our problems.

This new view of the role of immigration means that we will have to rethink how immigration policy is drafted. In the past, immigration policy, with the exception of its role within the National Policy (that trio of policies embracing western settlement, railway building, and tariffs that dominated Canadian economic policy in the late 19th and early 20th centuries), has been largely designed independently of other key economic and social policies. The shift toward a more social, humanitarian approach will reduce even further the role of the point system in assessing who will and who will not be admitted. Hence, closer attention will have to be paid to the impact that immigration plays on such social policies as unemployment, welfare, local education needs, etc. This will be particularly critical if the government continues with its policy of setting annual target levels independent of short-term economic conditions.

This shift in policy orientation in no way suggests an end to immigration. Immigrants have played, and will continue to play, an important role in the evolution of this country. However, this shift in emphasis opens the door for discussion about the appropriate level of immigration. The shift to a social/humanitarian base means that the current policy posture of using immigrants to solve economic problems is no longer valid.

As a contribution to this debate over levels, I would like to suggest a formula first set out almost 40 years ago by a leading American labour economist, Melvin Reder (1963). In the early 1960s the United States was in the midst of reviewing its immigration policy (ultimately revised in 1965). As mentioned earlier, the Quota Act of 1924 had set a limit on the number of immigrants that could be admitted in any one year. With the abandonment of this policy new guidelines were being sought to determine the "optimal" level of annual inflow. Reder came up with the following formula. Immigration levels should be allowed to rise until the new entrants threatened to lower the following ratio:

$$\frac{\text{per family income of the lowest decile of native families}}{\text{per family income of median of family income.}}$$

(Reder, 1963:230)

At the very least, this formula provides us with an objective measure around which to debate the sensitive issue of how many immigrants are to be admitted over a period of time.

An examination of the long-term evolution of Canadian immigration policy suggests that, in this case, the past is not a prologue to the future. We are long past the time when a fundamental re-evaluation of the current goals of immigration policy is needed.

● ●

CRITICAL THINKING QUESTIONS

1. What sort of impact does immigration have on Canada's growth and population aging? Why is this the case?
2. Canada faces in the future slowing population growth, potential labour shortages, and an aging population. To what extent can immigration alleviate potential problems associated with these trends?
3. What sort of role should social and humanitarian issues serve in developing Canadian immigration policy? From this point of view, critique Canada's current immigration policy.

● ●

CHAPTER 13

THE DETERIORATING ECONOMIC WELFARE OF IMMIGRANTS AND POSSIBLE CAUSES: UPDATE 2005

Garnett Picot and Arthur Sweetman

● ●

INTRODUCTION

Host countries such as Canada look to the skills and initiative of immigrants to promote economic growth. Immigrants, in turn, look to the host country for opportunities to gainfully employ their skills and abilities. These considerations are particularly important when immigrants are highly educated. Host countries are increasingly seeking highly educated immigrants to drive economic growth in the knowledge-based economy, and immigrants look to use their higher education levels to achieve high economic standards of living.

Immigrants arriving in Canada during the late 1990s were definitely highly educated. In 2001, fully 42 percent of adult "recent" immigrants (those arriving during the previous five years) had a university degree, and a historically high 54 percent entered under the "economic" admissions class (only 31 percent in the family class). The situation was very different 20 years earlier. In 1981, only 19 percent of recent immigrants had degrees, and during the early 1980s, 37 percent entered in the "economic" class, with 43 percent in the family class. Immigrants of the late 1990s were increasingly selected because of their potential contribution to the Canadian economy.

However, if immigrants are unable to convert their training to productive use, the expectations of both the host country and the arriving immigrants remain unmet. Immigrant contributions to the host country, which are central to the economic justification for relatively open immigration policies, may not be fully realized. In light of these considerations, there is considerable concern regarding the deteriorating economic outcomes among recent immigrants over the past two decades.

The analysis of employment *earnings* of immigrants is the most studied area of immigrant economic integration in Canada. Early findings indicated that newly arrived immigrants had lower earnings than comparable non-immigrant workers, but their initial earnings gap narrows significantly as they adjust to the labour market in the receiving society (Chiswick, 1978; Meng, 1987). More recent research suggests that the initial earnings gap may not close as quickly as earlier thought, even among groups entering during the 1970s (Hum and Simpson, 2003). Whatever the earnings gap at entry, and in the years following entry, during, say, the 1970s, these gaps increased in the 1980s and 1990s.

Subsequent research indicated an emerging trend during the early 1980s of declining earnings among successive waves of immigrants relative to the Canadian-born (Abbott and Beach, 1993; Bloom and Gunderson, 1991). A number of studies then asked if the decline was associated primarily with recessions, or the changing mix of immigrants by source country, and if this decline had abated during the late 1980s (Baker and Benjamin, 1994; Grant, 1999; McDonald and Worswick, 1998). More recent studies have concluded that the decline in entry-level earnings of immigrants did continue through the early 1990s (Reitz, 2001). Research studies initiated by the research groups of Citizenship and Immigration, and Statistics Canada, using even more recent data, observe relatively little improvement during the late 1990s (Frenette and Morissette, 2003; Green and Worswick, 2002). Some studies note that although there has been a large decline in entry-level earnings, the rate of growth in earnings with years in Canada is faster than among earlier cohorts (Li, 2003).

As important as studies of employment earnings are, they provide only part of the picture. They exclude the unemployed and those out of the labour market. They also exclude changes in all sources of income other than earnings, such as social transfer benefits. During periods of deteriorating labour market outcomes, such studies may underestimate the decline, in particular because they exclude the effects of possibly rising unemployment or the discouraged worker effect.

This paper briefly reviews the earnings decline among immigrants through the 1980s and 1990s. To provide a better overview of economic welfare outcomes among immigrants, the paper also reviews low-income trends among immigrants, recent immigrants in particular. The low-income rate[1] is a simple yet comprehensive measure of changing economic welfare among families at the bottom end of the income distribution. It reflects changes in unemployment, earnings, social transfers, and other income sources.

This paper focuses on the late 1990s, a particularly important period. Given the increasing "economic" nature of immigration and the very significant economic recovery in the late 1990s (as unemployment fell from 9.4 percent to 6.8 percent between 1995 and 2000), one might have anticipated a marked improvement in immigrant economic outcomes. If the deterioration was simply related to the recessions of the early 1980s and 1990s, then by 2000, there may well have been a return to the better outcomes observed in the late 1970s. The late 1990s is, in this sense, a sort of watershed, a period during which one looks for a return to the "good old days" of immigrant labour market outcomes.

This paper also focuses on outcomes of highly educated recent immigrants. One might expect this group to convert their training to productive use during a period of rapid economic growth, the expansion in the information and communications technologies sector, and the general expansion in the knowledge-based economy.

THE DECLINING ENTRY-LEVEL EARNINGS AMONG IMMIGRANTS

In spite of the increasingly economic nature of immigration during the late 1990s, earnings among male adult "recent" immigrants who worked full-time full-year fell by 13 percent between 1980 and 2000, two years that are in roughly the same position in the business cycle (Frenette and Morissette, 2003). Among recent female immigrants, earnings rose 6 percent. During the same period, earnings among Canadian-born working full-time full-year rose by 10 percent for men, and 11 percent for women.

These numbers can be put in a longitudinal perspective by focusing on particular entry cohorts of immigrants. These cohorts consist of immigrants who entered Canada during a five-year period, say, between 1975 and 1979, or 1990 and 1994. The earnings of the immigrants in each cohort are computed (as a proportion of the earnings of the Canadian-born) for the cohort after one to five years in Canada, six to 10 years in Canada, and so on. In this way, one can determine: (a) the extent to which the earnings gap at entry between immigrants and Canadian-born is reduced with years spent in Canada, and (b) whether the earnings gap at entry is increasing.

The horizontal axis of each of the four plots in Figure 1 measures years since immigration, and the vertical axis measures earnings relative to some group of Canadian-born workers. Relative earnings are represented as a proportion. When the proportion is, say, 0.9, immigrants earn 90 percent of what the Canadian-born do, whereas when it is 1.0 the two groups have the same earnings. Each cohort is followed over time in Canada using data from the Censuses that are conducted every five years.

Figure 13.1 suggests that the earnings gap for the cohort of the late 1970s was more than closed after 20 years in Canada. After 21–25 years, adult immigrants working full-time full-year earned about 8 percent more than the Canadian-born (both men and women). However, the earnings gap at entry has been increasing with successive cohorts. Among men, the cohort of the late 1970s earned 90 percent of that of the Canadian-born at entry and among the early 1990s cohort, this number had fallen to 67 percent. Among the late 1990s cohort, however, the entry earnings gap appears to have been reduced significantly (compared to the early 1990s cohort, for example), as recent immigrants earned 77 percent of that of the Canadian-born. The gap remained much greater than in the 1970s.

However, these figures compare all Canadian-born with all immigrants. We know that these two groups are very different regarding characteristics that affect their earnings potential. In particular, immigrants have been more highly educated than Canadian-born for many years, and their education level has increased rapidly, particularly during the late 1990s. A more appropriate analysis compares recent immigrants to "like" Canadian-born, along dimensions such as age, education, visible minority status, marital status, and region of employment (including major city). This is typically done within a regression format that computes the log of the ratio of the earnings of immigrants to those of the Canadian-born. The results of such an analysis by Frenette and Morissette (2003) are given in Figure 13.2. The log earnings ratio is an approximation of the earnings of immigrants as a proportion of those of comparable Canadian-born when the differences are small (say 10 percent to 20 percent), but when they become large (say 40 percent to 50 percent), the log (earnings ratio) overestimates the percentage difference.

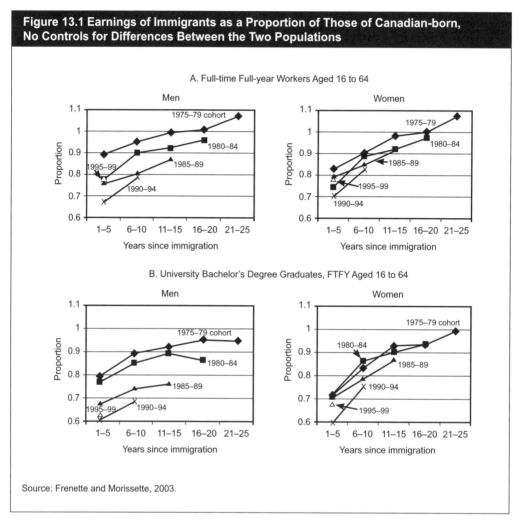

Figure 13.1 Earnings of Immigrants as a Proportion of Those of Canadian-born, No Controls for Differences Between the Two Populations

A. Full-time Full-year Workers Aged 16 to 64

Source: Frenette and Morissette, 2003.

This analysis provides a somewhat different picture (Panel A of Figure 13.2). As in Figure 13.1, the earnings gap has been increasing significantly with each successive cohort, both at entry and after many years in Canada. However, this increase is greater after accounting for the differences between immigrants and Canadian-born. Among males, the log earnings ratio at entry declined from .83 among the late 1970s cohort to .55 among the early 1990s cohort. Furthermore, in this analysis, one sees only a minor improvement in the earnings gap at entry between the cohorts of the early and late 1990s (log earnings ratio increased from .55 to .60). The relatively little improvement seen here compared to Figure 13.1 is likely because the late 1990s cohort was much more highly educated. After accounting for this higher education level and the associated higher earnings expectation, little improvement in entry-level earnings is observed. The earnings gap at entry remained much greater than among the cohorts of the 1970s or 1980s.

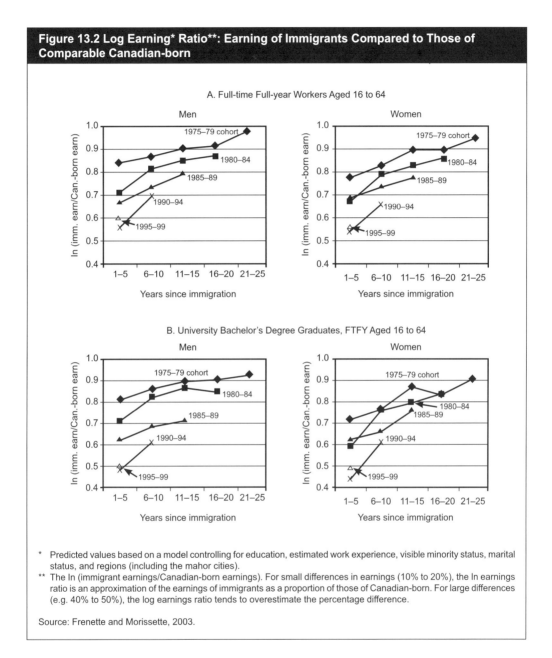

Figure 13.2 Log Earning* Ratio**: Earning of Immigrants Compared to Those of Comparable Canadian-born

A. Full-time Full-year Workers Aged 16 to 64

B. University Bachelor's Degree Graduates, FTFY Aged 16 to 64

*   Predicted values based on a model controlling for education, estimated work experience, visible minority status, marital status, and regions (including the mahor cities).
** The ln (immigrant earnings/Canadian-born earnings). For small differences in earnings (10% to 20%), the ln earnings ratio is an approximation of the earnings of immigrants as a proportion of those of Canadian-born. For large differences (e.g. 40% to 50%), the log earnings ratio tends to overestimate the percentage difference.

Source: Frenette and Morissette, 2003.

As noted earlier, the traditional "economic assimilation" story among immigrants is that they earn less at entry, but after a number of years in Canada, the earnings gap with comparable Canadians narrows, or disappears (Borjas, 1985; Carliner, 1981; Chiswick, 1978; Meng, 1987). In Figure 13.2, the traditional pattern is observed among cohorts entering in the late 1970s, but this is the last cohort to display any signs of eliminating the earnings gap after many years in Canada. Even among this cohort, earnings do not surpass the earnings of the Canadian-born (as they did in Figure 13.1), but they do almost catch up, reaching about 97 percent of the earnings of "like" Canadian-born after more than 20 years (Figure 13.2). But among the more recent cohorts, elimination of the earnings gap will be more difficult. The cohorts entering during the 1980s, even after 16 to 20 years in Canada, were earning approximately 85 percent of their Canadian counterparts (Figure 13.2). For the 1990s cohort, after six to 10 years in Canada, the early 1990s cohort was earning roughly 70 percent (log earnings ratio of .7) of Canadians. It is not clear that they can "catch up" to Canadians in 20 years. Again, the pattern is similar for women.

However, it is important to note that the greater the earnings gap at entry, the faster the improvement in earnings (Figure 13.2). Hence, the rate of improvement in earnings (i.e., the slope of the line in Figure 13.2) was much greater among the 1990–1994 cohort than the 1980s cohorts. In spite of this, however, earnings remained lower among the more recent cohorts than among earlier cohorts, no matter how long they had been in Canada.

EARNINGS DECLINES AT ENTRY WERE AS GREAT AMONG THE UNIVERSITY EDUCATED

The bottom panels of figures 13.1 and 13.2 display similar results for immigrants with bachelor's degrees. Among men working full-time full-year, immigrants entering during the late 1970s earned about 82 percent of their Canadian-born counterparts (log earnings ratio of .82, controlling for estimated years of work experience, and geographical region of employment). By the 1990s, the log earnings ratio had fallen to around .5. Some minor improvement was observed between the early and late 1990s, but relative entry-level earnings remained well below that of the cohorts of the 1970s or 1980s. Once again, the pattern is similar for women. "Recent" immigrant university graduates were increasingly unable to convert their education and experience into earnings in the way that earlier cohorts had. As with all immigrants, however, the larger the earnings gap at entry, the faster the growth in earnings (with years spent in Canada).

THE DETERIORATING LOW-INCOME POSITION OF RECENT IMMIGRANTS

Earnings represent the major income source for most families, so it is not surprising that the decline in relative entry-level earnings is reflected in the low-income rates. The proportion of recent immigrants with family incomes below the low-income cutoff rose from 24.6 percent in 1980 to 31.3 percent in 1990 and 35.8 percent in 2000. These years are roughly at business cycle peaks, and hence are reasonable indicators of longer-term trends. During this period, the low-income rate among the Canadian-born fell from 17.2 percent in 1980 to 14.3 percent in 2000. Hence, it was not a general deterioration in economic conditions affecting all Canadians that was responsible for the rising low-income rates. Recent immigrants had low-income rates 1.4 times that of the Canadian-born in 1980, and by 2000, this had increased to 2.5. There was improvement between 1995 and 2000 in the low-income rate among recent immigrants (falling from 47.0 percent to 35.8 percent). However, most of this change did not represent a longer-term trend in improved outcomes, but simply the expected decline during a very strong economic recovery. The *relative* low-income rate of recent immigrants (relative to Canadian-born) improved only marginally (falling from 2.7 to 2.5 times higher). This deterioration in low-income rates over the past 20 years was not restricted to recent immigrants. It was observed among all immigrant groups, no matter how long they have resided in Canada (Table 13.1), with the exception of immigrants living in Canada for more than 20 years. *New immigrant*

The deterioration in family economic welfare among recent immigrants may have been concentrated among particular groups. However, Picot and Hou (2003) concluded that, by and large, this was not the case. The increasing low-income rate was observed among all education groups, all age groups, all family types, and those whose home language was either French/English, or "Other." Source region was the one dimension along which some differences were observed. The low-income rate actually fell between 1980 and 2000 among recent immigrants from a few source regions, such as the U.S., western Europe, southeast Asia, and the Caribbean (even after controlling for differences over cohorts in education, home language, family type, and age). However, among the source regions from which three-quarters of all recent immigrants originated in 2001, rates were rising (Table 13.2). This included most parts of Asia, northern, eastern, and southern Europe and Africa. These results suggest that some factor (e.g., recognition of work experience or schooling, language skills, school quality, etc.) associated with source regions may play a significant role in the declining economic outcomes of immigrants. More of this later.

Given the widespread nature of the rise in low income, it is not surprising that Picot and Hou (2003) conclude that less than one-half, and quite possibly much less, of the rise in low-income rates among recent immigrants was associated with their changing characteristics as measured in the Census data. They could not be more precise because of limitations of the analytical techniques used to determine this effect. The paper focused on the changing mix of immigrants by source region, education, home language, age, and family status. More is said of this finding in the summary discussion at the end of this chapter.

Just as the earnings results reported above focused on university graduates, so too did the low-income analysis. Although recent immigrants with university degrees had lower levels of low income than, say, those with a high school diploma, the rate of increase in low income during the 1990s was higher among the university-educated immigrants. Among adults with high school graduation as the highest education level, the rate rose 25 percent. Among university-educated *recent* immigrants, it rose from 19.1 percent in 1990 to 27.5 percent in 2000 (Table 13.3), an increase of 44 percent. And there seemed to be no major difference by degree type. Among engineering and applied science degree holders aged 24 to 44, low-income rates rose from 14.7 percent in 1990 to 24.2 percent in 2000, in spite of the technology boom that was in place leading up to 2000. In 1990, these recent immigrant degree holders had low-income rates 4.6 times that of their Canadian-born counterparts; by 2000 this was 7.0 times higher. Similar stories are observed for other disciplines. For example, among prime age recent immigrants with teaching, social sciences, and commerce degrees, rates rose from 18.2 percent to 27.7 percent.

The focus to this point has been on the outcomes for immigrants at entry. What happens as they reside in Canada for a number of years? It was noted earlier that the earnings gap (with Canadian-born) does narrow.

Table 13.1 Low-income Rates by Immigration Status, Canada, 1980–2000

| | Total Population | Non-immigrants | All immigrants | Low-income rate* Years of residence in Canada | | | | | All immigrants | Low-income rates relative to Canadian-born Years of residence in Canada | | | | |
				<=5	6–10	11–15	16–29	>29		<=5	6–10	11–15	16–29	>29
1980	0.171	0.172	0.170	0.246	0.187	0.144	0.147	0.167	1.0	1.4	1.1	0.8	0.9	1.0
1985	0.187	0.185	01.93	0.342	0.280	0.198	0.159	0.165	1.0	1.8	1.4	1.1	0.9	0.9
1990	0.155	0.151	0.171	0.313	0.242	0.190	0.152	0.126	1.1	2.1	1.6	1.3	1.0	0.8
1995	0.191	0.176	0.247	0.470	0.353	0.272	0.221	0.155	1.4	2.7	2.0	1.6	1.3	0.9
2000	0.156	0.143	0.202	0.358	0.283	0.227	0.191	0.133	1.4	2.5	2.0	1.6	1.3	0.9

* After transfer, before taxes; based on the 1992 LICO updated for change in CPI only.

Data sources: The 1961 to 2001 Censuses (20% sample data).

Source: Picot and Hou, 2003.

Table 13.2 Percentage Change in the Low-income Rate by Source Region, Canada, 1980–2000

Source Region	Raw data	Controlling for age, education, language, and family type
Southeast Asia	-35%	-25%
Western Europe	-24%	-16%
U.S.	-18%	-12%
Caribbean	-2%	-5%
South & Central America	-2%	+1%
Northern Europe	+14%	+24%
Eastern Europe	+22%	+34%
Western Asia	+52%	+64%
Southern Europe	+61%	+115%
East Asia	+68%	+90%
South Asia	+82%	+86%
Africa	+121%	+94%

Source: Picot and Hou, 2003.

Table 13.3 Low-income Rates Among Recent Immigrants Aged 25 to 65 by Education Level, Canada, 1990 and 2000

Highest education level	1990	2000	% change in rate 1990–2000
Less than high school	34.3	38.4	13.1%
High school graduate	31.0	38.8	25.2%
Some post-secondary	26.4	33.7	27.6%
University degree	19.1	27.5	44.0%

Source: Picot and Hou, 2003.

WHY THE DECLINE IN RELATIVE ENTRY-LEVEL EARNINGS AND RISING LOW INCOME AMONG RECENT IMMIGRANTS?

Researchers have, for some time, been attempting to determine the cause of the decline in entry-level earnings in particular. There is no shortage of possible explanations; however, not all have been found to be empirically important. While we do not fully understand the mechanisms by which earnings have fallen, several recent studies are in broad agreement that particular issues have sizable impacts while other issues are less important. It is worth mentioning at the outset that these various explanations are neither exhaustive nor mutually exclusive.

THE CHANGING CHARACTERISTICS OF IMMIGRANTS ENTERING

As is well known, immigrants are entering Canada from very different countries now than was the case in, say the 1970s. Between 1981 and 2001, a decreasing share of immigrants came from the U.S., northern Europe, southern Europe, the Caribbean, South and Central America, and southeast Asia. The share of "recent" immigrants from these areas fell from 65 percent to 28 percent. Regions increasing their shares included eastern Europe, south Asia (India, Pakistan), east Asia (China, Korea, Japan), western Asia (Iraq, Iran, Afghanistan), and Africa. Collectively, the share of recent immigrants from these regions rose from 35 percent in 1981 to 72 percent in 2001. Immigrants from these source regions may have lower earnings at entry, even with comparable levels of education and experience. Their human capital may initially be less transferable due to potential issues regarding language, cultural differences, education quality, and possibly discrimination.

OTHER FACTORS POSSIBLY ASSOCIATED WITH THE SHIFT TO THE NEWER SOURCE REGIONS: EDUCATION QUALITY, LANGUAGE SKILLS, AND DISCRIMINATION

Related to the above mentioned shift in source countries, there have been changes in the characteristics of immigrants associated with a decline in entry earnings; for example, fewer entering immigrants have a home language and mother tongue that is either English or French (although unfortunately we do not have measures of actual language ability at entry). Language and communication skills are related to productivity and hence the wages of workers; any decline in language skills among entering immigrants can, therefore, clearly affect earnings. Studies such as those by Baker and Benjamin (1994), Frenette and Morissette (2003), and Aydemir and Skuterud (2004, 2005) suggest that perhaps one-third of the decline in entry-level earnings is associated with these changing characteristics of entering immigrants, particularly the shift in source regions and home language. This is an important amalgam of factors that together explain about a third of the observed decline in earnings. However, it is very difficult to disentangle the highly interrelated set of characteristics, such as language ability and visible minority status, associated with changing source countries.

Unfortunately, while we have good data on self-reported current home language and mother tongue, good-quality data on change through time in the language skills (in either official language) of recent immigrants does not exist. Hence it has been difficult for researchers to assess the impact using objective measures of language skills. Even if conversational skills appear adequate, it may be that immigrants' ability to work in either of the official languages when performing more complex tasks has declined among entering immigrants. A recent paper by Ferrer, Green, and Riddell (2003) uses data on language skills as measured by a test of adult literacy and finds clear differences between immigrants and the Canadian-born at the survey date. With or without taking education into account, immigrants have, on average, poorer English and French language skills by this measure.

This does not imply that all immigrants have poor skills, or that some immigrants do not fare better than some Canadian-born test takers, but the distribution of immigrants scores is usually lower than the distribution of scores for the Canadian-born. However, the paper goes further and asks whether the *decline* in returns to foreign experience (discussed later) may be related to increased relative (to younger immigrants) literacy or numeracy issues among older immigrants by looking at immigrants from different entry cohorts at a point in time. Despite using detailed data with test scores on literacy and numeracy, Ferrer, Green, and Riddell find little evidence to support this notion.

Increased ethnic, racial, or cultural discrimination is also possibly related to changing source countries; the number of immigrants who are visible minorities has increased significantly. Here again, the data to reliably estimate the effect of this factor, and changes in its importance over time associated with the observed decline in earnings, are scarce, although there is evidence of ethnic discrimination in society more broadly. It may be that some of these issues (e.g., language or discrimination) are more prevalent among immigrants from the more recent source countries (eastern Europe, Asia, Africa), and a shift to immigration from these countries has increased the importance of these issues for immigrants as a whole, resulting in a decline in entry-level earnings. If this were so, then the effects would be picked up in the type of statistical analysis reported above, which indicated that roughly one-third of the earnings decline is related to the changing composition of immigrants by source country and other factors.

THE RETURNS TO YEARS OF SCHOOLING AND THE CREDENTIALISM ISSUE

Immigrant average economic returns to schooling relative to the Canadian-born appear to have been fairly stable in recent years (Aydemir and Skuterud, 2004, 2005; Ferrer and Riddell, 2003). These returns are lower than that of the Canadian-born, and vary with whether the immigrant was educated in Canada or not (e.g., McBride and Sweetman, 2004), but they have probably not changed very much over the past two decades. Schaafsma and Sweetman (2001) show that those who arrive young and are educated in Canada have returns to education comparable to or higher than the Canadian-born, but those who arrive later in life tend to have quite low returns. Hence, our current understanding of the evidence is that the economic value of education cannot explain much of the decline in earnings over time. Still, it is a topic worth discussing in some detail.

Researchers studying the credentialism issue have posed the question in a slightly different manner from that most commonly observed in economic analysis, which focuses on years of schooling. They ask, after accounting for years of schooling, how much is the fact of having the university credential (i.e., degree) itself worth to an immigrant. This is referred to as the "sheepskin" effect. Is the earnings advantage of having a university degree (relative to not having it) changing? This credentials concern has been expressed for a number of years. However, to contribute significantly to the *decline* in entry-level earnings, this effect would have to have become more important in recent years.

Based on recent evidence from two sets of authors (Aydemir and Skuterud, 2004, 2005; Ferrer and Riddell, 2003) and consistent with that of others, it seems that the return to education for individuals within source countries has not declined. Individuals from non-traditional source countries do receive a lower return to their years of schooling (independent of degree completion) than those from traditional source countries, but workers from those same countries receive a larger economic return from degree completion. Thus, the change in the mix of source countries is not associated with much of the overall decline in earnings. Partly, the lack of impact of education on the aggregate decline in economic outcomes follows from many immigrants receiving their education in Canada and, therefore, having the same or higher economic return to education as the Canadian-born, and from the nature of the economic value of educational degrees/ certificates, as opposed to years of study, for immigrants.

Ferrer and Riddell's research, in particular, focuses on the "sheepskin" effect, the value of a university degree itself (independent of the number of years of schooling required to obtain the degree, but the fact of having this credential). The research does not distinguish between degrees in fields that are licensed (e.g., medicine and engineering) and those that are not (e.g., history and economics). Nonetheless, the results are very instructive. Overall, they find that having a degree increases immigrants' earnings significantly (relative to not having a degree), and that this effect is at least as strong or stronger for immigrants than for the native-born. However, they conclude that this credential advantage has changed little since the early 1980s for immigrants. The only evidence of a change is that the value of postgraduate certification has *increased, not decreased*, for immigrants who landed more recently. They do find that immigrants from non-traditional source countries have a lower return to years of schooling (independent of completion), but the "changing composition of immigration is therefore resulting in imported human capital that is less valued on one dimension (years of schooling) and more valued on the other (credentials)" (Ferrer and Riddell, 2003:20).

Overall, this suggests that, across all disciplines, the "credentialism" issue has not worsened (although it may or may not have in specific fields). Degree holders have not been exempt from the deterioration in earnings outcomes; however, the decline is not obviously associated with credential recognition or changes in the value of foreign education in the Canadian labour market. This does not imply that policy should not be focused on improving credential recognition. The economic return to education for immigrants educated outside of Canada is clearly lower than that for the Canadian-born or for immigrants educated in Canada, and government programs may improve the return to foreign education if the "recognition" problem is substantial. However, these programs should be aware that they are addressing a problem that has been close to stable for at least two decades.

There are other, usually immeasurable, effects that are also associated with the economic return to education. One factor, for example, relates to the variety that exists in the "quality" of education systems across countries. Sweetman (2004) has attempted to focus on this issue by using the test scores from international literacy and numeracy surveys to proxy for the quality of a country's education system. He finds support for the notion that lower school quality is associated with lower returns to education for immigrants educated prior to landing in Canada (those who arrive at a young age and are educated in Canada are unaffected by the quality of their source country's educational system). This implies that not all superficially similar degrees are of equal value in the labour market and points to the complexity of the policy issue.

DECLINING RETURNS TO FOREIGN LABOUR MARKET EXPERIENCE

Another factor that is taking on increasing importance is referred to as "declining returns to foreign experience." Human capital consists largely of education/ training and the skills developed through work experience. One typically expects some return to this human capital when entering employment, but immigrants from non-traditional source countries receive close to zero economic benefits from pre-Canadian potential labour market experience. Importantly, "potential" is a key word in the formulation of the measure of labour market experience employed in all recent studies. Actual labour market experience is not measured in the data, so "potential experience" is calculated as *age – years of schooling* – 6 (or minus 5 in some studies). Put another way, therefore, one could think of the phenomenon of declining returns to foreign labour market experience as being associated with an earnings decline at entry among older immigrants. Age could be employed instead of potential experience to address this issue, but the latter fits the data better since it appears to be post-schooling labour market experience that matters for employment earnings (among those for whom it does matter).

A number of recent studies indicate that the foreign work experience of entering immigrants is increasingly discounted in the Canadian labour market (Aydemir and Skuterud, 2004, 2005; Frenette and Morissette, 2003; Green and Worswick, 2002; Schaafsman and Sweetman, 2001). Older immigrants entering Canada, who in the late 1970s or early 1980s earned significantly more than their younger counterparts, presumably because of their experience (controlling for education, etc.), now have much less of an advantage. Their foreign work experience appears to be more heavily discounted now as compared to, say, 20 years ago. Relatedly, Schaafsma and Sweetman (2001) observed that age at immigration is a very important predictor of the earnings of immigrants. Using Census data from 1986 to 1996, they found that older workers experienced, on average, lower returns to both foreign labour market experience and foreign education than both the Canadian-born and Canadian-educated immigrants who land at a young age. As part of the research program initiated by the research arm of Citizenship and Immigration Canada, Green and Worswick (2002) observed that returns to foreign experience were falling for successive entering immigrant groups. Moreover, the credibility of the finding was enhanced since they made the same observation using a different data set. Their data allowed immigration category to be observed, permitting them to extend the analysis. They observed this effect among both family and economic classes, so it is not driven by a shift in immigrant class.

Green and Worswick (2002) concluded that the declining returns to experience is one of the major factors, if not the most important, associated with the decline in earnings among recent immigrants. Subsequent work by Aydemir and Skuterud (2004, 2005) and Frenette and Morissette (2003) provide support for this notion. However, it has been concluded that this decline in returns to foreign experience is not evident among immigrants from the traditional source regions (e.g., northwestern Europe, the English-speaking countries) and is concentrated among immigrants from the newer source regions. Aydemir and Skuterud find that the decline in returns to foreign labour market experience are observed only among immigrants from eastern Europe, Asia, and Africa. Aydemir and Skuterud find that foreign experience has become almost worthless in the Canadian labour market for immigrants from these regions. Aydemir and Skuterud conclude that among recent immigrants, the decline in the return to foreign experience accounts for roughly one-third of the decline in entry-level earnings reported earlier.

DETERIORATING LABOUR MARKET OUTCOMES FOR NEW LABOUR MARKET ENTRANTS IN GENERAL, OF WHICH IMMIGRANTS ARE A PART

Labour market outcomes for young labour market entrants, particularly males, have been deteriorating in Canada through the 1980s and 1990s. Earnings of young men have been falling through these decades (Beaudry and Green, 2000; Picot, 1998). Entering immigrants are themselves new labour market entrants, and it may be that whatever is causing the decline in earnings of the young in general (and that is not well understood) may be also affecting the earnings of "recent" immigrants. Green and Worswick find that for recent immigrant men, this may account for 40 percent of the decline in entry-level earnings. They also find, however, that this effect was concentrated in the 1980s; it was less important for the 1990s. Frenette and Morissette also conclude that this is a significant factor, as do Aydemir and Skuterud.

FLUCTUATIONS IN MACROECONOMIC CONDITIONS

Canada experienced two severe recessions during the early 1980s and 1990s. It was during the early 1980s that a major decline in entry-level earnings was first observed. Furthermore, the position of recent immigrants declined very significantly again in the early 1990s when immigration levels remained high during the recession. This has caused a number of researchers to speculate that changing macroeconomic conditions played a major role in the earnings trends.

Bloom and Gunderson (1991), and McDonald and Worswick (1998) noted the effect of the decline was concentrated among male immigrant workers over age 30. Green and Worswick, when first observing this effect, suggest that it may be related to both the shift in the composition of business cycle on immigrant earnings, and the latter concluded that immigrants are more negatively affected by recessions than are the Canadian-born. In a 1997 paper on unemployment rate differentials between immigrants and the Canadian-born, McDonald and Worswick (1997) conclude that the unemployment gap is much larger in recessions, and much less, or near zero, in expansions. However, Reitz (2001) concluded that fluctuations in macroeconomic conditions could not fully explain the general downward trend in immigrants' economic performance.

STRONG COMPETITION FROM THE INCREASINGLY HIGHLY EDUCATED CANADIAN-BORN

The supply of highly educated workers in Canada has been increasing at a very rapid pace. The number of women in the labour force with a university degree quadrupled over just 20 years. For every woman in the labour force with a degree in 1980, there are now four. The comparable number of men with a degree more than doubled. In studies on the wage premium associated with a university degree (i.e., the earnings of university graduates compared to high school graduates), it has been observed that, in general, this premium has increased significantly in the U.S., but little in Canada over the past 20 years (Burbidge et al., 2002). In the face of an apparently increasing demand for more highly educated workers, why have the relative wages of university graduates risen in the U.S. but not in Canada? Two high-profile papers argue that it is differences in the supply of highly educated workers; this supply (relative to the high school-educated) has been increasing much more rapidly in Canada than in the U.S. (Freeman and Needels, 1993; Murphy, Romer, and Riddell, 1998).

Reitz (2001) argues that in spite of the rising educational levels of immigrants, their *relative* advantage in educational levels has declined as a result of the more rapidly rising levels of education among the Canadian-born. He also argues that immigrants did not benefit to the same extent as the Canadian-born from increases in education. This fits with other findings that suggest that although the "sheepskin" effect (the fact of having a degree) has not diminished among immigrants, the returns to years of education have been falling among "recent" immigrants, and that if anything, labour market outcomes among university-educated immigrants have been declining faster than among others (controlling for age), as noted above. It may be that in a very competitive labour market for new entrants' foreign experience and years of schooling from the "new" source countries are increasingly discounted, and that language and other factors associated with the new source regions place "recent" immigrants, even the highly educated, at a relative competitive disadvantage.

CONCLUSION

The economic welfare of recent immigrants deteriorated through the 1980s and 1990s. It seems unlikely that the rate of economic assimilation will be such as to allow many of these immigrants to achieve earnings or low-income rate levels comparable to the Canadian-born, or even those of earlier immigrant cohorts (Frenette and Morissette, 2003). Reasons for this decline are numerous and are not, of course, necessarily independent of one another, but some issues have been found to be quite empirically important, while others are not observed to contribute much to the decline. Three central factors are found to be crucial. First, the changing composition of source countries, mother tongue and/or language used at home, visible minority status, and other related issues are associated with about one-third of the decline. It is worth noting that this set of factors is so highly intercorrelated that it is difficult to separate the independent influence of each in the data that are commonly available. Second, there has been a substantial decline in the economic return to pre-immigration potential labour market experience for those from non-traditional source countries. This explains about another third of the decline for men, and slightly less for women. An implication of this phenomenon is that age at immigration is becoming increasingly important for labour market outcomes, with those who arrive at an older age having poorer outcomes. Third, there has been a very general decline in labour market outcomes for new entrants to the labour market, especially males. Immigrants, regardless of their age at arrival, appear to be treated like new entrants by the labour market. This accounts for at least another third of the observed decline. Related issues are the long-term labour market impact of immigrants arriving during a recession, and that immigrants appear to have labour market outcomes that are more sensitive to the business cycle than the Canadian-born.

Overall, increased competition from domestic labour sources, combined with a shift in the source regions of immigrants, may together result in a reduced ability of immigrants to convert their experience into earnings. It may also be that declining returns to foreign experience, decreasing language ability (if this is the case, which is largely unmeasured), and changes in discrimination may themselves be related to changes in the source countries of immigrants. While the debate over the possible reasons for the decline in immigrant labour market outcomes will undoubtedly continue, progress has been made in understanding some aspects of this decline while ruling out other factors.

NOTE

1. The proportion of the population with family incomes below Statistics Canada's Low-Income Cutoff (LICO), fixed at the 1992 level, and adjusted only for changes in the CPI. Hence, over the period of study this is a "fixed," not a relative low-income measure.

•••••••••••••••••••••••••••••

CRITICAL THINKING QUESTIONS

1. Discuss recent changes in the relative economic well-being of newly arrived immigrants to Canada. How has the situation changed over the last several decades?
2. Many immigrants encounter major hurdles in establishing a foothold in Canada's knowledge-based economy. A particularly difficult issue relates to the recognition in the Canadian labour market of foreign educational credentials and work experience. What might be done to remedy this situation?
3. On the basis of theory and evidence, which factors do you think are most important in explaining the deteriorating earnings of new Canadians? To what extent do you think discrimination is relevant to recent trends?

•••••••••••••••••••••••••••••

CHAPTER 14

MIGRATION AND THE DEMOGRAPHIC TRANSFORMATION OF CANADIAN CITIES: THE SOCIAL GEOGRAPHY OF CANADA'S MAJOR METROPOLITAN CENTRES IN 2017

Daniel Hiebert

● ●

INTRODUCTION: IMMIGRATION AND THE POPULATION OF CANADIAN CITIES

The relationship between immigration and the population dynamic of Canada is unmistakable. As demographers and media commentators frequently remind us, immigration is responsible for the lion's share of population growth. It is interesting to note that this balance only arose recently, in the early 1990s. Before that, domestic births were the key determinant of population growth. Not any more. According to the latest figures, the number of births in Canada exceeded the number of deaths in the year ending on June 30, 2004 by around 97,000 people; net international migration during the same period added twice that number to Canada, about 193,000 people. According to demographic projections, the contribution of net migration to total population growth will reach 100 percent some time between now and 2025 (Statistics Canada, 2005). There are two corollaries to this demographic shift that are already well known: the cultural composition of immigrants to Canada has become remarkably globalized in the past few decades; and the process of immigrant settlement in Canada is geographically uneven, and highly concentrated in the largest metropolitan centres, especially Montreal, Toronto, and Vancouver. Metropolitan regions in general, and these three in particular, are therefore at the forefront of Canadian population change, and are becoming more diverse every day.

This brief chapter will consider the scale and significance of population change, assuming that immigration is the driving factor in bringing about greater ethnocultural and religious diversity among those Canadians living in metropolitan centres. I begin by summarizing demographic and socio-economic developments that have occurred in the late 20th century, and then provide a basic snapshot of the contemporary scene. In discussing the recent

197

past and the present, I concentrate on the relationship between diversity and social equity, and show that there are aspects of this relationship to celebrate, but also aspects that suggest fundamental concerns. With these issues in mind, the remainder of the chapter will consider ways to minimize the possible negative consequences that could accompany this shift to greater diversity. I argue that the benefits of increasing diversity will best be reached by a combination of strategic intervention by government; initiatives that ensure an open labour market; and the activities of non-government organizations.

LOOKING BACK: IMMIGRATION AND THE TRANSFORMATION OF CANADIAN METROPOLITAN CENTRES

Before discussing the significance of immigration in recasting the socio-cultural composition of Canadian cities, it is instructive to remember that immigration is just one of several cross-cutting transformations that have been under way in the postwar period. The Canadian economy has shifted dramatically in these years from an overwhelming emphasis on resources, manufacturing, and commodity trade to the higher-order services that now propel growth (the proverbial shift from an economy based on bricks to one based on clicks). In general, the new economy is characterized by heightened socio-economic polarization that has been exacerbated by a reduction in spending on non-health-related social programs by all levels of government.

The nature of families and households has also changed in ways that were largely unanticipated. Certainly, even by the 1960s, commentators began to expect falling birth rates, but few (if any) understood the impacts that would arise from the combination of higher rates of female labour market participation, more prevalent divorce, more prevalent common-law relationships (both heterosexual and same-sex), and declining fertility. Together, these have led to new configurations of households, a restructuring of housing demand, and a concomitant reappraisal of the desirability of residential settings. While many Canadians remain dedicated to acquiring detached suburban homes in upscale subdivisions, this enthusiasm is far from universal.

Land developers and real estate agents have capitalized on emerging sensibilities by upgrading or redeveloping inner-city neighbourhoods to accommodate the growing interest of the new middle class in these settings. In a number of cities, but notably Toronto and Vancouver, this has led to affordability issues for the groups that have traditionally found housing in inner city locations, including immigrants and members of various minorities. Suburban neighbourhoods have also changed. Some retain the traditional landscape of detached houses surrounded by landscaped lawns, but others have come to specialize in the populations formerly associated with the inner city. Significantly, there are food banks operating now in nearly all the suburban municipalities of Greater Vancouver, an outcome that would not have been predicted half a century ago. As suggested by this final point, metropolitan areas are now characterized by variegated social landscapes that include affluence in central areas and poverty in the periphery.

The first point to emphasize in this section is that immigration, and the growing population diversity that results from it, is just one of several dimensions of significant change. Even if immigration slowed to zero, economic change would still take place, as would the reconstitution of family relationships, and the reconfiguration of residential patterns. Secondly, immigration and growing diversity intersect with these other transformations. For example, immigrants entering Canada half a century ago encountered a postwar economy that was booming and that had a high demand for blue-collar workers in resources, manufacturing, and construction. Employers were not especially concerned with educational achievement or even language skills beyond a rudimentary level. Under these circumstances, adult men quickly found work that paid enough to sustain whole families in modest houses near the inner city. Every major Canadian city that received large numbers of immigrants in that era had immigrant districts, such as the St. Lawrence Boulevard corridor of Montreal, and the areas surrounding Spadina Avenue in Toronto, Selkirk Street in Winnipeg, and Commercial Drive in Vancouver. Each of these streets emerged as cultural, social, and commercial hubs of newcomer communities, and in the process, became symbolic of the settlement process itself.

In recent years, however, the large volumes of newcomers arriving in Canada have contributed to urban change by settling in new patterns. Suburbs have become primary reception zones in many cases, particularly in Montreal, Toronto, and Vancouver. In fact a significant number of Punjabi-speaking immigrants have elected to settle outside the metropolitan boundaries of Greater Vancouver entirely, for example, both to the north and east, as have new Chinese-Canadians in the Toronto region. Recent immigrants are therefore bringing global diversity to these locations on the periphery (or beyond) of metropolitan regions. In the process they establish places of worship, cultural institutions, and commercial centres. Mosques, Gurdwaras, and Hindu temples are therefore now as common in the suburbs as they are in the inner city, as are the Asian-theme malls of Richmond, British Columbia, or Markham, Ontario.

There are two radically different ways of interpreting these emerging landscapes: they could be seen as an indication of cultural mixing between host and newcomer (or, in effect, European and visible minority) groups; or they could be seen as new forms of enclave formation. Further, if minority groups are forming enclaves, the extent to which they are economically marginalized is critical. A combination of residential concentration and economic marginalization can lead to the unfortunate result of ghettoization. Before turning to this important question, it is worth pausing to consider the dynamics at work here. What is the relationship between the settlement choices being made by newcomers and members of visible minority groups on the one hand and, on the other, those made by long-term residents of Canada who are mainly of European descent? In the U.S., researchers have identified counter-cyclical migration trajectories. In that country, immigrants are mainly settling in a small number of large cities, while the American-born are leaving the same places. That is, international and internal migration systems are moving in opposing directions, leading to a widening gap in the location of immigrants versus the native-born. The resulting, uneven ethnocultural patchwork is often interpreted as evidence of White flight (though this conclusion is not universally shared).

Similar counterposed systems appear to be operating in Canada. Between 1991 and 1996, for example, all three of Canada's largest metropolitan centres experienced negative net internal migration and positive international migration. Immigration is accounting for nearly all of the population growth in these centres, since natural increase rates are not much higher than the number leaving them for other parts of Canada. In analyzing these patterns, Ley (2003) is reluctant to invoke a cultural explanation, that is, to see them as evidence of White flight. Instead, he focuses on economic factors and argues that they affect immigrant and Canadian-born populations differently. He finds a high correlation between the volume of immigrants into Canadian cities (specifically Toronto and Vancouver) and house prices. The Canadian-born respond to this development either by avoiding the high-priced metropolitan market or, if they already live there, by cashing in on their rising equity. Immigrants, on the other hand, adjust to rising land and rent costs by adding to their household size and pooling their income. They therefore are able to manage in circumstances that deter most Canadian-born households, although it involves a considerable financial burden. Why do they sacrifice so much to live in expensive housing that they can barely afford? The Longitudinal Survey of Immigrants to Canada suggests an answer: The drive to live near friends and relatives is particularly strong for newcomers, and is the most commonly declared reason for the choice of settlement location. As approximately three-quarters of the immigrants arriving since the 1980s have been visible minorities, the processes that shape immigrant settlement, by default, also shape the social geography of European-origin versus visible minority groups.

We see particularly complex dynamics at work by turning our attention to the intra-metropolitan scale. Actually, given the changes that have occurred in the way that Statistics Canada classifies cultural ancestry—some subtle and others dramatic—there is no easy way to chart statistically the evolving social geography of Canadian cities. It is therefore impossible to construct comparable ethnocultural categories across Census years in the crucial period of the past 30 years. In other projects, I have tried to do this and have found that, in the Vancouver case, the situation is extremely complex. Most ethnocultural groups appear to be slowly becoming more distinct or concentrated in terms of their residential location, but there are also some that are becoming more dispersed (Hiebert, 1999). The extent to which these patterns are meaningful versus statistical artifacts, though, is debatable.

While it is difficult to chart change over time, current Census figures offer an instructive snapshot of the emerging social geography of Canada's major metropolitan centres. Across the three largest centres, the degree of residential separation between visible minority and European-origin groups is approximately equal, though there is a tendency for groups to be slightly more spatially concentrated in Montreal than Toronto, which is again a little higher than Vancouver. There is also considerable variation between groups, as suggested in the indices portrayed in Table 14.1. The most common measure of residential concentration is the so-called Index of Segregation, which ranges from 0 to 100 and indicates the proportion of a group that would have to relocate for that group to have the same residential distribution as the rest of the population. A value of 0 means the group has exactly the same distribution as the rest of the population, while 100 means the group is completely ghettoized and resides in an area exclusive to itself. Values less than 30 are generally believed to suggest that a group is widely dispersed; values from 30 to 50 are seen as ranging from a low to medium level of concentration; values between 60 and 80

Table 14.1 Geographical Concentration by Visible Minority Group, Montreal, Toronto and Vancouver, 2001

	Montreal		Toronto		Vancouver	
	Population	Ind. Seg.	Population	Ind. Seg.	Population	Ind. Seg.
Total—all groups	3,380,640		4,640,330		1,967,520	
Total visible minority population	458,335	46.5	1,710,110	43.5	725,700	41.1
Chinese	52,115	53.3	408,935	53.1	342,620	50.0
South Asian	57,940	63.9	473,635	44.9	164,320	52.8
Black	139,300	45.9	309,910	39.7	18,460	32.8
Filipino	17,890	74.4	133,310	40.4	57,045	37.8
Latin American	53,160	46.6	75,815	43.0	18,765	36.4
Southeast Asian	39,565	53.9	53,385	48.9	28,550	48.4
Arab	67,830	50.7	42,640	46.1	5,855	53.7
West Asian	11,585	66.5	53,010	50.8	21,415	54.1
Korean	3,760	80.7	42,570	49.4	28,880	44.5
Japanese	2,295	82.4	17,385	45.0	24,025	32.7
Visible minority, n.i.e.	6,780	65.9	66,340	40.2	3,290	56.3
Multiple visible minority	6,110	65.7	33,110	34.9	12,450	36.3
All others (non-visible minority)	2,922,315	46.5	2,930,185	43.5	1,241,815	41.1
Average, weighted	47.4		44.3		43.6	

are seen as high concentration; and anything over 80 is seen as extreme concentration. To put this into perspective, index values for Black/White groups in U.S. cities typically are in the 80 range, which is the highest general level of residential segregation anywhere in the industrialized world.

Weighted average Segregation Indices for visible minority groups across the three metropolitan areas suggest that these groups have a greater degree of concentration: West Asians (53.7); Chinese (51.8); Southeast Asians (50.4); Arabs (49.2); Koreans (49.1); and South Asians (48.3). These groups reside in more dispersed patterns: Latin Americans (43.4); Visible minorities (n.i.e.) (43.1); Filipinos (42.6); Blacks (41.3); Japanese (40.1); and Multiple visible minorities (38.9). This spectrum of socio-spatial tendencies defies simple analysis. There is no easy socio-economic logic at work either as, for example, there are groups with similar incomes that have quite different geographic patterns (e.g., Filipinos and South Asians).

The complexity of residential patterns makes it virtually impossible to answer an old question that seems to arise with each new generation of immigrant reception: Are residential concentrations of immigrants (or visible minorities) good or bad? It is worth noting that several prominent critics of Canadian immigration and multiculturalism policies believe that these concentrations indicate a lack of social cohesion and are likely to lead to social strife (Collacott, 2002; Francis, 2002; Stoffman, 2002). The recent adoption of regionalization policy—which seeks to redistribute immigrants to centres outside Montreal, Toronto, and Vancouver—also appears to be based on the logic that concentrated settlement is a problem. Moreover, the 2003 study conducted by the United Way and Canadian Council on Social Development (poverty by postal code) reports high poverty rates in areas settled by immigrants and visible minorities in the Greater Toronto Area. In 1981, 45 percent of the residents of the most impoverished Census tracts in the Toronto CMA were immigrants, and 37 were members of visible minority groups; by 2001, those figures had risen, respectively, to 65 and 78 percent. The absolute number of visible-minority individuals experiencing low income is perhaps the most disappointing statistic of all: It jumped from 60,500 in 1981 to 278,700 in 2001. To put this number into perspective, it exceeds the total population of individuals experiencing low income in Newfoundland and Labrador, Prince Edward Island, and Nova Scotia combined, as recorded in the 2001 Census.

Several points are important to build a more comprehensive understanding of ethnic enclaves and, more generally, the social geography of metropolitan areas. First, the Segregation Indices reported in Table 14.1 reveal that immigrant and minority groups are not living in exclusive areas in Montreal, Toronto, or Vancouver. No group, for example, approaches the Black/White division of social space in many U.S. cities. Secondly, ethnocultural congregation is a double-sided process, on the one hand crystallizing social differences in spatial terms, but on the other providing opportunities for social and economic development (e.g., Peach, 1996). Thirdly, as implied in the previous statement, the relationship between ethnocultural enclaves and socio-economic marginalization is far from clear (an issue I examine in greater detail in the next section).

Summarizing these last points, the degree of ethnocultural concentration in Canada is actually much less than has been assumed in the popular press or by recent critics. In any case, the development of enclaves may even be seen as a by-product of multiculturalism. I conclude from this that concern over immigrant/minority residential concentration is largely misplaced. True, there are far-reaching transformations of urban spatial structure under way, and these intersect with immigration, but the specific social geography of settlement is not a problem. The more pressing issue, to which I now turn, is that of marginalization of immigrant and visible minority populations.

DIVERSITY AND EQUITY IN MONTREAL, TORONTO, AND VANCOUVER

Researchers in the late 1980s began to detect a decline in the relative economic well-being of recent immigrants, and these concerns became amplified through the 1990s (Li, 2000). Results of the 1996 Census only added to this worry because it was clear that labour market participation rates had fallen for newcomers, as had earnings and overall incomes. The 2001 Census, taken at a time of relative economic buoyancy, was seen as a key moment to see whether the pattern of declining fortunes was temporary, related to the weak economy of the early 1990s, or structural. Early analysis of 2001 Census figures have yielded results that do not easily lead to a definitive answer to this burning question (Chiu and Zeitsma, 2003). On the more optimistic side, the gap between immigrant and Canadian-born earnings and incomes, which had been growing from 1981–1996, did not increase further. In fact, the situation of male immigrants appears to have been improving relative to the non-immigrant population. But, on the other hand, the situation for female newcomers has actually worsened, relative to the Canadian-born (Badets, 2003), and the overall gap in earnings (for men and women together) has only improved marginally.

Picot and Hou (2003) have added an important insight into the dynamics of well-being among Canadians. Using the main base of the 1981, 1991, and 2001 Censuses, they show a pronounced deterioration in the economic situation of newcomers, defined in their terms as immigrants who arrived in the five-year period before the Census was taken. In the early 1980s, recent immigrants were 1.44 times more likely to experience low income than the population as a whole; by 2000 the corresponding figure had risen to nearly 2.3 times. Immigrants who have lived in Canada longer than five years did not fare quite so poorly; their relative rate of low income rose from 1.0 to 1.4 times higher than the total population. Significantly, the situation of the Canadian-born improved dramatically over the same period, with a drop in both their absolute and relative rates of low income. In other words, immigration appears to be associated with an improvement in the level of economic well-being for the Canadian-born, but the opposite is true for immigrants.

Of course, given the different ethnocultural profiles of the Canadian-born and immigrant populations, these economic trajectories are also registered in terms of those of European origin vs. visible minorities. That is, low-income rates are much higher, in general, for Canadians of non-European origin than for the total population, in part because such a high proportion of that group are immigrants. In Canada as a whole, and in each of the three major metropolitan centres, the percentage of the population experiencing low income is almost twice as high for visible minorities as for those not in that category (which includes individuals of European and Aboriginal heritage; Table 14.2). As these figures imply, this means that even Canadian-born members of visible minority groups face high rates of poverty. Pendakur and Pendakur (2004) have used the main base of each Census from 1971 to 1996 to track the earnings rates of visible minority versus other Canadians. In each case, they confined their analysis to those born in Canada. After controlling for key personal features (age, sex, and education), they find that members of visible minority groups suffer a substantial penalty in earnings.

The scale of this penalty declined somewhat over the 1970s, but increased in the 1980s and early 1990s. They have also just completed an update of their analysis which shows that little changed in the late 1990s (though the situation did not deteriorate further). This is a rather sobering point. In the period between 1971 and 2001, Canada adopted official multiculturalism, passed the Human Rights Act and the Employment Equity Act, established the Human Rights Commission, and initiated other measures designed to ensure equitable treatment for all, including members of visible minority groups. However, despite all these measures and regulatory structures, the gap between visible minority and White earnings—with age, gender, and education controlled—is actually larger in 2001 than it was in 1971.

Before turning to consider the future, I believe it is essential to acknowledge a particularly positive aspect of immigrant settlement in Canada, one that also has implications for minority groups. There is growing evidence showing that Canadians have developed uniquely favourable attitudes to immigration and immigrants compared with the residents of every other country that is surveyed on these issues. In part, this widespread attitude reflects the fact that there are no significant anti-immigration or anti-minority political

Table 14.2 Percentage of Primary Household Maintainers Below LICO, 2001

	Canada		Montreal		Toronto		Vancouver	
	Total	Im91–01	Total	Im91–01	Total	Im91–01	Total	Im91–01
Total	19.1	38.3	26.5	52.6	18.8	34.8	23.2	42.8
Non-Vis.Min.	17.8	29.3	24.1	41.1	15.0	27.6	19.3	27.8
Visible Minorities	31.1	42.0	46.9	58.4	27.7	37.1	33.2	46.0
Black	36.7	51.4	48.4	62.5	32.9	46.0	32.5	53.2
South Asian	25.4	35.6	48.3	59.6	25.9	35.1	23.2	31.6
Chinese	30.1	43.6	44.9	60.5	26.8	38.1	35.5	50.3
Southeast Asian	31.7	43.0	36.6	52.2	26.5	35.2	43.3	55.2
Filipino	18.9	23.9	34.8	41.0	15.7	19.9	21.2	25.7
Arab/West Asian	43.5	52.5	52.3	60.5	37.8	45.3	46.5	54.7
Latin American	36.0	41.6	49.0	54.8	27.9	30.3	41.4	43.0

Source: Statistics Canada, Metropolis Core Tables, Part 3, Table 2.

parties operating in Canada, as opposed to the case of many other countries (e.g., Smith, 2005). But we can turn this point around: No major movement against these groups has arisen in Canada because there is no political constituency for it. When asked by the Pew Council on Global Attitudes in 2002 whether immigration yields, on balance, more good or bad results, the ratio of Canadian respondents on these answers was 77:18 (Pew Global Attitudes Project, 2002). This result was unique among the countries surveyed. The good side was supported by less than 50 percent of respondents in every other country, though respondents in the U.S., France, and Bulgaria came close, with 49, 46, and 42 percent, respectively, expressing this view. Russia represented the opposite extreme of Canada, with only 13 percent believing that immigration brings about positive outcomes. Results of a 2004 IPSOS study were similar, with Canadians much more positive in their assessment of immigration than respondents from any other country (IPSOS-Public Affairs, 2004). In a project documenting public opinion in Vancouver, I found that the favourable attitudes about immigration and immigrants were echoed in public perceptions of multiculturalism (Hiebert, 2003). For example, 93 percent of respondents agreed with the statement that Canadians should accept cultural variety, and 91 percent agreed that Canadians should celebrate diversity.

LOOKING FORWARD: TOWARD NEW METROPOLITAN SOCIETIES

According to projections provided by Statistics Canada, metropolitan centres in Canada will clearly attract the most immigrants over the next several decades and will therefore house the most diverse populations. For example, Statistics Canada has projected that by 2007 the visible minority population may very well increase to as much as 3.2 million in Toronto (more than half the metropolitan total), 1.4 million in Vancouver (also more than half), and 750,000 in Montreal (Statistics Canada, 2005). The emerging social landscapes of Canadian metropolitan centres are unlike anything we have seen before in this country. There are few precedents worldwide, in fact, to the level of diversity that will characterize Canada's future.

The first and most important policy response to the problems presented in this paper is already firmly in the public eye and has been discussed at length by others (e.g., see Reitz, 2001, 2004). On the subject of immigrants, commentators from a wide variety of backgrounds make the same point: Credentials and labour market experience gained before arrival in Canada need to be acknowledged. Arguably, nothing would do more to promote effective integration and social justice for newcomers. The labour market must also become more accommodating to Aboriginal peoples and members of visible minority groups. Processes of discrimination—whether blatant or subtle—operate throughout the job cycle, from the assessment system of applicants at the moment of hiring all the way through to high-level promotions.

The human capital brought by immigrants will best be realized if they acquire an official language, and the provision of English and French training is therefore essential. Unfortunately, the availability of these critical services varies across the country as provincial jurisdictions are involved. Strange as it might seem to a newcomer to this country, the level of language training provided for immigrants arriving in Newfoundland and Labrador or Manitoba, for example, is much higher than that offered in British Columbia. In my opinion, this differential is hard to justify.

The issue of housing is also crucial. In Canada the stock of social housing is small relative to European countries and its administration is under piecemeal jurisdiction. In Toronto alone, there are reputed to be approximately 70,000 households on the social housing waiting list, and average time spent on the list is more than seven years. The combination of rising housing prices and rents, with rising poverty rates among immigrants and visible minority groups, have led to critical affordability issues (Rose, 2004; United Way and Canadian Council on Social Development, 2003). As noted earlier, immigrant and visible minority households have responded by adding more people to each unit in an effort to assemble higher incomes, but this strategy is associated with crowding and precarious financing. Increasing the stock and availability of social housing, especially in the largest metropolitan centres, would alleviate these problems. Clearly, the emerging cities initiative ought to include social housing as a core element.

Beyond the economy and the bricks and mortar of the housing system, and turning to the local scale, there is also a need to address the way urban societies function. Research in Montreal and Vancouver has been instrumental in exploring the social networks that operate to both help and hinder immigrants (and, by extension, members of visible minority groups) (cf. Germain, 2002). Extrapolating from the work of sociologist Mark Granovetter, individuals rely on two types of social relationships to find their way in society (including entering the housing and labour markets as well as educational systems). Most people are embedded in a network of strong ties that are shared with family members, close friends, and others who are trusted implicitly. For the most part, strong ties are contained within ethnocultural or ethnoreligious communities, but there are also many exceptions to this generalization. Strong ties nurture the individual, especially in times of difficulty, and provide a basis for psychological well-being. Weak ties connect people outside this circle of intimacy, and are built out of acquaintances and casual friendships that emerge in school, work, neighbourhood, and other social settings. Networks of weak ties are typically broad and can extend into many groups. They therefore have a great potential to provide vital information about the world. Strong ties exist in close social networks and therefore tend to include people who know similar things—that is, people who have the same social limits.

Social policies will be most effective when they reinforce the networks of both strong and weak ties (Rose, 2004). For immigrants and refugees, this translates, first and foremost, to rebuilding family structures in Canada (strong ties). There is also a need to foster the interaction between people from different backgrounds, or the development of weak ties. Above all, this means that members of the host society need to welcome newcomers, and to adjust their frame of mind to include diverse groups within their commonplace understanding of who belongs. As Sandercock (2003) argues, this entails a first step of enhancing civility, and a second of enhancing conviviality. She sees the Vancouver system of neighbourhood houses (supported by the municipal government) as instrumental in building conversations and everyday understandings across different groups. These arise out of daycare and seniors' programs, recreation, and so on—in essence, in daily engagement over local issues. In her work, Sandercock (2003:26) advocates a normative ideal of urban citizenship that is based on "the ethnographic reality of intercultural co-existence, the willingness of host society and immigrant groups and individuals to work together across cultural divides without the fear of losing their own identity."

In a fundamental sense, the policy and legal framework of multiculturalism is key for both strong and weak ties, and for the type of citizenship advanced by Sandercock. On the one hand, by enabling cultural retention, systems of strong ties can be nurtured. On the other hand, multiculturalism can foster interaction across cultures in an atmosphere of respect. As Sandercock effectively reminds us, however, local governments have yet to meet fully the challenge of multiculturalism. In particular, the planning system retains, at its core, rules and codified practices that were created out of the European-Canadian experience. Planners conduct their work with sensibilities that are, understandably, shaped by these inherited views. The interests of newcomers, especially those from ethnoreligious minorities, are not easily seen or understood within this inherited mindset.

Those who frame local policies and programs need to be aware of several constraints. First, throughout this chapter I have emphasized that many immigrants and members of visible minority groups encounter Canadian, or mainstream, society from a position of economic vulnerability. In other words, there is a class dimension that pervades the interaction that takes place between planners and other government officials and society, and between social groups. For the particular groups under consideration here, the issues of immigrant credentialization and the openness of the labour market to visible minorities are ever present. Encouraging social interaction is a noble goal, but will not replace these larger issues. Enhancing strong and weak ties will not help very much if the labour market systematically channels immigrants and visible minorities to second-class jobs. Secondly, the reduced scope of government in Canada has meant that the sorts of institutions that are vital to promoting cross-cultural interaction have seen substantial budget cuts in recent years. This has been particularly problematic for the NGO sector, which carries much of the responsibility of delivering settlement services to immigrants, and conducts advocacy on behalf of visible minorities. Reinvestment in civil society ought to be an essential ingredient in any plan to improve the socio-economic situation of immigrants and visible minority groups. This reinvestment should be conducted between governments and NGOs in partnerships that are based on mutual trust.

Finally, I must return to modify, at least slightly, my earlier dismissal of the geographical concentration of immigrants and minority groups as an issue. The suburbanization of immigrant settlement, minority enclaves, and poverty has taken place quickly and service organizations have yet to catch up. In Greater Vancouver, for example, most of the large settlement organizations are located in the City of Vancouver (though several also have suburban subsidiary offices, and there is one large agency specializing in the Delta/Surrey region in the southeast quarter of the metropolitan area). The level of service in most outlying areas is small relative to the number of potential clients living there, meaning that clients have to deal with a journey to service to obtain the information and help they need. Many newcomers and members of minority groups in these areas rely on public transportation, and the quality of that system is critical to their access to services and therefore their well-being. More fundamentally, providing resources for NGOs to reach out to suburbanized immigrant and minority groups should be prioritized.

CONCLUDING THOUGHTS

In this chapter I have tried to generate a sense of urgency without descending into a sense of despair. The situation is too complex for the latter, but there are definitely sufficient worries to justify the former. If 2017 yields outcomes that simply extend the 1981–2001 trajectory of increasing poverty among newcomers and members of visible minority groups—that is, if things just continue in their present direction—Canadian metropolitan centres will be places of even greater vulnerability and polarization. Without effective intervention, levels of marginalization will surely increase. This intervention has to involve all levels of government and bring in a wide network of institutions, including, of course, those outside government. There are three strengths to build upon in this respect, in my opinion. The first is the remarkably positive level of public support for immigration, diversity, and multiculturalism. This is fundamental. Unlike the case in so many countries, advocacy organizations and governments in Canada do not have to act against the grain of public opinion to improve the well-being of designated groups. The second is the breadth and depth of Canadian civil society, especially the organizations dedicated to the cause of immigrants and minorities. It is perhaps unfair to select just one of these organizations as an example, but it is also instructive. The largest (in terms of budget) NGO that provides services to newcomers in Greater Vancouver, SUCCESS, employs about 350 people and benefits from the efforts of 9,000 volunteers. Clearly, the public is engaged in these issues. The third is the patchwork of institutional jurisdictions and systems across Canadian metropolitan areas. Montreal, Toronto, and Vancouver (and other centres, of course) are under different provincial jurisdictions, have different administrative systems, different NGOs, different urban cultures, and so on. This is fertile ground for experimentation with new policies and programs, as long as there is dialogue between the centres and a will to take up successful initiatives regardless of their origin.

● ●

CRITICAL THINKING QUESTIONS

1. What are some of the potential negative consequences of current immigration patterns to Canada? Correspondingly, what are some of the potential gains or benefits?
2. What might Canadians do to minimize negative consequences of high levels of immigration?
3. Hiebert considers in detail some of the interrelationship between immigration, new settlement, and residential patterns in Canada. In so doing, he is particularly concerned with the potential for ghettoization. What do we mean by ghettoization, and why should it be considered particularly problematic?

● ●

SECTION 4
POPULATION AGING

● ●

HAVING STUDIED THE COMPONENTS OF POPULATION CHANGE (mortality, fertility, and migration), the current section moves on to consider one of the most fundamental consequences of past change in terms of these components, i.e., population aging in Canada. At the national level, this transformation in age distribution has had profound consequences for Canadian society. A shift toward below replacement fertility has been particularly important in this context, as have significant reductions in mortality at older ages. Légaré's contribution to the current collection demonstrates the utility of demographic projections in predicting further aging of the population well into the 21st century. For example, reasonably robust projections suggest an increase in the size of Canada's elderly population (65 years and older) by a factor of 2.5 between 2000 and 2050.

As Canadian society continues to age, Légaré argues that this will necessitate significant reforms in both the funding and delivery of social security, pensions, and health care programs. While Canada might not be facing an "aging crisis" in the near future, Légaré makes a convincing argument that without proper planning well in advance, Canada could face a "crisis" over the longer term. In terms of intergenerational equity, future generations could be unfairly burdened with the costs of population aging. As merely one example, Canada's social security system has long been criticized as being largely "pay as you go" whereby contributions by workers are not invested for future return, but go directly to pay benefits to retirees. While such a system can work relatively well when there are few retirees relative to people of labour force age, actuaries worry about a future whereby a much higher proportion of the population will be retired and no longer active in the labour force.

At the national level, past fertility and mortality trends have been particularly important in determining Canada's age structure, whereas net international migration has had a relatively modest effect. Simulations with various types of population models have demonstrated this insight, which is now taken for granted by demographers, i.e., international migration is of relatively little importance in influencing age structure. Without a significant upturn in fertility, Canada's population will inevitably age, and Canadian society will have to adjust to this simple fact. In this context, Moore and Pacey's chapter on the geographic dimensions of aging demonstrates how migration, while relatively unimportant at the national level, can have a particularly strong impact on age structure at the local level. There are clearly important differences across regions and provinces in Canada in terms of age structure as migration can both accelerate and slow down the pace of population aging.

These regional differences in age structure imply important differences in terms of the demand for health care and social services. For example, consider Alberta (with about 10 percent of its population 65 years or older) relative to its neighbour Saskatchewan (with about 15 percent of this age group). Provinces and communities with the most buoyant local economies have attracted young in-migrants and as a result experience slower rates of aging. It is an oversimplification to think that the national age structure is one and the same as what is observed provincially and/or locally. From a public policy and planning viewpoint, this geography of aging has particularly important ramifications for all levels of government.

While there is little doubt that population aging will add to the costs of health care and social security, there is considerable uncertainty to the extent to which this will occur and our ability to accommodate this shift. While population aging is important, there are many other factors beyond demographic change that are arguably as important, if not more important, in this regard. For this reason, we have included Gee's essay, which makes precisely this point as she suggests there is much misinformation and exaggeration in both academic and policy debates on population aging. Building on her earlier work, Gee points to what she labels as "apocalyptic thinking" on population aging, suggesting that neo-liberal arguments frequently point to demographic trends as justification for retrenchment of the welfare state. While population change is important, there are obviously many other political and economic factors that should enter into debates on public policy, in defining and identifying social problems, with the appropriate response from government and civil society.

RECOMMENDED READINGS

Cheal, David (ed.). (2003). *Aging and Demographic Change in the Canadian Context*. Toronto: University of Toronto Press. This edited collection of Canadian research considers the various implications of aging and demographic change.

Connidis, Ingrid. (2001). *Family Ties and Aging*. Thousand Oaks: Sage. This book demonstrates how family ties continue to remain important in societies with low fertility and significant population aging.

Gee, Ellen, and Gloria Gutman. (2000). *Overselling Population Aging: Apocalyptic Demography, Intergenerational Challenges, and Social Policy*.Toronto: Oxford University Press. This book was meant as a critique of arguments that overstate the problems associated with population aging. Briefly, it argues that population aging should not be used as a justification for recklessly reforming the welfare state.

Stone, Leroy O. (ed.). (2006). *New Frontiers of Research on Retirement*. Ottawa: Statistics Canada. Cat. no. 75-511-XPE. This edited collection of empirical research contributes information on the many institutional adjustments that Canadian society will need to make given the upcoming wave of retirements among baby boomers.

Zeng, Y., E.M. Crimmins, Y. Carrière, and J.-M. Robine (eds.). (2006). *Longer Life and Healthy Aging*. International Studies in Population. Dordrecht: Springer. The focus of this book is on theoretical issues and empirical findings related to trends and determinants of healthy aging, including factors related to "healthy longevity" of the oldest-old, aged 80 and over.

RELATED WEB SITES

Canadian Association on Gerontology
<http://www.cagacg.ca>
   The Canadian Association on Gerontology encourages studies in gerontology and disseminates information among the many professions and disciplines whose mandate includes the elderly.

International Association of Gerontology
<http://www.iagg.com.br>
   The International Association of Gerontology encourages interdisciplinary research on aging across member organizations from over 60 countries.

International Programs Center
<http://www.census.gov/ipc/www/idbpyr.html>
   Shows a series of dynamic population pyramids for different countries, created by the International Programs Center at the U.S. Census Bureau.

National Advisory Council on Aging
<http://www.naca-ccnta.ca>
   This Web site includes much material on matters related to the aging of the Canadian population and the quality of life of seniors.

Statistics Canada
<http://www.statcan.ca/english/kits/animat/pyone.htm>
   Shows animated population pyramids illustrating the changing age structure of Canada's population from 1901 through to 2001. It also provides an animated projection through to 2056.

CHAPTER 15

AGING AND SOCIAL SECURITY PROGRAM REFORMS: CANADA IN INTERNATIONAL PERSPECTIVE

Jacques Légaré

● ●

INTRODUCTION

In the century between the end of World War II and the year 2050, the total population of the UN Economic Commission for Europe (UNECE) countries studied here is expected to multiply by 1.5, growing from 741.2 million to 1,129.7 million. During the same period, however, the number of people aged 65 years and over will increase three times as quickly, multiplying 4.7 times (Figure 15.1) and almost 10 times in Canada; inevitably, these changes raise important issues for policy makers.

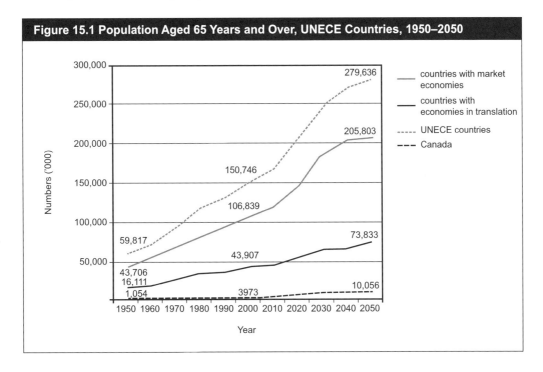

Figure 15.1 Population Aged 65 Years and Over, UNECE Countries, 1950–2050

THE AGING OF THE TOTAL POPULATION

For our analysis, we group UNECE countries into two broad categories: those with market economies and those with economies in transition. Both groups will see their number of elderly almost double between 2000 and 2050. In regions with market economies, these trends are projected to level off and even decrease in some cases, while for those with economies in transition, the proportion of elderly people continues its upward trend, but at a slower pace. Regions that at the present time have younger populations, such as North America and southern Europe, will see their elderly population more than double (by a factor of 2.5 in Canada). In western and northern Europe, as well as the Commonwealth of Independent States (CIS) and Baltic states, numbers will multiply by only about 1.5.

These trends on absolute numbers are reasonably robust as they are based on people who have already been born—those who will be 65 and over in 2050 were born before 1985; variations in mortality and immigration will have only a minor impact on these crude numbers. Yet when we consider the percentage aged 65 and over in the total population, however, the long-term projections are more risky as they have to take into account the fertility behaviour of couples who have not yet been born!

Nevertheless, assuming that the UN projections are accurate, we estimate that the percentage of those aged 65 and above will also double, moving from about 13 percent now to 14 percent in 2010, 20.5 percent in 2030, and to nearly 25 percent in 2050 (United Nations, 1999). This overall picture obscures the rapid rate of aging in Europe (Figure 15.2). Already by 2010, in some countries (Germany, Greece, Italy, and Sweden), one-fifth of their predicted total population will be aged 65 and over. By 2030, this percentage is expected to reach 25 percent, as is also expected to be the case in Austria, Belgium, the

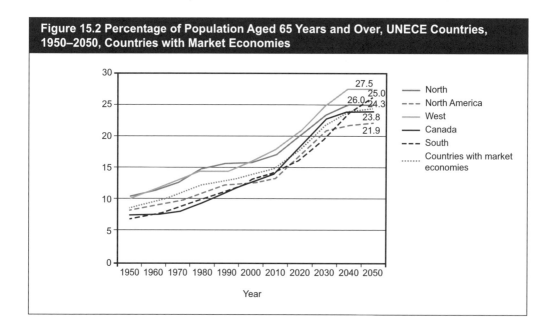

Figure 15.2 Percentage of Population Aged 65 Years and Over, UNECE Countries, 1950–2050, Countries with Market Economies

Czech Republic, Finland, Netherlands, Slovenia, Spain, and Switzerland. Even further, in the absence of drastic changes in demographic behaviour, more than one-third of the population will be 65 and over by 2050 in the Czech Republic, Greece, Italy, and Spain. During the same period, the elderly population is only expected to reach one-fifth of the total population of North America—23.8 percent in Canada. In an era of globalization, such sharp differences in population age structures could have important political, social, and economic repercussions.

THE OLDEST OLD: THE MOST RAPIDLY INCREASING GROUP

Challenges facing aging societies cannot be properly studied when old age is taken to begin at 65; old age in the past as well as in the future should be linked to dependency, both in terms of health and income security. There is no doubt that it is almost impossible to fix a threshold corresponding to dependency. Since the majority of people over 65 are not dependent in most respects, only people aged 80 years and over will be classified here as the oldest old. This group is the fastest-growing portion of the elderly population in UNECE countries, for those with market economies as well as for those with economies in transition. For both groups of countries, the oldest old will multiply threefold in the first half of the 21st century, and fourfold in Canada, where the population has evolved differently. Germany and the CIS, for example, are expecting to each have about 8 million people over age 80 in year 2050, which is more than the total population of many UNECE countries!

Of course, this is a long-term outcome, reaching a peak when all the cohorts of the baby boom are over 65 and the baby bust generations are joining their ranks. When we look at percentages of those aged 80 years and over in the total population, however, the situation is different for the two groups of countries. Market economies are expected to have significantly higher proportions of their populations over 80 by 2050 than are economies in transition, between 8 percent and 11 percent, as compared with 6 percent and 8 percent (Figure 15.3). Nevertheless, these calculations are based on predictions of future mortality that may be highly unreliable in countries with economies in transition.

In 2050, about one-tenth of the population of western Europe as a whole will be aged 80 years and over, a percentage equivalent to the proportion of persons aged 65 and over in most UNECE countries, up until very recently.

THE ELDERLY: A WOMEN'S WORLD

One of the features of the 20th-century mortality decline in the Western world has been the increasing gap between male and female mortality, as mortality has declined more rapidly for women than men. A second important element is that far more men than women died during the two world wars. Added to these direct mortality effects is the age difference between spouses, as wives tend to be younger than their husbands. All these factors contribute to the fact that women make up the majority of the elderly population, a situation that seems likely to continue.

If we consider the percentage of women in the total population (Figure 15.4), we appear to be living through a transitional period. In 1950, women comprised about 58 percent

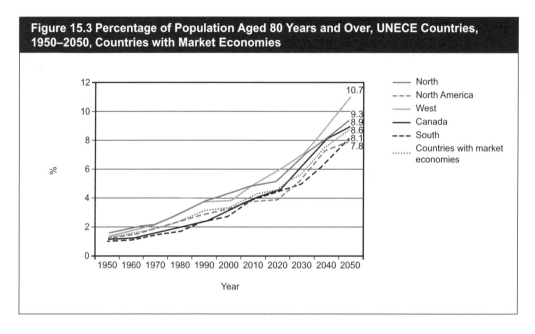

Figure 15.3 Percentage of Population Aged 80 Years and Over, UNECE Countries, 1950–2050, Countries with Market Economies

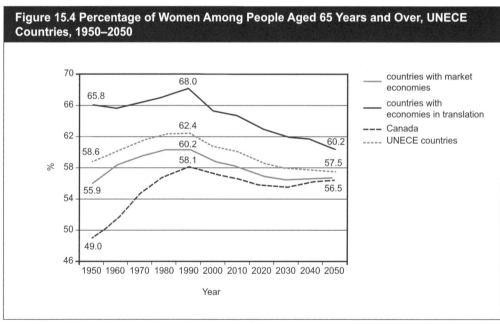

Figure 15.4 Percentage of Women Among People Aged 65 Years and Over, UNECE Countries, 1950–2050

of the elderly population, with this percentage rising through to the present and then expected to return by 2050 to a level equivalent to the 1950s. In the interval, especially in countries with economies in transition, not to mention the CIS and the Baltic states, the last 50 years have been characterized by important disparities with more than 70 percent of elderly people being female in the 1990s—and most of them not married. Even if the situation is now improving a little, short-term economic and social issues will still have to be faced and adjustments made.

Furthermore, the gender imbalance increases with age, reaching a peak for the age group 90 and over. The majority of these women have spent little time, if any, in the labour force, a situation potentially creating many problems of income security. Now, and in the year 2050, nearly 75 percent of the oldest old will be women, these percentages being well over 80 percent in countries with economies in transition.

THE AGING OF THE WORKING AGE POPULATION

For the second half of the 20th century, the median age of the working-age population hovered around 39, reaching 40 by the end of the century for UNECE countries as a whole (Figure 15.5). In the near future, this figure will rise rapidly in all regions, levelling off by 2030 in market economies but not in economies in transition. This process could raise the overall median age in year 2050 to about 42 for Canada and 43 for the UNECE countries. This is very close to 42.5 years, the midpoint age of the large age group 20 to 65, a situation that would be observed in a stationary population with all birth cohorts about the same size and very few deaths before old age.

AGING INDEXES

The aging index most commonly used by demographers and others is the dependency ratio, relating dependants—the population under age 20 and over age 65 (occasionally

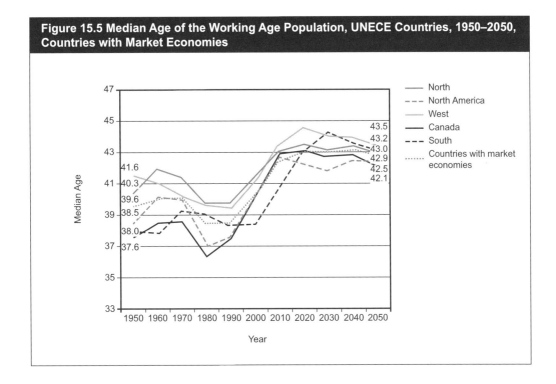

Figure 15.5 Median Age of the Working Age Population, UNECE Countries, 1950–2050, Countries with Market Economies

over age 60)—to the population of working ages. Sometimes, the dependency ratios of the elderly population are compared to the dependency ratios of youngsters. As people intuitively think in terms of economic burden, such an index can be highly misleading when applied to the older population. There may be an economic cost for supporting retired people, but it is important to remember that most elderly people are taxpayers and have financial assets, so that, unlike children, they are not necessarily dependent (International Social Security Association, 1998). Even though nowadays we more often use the term "demographic dependency" to avoid this confusion, these indexes can be proplematic as indicators of change in population age structure. Accordingly, we will now present alternative aging indices.

To illustrate how the age "pyramid" is becoming more and more an age "cylinder," we compare the population aged 65 years and over to the population under age 20. During the 1950s, there were some 23 elderly for 100 young people; the figure is now closer to 50—slightly more in countries with market economies, and less in those with economies in transition. By 2050, this ratio it is expected to reach about 110 elderly for 100 youngsters (a situation which could even be true for Canada). We will likely have a cylinder with a top on it.

As mentioned earlier, dependent elderly people are chiefly to be found among those aged 80 years and over, especially in terms of health. The weight of this group in the elderly population as a whole has been increasing for the last 50 years and will accelerate after 2025. This will be particularly true in Canada and in the other countries with market economies, when the first baby boomers reach this threshold (Figure 15.6).

The relation of the population aged 80 years and over to those in the age group 50 to 64 years (Figure 15.7) is probably a more meaningful indicator, as the children of the oldest

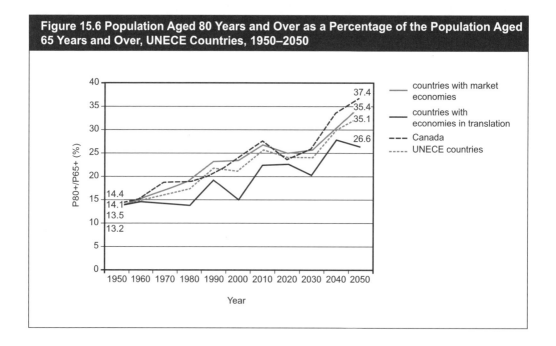

Figure 15.6 Population Aged 80 Years and Over as a Percentage of the Population Aged 65 Years and Over, UNECE Countries, 1950–2050

old belong mainly to this age group. Many policies currently designed to face the problems of population aging imply a greater reliance on the family than on public services, and some involvement in dealing with their dependent parents is expected of this age group. In 1950, there were only eight older parents per 100 mature children, and many of the latter still had children at home. Between 1980 and 2020, 100 mature children, mostly at the empty nest stage of their life cycle, may have to take care of 20 elderly parents. By 2050, the number could more than double in countries with market economies and increase by more than 50 percent in countries with economies in transition. In Canada, there could be one oldest-old person for every two mature children. Policies that tend to shift burden from the public sector to the family deserve close scrutiny, especially when we know that it is mainly women who will be affected by this shift.

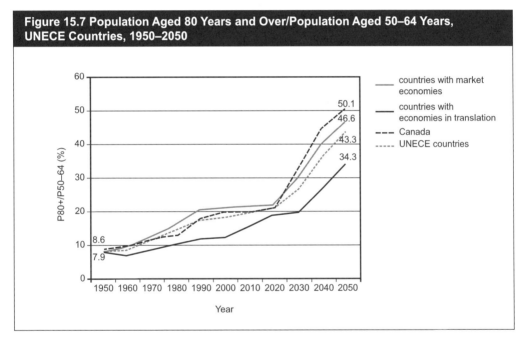

Figure 15.7 Population Aged 80 Years and Over/Population Aged 50–64 Years, UNECE Countries, 1950–2050

Finally, to enable an understanding of changes in the age structure for the working-age population, an additional aging index relates the number in pre-retirement age (aged 50 to 64 years) to those of labour force entrance age (20 to 34 years) (Figure 15.8). The graph of this index largely replicates the trends in the median age of the working-age population (see Figure 15.5), but this time in a more meaningful way. Presently, there are about six older people for 10 younger people available for the labour market, but by 2050 this could fall to one for one in Canada and even more than one for one in UNECE countries as a whole. This movement reflects a pattern observed with the median age of the working-age population—the upward trend (from 39 to 43 years). Of course these are median values: For some countries or regions, the situation envisaged could be catastrophic. For example, the Baltic states could see this index rise to 135 by the year 2050, which could be a nightmare situation from the point of view of human resources development and planning.

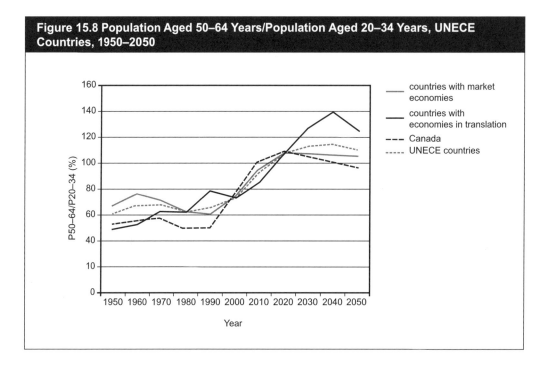

Figure 15.8 Population Aged 50–64 Years/Population Aged 20–34 Years, UNECE Countries, 1950–2050

THE IMPACT OF DEMOGRAPHIC DETERMINANTS OF AGING AND CHARACTERISTICS OF OLDER POPULATIONS ON SOCIAL SECURITY PROGRAMS

The demographic aging process we have just outlined was, initially, totally linked to reductions in fertility, not mortality. Indeed, in the past, it was mostly infants and children whose numbers increased because of lower child and infant mortality rates. Yet when most premature deaths have been eliminated, the decline in mortality rates becomes largely restricted to older ages and subsequently has a major impact on age structure and aging. And, even if immigration flows slow the demographics of the aging process, as illustrated here in Canada and North America, it cannot stop population aging and can only provide a salve to the wound (George et al., 1991).

FERTILITY AND PAYG PENSIONS AND HEALTH SCHEMES

When public social security programs in industrialized countries were subjected to radical restructuring after World War II, pay-as-you-go (PAYG) schemes were generally adopted, reflecting assumptions that strong economic and demographic growth would remain the norm. However, economic growth stalled in the early 1970s, and cohort fertility (or family size) has been considerably below replacement level in Canada for more than 20 cohorts, as it has been in most UNECE countries.

PAYG schemes imply that those who pay taxes—mainly workers—in any period assume the costs of health and pension schemes of the same period. These workers tend to be the children of the seniors. As there are—and will continue to be—growing numbers of beneficiaries and declining numbers of workers, the share of total social security benefits coming from PAYG schemes should decrease accordingly if we want to secure solidarity between generations. This change should occur at the pace that cohort fertility indexes decline (not period fertility indexes); these rates have been well documented for the past and are relatively easy to predict for the future.

Indeed, when family size—i.e., the cohort total fertility rate—drops by 50 percent over a certain period of time, the proportion of social security benefits coming from PAYG schemes should also drop by 50 percent if these benefits remain constant. This means that part of the benefits will have to come from other sources, mainly from the beneficiaries themselves, as it is they, and not society, who have decided to have fewer children (Le Bras, 1990). Some may protest that society is then breaking the social contract, but they need to remember that they themselves broke the contract by not having the expected number of children—that is, a sufficient number to ensure replacement levels. It is not our role to assess the merits of such a behaviour, but societies—and seniors—should proceed in an ethical way; this means not putting too heavy a burden on the working age population whose numbers are declining as a result of past fertility behaviour.

MORTALITY AND PENSION SCHEMES

As mentioned earlier, current contractions in mortality rates will have an important impact on the number of older people and on their proportion in the population. Crude numbers can only be on the increase. If we want to keep a fair share between population subgroups in PAYG schemes, we have to keep the ratios stable between workers and retirees and raise the age of access to public social security programs—an age that could be different from the age of retirement from the workplace.

In regard to funded pension schemes, benefits will either have to be reduced or contributions increased to cope with a longer life expectancy. These additional expected years of life, rather than the death rate, should guide decision making, as the death rate will increase in the future due to population aging, even if mortality still abates. For example, relatively conservative mortality scenarios suggest that life expectancy at age 65 in Canada has moved from 17 years for the 1901 birth cohort to 20 years for the 1941 birth cohort (Bourbeau et al., 1997). Meanwhile the crude death rate is expected to rise from 7.5 per 1,000 in 2000 to 12.8 per 1,000 in 2050. Encouraging early retirement in recent years has only worsened the problem. Even if early retirement is usually penalized actuarially, departure lump-sum payments—costly for governments and firms—keep early retirement attractive. Unless very favourable economic conditions prevail, early retirement will have to be seriously questioned in the interests of the larger society.

MORBIDITY AND HEALTH STATUS

While it is clear that mortality rates have improved considerably, especially at older ages, the question remains as to whether the elderly population is in better health. To ascertain more fully the health status of a population, epidemiologists and demographers have developed morbidity indexes to measure what is usually termed "healthy life expectancy." For example, the "disability-free life expectancy" is estimated by subtracting those years lived with a disability from "all health status combined" life expectancy. Even if all problems with definitions and data related to this measure have not yet been completely solved, breakthroughs have been achieved in the last 10 years due to the efforts of international researchers—Réseau Espérance de Vie En Santé (Robine and Romieu, 1998).

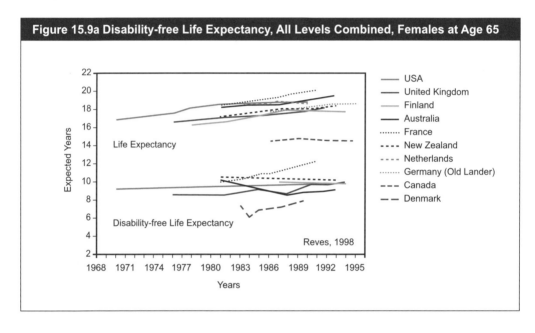

Figure 15.9a Disability-free Life Expectancy, All Levels Combined, Females at Age 65

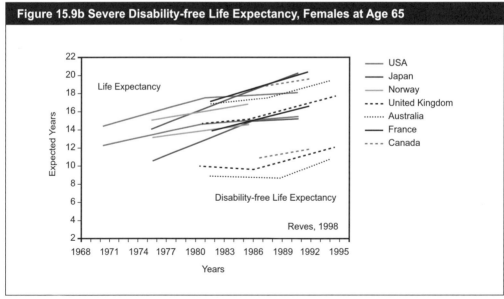

Figure 15.9b Severe Disability-free Life Expectancy, Females at Age 65

The links between mortality and morbidity are not self-evident, and researchers in the field champion one of three possible scenarios. The first one predicts pandemic disabilities at older ages, which means that life expectancy would increase more rapidly than disability-free life expectancy. At the opposite extreme, a second scenario forecasts a faster decline in morbidity than in mortality, resulting in fewer years in bad health. Finally, a third scenario predicts what is called a "dynamic equilibrium" between mortality and morbidity.

The experience of the last 30 years in industrialized countries (Canada and many UNECE countries, Japan, Australia, and New Zealand) supports the first scenario (Figure 15.9a): disability-free life expectancy has stagnated, if not worsened, while life expectancy improved greatly, a situation that reflects the worst scenario, namely, pandemic disabilities. However, if only severe disabilities are taken into account (Figure 15.9b), both indices improve. Only trends for women at age 65 are displayed here, but the pattern is similar for men at age 65, and for both women and men at birth. However, some progress has been observed for the most recent past in Canada (Martel and Bélanger, 1999).

WHAT ABOUT THE FUTURE?

In our opinion, as a society, we should not passively accept any of these scenarios, but we should reform the health system so as to make sure that we gain in quality as well as in quantity of life (Légaré and Carrière, 1999). In aging societies, in order to improve quality of life, future health investments should be directed principally at improving home services and fighting chronic diseases rather than devoting a disproportionate amount of resources to fighting fatal diseases.

MORTALITY, MORBIDITY, AND HEALTH COSTS

If we exclude the costs incurred at birth, it is now acknowledged that the older the person, the higher the per capita health costs. These costs have escalated exponentially in recent decades at the same time as the aging process has accelerated. For many people, the link between these two phenomena is evident. However, in-depth studies have clearly demonstrated that, up to now, population aging—or demography—has had very little to do with this explosion in health costs: paradoxically, supply—specifically in terms of technology—has been much greater than demand, particularly for the elderly (Barer et al., 1995; Hourriez, 1993).

The sharp increase in the projected proportion of elderly people raises critical questions about the pace of rising health costs, even if the per capita and per age costs are held constant at their present level. How, by diminishing morbidity levels, can we challenge the spectre of pandemic disabilities at older ages, too plausible a consequence of reduced mortality and increased aging. The fact that health expenditure apparently increases with age is mainly related to costs incurred at the time of dying, whatever the age at which death occurs (Zweifel et al., 1999). Accordingly, costs for younger elderly people could eventually decrease, but only if the reduced numbers of deaths resulting from lower mortality are not offset by increased numbers of seniors. To better predict future health costs, therefore, we should put more emphasis on the future numbers of *deaths* among the elderly than on the increase in the number of elderly themselves. Whatever the mortality scenario used, the former increase is much slower than the latter, thus presenting a less catastrophic, though still relatively serious, situation in terms of future health costs. In Austria, for instance, the numbers of deaths will increase twofold between now and 2030, while the proportion of elderly will increase by *five* (Prinz, 1997).

All these considerations apply mainly to health *cure* (medical and hospital services) costs. For long-term health *care costs* (where social services become important), only important gains in terms of morbidity are likely to modify the impact of population aging. This has important public health policy implications both for future fundamental and applied biomedical research, as well as for ethical attitudes when facing death (Légaré and Carrière, 1999).

SEX RATIOS AND PENSION SCHEMES LINKED TO PREVIOUS LABOUR FORCE PARTICIPATION

In discussions of present and future income security for the elderly, most studies use existing information on pension schemes, based largely on the past labour force involvement of men. However, as previously shown, population aging into the future implies largely a female world, especially at the oldest ages. To forecast the situation more realistically, efforts should be made to understand the real impact that private and public pension schemes will have on a retirement income based on the past and current labour force participation of men and women.

There is no doubt that the proportion of women in the labour force has increased at a rapid pace; in the early 1980s it was expected that such a change would eventually solve the expected problems of PAYG pension schemes and population aging in general (Fellegi, 1988). However, observed participation rates for female cohorts have now levelled off across most countries (Figure 15.10). Furthermore, these participation rates veil important differences between men and women in terms of real income, partly because women are paid less and work more often part-time. The estimated future income of women from pension schemes linked to previous labour force participation will thus be proportionally lower.

Accordingly, in terms of equity, basic pension schemes that mostly have a PAYG format should be indexed to take into account these different patterns of labour force involvement. This kind of flexibility will also soon have to be applied to men who are also increasingly following unconventional career paths.

MORTALITY, MARITAL STATUS, AND SUPPORT FOR ELDERLY PEOPLE

In aging societies, the elderly are living increasingly autonomous lives. Nowadays, the elderly do not wish to be dependent on their children or their community, at least as long as they are healthy; and even as their health deteriorates, their spouse is generally the best source of support. Thus, the joint survivorship of spouses should be optimized. However, with current discrepancies in life expectancies of men and women and with divorce on the increase, recent trends often make this situation difficult to achieve. The problem of divorce is mitigated by the fact that people continue to prefer living with a

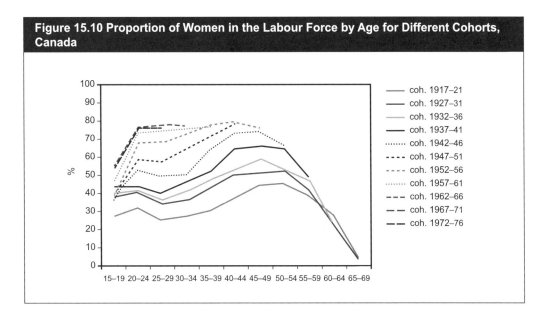

Figure 15.10 Proportion of Women in the Labour Force by Age for Different Cohorts, Canada

partner and often enter a new conjugal union following the breakdown of an earlier one. We should therefore focus our efforts on reducing the gap between male and female mortality, or in other words, further reducing it since the gap is already narrowing for Canada (Nault, 1997). Male mortality rates should be reduced to at least the level of female mortality rates.

This could achieve two things: First, it would postpone institutionalization for those with impaired health by encouraging living arrangements in private households. Second, it would minimize some of the drawbacks described in the previous section regarding income security for older women.

CONCLUSION

Even though population aging will be less smooth than it might have been had we followed the course predicted by demographic transition theory, it would be incorrect to talk of an aging crisis.

Reforms to social security programs should be based on in-depth studies of successive cohorts, as the cohorts entering old age differ widely, both in numbers and characteristics. In Canada, as in many other countries, the steady 20th-century decline in the birth cohort size was interrupted by the baby boom, when the number of babies almost doubled. The baby bust simply brought birth cohort size back in line with a longer term secular trend. Nevertheless, these changes in numbers have implications that must be faced. The fact that these successive cohorts have very different characteristics is also crucial. Older people of tomorrow will differ from those of today (Marcil-Gratton and Légaré, 1987); women in particular will be far more educated. We can, therefore, expect that, in the future, older women will be a great deal more autonomous, as they have been throughout their lives.

In an era of globalization, however, can we expect industrialized countries to remain indifferent to the fact that some will have growing populations while others will start to decline? Certainly, all these societies will age, but at very different speeds. If we recognize that any major change in fertility behaviour is unlikely, it is clear that some countries may have to rely on immigration policies that will at least slightly slow the pace of aging, while not preventing it. Immigrants can pay the contributions that would have been paid by the babies who were never born.

Some consider the postwar social contract to be of great worth and beyond question. Will the reforms envisaged in our social security programs really threaten it? From a demographic point of view, a mixture of PAYG and funded schemes may prove to be a solution that may save social cohesion against individualism.

For this to be the case, it may be a good strategy to rely on generational accounting, even if it has to be based on a very long-term longitudinal perspective. Any reform should try to measure the implications of its new rules for intergenerational equity. We have certainly benefited from the gender revolution during the second half of the 20th century, but we must definitively avoid an old-age crisis as we move into the 21st century.

● ●

CRITICAL THINKING QUESTIONS

1. What do current population projections suggest in terms of the future age structure of Canadian society? In considering these trends, do you think we are facing an aging crisis?
2. What is meant by PAYG (pay-as-you-go) pensions and health care schemes? Why should this be considered problematic in a context of population aging?
3. Envisage a Canada whereby one in four people are over the age of 65. How do you think Canadian society might differ? How do you think that population aging might have a bearing on your own life course?

● ●

CHAPTER 16

GEOGRAPHIC DIMENSIONS OF AGING IN CANADA, 1991–2001

Eric G. Moore and Michael A. Pacey

● ●

INTRODUCTION

The rapid increase in population aging in Canada, triggered by the end of the baby boom in the 1960s, continued with little abatement throughout the 1990s. As the overall rate of population growth declined, fertility remained below replacement level and life expectancy continued to improve, with immigration providing the primary mechanism for even modest growth. The result was that the population aged 65 and over (and even more markedly the population aged 80 and over) continued to grow at a faster rate than the rest of the population. From 1996 to 2001, while total population growth fell to 0.9 percent a year, the population aged 65 and over continued to grow at 1.8 percent a year and the population aged 80 and over grew at 3.5 percent a year. By 2001, 12.6 percent of Canada's population were 65 and over and 3.1 percent were 80 and over.

While the major focus in the policy literature continues to be on the macro-level effects of increasing proportions of older people at the national level, particularly in regard to implications for health care, pensions, and social security, attention is also being given to the geographical consequences of aging (Moore and McGuinness, 1999; Moore, Rosenberg, and McGuinness, 1997; Rogers, 1992). The distribution of older adults in both absolute and relative terms is far from even, with the result that jurisdictions at all levels of government face different demands for local goods and services by seniors in different places. In this paper, we extend earlier work on the aging of the Canadian population during the 1980s and early 1990s (Moore and McGuinness, 1999; Moore, McGuinness, Pacey, and Rosenberg, 2000) to include the most recent population estimates (for 2001) for provinces and large census metropolitan areas (CMAs).

Population aging refers specifically to the relative size and attributes of those aged 65 and over in the population as a whole. While trends in population aging clearly reflect temporal shifts in the experiences of older individuals, they are sensitive to changes in all segments of the population, young and old. Conventional wisdom has focused on the age of 65 as the significant dividing line between *young* and *old*, largely because of its traditional and

227

institutionalized links to separation from the labour force and the initiation of a range of social benefits. The proportion of the population aged 65 and over is the most common measure of population aging (McDaniel, 1986; Rogerson, 1996) and it is extensively used in this chapter. However, there is no necessary transition in the life of an individual at that age, and it is clear that the great majority of seniors consider themselves active, healthy, and contributing to the larger society (Stone and Fletcher, 1986). The most significant changes in the likelihood of experiencing major health problems, loss of independence, and institutionalization tend to occur much later and increase sharply over the age of 80 (Moore, Rosenberg, and McGuinness, 1997:Chapter 4). However, in this chapter the analysis deals primarily with the population aged 65 and over.

The major focus of this paper is on the geographic dimensions of aging in Canada during the 1990s, with specific emphasis on changes at the provincial and metropolitan scales and the demographic processes that underlie them. Canada is an urban society, with 63 percent of the population living in the 25 largest cities in 2001. The question we address is how the proportion aged 65 and over changed in the period from 1991 to 2001 and how these changes relate to the demographic and socio-economic attributes of different jurisdictions.

There are several ways in which the proportion of the population aged 65 and over changes in any given geographical area. Given that we are concerned with the *proportion* of the population that is aged 65 and over, it is clear that this measure must be sensitive to changes in both the numerator and denominator, namely, to changes that occur to the segments of the population both who are 65 and over and who are under 65. Forces that act on each of these population segments produce changes *within* the geographical area arising from local fertility, aging, and mortality, and changes that derive from *external* flows of immigrants and out-migrants of different ages. Although there is some variation in terminology in the literature, there would appear to be a convergence on the concept of *aging in place* as referring to the processes of change that accrue from births, individual aging, and deaths within a given area and *net migration* as the summation of changes arising from external flows (Graff and Wiseman, 1978; Rogers and Raymer, 2001). Here we focus specifically on the relative roles of aging in place and net migration in population aging at different scales. Scale plays an important role in understanding population aging. As an example, a large urban area may be surrounded by smaller communities, all of which have significant net migration to the urban core. At the larger, regional scale, however, these net migrations are subsumed into the aging-in-place component of the region. It follows that the relative importance of net migration for population aging tends to be greater for smaller areas.

In this chapter, we utilize the accounting framework in Moore and McGuinness (1999), which is built on earlier work by McCarthy (1983) and Rogerson (1996). Not only are the demographic accounts of interest, but the parameters of these accounts reflect underlying changes in the characteristics of regions and communities. In particular, communities with more active and growing local economies are particularly attractive to younger migrants, while those communities with declining economic opportunities are likely to see younger populations depart at a faster rate than older individuals. Sustained over longer periods of time, these processes produce shifts in the age structure of local communities and, as established in earlier work (Moore, Rosenberg, and McGuinness, 1997), both the structure and the processes of population aging are intimately linked to the economic geography of the national landscape.

The formal accounting of the processes of population aging is developed in Moore and McGuinness (1999). The components of aging were derived in Moore and McGuinness (1999) for Canada at the provincial and local (county) level for 1986 to 1991. In this chapter, the corresponding components are constructed for 1991 to 1996 and 1996 to 2001. The aging profiles are constructed for provinces and census metropolitan areas (CMAs) and the relations between the structure and processes of aging at the CMA level, on the one hand, and their socio-economic characteristics, on the other, are assessed for both five-year periods.

POPULATION AGING IN CANADA

Geographical differences are played out within the framework of the national experience. Social values with respect to fertility and reproduction, advances in medical knowledge influencing mortality and morbidity, and controls over immigration are common factors that influence population aging across the country; geographic differences arise within this larger context and are particularly sensitive to patterns of interregional migration and regional variations in attractiveness to immigrants.

Canada's population has experienced one of the largest growth rates in the developed world since the end of World War II fuelled by the *baby boom*, which lasted from the late 1940s to the early 1960s (Romaniuc, 1994). The total population was 14.0 million in 1951 and reached 31.1 million in 2001. The peak growth rate reached 2.8 percent a year during the height of the baby boom between 1951 and 1956 and declined steadily until the early 1980s, when it fell to just under 1.0 percent a year. However, with a marked increase in immigration levels and the stemming of the free fall in fertility rates at the end of the 1980s, the growth rate for 1986 to 1991 increased again to 1.5 percent a year. From 1991 to 1996, with rates of immigration declining slightly and fertility relatively constant, the growth rate settled back to 1.1 percent; it fell to 0.9 percent a year in the second half of the 1990s.

As in all other developed countries experiencing declining fertility and mortality, the older population is growing at a considerably faster rate than the total population. In 1951, the population aged 65 years and over totalled 1.4 million and constituted 8.0 percent of the total population. Of the population aged 65 years and over, 149,000 were 80 years of age and over and comprised 1.1 percent of the population. By 2001, the population aged 65 years and over had reached 3.9 million or 12.6 percent of the total population and the population aged 80 and over had grown more than sixfold to 954,000 or 3.1 percent of the population. The population aged 65 and over had sustained a growth rate of over 3 percent a year for the entire 45 years, while for those aged 80 and over, it was close to 4 percent a year. Not only has the Canadian population been aging steadily, but the internal composition of the group of older people conventionally defined as those *aged 65 and over* has itself changed and contains a progressively higher proportion of *very old* individuals (i.e., 80 and over), with a range of important consequences for public policy.

At the national level, the proportion of the population who are seniors has increased steadily for both women and men since 1951 (Figure 16.1). The basic measure of change in population aging between two Censuses is the ratio of the percentage aged 65 and over in each Census, a measure that we call C65, which essentially measures the rate of population aging between Censuses. If C65 is greater than 1, population aging is increasing, and if it is less than 1, population aging is decreasing. The rate of population aging has slowed in the last decade, as is shown more dramatically in the series for C65 at the national level (Figure 16.2). The peak rate of growth of the proportion 65 and over was in the latter half of the 1970s. The rate of increase was slower in the 1980s and dropped quite markedly in the first half of the 1990s. This drop reflects the larger demographic trend of changing fertility over the years; those becoming 65 during the 1990s are from the smaller birth cohorts of the late 1920s and the Depression years of the1930s. The relative sizes of birth cohorts provide a major driving force behind population aging. Figure 16.3 shows the relative sizes of successive five-year age groups at the time of the 1996 Census and the date at which these relative sizes would affect the rate at which people turn 65. It indicates the impact of the arrival of the baby boom cohorts after 2010 and the sharp decline in pressures on aging between 2020 and 2030. Immigration will have only a small effect on the timing of these demographic impacts on population aging (Mitra, 1992), since immigrants themselves become the seniors of the future.

GEOGRAPHIC DIMENSIONS OF POPULATION AGING IN CANADA, 1991 TO 2001

The national picture embraces a great deal of geographical diversity in both the distribution and the rates of growth of the population aged 65 and over. The underpinnings

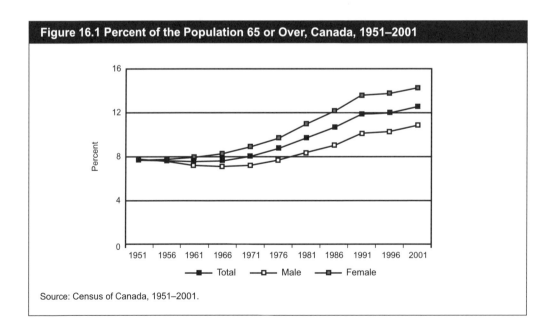

Figure 16.1 Percent of the Population 65 or Over, Canada, 1951–2001

Source: Census of Canada, 1951–2001.

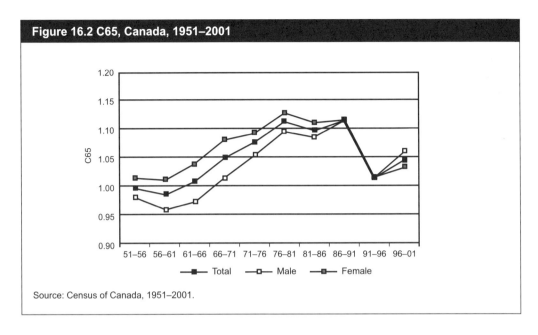

Figure 16.2 C65, Canada, 1951–2001

Source: Census of Canada, 1951–2001.

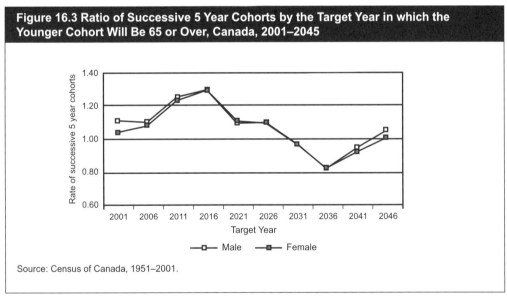

Figure 16.3 Ratio of Successive 5 Year Cohorts by the Target Year in which the Younger Cohort Will Be 65 or Over, Canada, 2001–2045

Source: Census of Canada, 1951–2001.

of the differences lie primarily in regional disparities in both economic opportunity and access to amenities, which generate migration flows that are strongly age-selective (Rogers, 1992; Shaw, 1985). The foundations of migration decision making in human capital investment imply much higher propensities to migrate among younger adults and, therefore, in general, significant out-migration for the population as a whole will be associated with increases in the rate of population aging, while substantial in-migration has the opposite effect. There is a secondary effect that receives little attention, and that is the impact of migration decisions on fertility; often the decision by females to pursue tertiary education or to join the labour force elsewhere is also a decision to forego earlier marriage and child-bearing (Moore, 1993). Spatially, these decisions are particularly important in increasing fertility in rural areas and small towns, with a small effect in reducing the rate of population aging, although this effect is offset by the much larger migration effects associated with young people leaving rural areas. However, the relative size and importance of these effects varies considerably from region to region, as both age and sex profiles of local populations and the impacts of local social and economic conditions on the decision to move or stay differ from place to place.

CHANGE IN POPULATION AGING AT THE PROVINCIAL LEVEL

For any set of sub-national regions, such as provinces or metropolitan areas, not only does the degree of population aging vary considerably between areas but the relative importance of different components of change also tends to shift. Because, for any origin population, the likelihood of migrating declines strongly with distance, it follows that the smaller the region, the greater the potential role to be played by migration. Thus, interprovincial migration plays a role in changing provincial population distributions, while that role is magnified for the smaller entities, both provinces and metropolitan areas.

Table 16.1 Percent of Population Aged 65 and Over by Province, 1991–2001

Province	1991	1996	2001	% Increase in Proportion over 65
Newfoundland	9.6	10.7	11.8	23.0
Prince Edward Island	13.1	12.9	13.3	1.3
Nova Scotia	12.5	12.9	13.4	7.0
New Brunswick	12.0	12.5	13.0	8.4
Quebec	11.1	12.0	13.0	17.1
Ontario	11.6	12.2	12.6	8.7
Manitoba	13.3	13.5	13.5	1.6
Saskatchewan	14.1	14.5	14.6	3.5
Alberta	9.0	9.8	10.2	13.0
British Columbia	12.7	12.5	13.2	3.9
Yukon Territory	3.8	4.4	5.7	48.2
Northwest Territories/Nunavut	2.7	34.0	3.6	32.9
Canada	11.5	12.1	12.6	9.8

Source: Census of Canada, 1991, 1996, 2001.

Since population change is a function of births, deaths, and migration, variation in population aging in a region is attributable to long-term differences in fertility, mortality, and migration rates. Change is cumulative, so that, for any five-year intercensal period, the rate of population aging is dependent primarily on two demographic influences:

1.　the demographic structure of the area at the beginning of the period, which determines the magnitude of *aging in place* (α). Aging in place is the increase in the proportion of the population aged 65 and over that is attributable to births and age-specific deaths occurring in the population at the beginning of the period. In a given five-year period, the dominant predictors of the increase in the proportion aged 65 and over due to aging in place are: (a) the ratio of the population aged 60 to 64 to that aged 65 to 69, which represents the potential for those about to be seniors to increase that segment of the population; if the younger age group is significantly larger, it will more than offset the accumulated number of deaths in the elderly population. Figure 16.3 indicates the general pattern of variation in this ratio for the next 40 years. (b) the proportion of those aged 65 and over who are 80 and over. This variable defines the shape of the age pyramid for seniors; the smaller the ratio, the younger the population of seniors and the greater the potential for rapid increase.

2.　the impact of the demographic structure of migration into and out of the area during the five-year period, which defines the *net migration* effect (η) on population aging. The relationship between migration for those in the labour force years and that for older Canadians is complex. Younger individuals are more strongly influenced by economic opportunity, with limited job opportunities in the local economy encouraging out-migration and flourishing local economies encouraging in-migration or retention of the current population. Significant out-migration will tend to increase population aging in the originating communities, while out-migration of older individuals has the opposite effect. The converse effects are associated with in-migration. The overall effect of migration will depend on the detailed balance of in-migration and out-migration for older and younger populations. In British Columbia, for example, although the province is noted for its attractiveness as a retirement destination, the attraction for younger Canadians has been even stronger, producing a net migration effect that actually slows the rate of aging in the province (Figure 16.4). In much of the Prairies, the dominant out-migration flows from small communities have been the driving force behind the high levels of aging in this region.

In the short run, these two factors are more important than local variations in fertility and mortality rates. In the longer run, however, sustained differences in regional fertility and mortality would produce differences in the aging experience. Higher mortality rates or higher fertility rates would tend to slow the aging process. It is also worth noting that, over longer periods of time, it is necessary to take into account the fertility, mortality, and subsequent migration experience of the migrants themselves (Rogers, 1995), which have

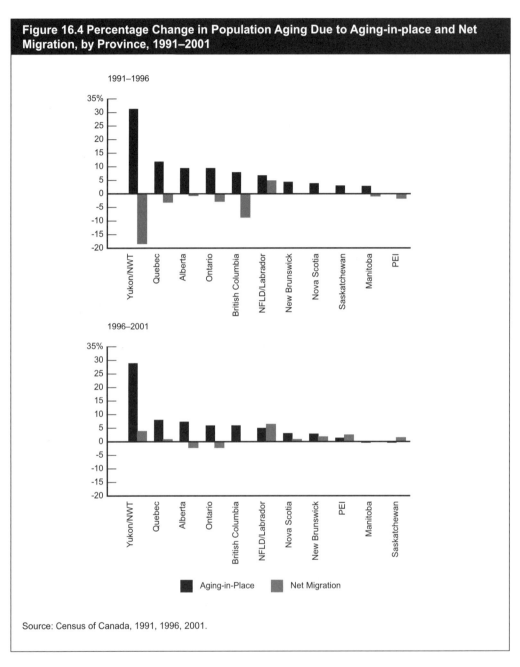

Figure 16.4 Percentage Change in Population Aging Due to Aging-in-place and Net Migration, by Province, 1991–2001

Source: Census of Canada, 1991, 1996, 2001.

the potential to change the rate at which local populations age. However, in a five-year period, the marginal effect of these differences is small.

The cumulative nature of population aging means that the demographic characteristics of an area at the beginning of an intercensal period reflect a complex history of prior fertility, mortality, and migration experience and may not necessarily be explained by any recent set of events or by current community characteristics. In large part, mortality and fertility effects are macro-scale influences that permeate every part of the country. However, there are also systematic demographic processes that have persisted for many decades, which produce geographic variations in the distribution of those aged 65 and over. The history of migration within Canada, as in other countries, has seen young adults moving from areas with limited economic opportunity to places where job prospects are more enticing. In general, these have been moves from rural and small town Canada to bigger towns and cities, and they have occurred at consistently higher rates than for older cohorts, whose established social networks and higher job security are associated with significantly lower propensities to migrate (Northcott, 1988). A prime consequence of this process has been that many parts of rural Canada, particularly in the Prairies and the Atlantic provinces, have experienced significant population aging as the older members of the community remain while the younger ones depart. In the most recent periods (1991–2001), we would still expect that those communities with the most buoyant local economies would continue to attract young in-migrants and experience slower rates of aging.

More recently, the increasing affluence of segments of the older population, many of whom have significant financial resources at retirement, has led to a greater emphasis on living in or moving to high-amenity areas, particularly those with moderate as opposed to harsh winters (Northcott, 1988; Serow, 1987). Again, however, selective migration by one group leads to the concentration of others who are less mobile; in this case, the less affluent older population tends to become concentrated in more disadvantaged origin areas. Finally, as a counter to this flow to higher amenities, the phenomenon of return migration (Newbold, 1993) to gain advantages from proximity to family and to other services would suggest that net flows by older people to less economically and climatically privileged areas will increase and lead to more rapid increases in the population aged 80 and over in many of these areas.

AGING AT THE PROVINCIAL LEVEL

In 2001, the variation in the proportion of the population aged 65 and over at the provincial level was substantial (Table 16.1). The Northwest Territories and the Yukon had less than 4 percent of the population in this category, while in Alberta, 10.2 percent of the population were seniors. Saskatchewan lies at the other end of the spectrum, at 14.6 percent. Although all provinces experienced an increase in the proportion aged 65 and over during the 1990s, there was much variation. The Territories had the largest increases, followed by Newfoundland, Quebec, and Alberta, while Prince Edward Island and Manitoba saw an increase of less than 2 percent in the proportion aged 65 and over.

The differentials tend to reflect the long-term patterns of age-selective migration away from rural and primary resource areas in the Atlantic provinces and the Prairies and toward the regions of economic growth in central Canada and the West. Alberta, in particular, benefited from a substantial in-migration of younger people in the 1970s and this was reflected in both low proportions and low rates of growth of the population aged 65 and over in the 1970s. The trend in the 1980s and early 1990s, however, was for a slow convergence in the interprovincial proportions. The higher rates of aging tended to be in those provinces with the lower proportions of seniors (Quebec, Newfoundland, and Alberta), which highlights the importance of the overall aging of larger pre-65 cohorts.

Return migration (Newbold, 1993) is more likely to occur at higher ages, particularly in those provinces that have been the origin of strong out-migration streams by adults during the labour force years. Superimposed on the return migration flows are the movements of retirees to high-amenity regions, with British Columbia, Ontario, and Prince Edward Island being the primary recipients. The net result is that migration produces differential aging effects across the nation, with the Atlantic provinces and British Columbia being the prime recipients of relative gains in older adults from these moves.

Table 16.2 Percent of Population Aged 65 and Over by CMA, 1991–2001

Province	1991	1996	2001	% Increase in Proportion over 65
Chicoutimi	9.0	10.7	12.7	40.7
Sudbury	10.3	11.6	13.5	31.3
Trois Rivières	11.7	13.1	15.1	29.0
Edmonton	8.4	9.6	10.5	24.3
Québec	10.6	11.6	12.8	21.0
Oshawa	8.9	9.7	10.6	19.4
Calgary	7.7	8.6	8.9	15.6
Thunder Bay	13.1	13.9	15.1	15.3
Montreal	11.1	11.9	12.7	13.8
St. Catharines	14.8	16.1	16.7	13.1
Ottawa-Hull	9.5	10.0	10.7	12.9
Regina	10.8	11.6	12.2	12.5
Hamilton	12.7	13.7	14.2	12.1
Halifax	9.4	10.0	10.5	11.5
Sherbrooke	11.4	12.1	12.7	11.5
Saskatoon	10.3	11.0	11.5	11.3
St. John's	9.2	9.9	10.2	10.4
Canada	**11.5**	**12.1**	**12.6**	**9.8**
Toronto	10.2	10.8	11.0	7.8
Kitchener	10.1	10.7	10.8	7.4
London	11.9	12.4	12.8	7.2
Winnipeg	12.7	13.2	13.3	4.6
Saint John	12.2	12.5	12.6	2.7
Vancouver	12.0	11.6	11.8	-2.3
Windsor	12.6	12.7	12.2	-2.6
Victoria	18.3	17.5	17.5	-4.8

Source: Census of Canada, 1991, 1996, 2001.

If we calculate, for the different provinces, net migration levels by age (aged under 65 vs. aged 65 and over) between 1991 and 2001, we see that the patterns for the younger and older ages exhibit important commonalities and differences (Table 16.3). During the first half of the decade, higher in-migration among younger populations in British Columbia and Ontario reduced the rate of aging, even if these regions were also attractive to older migrants. In Quebec, continued out-migration of older individuals, coupled with a net in-migration of younger people, produced additional slowing in the rate of population aging. Many of the rest of the provinces experienced small net outflows of younger individuals. In the period from 1996 to 2001, however, significant changes occurred, the most dramatic being large declines in the net in-migration of younger people to British Columbia and Quebec, together with a shift in the net flows of those aged 65 and over to Quebec from negative to positive. Ontario and Alberta retained their attractiveness for younger individuals, while the rest of the provincial flows were similar to those of the earlier five-year period.

The relative roles of aging in place and net migration changed somewhat between the two five-year periods. From 1991 to 1996, aging in place was the dominant force in most provinces (Figure 16.4). Only in Prince Edward Island and British Columbia did net migration have a larger effect on aging. In British Columbia, the large influx of younger individuals, including immigrants, more than offset both the arrival of older individuals and the aging of the population already residing in the province in 1991. In six provinces, especially in the West, net migration served to ameliorate the rate of aging. However, in the latter half of the decade, patterns shifted, and only two provinces—Ontario and Alberta (the two thriving regional economies)—experienced migration where the net effects

Table 16.3 Estimated Net Migration by Age and Province, 1991–2001

Province	1991–1996		1996–2001	
	n<65[a]	n≥65[b]	n<65[a]	n≥65[b]
Newfoundland	-26,052	-17	-32,734	-55
PEI	4,321	267	650	541
Nova Scotia	8,497	1,184	4,079	2,071
New Brunswick	-8,098	-619	-12,226	356
Quebec	99,906	-18,401	1,085	13,183
Ontario	418,021	10,903	515,167	33,180
Manitoba	-7	-1,076	-11,750	-149
Saskatchewan	-3,991	-554	-25.021	-1,438
Alberta	84,192	6,939	172,688	12,431
British Columbia	413,578	13,379	118,746	17,917
Yukon/NWT/Nunavut	-1,866	-340	-13,664	-397

[a] Net migration for population under 65.
[b] Net migrtaion for population aged 65 and over.
Source: Census of Canada, 1991, 1996, 2001 (calculation by author).

reduced the rate of aging. Most dramatic was the change in status of British Columbia, with the net effects of migration virtually eliminated. As indicated above, this reflects a change in the structure of migration, with very significant declines in the migration of younger people to the flagging economic environment of the West Coast. It shows, quite markedly, how shifting economic fortunes have rapid effects on population aging, with their own set of consequences for a broad range of services.

AGING AT THE CENSUS METROPOLITAN AREA (CMA) LEVEL

The percentages of the population aged 65 and over at the metropolitan level were as variable as those at the provincial level (Table 16.2). There are a number of different patterns that emerge. In a majority of cities (17 out of 25) the proportion of the population aged 65 and over increased at a faster rate than in the country as a whole. Those with the highest rates of increase tended to reflect two different scenarios: (a) cities such as Chicoutimi, Sudbury, and Thunder Bay, which are older industrial and resource-based towns with struggling economies; and (b) cities such as Calgary, Edmonton, and Oshawa, where aging was more a function of having small older populations to begin with, so that the aging of the 60-to-64 cohort produced high internal aging. The reverse of this situation occurred for cities experiencing low increases in the proportion aged 65 and over. Toronto and Vancouver are dynamic environments, with high levels of immigration that ameliorated aging, although the immigration of younger people to Vancouver declined sharply after 1996. In contrast, Victoria and, to a lesser degree, Winnipeg, had relatively high proportions of seniors in 1991 and regressed somewhat toward the national mean by 2001.

The net flows for younger and older individuals were dominated by the experience of Toronto and Vancouver, although, as might be expected from the provincial analysis, there was a significant decline in the attractiveness of Vancouver to younger people in the latter part of the decade (Table 16.4). Montreal also declined in its ability to attract those under age 65, while both Calgary and Edmonton increased their numbers substantially. The central Canadian cities—Regina, Saskatoon, Winnipeg, Sudbury, and Thunder Bay—had all experienced losses among the younger population by the latter part of the 1990s. The pattern of net migration of those aged 65 and over remained fairly stable for almost all cities during the 1990s, although Montreal lost population in this older group after 1996.

Aging in place was still the dominant influence on population aging in cities for both five-year periods (Figure 16.5). In most cities, the period 1991 to 1996 saw net migration ameliorating population aging, with the effect being particularly strong in Vancouver, Toronto, and Windsor. Net migration only tended to increase aging in the central Canadian and Atlantic cities. In the second half of the decade, significantly more cities experienced increases in population aging from net migration, largely due to out-migration of younger people. This phenomenon was particularly dramatic in Chicoutimi, Trois Rivières, Sudbury, and Thunder Bay. Regina, Saskatoon, and Winnipeg also illustrated this pattern. Oshawa experienced a similar situation, although the increase was produced by a net influx of older individuals rather than a loss of those under age 65. The ameliorating effects of net migration were confined to Calgary, Toronto, Vancouver, and Windsor.

Table 16.4 Estimated Net Migration by Age and Metropolitan Area, 1991–2001

Metropolitan Area	1991–1996		1996–2001	
	n<65[a]	n≥65[b]	n<65[a]	n≥65[b]
Calgary	52,169	3,116	89,378	5,135
Chicoutimi	-3,899	-331	-7,408	311
Edmonton	-314	2,023	39,957	5,151
Halifax	5,865	736	8,620	1,397
Hamilton	11,715	925	19,605	3,670
Kitchener	12,912	1,131	18,998	1,486
London	7,139	480	2,718	1,558
Montreal	83,763	-9,832	39,982	6,011
Oshawa	15,256	1,438	9,489	2,904
Ottawa-Hull	42,723	1,010	34,313	5,123
Quebec	21,336	345	-1,062	3,463
Regina	-30	161	-6,011	-115
St. Catharines	1,567	1,074	3,350	2,313
St. John's	-4,550	214	-4,309	-370
Saint John	-4,316	-484	-3,608	-335
Saskatoon	3,911	1,283	-3,325	457
Sherbrooke	4,094	670	1,292	848
Sudbury	-51	-541	-11,945	-55
Thunder Bay	-1,032	-366	-6,927	365
Toronto	290,182	7,070	332,931	11,923
Trois Rivières	2,851	148	-3,035	1,240
Vancouver	243,754	5,573	131,087	7,581
Victoria	24,069	1,444	3,195	2,383
Windsor	12,942	-874	18,190	-239
Winnipeg	-1,183	-444	-36.611	-33

[a] Net migration for population under 65.
[b] Net migrtaion for population aged 65 and over.
Source: Census of Canada, 1991, 1996, 2001 (calculation by author).

Existing knowledge of the processes of population aging suggests that the global aging produced by shifts in fertility and mortality across the country are geographically differentiated by a complex web of additional social, economic, and demographic variables. The dominant message, however, is that we would expect to find a strong association at the community level between population aging and local economic conditions. Communities with limited job opportunities, lower incomes, and higher unemployment are likely to experience greater growth in proportion of older individuals in the population than more prosperous areas. The situation in Canada, in examining the socio-economic context of migration, is largely consistent with these observations.

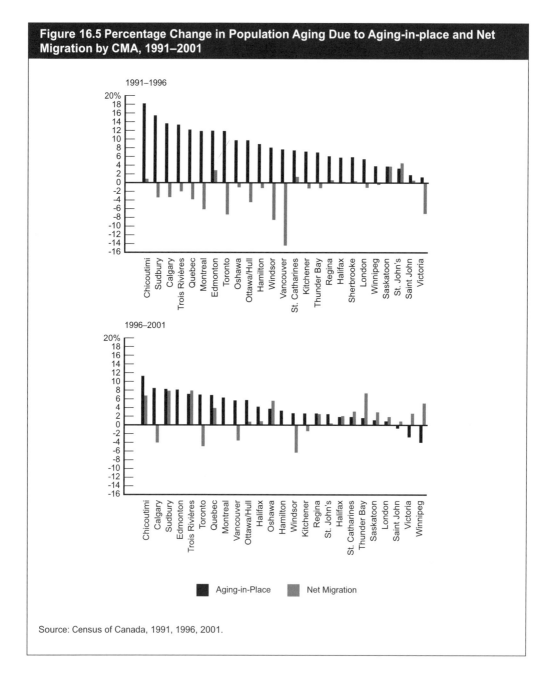

Figure 16.5 Percentage Change in Population Aging Due to Aging-in-place and Net Migration by CMA, 1991–2001

Source: Census of Canada, 1991, 1996, 2001.

CONCLUSION

The primary intent of the research reported here has been to underscore the complexity of the process of population aging at different scales. Population aging is a function of two elements: aging in place and net migration. As Morrison (1992) noted, aging in place is a critical component of aging in most communities, so the existing population structure is important to future patterns of change. Aging in place also increases in relative importance with average age of the older population. This means that future growth at the local level of the population aged 80 and over is significantly determined by the distribution of the population aged 65 to 79.

Net migration assumes much greater importance as a factor in population aging in those areas and communities where out-migration of the young is particularly dramatic. Manitoba, Saskatchewan, and the Atlantic provinces have long been the sources of much out-migration among the younger, working-age population, and this has had a consistent impact on accelerated rates of aging in those areas. Return migration of older persons to the Atlantic provinces and the eastern Prairies also increases population aging. The obverse of this situation is reflected in the strong inflows of younger migrants to Ontario and British Columbia, inflows that have had consistent ameliorating effects on population aging. Although migration decisions by both younger and older people are influenced by similar factors and both groups tend to be attracted to the same destinations, with British Columbia's dynamic economy and milder climate proving universally attractive, the net effects of migration are very different. In those areas with significant out-migration of the younger population, the rate of population aging in the community tends to increase greatly, while the obverse is true in areas with strong flows of in-migrants in the labour force years. These provincial differences are reflected in the experiences of the major cities, with Toronto and other cities in southern Ontario, Vancouver, Calgary, and Edmonton gaining younger populations, while cities in the Prairies, Quebec, and the Atlantic provinces did not, although some continued to draw younger migrants from their hinterlands.

Some significant changes occurred in patterns of population aging between the first and second half of the decade. Most important was the changing role of British Columbia, in general, and Vancouver, in particular. As the British Columbia economy struggled, the attractiveness of the region to younger migrants declined. The drop in positive net migration at younger ages produced increases in population aging after 1996. The other major change was the significant increase in the net migration component of population aging for the industrial and resource-based cities of Sudbury, Thunder Bay, Chicoutimi, and Trois Rivières, an increase that stemmed from increased out-migration of younger people.

The main conclusion is that, while aging in place continues to be the strongest force in population aging, changes in the rate of population aging are very much a function of the economic conditions that underlie differential growth in local economies. Those communities with higher incomes and the most rapid employment growth attract large numbers of people in the labour force years, while elevated housing costs are a deterrent to older migrants. The consequence is that population aging tends to occur in communities with fewer economic advantages. Because of these net migration effects, sudden shifts in regional economic performance produce noticeable changes in patterns of population aging.

From a public policy viewpoint, the changing geography of aging should be viewed as a national as much as a regional or local issue. Given the significant service demands of seniors, particularly in the areas of health care and social services, the changes in population aging generated by shifts in economic performance have widespread implications. For example, the growth in employment in Alberta not only means a larger labour force in relation to non-working populations, with important tax revenue and consumer spending implications in that province, but it also means an increase in the proportion of seniors in the populations of those provinces that have a net out-migration of younger people to Alberta. Similar arguments apply within provinces as net flows to larger cities produce corresponding increases in the rates of aging in smaller communities. Without serious attempts by central governments to address disparities among areas, the risk is enhanced that the landscape of *have* and *have-not* communities will become even more pronounced.

● ●

CRITICAL THINKING QUESTIONS

1. It is an oversimplification to think that the national age structure is one and the same as what is observed provincially and/or locally. Why is this the case?
2. Why is there less population aging in provinces and communities with the most buoyant local economies? Provide examples.
3. From a public policy and planning viewpoint, the geography of aging in Canada is an important consideration for all levels of government. How does this play out in the Canadian context?

● ●

CHAPTER 17

MISCONCEPTIONS AND MISAPPREHENSIONS ABOUT POPULATION AGING

Ellen M. Gee

● ●

THE LAST DECADE HAS SEEN the emergence of neo-liberal policies and agendas, and a parallel dismantling of the public provision of health and social services and programs in most Western countries. This neo-liberalism represents an endorsement of, or at the very least an accommodation to, the primacy of the individual and his/her efforts to ensure his/her own well-being, and a corresponding de-emphasis of conceptualizations of, and commitments to, shared risk, rights of citizenship, and the common good. Population aging has played a fundamental role in this transition; the public costs of population aging—particularly regarding health care and pensions—are purported to be unsustainable without considerable welfare state "reform." Reform is, of course, a process, and it has taken differing shapes in various Western countries. I focus on North America, and particularly Canada, examining the links between reform and (mis)perceptions about population aging, concentrating on the latter.

In the last few years, three monographs highlighting the fallacies of current, taken-for-granted understandings of population aging have appeared: *Demography Is Not Destiny* (National Academy on an Aging Society, 1999), published in the U.S.; the Canadian-based *The Overselling of Population Aging: Apocalyptic Demography, Intergenerational Challenges, and Social Policy* (Gee and Gutman, 2000), and *The Imaginary Time Bomb: Why an Aging Population Is Not a Social Problem* (Mullan, 2000) from the U.K. These monographs were preceded by a few journal articles with the same theme (Barer et al., 1995; Denton et al. 1998; McDaniel, 1987; Northcott, 1994; Robertson, 1997). While the still dim voices of these demographers and gerontologists are beginning to be heard, more people have to pay attention.

This chapter seeks to deconstruct the misperception that population aging is necessarily the social crisis/social problem that it is commonly believed to be; this will be done by illuminating untested and sometimes clearly wrong assumptions. This misperception contains (at least) four interrelated components that will be dealt with separately for the purposes of analysis.

DIMENSIONS OF "POPULATION AGING AS CRISIS" THINKING

As a preface, it is useful to recognize the historical precedence for demographic scapegoating in the 20th century, i.e., the blaming of social ills/problems on demographic phenomena. As I have discussed elsewhere (Gee, 2000), two examples provide evidence of earlier demographic alarmism. One example is the eugenics movement that focused on reproductive control as a way to preserve and improve the White race. In Canada, attempts were made to lower the fertility of non-Whites and less socially desirable Whites (eastern Europeans, for the most part) in the early part of the 20th century; the most egregious being the forced sterilization of people deemed to be "unfit," a highly disproportionate number of whom were of Aboriginal origins (McLaren, 1990). Coupled with negative views about the higher fertility of the non-Anglo-origin population were concerns about the unsuitability of immigrants of non-western European origins, concerns that culminated in the passing of the Oriental Exclusion Act in the 1920s (similar legislation was put into effect in the U.S. at the same time). Thus, as North America was wrought with the social and economic changes associated with industrialization and modernization, fertility and migration (two key demographic processes) were being used in an attempt to preserve an earlier version of society.

A second example of demographic alarmism is the formulation of the "population bomb" in the decades following World War II. While it is true that the population grew rapidly in the South at this time, it was the North that defined this growth as a "bomb"—a crisis of huge proportions. A massive infusion of Western (largely U.S.) money was put into the birth control movement, based on the simplistic notion that technology (i.e., methods of birth control) would lower the number of children that Southern women would have and on the assumption that lowered rates of population growth would stimulate economic growth. The birth control movement failed, in the sense that fertility was not significantly lowered; I remember hearing John Rockefeller—one of its major leaders—declare its failure in a very crowded and tension-filled auditorium at the 1974 World Population Meeting in Bucharest. However, when one recognizes that the U.S. political motivation behind birth control expenditures in the South was the exertion of Western influence on uncommitted countries of the Third World that could have been attracted to Soviet development models, the birth control movement did succeed on one level.

These examples may seem far from the topic of population aging, but they are instructive in showing that demography can be, and has been, used to reconstruct and redefine social problems in ways that fit a political agenda or, at the least, that calibrate with current and popular ideological positions. One reason for this is that demographic phenomenon and projections are viewed as having a "scientific" certainty that is not subject to question.

THE (UN)CERTAINTY OF DEMOGRAPHIC PROJECTIONS

Demographic crisis thinking depends on the acceptance of demographic projections. While no one is challenging that Western (and other) populations are aging (i.e., that the proportion of their populations aged 65 and over is increasing), demographic projections about the numbers and percentages of future elderly are based on assumptions about fertility, mortality, and net migration levels in the future. Assumptions are only assumptions, and many times in the past the assumptions built into demographic projections have proven to be off the mark. Similarly, there are uncertainties about future levels of mortality, fertility, and net migration. Mortality may not improve as much as projections assume based on: trends in new and emerging diseases (e.g., HIV/AIDS), re-emerging infectious diseases (e.g., a few decades ago, we thought that smallpox had been eradicated, and that tuberculosis had been eliminated, at least in the West), and now we face the real possibility of bioterrorism, as attested by the anthrax deaths in the U.S. in the months after the September 11 assault; the appearance of more and more antibiotic-resistant bacterial strains and the possibility that changes in the natural environment (even slight changes in temperature caused by, say, air pollution) can alter the relationships among microbes, hosts, and intermediate vectors, setting the stage for the development of new microbes or for an unexpected epidemic. On the other side of the coin, advances in genetic engineering/molecular biology may lead to significant improvements in mortality (Schwartz, 1998).

Future fertility levels are especially hard to predict, since fertility is subject to a complex interaction of forces. Projections tend to assume that fertility in the West will stay fairly close to its current low levels; however, any number of changes could alter fertility. For example, the introduction of truly family-friendly policies in the workplace, changes in laws affecting access to abortion, and a trend toward nationalism/patriotism—more likely after September 11—could significantly increase fertility. Given that fertility is the major determinant of age structure, any substantial increase would delay population aging. Since net migration does not play a large role in determining national age structures, changes in assumptions about it have a lesser impact. However, if political exigencies result in the West having to absorb large numbers of refugees, the effect would be to "young" the population. Although much less likely, if huge numbers of Western youth moved to the South, the effect would be to accelerate population aging in the West.

Since population projections are dependent on the assumptions upon which they are based, three projections—termed high, medium, and low variants—are usually calculated by demographers. For example, projections of the size of the American population aged 65 and over in 2040 range from 92 million (high variant) to 59 million (low variant)—a difference of 33 million people. Similarly, projections for the size of the U.S. population aged 85 and over in 2040 range from 20.9 (high variant) to 8.3 (low variant) million people (National Academy on an Aging Society, 1999). However, these substantial differences are rarely reported, and we are led to believe that there is real certainty about how many older people there will be in the future.

Even using medium variant assumptions, different agencies can produce quite different projections. To provide an example, the U.S. Bureau of the Census estimates the population aged 65 and over in 2030 to be 69.3 million while the Urban Institute's projected figure is 64.3 million. This approximate 5 million discrepancy may not seem very big, but it translates into a difference of $76 billion in Social Security benefits (in 1998 dollars) (National Academy on an Aging Society, 1999).

RELIANCE ON DEPENDENCY RATIOS

Apocalyptic thinking about population aging depends on, perhaps more than anything else, the acceptance of dependency ratios as meaningful measures of the economic and social impact of aging. Dependency ratios measure the ratio of people in so-called dependent ages (arbitrarily defined as 0–15 or 0–18 or 0–20 and ages 65 and over) to people in the working ages of 15 (or 18 or 20) to 64. These dependent age groups can be separated to construct a youth dependency ratio and an aged dependency ratio, with their sum equaling the total dependency ratio. Crisis thinkers focus on the aged dependency ratio, and see a substantial increase over the past decades, and an even greater increase in the decades to come, especially in countries that experienced a significant post-World War II baby boom (such as Canada, the U.S., and Australia/New Zealand). However, it is important to look at youth and total dependency ratios, and not fixate on the aged dependency ratio only. This is necessary because the youth and aged dependency ratios have counterbalancing effects on the total dependency ratio.

Canada provides a particularly good example of these counterbalancing effects. In 1951, the total dependency ratio in Canada was 0.83 (i.e., there were 83 dependants—old and young people—for every 100 people in the working ages (Denton et al., 1998). In 2041, it is expected to be 0.82 (subject to the provisos of projections). This basically unchanged situation is caused by a large increase in the aged dependency ratio (from 0.14 to 0.46) accompanied by a large decrease in the youth dependency ratio (from 0.69 to 0.36). It is also interesting to note that now (2001)—at approximate midpoint between 1951 and 2041—the overall dependency ratio is at an historical low point (0.62). This knowledge makes it difficult to accept the commonplace view that many of the social problems of the day (such as government debt and deficit, a crumbling health care system) are due to changes in the Canadian age structure, and population aging in particular.

Some may argue that it is misleading to equate youth and aged dependency, seeing as the elderly are bigger users of social programs. This point has some validity, given that pensions and health care comprise the largest portion of the social envelope. It has been estimated that public expenditures are approximately two to three times higher for the aged than for the young (Clark and Spengler, 1980; Foot, 1989). However, it is also important to remember that transfers are both public and private; as researchers, we tend to focus on public transfers only, often because of data availability (McDaniel, 1997). Denton et al. (1998), in one of the first attempts to estimate the relative social (public and private) costs of the young and old, conclude that the total social costs of the elderly would have to be three times higher than for the young in order for Canada's future overall dependency to be higher than what the country has already experienced. Seeing that public costs are two to three times higher for the elderly and that the elderly make economic and social contributions that are not counted in public transfer calculations, it does not appear that Canada faces much of a dependency problem due to population aging.

I have used dependency ratios to counter "population aging as crisis" thinking, because they are the arithmetic tool commonly used to illustrate/forecast the upcoming aging predicament—in other words, to fight fire with fire. However, dependency ratios themselves are problematic for a number of reasons. First, they make the arbitrary assumption that people below and above a certain age are dependants. There are many in the so-called dependent age groups who are not dependent, such as people who engage in paid labour after the age of 65—a percentage that is bound to increase as mandatory retirement at 65 legislation/policy begins to fall by the wayside. Similarly, there are people in the "working ages" who are dependent for various reasons. (As an aside, the disability movement may end up moving some of these people into waged labour, which would soften the impact of population aging.) Second, dependency ratios do not count unwaged labour, and it is well established that older women do a significant amount of caregiving for their spouses (as do elderly men, but this is statistically rarer). Also, many elderly people do a considerable amount of volunteer activity (Prince and Chappell, 1994) that is similarly not factored into dependency ratios. Last, Robertson (1997) suggests that dependency ratios create a false dichotomy—between people who are dependent and those who are not—that ignores the relations of interdependence and reciprocity that make up the fabric of social life.

Conceptualizing populations in terms of dependent and independent subgroups has facilitated what is termed the intergenerational equity debate. On the one (and dominant) side are those who argue that the aged are getting more than they deserve from the public purse. Along with some academic research/writing—such as Samuel Preston's (1984) presidential address to the Population Association of America in the early 1980s and the work of economists on what is called generational accounting (Kotlikoff, 1993)—a U.S. political movement (AGE—Americans for Generational Equity) has become quite influential (Longman, 1987). By pitting age groups against one another with regard to public resources, the proponents of generational equity have been an important force in welfare reform that is based in demographic alarmism. Assisting in this process has been the tendency to homogenize people on the basis of age.

HOMOGENIZATION OF THE ELDERLY POPULATION

Too often the aged are viewed as sick and frail non-contributors to society—as users of social programs who give nothing in return. This fallacy has been alluded to above, with countering evidence of the unwaged domestic and volunteer work performed by seniors. Interestingly, this stereotype of the elderly exists side by side with another quite different one—that of older people as "greedy geezers" who are financially well off and healthy people with leisure time (especially tourists), taking advantage of social services they can afford to pay for themselves (Binstock, 1994). Neither of these stereotypes of the aged are correct; the aged are much more diverse than they allow for. While some elders are well off, the majority are not, and approximately 10 percent are poor (National Academy on an Aging Society, 1999). The poor are disproportionately likely to be unmarried (typically widowed) women (McDonald, 2000). While some of the aged are frail, more than 60 percent have no disability, and disability rates among the American elderly are decreasing steadily (Manton et al., 1997).

When thinking about the future, it is similarly important not to homogenize the elderly. It is expected that the baby boomers will be generally better off financially and healthier than today's elderly (National Academy on an Aging Society, 1999). However, we must keep in mind that the baby boomers are a diverse group now, and will continue to be in later life (Gee, 1997). Some of the social policy changes currently being implemented may increase inequality in old age. The move toward pension privatization will favour the baby boomers whom we called yuppies, but will disadvantage those without access to private pensions. In Canada, the virtual certainty of the dismantling of universal medical care will differentially affect baby boomers' access to health care based on income. In an ironic way, then, actions taken based on fear of the costs of population aging may actually operate to increase the costs of the aged in the future (and/or adversely affect people who have not been able to accumulate resources over their life course).

"COMMON SENSE": AGING AND PUBLIC HEALTH CARE COSTS

One of the major contributors to demographic crisis thinking regarding population aging is its fit with common sense notions about the elderly (as an homogenized group). For example, older people are sicker and frailer than younger people—therefore their increasing numbers and percentages will place strain on the health care system; older people rely on pensions—therefore, their increasing numbers and percentages will stress the public retirement income provision system. Here, space allows only for a consideration of aging and health care utilization. A considerable amount of research, much of it conducted by Robert Evans and his colleagues at the University of British Columbia, shows that population aging itself will account for only a small part of future health care costs and will require little, if any, increase in public expenditures for health care (Barer et al., 1987; Barer et al., 1995; Barer et al., 1998; Carrière, 2000; Evans et al., 2001). Using administrative data from the province of British Columbia for the period from the mid-1970s to the late 1990s, Evans et al. (2001) found that: acute-care hospitalization use rates fell dramatically, the result of declines in age-specific use rates; the use of physician services increased substantially, resulting from rises in age-specific use rates that are associated with increases in the number of physicians per capita and in billings per physician (especially among specialists); per capita expenditures on prescription drugs (for which there is comprehensive coverage for only certain categories of people in British Columbia, including all those aged 65 and over) rose far faster (over the period since 1985, the only data available) than would be projected on the basis of changes in the age structure, even if one focuses on the elderly population alone.

What then has led to increased health costs (that are so often assumed to be the result of an aging population)? An important component is rapidly rising costs for pharmaceuticals, the result of a combination of inflation and shifts in prescribing more expensive medications without scientific evidence of therapeutic benefit. The pharmaceutical industry is an important cost driver; one publication dedicated to this issue is the cleverly titled *Tales from the Other Drug Wars* (Barer et al., 2000). Other factors include cost increases present in the pricing and rate of uptake of new technologies, and an oversupply of physicians (Evans et al., 2001). Thus, while it makes "sense" that an aging population leads to increased health care costs, the evidence—at least in terms of hospital use, physician use, and pharmaceuticals—strongly negates the importance of age structure in affecting health care costs.

SUMMARY

Misperceptions about the elderly and about population aging abound. This chapter has attempted to deconstruct these misperceptions, which are important because they play a dominant role in current and future-oriented welfare reform. To varying degrees, all Western countries are retrenching in the expectation of unsustainable costs caused by the needs of an older population. That this expectation is highly unlikely is rarely considered, perhaps because it meshes so well with neo-liberal interests. Sometimes, even evidence that population aging is not particularly influential for future public costs gets lost in the rhetoric of demographic alarmism. For example, a recent Conference Board of Canada publication estimates that public heath care costs will increase by 5.2 percent per year over the period from 2000 to 2020, of which 0.9 percent will be due to population aging; this same publication speaks of "a growing and aging population washing onto the shores of the health care system" (Conference Board of Canada, 2000). The discourse of apocalyptic demography seems to have such sway that it overrides reason at times. People seeking a future that includes a well-functioning social safety net, beware.

● ●

CRITICAL THINKING QUESTIONS

1. There are several examples of *crisis thinking* in demography or what Ellen Gee refers to as demographic scapegoating. Provide a few examples. How does this relate to the debate on population aging?
2. What is meant by the concept of *intergenerational equity* in demography, and how is this related to current demographic trends? What is the utility in placing emphasis on intergenerational equity, and how does this relate to future public policy?
3. There are some who argue that population aging is perhaps one of the most serious challenges facing Canadian society as we move into the 21st century. Would you agree with this argument? Why or why not?

● ●

Section 5

Population Composition

• •

POPULATION COMPOSITION CONCERNS THE CHARACTERISTICS of a given population, including age and sex structure, but also marital status, household and family structure, living arrangements, ethnicity, language, education, and income, among other socio-economic variables. The popular term "demographics" has been used widely by non-demographers to denote population composition, as there has been a growing appreciation of how a society's *demographics* can hold fundamental implications for individuals, families, social groups, markets, and governments alike.

Bourne and Rose's chapter on the changing face of Canada considers change in the level of social and cultural diversity in Canada (as driven by immigration), as well as fundamental transformations in family structure and living arrangements, in labour force participation, and corresponding shifts in the linkages between the sphere of work and the domestic or household sphere. As geographers, they are particularly interested in how many of these changes have been far from geographically even, with important differences across provinces, municipalities, and local areas. Canada is increasingly marked by an uneven geography of growth, as many peripheral regions of the country lag behind its major metropolitan areas, as both internal and international migrants move to places that provide economic opportunities. As a result, some parts of Canada have become remarkably diverse, as influenced by cultures and nationalities from all over the world, whereas others continue to remain relatively homogeneous.

Bourne and Rose also sketch some rather broad demographic changes that have characterized Canada in terms of family structure, conjugality, and living arrangements, all with important implications for how Canadians share and consume resources. Changes in births, marriage, divorce, and cohabitation have brought fewer children, but also a higher level of diversity in the living arrangements and family life. Again, these changes have been far from geographically even, as there are important differences across provinces and regions. Le Bourdais and Lapierre-Adamcyk pick up on this theme by documenting major differences in conjugality of Quebec relative to elsewhere in Canada (i.e., cohabitation is far more common in Quebec). As of 2001, the incidence of cohabitation in Quebec was as widespread as in Sweden, where 30 percent of couples were cohabiting. Canada outside of Quebec (at 12 percent) is closer to the broader North American pattern in this regard, as for example, 8.2 percent of couples in the United States are cohabiting. The distinct culture and language of Quebec continues to be fundamental in shaping demographic behaviour in this country.

As demographers and other social scientists are concerned with carefully documenting population composition, one should not lose sight of the fact that there are many methodological and definitional issues that can at times seriously undermine the validity and reliability of demographic measurement and analyses. In this regard, the chapter by Goldmann carefully examines ethnicity data from Canadian Censuses. There are clearly several difficulties as associated with the Census –or, for that matter, any large-scale survey interested in documenting population composition. While ethnicity, at first glance, might be thought of as a relatively fixed, ascribed characteristic to be easily measured through a Census, Goldmann demonstrates how in fact this is often far from the case. As it is people, not nature, that create our identities, the reality is such that ethnicities are largely cultural and historical constructs, and subsequently not necessarily stable in measurement. In societies like Canada, with a long history of immigration and intermarriage, racial and ethnic identities are far from stable, such that it is becoming increasing difficult to establish fixed boundaries in the delineation of ethnicity or cultural origins.

These issues of measurement and definition are briefly addressed by Maynard and Kerr in their sketch of demographic change and the Aboriginal population in Canada. Several centuries of cultural exchange, assimilation, and intermarriage make identifying what constitutes the modern Aboriginal population somewhat elusive. Measuring the demographic states and processes of the Aboriginal population has never been easy, and in certain ways has become more difficult. Aboriginal peoples are spread across Canada, living in urban and rural areas, on reserves, and in the far North.

Despite the difficulties, data from a variety of sources show clear demographic and socio-economic patterns. This includes a relatively rapid rate of population growth, particularly over recent decades. The population is considerably younger on average, as both fertility and mortality (including infant mortality) have been consistently higher than that of other Canadians. Many of the demographic characteristics and patterns of change for the Aboriginal population deviate in quite a pronounced manner from those of the Canadian population as a whole. In addition, outside of urban Canada, the Aboriginal population experiences a high level of segregation, as many live on reserves and in settlements that are relatively isolated. The Aboriginal population in Canada continues to be unique in terms of its demographic development, with important implications for cultural continuity, public policy, and socio-economic development.

The final chapter in this section, by Balakrishnan and Gyimah, returns to a theme that is common throughout many of the chapters in this book, i.e., the remarkably high level of cultural and ethnic diversity that characterizes contemporary Canada. The growing number of immigrants, and this diversity, suggests various challenges and is truly a test for Canada's multiculturalism policies. In effect, these policies set out to assist new arrivals in their acculturation to Canadian society (and in particular, in establishing themselves economically) while preserving cultural heritage and community ties. In this context, Balakrishnan and Gyimah examine patterns of residential segregation in Canada's largest cities, and how this might relate to the successful integration of new Canadians.

Various hypotheses are reviewed in examining the relevance of social class, social distance, and ethnic identity. To the extent that residential segregation of ethnic groups is a by-product of social class and/or social distance, there are rightful concerns as to the economic marginalization of selected ethnic groups and/or discrimination. On the other hand, if these patterns are a by-product of ethnic identity (i.e., people of common heritage merely preferring to live in close proximity with others of the same background), then residential segregation is not necessarily problematic, particularly as new Canadians first attempt to establish themselves in Canada. As Balakrishnan and Gyimah emphasize, as we attempt to understand the dynamics of ethnic diversity in Canada, this spatial dimension is an integral part of the overall picture.

RECOMMENDED READINGS

Driedger, Leo. (1996). *Multi-ethnic Canada: Identities and Inequalities.* Toronto: Oxford University Press. Canadian ethnicity is examined from the perspectives of identity and inequality, theories of ethnicity and change, demographic history, regionalism, class, and socio-economic status.

Fong, Eric (ed.). (2003). *Inside the Vertical Mosaic.* Toronto: University of Toronto Press. Edited collection of research on immigration and its social impact, with Toronto as a case study.

Gauthier, Anne Hélène. (1996). *The State and the Family.* Oxford: Clarendon. This book analyzes the various ways in which policy seeks to influence family behaviour and support families.

Romaniuc, Anatole. (2000). "Aboriginal Population of Canada: Growth Dynamics under Conditions of Encounter of Civilizations." *The Canadian Journal of Native Studies* 20:95–137. A very useful summary of past research and evidence on the demography of this population.

Wu, Zheng, (2000). *Cohabitation: An Alternative Form of Family Living.* Toronto: Oxford University Press. A summary of the empirical and theoretical literature on cohabitation in Canada, among other family and demographic changes.

RELATED WEB SITES

Assembly of First Nations
<http://www.afn.ca/>.
    Web site for the Assembly of First Nations, a political organization that represents registered Indians in Canada.

Canadian Council on Social Development
<http://www.ccsd.ca/>
    The Web site of the Canadian Council on Social Development, a non-profit social policy and research organization focusing on such issues as poverty and social inclusion.

Canadian Ethnic Studies Association
<http://www.ucalgary.ca/CESA/>
    The Canadian Ethnic Studies Association is an interdisciplinary organization devoted to the study of ethnicity, multiculturalism, immigration, and the cultural life of ethnic groups in Canada.

Department of Indian and Northern Affairs (INAC)
<http://www.ainc-inac.gc.ca/>
    The Department of Indian and Northern Affairs (INAC) is responsible for meeting the federal government's constitutional, treaty, political, and legal responsibilities to First Nations, Inuit, and northerners.

Heritage Canada
<http://www.pch.gc.ca/>
   The official Web site of Heritage Canada, the federal department responsible for promoting Canadian culture.

Vanier Institute of the Family
<http://www.vifamily.ca/>
   This Web site of the Vanier Institute of the Family, a national charitable organization, is dedicated to promoting the well-being of Canadian families.

CHAPTER 18

THE CHANGING FACE OF CANADA: THE UNEVEN GEOGRAPHIES OF POPULATION AND SOCIAL CHANGE

Larry S. Bourne and Demaris Rose

● ●

SETTING THE AGENDA

Viewed from a satellite, Canada represents a vast and colourful slice of territory almost 10 million square kilometres in size. At an average density of only three people per kilometre, however, much of that territory, depending on the season, is green, brown, or white, and very thinly populated. Most of the 32 million residents live on a small segment of the country (roughly 15 percent), and over 84 percent now live in cities, towns, and metropolitan areas (Figure 18.1) that combined represent only 5 percent of the country's surface area. The population face of the country obviously differs from the physical map face, and increasingly from the political face. Viewing Canada as a social entity, therefore, effectively requires the use of different lenses and spatial scales of analysis.

This chapter focuses on Canada as a social space, and specifically on changes in Canadian population characteristics and living conditions. We offer a broad-brush picture of the changing face and place of the Canadian population and the implications of those changes for individuals, social groups, and regions, as well as for markets, governments, and service providers. We review the transformations that have swept over the social fabric and landscapes of the country in the last half-century, and identify some of the key issues that flow from those transformations. We do not attempt, in the limited space available, to provide detailed information on any of these transformations, or on any specific places or groups. Instead, we seek to convey a sense of the increasing centrality of the "population question" writ large, and to provide a summary of principal trends in the character, living conditions, and social well-being of the population. The chapter concludes with a look ahead, to evolving population patterns and emerging social issues and policy problems, over the next two decades and beyond.

This chapter emphasizes several parallel themes: the combination of rapid social change with social continuity; the changing environments, especially metropolitan environments,

Figure 18.1 The Canadian Urban System

in which Canadians live and work; the "downstream" consequences of the demographic transition, population redistribution, and the increasing unevenness of growth and change; the tensions, challenges, and opportunities associated with increasing social and ethnic diversity; and the uncertainty of both future population trajectories and the macro-social geographies that emerge from these trajectories.

Few readers would question the assertion that population questions are a fundamental element in defining the future of the country and the quality of life it provides to its residents. The processes of social and demographic change set in motion after World War II are historically unique, but, of course, build on trends inherited from earlier periods. In combination, these have reshaped the country's societal structure and will continue to do so for another half-century or more. We also know that the outcomes of those processes are highly variable over space and time. They affect certain regions and localities, and certain individuals and segments of society, more profoundly than others. These outcomes, in turn, are influenced by parallel shifts in the economy and labour market conditions, in social needs and consumer preferences, in political attitudes and institutions, and in the relative distribution of wealth and power.

WAVES OF SOCIAL TRANSFORMATION

The last half of the last century has been characterized by the intersection of a series of linked and often dramatic social transformations. Four such transformations are reviewed here: first, the demographic transition and the changing components of population growth; second, changes in family structure, domestic relations, and household composition; third, immigration and the increasing level of social and cultural diversity; and fourth, shifts in the linkages between the domestic or household sphere, the sphere of work and production (e.g., local labour markets), and the changing nature of the state and civil society.

POPULATION AND SPATIAL DEMOGRAPHY

The first of these critical transformations is demographic. Although Foot and Stoffman's (1996) view that demography explains roughly three-quarters of everything is somewhat exaggerated, it is clear that demographic change is one of the key underlying dynamics reshaping the country's social system. Canada, like most other Western countries, but to an even greater extent, underwent a fundamental demographic transition in the immediate postwar period. This period, the baby boom, lasted until about 1963. It was characterized by high fertility levels (birth rates), declining death rates, earlier marriages, higher marriage rates, and increased levels of family and household formation. This period was followed (with the notable exception of Aboriginal communities) by the baby bust, a period of rapidly declining birth rates, higher divorce rates, and increased longevity that coincided with a stabilization of marriage rates and family formation.

One obvious result of this transition has been significant differences in the relative size of each generation or age cohort. The sharpest contrast is between the generation of boomers (those aged 40 to 60 in 2005), those in the older cohort (over 60), and those in the youngest cohort (aged 24 and under). As each cohort passes through the life cycle, it sends variable wave-like effects through the social order and the economy. These immense cohort size differences alter labour market dynamics, influence the demand for commodities ranging from the starter home to running shoes to the recreational vehicle, and modify the structures of need for public goods and services such as school classrooms and health services. They will also continue to shape and reshape the policy agenda for decades to come.

These demand shifts also have a direct spatial expression. For example, in the context of the increased affluence that characterized the postwar period, the parents of baby boomers led the initial explosion of the suburbs. Their children, when they reached young adulthood, fuelled the high-rise apartment boom in Canadian cities in the 1960s and early 1970s before founding their own families, typically in newer, more far-flung suburbs. Some members of both boom and bust generations, however, eschewed suburban lifestyles and contributed to the upgrading of selected parts of the inner city. Increasing numbers of empty nesters also began to move during the 1980s and 1990s, leading to a growth in the demand for low-maintenance condominium housing arrangements. Meanwhile, the echo-boom cohort provided some of the greying suburbs with a re-infusion of young families.

LIFESTYLES, FAMILIES, AND LIVING ARRANGEMENTS

The second and related transformation is reflected in the changing nature and increasing diversification of Canadian households, including the processes by which individuals choose their partners and their living arrangements, and in major shifts in the roles of women in Canadian society. In 1960, 8.9 percent of all households were non-family households. By 2000, in contrast, about one in four were non-families. Much of the increased rate of household formation noted above was due to the greater propensity of both the young and the elderly to live alone. In fact, in the second half of the 20th century, these were the two most rapidly growing types of households. Average household size has also decreased—in part as a result of lower fertility and higher divorce rates—from over four people in 1950 to about 2.8 people by the turn of the century, an overall decline of more than 30 percent.

More broadly, Canada's social fabric has become one of increasingly fluid conjugal relationships. For example, whereas only one-quarter of women aged in their sixties in 1995 had experienced relationship breakups in their lifetimes, the corresponding figure for those in their thirties was 43 percent. Almost three out of five women aged in their twenties in 1995 had lived in at least one common-law union, and couples who began their conjugal life in a common-law union were twice as likely to separate as those whose first union started with marriage (Le Bourdais et al., 2000). As couples move in and out of relationships more frequently, shared custody arrangements and blended families have become more common. These are trends that may once again increase the demand for larger family housing units and for daycare. Moreover, women's increased control over their fertility, as well as the greatly expanded labour market opportunities to which they have gained access since mid-century, have much to do with these trends. That is, women who are in a stronger economic position are less dependent on the institution of marriage (Le Bourdais et al., 2000), and as wives/partners today their direct financial contribution to the household is much greater than that of their peers in the 1950s and 1960s.

These transformations in living arrangements reflect several parallel social processes that include rising levels of affluence and improved health care, as well as changes in how we view social relationships, including family ties and gender responsibilities. Whatever the specific sources, the overall effects have already been substantial, notably on the demand for housing and services, and also (as we shall discuss below) for the changing distribution of income and well-being across household types.

SOCIAL DIVERSITY IN THE URBAN SYSTEM: IMPACTS OF IMMIGRATION AND MIGRATION

International immigration has always been the most variable component of Canada's population growth, exhibiting a strongly cyclical profile over time as government policy has responded to changes in the demand for labour, in social attitudes, and in conditions abroad (Beaujot, 1991; Beaujot and Mathews, 2000; Halli and Driedger, 1999). In the last two decades, however, the country has increasingly come to rely on immigration to ensure a supply of skilled workers and continued population growth. These pressures are likely to increase in future decades as the effects of the decline in fertility ripple through the age pyramid, and in response to emigration to the United States. Between the early 1980s and the late 1990s, annual immigration flows increased from only about 85,000 (a figure representing a dramatic dip from the high levels of most postwar years) to an average of

200,000. While even this figure falls far short in absolute numbers and even further short in relative terms of those of the early 1900s and the 1950s when Canada's population was much smaller than it is now (Figure 18.2), immigration nonetheless now accounts for well over half of population growth and over 70 percent of labour force growth in Canada (Figure 18.3).

At the same time, fundamental shifts have taken place in the sources of immigration flows to Canada. In the immediate postwar period, roughly 80 percent of all immigrants came from traditional European source countries. As these flows began to wane after the 1960s with rising prosperity in Europe, immigration and refugee policy changes increasingly opened the door to those from non-traditional source countries in Asia, Africa, the Caribbean, and Latin America. These countries were often experiencing economic and/or political upheavals. By the 1990s these regions were furnishing almost 80 percent of Canada's new immigrants, who are drawn from a wide range of social and economic backgrounds.

The changed composition of contemporary immigration flows has profound implications for the regional and urban geographies of Canada. For some regions and urban areas, where domestic net out-migration exceeds levels of natural population increase, immigration is the only source of growth, yet most parts of the country receive few immigrants. Recent flows of immigrants have become increasingly focused on a few larger metropolitan areas, including the metropolitan areas of Toronto, Vancouver, and Montreal. Although these cities have historically been "gateway cities" for immigration to Canada, the evidence available to date (from the National Immigration Data Base) suggests that a distinguishing feature of contemporary immigrants is their propensity to remain in these cities rather than fanning out to smaller urban centres and other regions as many did in the past. This is perhaps not surprising in view of changes in the country's economy, and given the well-known role of linked or chain migrations in encouraging spatial concentration as immigrants use their social networks to obtain jobs and housing. Moreover, because immigrant groups are still often defined by the established population as being "different" or "Other" in terms of their visible minority status, their religion, or their cultural traditions, it is to be expected that today's new immigrants would seek to make their homes in the most cosmopolitan and socially diverse urban regions of the country.

Is this extreme geographical concentration a transitional condition likely to diminish over time as the recent immigrant cohorts become more established? No one really knows, but indeed, the reverse may be happening. Regions of the country with lower incomes and limited employment opportunities are experiencing increased difficulties in retaining the immigrants they do receive, and those who remain tend to be poorer than those who leave. Immigrant retention rates tend to be especially low in the eastern provinces, Quebec, the Prairies, and the northern resource-based periphery. In this sense, immigrants as migrants behave much like their native-born counterparts, but with even more selectivity in their choices of destinations. Thus, immigration seems to be driving the process of a continued concentration of population in Canada's large metropolitan areas.

The regional impacts of immigration cannot, however, be assessed independently of other processes of population redistribution, notably domestic migration. As fertility

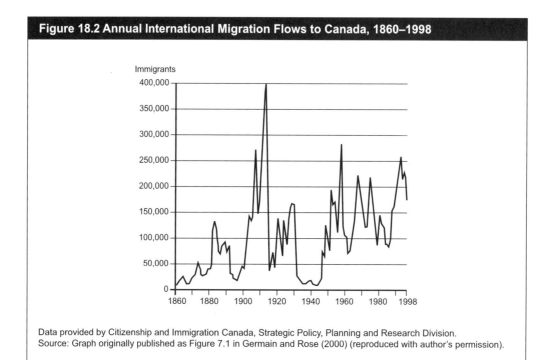

Figure 18.2 Annual International Migration Flows to Canada, 1860–1998

Data provided by Citizenship and Immigration Canada, Strategic Policy, Planning and Research Division.
Source: Graph originally published as Figure 7.1 in Germain and Rose (2000) (reproduced with author's permission).

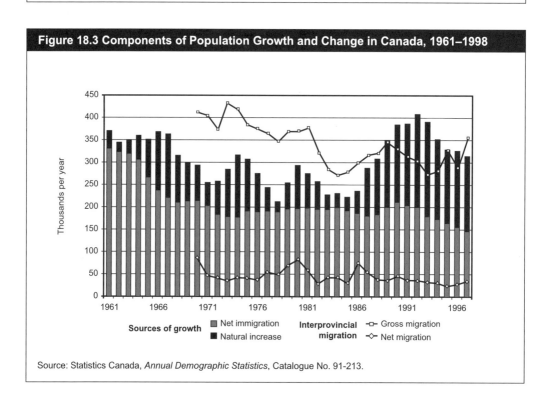

Figure 18.3 Components of Population Growth and Change in Canada, 1961–1998

Source: Statistics Canada, *Annual Demographic Statistics*, Catalogue No. 91-213.

levels have declined, and then became relatively uniform across the country, the role of redistribution processes—internal (domestic) migration and especially immigration—in accounting for differential population growth and decline, has increased. We know that internal migration, at various geographical scales, is the primary means by which the supply of labour adjusts to demand, and vice versa; and it is the dominant mechanism by which people adapt to changes in life course needs and lifestyle choices. Internal migration, in other words, measures the degree to which the population is undergoing selective redistribution, and thus it mirrors the potential for change in the country's macro-social geography. Fully 45 percent of the population move every five years (11.5 million people, or 43 percent of the nation's population over the age of five during the 1991–1996 period), and half of those (21 percent) move across municipal boundaries, while under 4 percent change provinces. Interprovincial moves during the same five-year period numbered some 900,000 people, roughly the same number as were admitted through immigration.

Although the numbers are similar, the temporal and spatial dimensions of immigration and domestic migration differ. While the overall rate of internal migration has remained much the same for the last 50 years, excluding minor fluctuations due to the business cycle, the specific urban destinations—the macro-geography of domestic migration—have not remained constant. The reverse is true for immigration; it has exhibited a more variable rate over time and a more constant and focused geography. Migration and immigration are also more important as social processes than is indicated by the simple numbers of people involved. They also shift the location of wealth, income, skills, and labour, as well as voters and the future generation.

Contrary to popular perceptions, the country's 25 metropolitan areas (CMAs) have had a net migration loss among domestic migrants for most of the last 20 years. Over the 1991–1996 period alone, the CMAs had a migration loss of some 156,000 people in their exchanges with non-metropolitan areas (Bourne and Flowers, 1999). The largest losses were recorded for Toronto (–87,000), Montreal (–47,900), Edmonton (–23,600), and Winnipeg (–17,000). Nevertheless, in total, foreign immigration more than made up for the loss in net domestic migrants.

What is unclear, however, is whether immigration and migration flows are related and, if so, how? Has increased immigration, given its concentration in four large metropolitan areas, become a factor in the relatively high levels of out-migration of the resident population to non-metropolitan areas? Is there a displacement effect operating in terms of housing and labour markets? Is it the case, for example, that a proportion of the resident population takes this inflow of new immigrants as an opportunity to cash in their increased housing equity by moving to less expensive places, including "exurbs" not (yet) formally defined as part of the metropolitan realm? Or, are we seeing internal movements completely unrelated to the dynamics of international immigration, for instance, an increase in retirement or amenity-oriented migrations out of large urban areas, as well as—more speculatively—a decrease in geographic ties to metropolitan labour markets linked to the growth of self-employment and an increase in the number of people working from home among the nation's increasingly more professionalized labour force?

THE LABOUR MARKET NEXUS

The fourth transformation involves the changing relationships between population and demography, family and household composition, and the country's labour markets, both local and national. In the research and policy literature, this complex intersection is acknowledged, but its implications are typically ignored or downplayed. It is true that social well-being—as well as access to full social citizenship in Canada (see Bakker and Scott, 1997)—is primarily a function of the individual's position with respect to the world of paid work. This position, in turn, is influenced by the changing structure of the economy, in terms of sectors of employment, occupation, skills requirements, and the demand for full- and part-time workers, and by differences in levels of education and training, i.e., individual human capital, as well as by location.

Yet changes in demography, household structure, and lifestyle choices also play a significant role in enhancing or ameliorating inequalities attributable to differences in earnings (wages and salaries) and working conditions. Individuals perform unpaid and paid work, and earn monetary income from the latter. Yet it is usually the household or family that serves as the unit that collects these monetary resources, negotiates their allocation, and then spends them. Households and families are, in effect, the basic units of consumption, social reproduction, and collective decision making.

Consequently, changes in the size and composition of the household, including the relations among individuals within those collective units, have substantially redefined the distribution of income and social capital. Smaller household sizes, for example, tend to both offset and reinforce the advantages of higher labour force participation rates, depending on household composition. Indeed, the faster-growing household types are those with no one in the labour force and those with two or more income earners. The latter are largely, but not exclusively, a reflection of the increasing participation rate of married women referred to earlier. One significant result of household fragmentation, and of the feminization of paid work, is an increase in disparities in employment income and accumulated wealth between two-earner households and those with one earner or none (Péron et al., 1999). Perhaps the most seriously affected groups, other than the unemployed, are unattached individuals, the elderly, especially women living alone (Brotman, 1999), those with major disabilities, and single-parent families. Substantial proportions of each of these groups fall below the low-income cut-offs as defined by Statistics Canada. These differences between two-earner households on the one hand, and one- or no-earner households on the other hand, are likely to reinforce the polarization between rich and poor neighbourhoods of major metropolitan areas that has been documented with respect to individual employment earnings (see Myles et al., 2000).

THE UNEVEN GEOGRAPHIES OF SOCIAL CHANGE

It is the uneven geographies of these social transformations that are of particular interest here. Of course, population change is almost always geographically uneven, and there is no reason in theory, no evidence in the historical record, to expect it to be otherwise. The history of Canada mirrors a number of processes of population redistribution and social change that, in combination, underlie the country's changing face. From the beginnings of

European colonization, population has shifted from East to West, from the Atlantic region to Quebec and Ontario, from Quebec to Ontario and the West, and later from Ontario to the far West, and from Manitoba and Saskatchewan to Alberta and British Columbia. Ontario, then as now, serves as the migration lynchpin or "swing" region, attracting migrants from the East and sending others to the West. Since 1951, all provinces east of the Ottawa River, as well as Saskatchewan and Manitoba, have witnessed net out-migration. Ontario and Alberta have swung between positive and negative migration balances depending on their relative economic performance. Only British Columbia has had consistently positive domestic migration balances through the half-century (Table 18.1). In an abstract sense, these internal migration flows can be seen as a structural correction for the initial decisions to settle the East first.

Other forms of population redistribution in Canada, in addition to the traditional East-West flow, are also well known (Bunting and Filion, 2000). The population has shifted from being 30 percent urban in the early 1900s to over 84 percent urban today. Rural residence, moreover, has been largely dissociated from agricultural-based livelihood. The net effect is that less than 3 percent of the population is now classed as rural farm. Within the country's

Table 18.1 Net Migration by Province, Canada, 1956–1996

Province	Net Migration Rate (%)							
	1956–61	1961–66	1966–71	1971–76	1976–81	1981–86	1986–91	1991–96
NF	-1.1	-3.3	-3.1	-1.3	-3.6	-2.9	-2.3	-4.1
PE	-1.0	-2.9	-0.6	2.3	0.0	1.2	-0.1	1.1
NS	-2.2	-3.7	-1.0	0.7	-1.0	0.7	-0.1	-0.7
NB	-1.0	-4.3	-1.0	1.5	-1.3	-0.2	-0.5	-0.2
PQ	-0.2	-0.4	-1.2	-1.0	-2.3	-1.0	-0.6	-0.5
ON	0.7	1.4	0.8	-0.6	-0.9	1.2	0.7	-0.4
MB	-1.8	-2.9	-3.0	-2.5	-4.3	-0.1	-3.3	-1.8
SK	-3.7	-4.5	-7.0	-3.1	-0.6	-0.2	-6.6	-2.0
AB	1.6	0.2	-1.8	4.0	10.8	-1.2	-1.5	0.1
BC	2.5	4.8	6.6	4.6	4.5	0.3	4.6	4.6
Net Change	0.55	0.89	1.03	0.85	1.34	0.48	0.78	0.57
Mean	-0.6	-1.6	-1.1	0.5	0.1	-0.2	-1.0	-0.4
SD	1.75	2.82	3.26	2.49	4.21	1.18	2.74	2.14
COV	-2.82	-1.76	-2.88	5.41	32.4	-5.36	-2.82	-5.49

Notes:
Net migration rate exressed as a percentage of base population for each period.
Net change = Sum of all positive net flows over the national base population for each period.
SD = Standard Deviation
COV = Coefficient of Variation (Standard deviation divided by the mean)

Source: Statistics Canada, Census of Population, various years.

extended urban system, population has continued to move upward through the size hierarchy to the larger cities and metropolitan areas, and in the process has become more geographically concentrated, despite the role of net domestic out-migration. In 1930, for example, no Canadians lived in large metropolitan environments (i.e., those with over 1 million population); by 2000, over 12.5 million did.

Within those metropolitan areas, the imprints of the social transformations sketched out above tend to be magnified. Populations have continued to decentralize to suburban and exurban locations, often creating ruralized landscapes but without cutting the umbilical cord to the metropolitan job market. As a result of the reduced number of children per family, the increased proportion of non-family households, and an aging population, almost all older, established neighbourhoods have seen a dramatic thinning of their population. Intra-urban contrasts in age structure have increased: inner city neighbourhoods tend to be dominated by young, non-family households; the older suburbs by "greying" households. The new suburbs, in contrast, continue to be dominated by younger families, but with an increasing mix of housing and household types (Evenden and Walker, 1993).

Perhaps even more striking, as noted above, has been the ethnocultural transformation of the larger cities through immigration. Whereas the process of inner-city neighbourhood revitalization in Canada was in large part initiated by the postwar waves of European immigrants, today—especially in the Toronto and Vancouver regions—many new immigrants go directly to middle-class suburbs without passing through traditional reception areas. In suburban municipalities such as Richmond and Surrey (Vancouver CMA), and Mississauga, Vaughan, and Markham (Toronto CMA), the proportion of immigrants has reached 25–40 percent, and is likely to go much higher. Older suburban areas with a large stock of low- to modest-income rental housing also draw large numbers of low-income immigrants, Toronto's Scarborough being the most telling example. While Canadian suburbs have never been as homogeneous as conventional wisdom portrayed them to be, these suburbs, and our images of suburban life and culture, will never be the same. Diversity has suburbanized.

SOCIAL CONCERNS AND POLICY ISSUES

The changing character, growth, and distribution of the Canadian population raise numerous issues of immediate and long-term interest and concern. The first is the country's slower rate of population growth in combination with continued redistribution through internal migration and immigration, processes that are regionally selective. Although still relatively high by western European standards, the overall rate of growth is now only 0.9 percent annually, and will be near 0 by 2030, even if levels of immigration increase to 300,000 per year.

This declining population growth rate is also coincident with a markedly uneven geography of growth. Although not new, that unevenness is also likely to increase since the veneer of high fertility levels has been removed. Immigration, as argued above, is almost certain to compound the spatial concentration of growth, as well as to increase the degree of uncertainty in the broader spatial demography, irrespective of policy targets. Both the levels of immigration and the socio-economic trajectories of immigrants are inherently unpredictable.

Slower population growth is, of course, not necessarily a problem. In some instances, it may allow for regions and local municipalities to catch up with the demands for new infrastructure and social services, and to address the need for environmental sustainability. In other and less economically favoured regions, however, a decrease in national population growth will result in zero regional growth, or even sharper population declines than in the past. For these regions it will be an increasingly difficult struggle to maintain a basic level of public services, jobs, and infrastructure, and thus to retain their younger and more mobile populations. Population decline, therefore, is a problem if it limits opportunities, increases unmet expectations, reduces public services, and depreciates the quality of everyday life. These conditions, in turn, may rekindle the tensions between the have and have-not regions, provinces, and municipalities that have dominated policy debates for decades. The ongoing decline in the relative weight of the French-Canadian population, and specifically that of Quebec, within Canada is a telling example of how demographic issues can pose fundamental challenges to a country's political fabric. At the same time, the rapid increase in the Aboriginal population will pose a completely different set of policy challenges in the coming decades.

Population loss in the more peripheral regions of Canada is fundamentally linked to the relative decline and/or restructuring of traditional primary resource-based industries (logging, grain farming, fishing, and mining). This decline is taking place in the context of technological change and the economic and political pressures deriving from trade liberalization and globalization, all of which pose major challenges to the long tradition of regional policies that have helped to sustain population numbers, for better or worse, in peripheral areas (Brodie, 1997). For example, do Canadians, whose individual mobility rights are enshrined in the Constitution, also have the collective right to immobility — that is, to remain in place rather than permanently moving away from those peripherally located communities undergoing economic decline (Blomley, 1992)? The dual challenge will be to maintain a social fabric and social service base over vast territories that are remote, sparsely inhabited, and consequently difficult to service, and where it is difficult to find appropriate ways of diversifying local and regional economies so as to make such regions economically and environmentally sustainable once again (Villeneuve and Preston, 2001), or perhaps, where such policies prove impossible, to find humane ways of managing population decline. Growth, on the other hand, will also continue to be geographically concentrated in a large few urban regions. Although levels of metropolitan concentration in Canada will remain much lower than those in comparable countries (e.g., Australia, Sweden), the process of adjusting structures of government and modes of governance to these new urban realities will be difficult and painful (Polèse and Stren, 2000).

The third trend is the increasing average age of the population. This process will likely continue until the middle of this century. Increased longevity, a sign of social (or at least medical) success, and a rapidly aging population base will pose a series of fundamental challenges to public policy and to the social order. The dependency ratio, measuring essentially the number of tax-paying workers divided by the number not in the labour force, will increase markedly, even with proportionately fewer children; nevertheless, it is unlikely to reach the high levels attained during the baby boom years (Denton et al., 1998). Although there are intense debates regarding the costs of this transformation, notably in terms of the potential drain on social services and the health budget (and although society seems to have been reasonably successful at reducing the high level of poverty among the elderly), there is little doubt that the relationship between the population and production spheres, and the welfare state, will need to be rewritten. The already-substantial burden of unpaid caring work assumed by working-age Canadians for their elderly and ailing relatives is set to increase, posing major challenges to which both employers and governments will need to respond. This adjustment will be complicated by the uncertainty regarding the geography of migration in a society growing older, a society that—in theory—will also be less mobile.

The fourth trend is primarily linked here to increasing immigration from non-traditional sources. While most aspects of the increasing diversity of the Canadian population have implications for the range of demands placed on the market and the public sector for goods and services, there is no doubt that ethnocultural diversification poses particular new challenges, but it also creates new opportunities. In many "gateway" cities, social service agencies, service providers, and municipal administrators are indeed struggling with the challenges posed by—and the claims for recognition of diversity made by—so many newcomers from so many different ethnic, cultural-linguistic, and "racial" backgrounds (*Canadian Journal of Regional Science*, 1997; Isajiw, 1999). In a context of inadequate government funding for settlement assistance programs and fiscal downloading from provinces to municipalities, these pressures are adding to the usual tensions and conflicts over the funding and allocation of scarce collective resources.

Other demographic trends have tended to make portions of the country's territory and population poorer, or at least more vulnerable to economic and social turbulence. The shrinkage of average household size and the revolution in living arrangements—entailing the fragmentation of families and households into smaller and smaller units of domestic production and consumption—as well as the feminization of the labour force, now seem to be largely complete. Their impacts will nevertheless continue to be felt for decades to come. Average household size, currently 2.7, is expected to decline but only marginally so, to 2.5 by 2016 (Statistics Canada, 1994). Smaller household sizes, and the ability of many individuals to live alone, even if paying high proportions of their income on rent, may be seen, to a degree, as a sign of social success. For others, it is clearly not.

A wide range of household types, social groups, and individuals are thus left in a precarious situation by economic restructuring, demographic change, and shifts in living arrangements and, for recent immigrants, by obstacles to a successful immigrant settlement experience. The face of poverty, of social disadvantage, in Canada has changed. Although there is intense and ongoing debate as to whether and by how much, inequalities in income have increased (Beach and Slotsve, 1996; Canadian Council on Social Development, 2000; Yalnizyan, 1998), there is little doubt that certain types of households, individuals, and places have suffered more than others as a result of these trends. The most obvious perhaps is the Aboriginal population, which continues to grow at above-average rates, and, though internally diverse in terms of socio-economic conditions (Armstrong, 1999), has yet to gain full access to the country's resources. Other vulnerable groups include certain segments of the immigrant population; notably, those who begin their life in Canada as refugee claimants awaiting the decision as to their status, those whose professional credentials are not recognized, and those with limited job skills, have found it particularly difficult to gain a foothold in Canada's increasingly post-industrial labour market (Kazemipur and Halli, 2000). Still other vulnerable groups include unattached individuals, and single-parent families, especially those headed by a female (Péron et al., 1999).

In those situations where increased income inequalities among population groups can be documented, three explanatory factors seem to be relevant. One, of course, is economic restructuring and the loss of significant numbers of blue-collar jobs beginning in the 1980s, followed by the loss of public sector jobs in the 1990s. A second source is the truncation of social assistance benefits, (un)employment insurance, and transfer payments to individuals and families in the mid-1990s. The third relates to the transformations in demographic structure and lifestyles, the effects of aging, and the proliferation of smaller, non-traditional households. It is possible to argue that demographic and lifestyle components are now of roughly equal importance in accounting for income inequalities as are workplace restructuring and revisions to the welfare net, although all four are inextricably interwoven.

OUR UNCERTAIN POPULATION FUTURE

We have argued that the country's future will be shaped more by population processes and conditions than by economic and political forces. We have shown how a series of linked social transformations have swept over the country's social fabric, altering patterns and images as they have evolved. The face of Canada has been redefined, in most instances in an irreversible fashion. Moreover, these same factors have also contributed to an increasingly uneven geography of population growth and social change. This unevenness is likely to be all the more obvious and more politically charged in the slow-growth scenarios that we anticipate in the future.

To a certain degree our demographic future is here now. One obvious example is that most senior citizens of 2020 are here now, aged 50 and older. This group will be an economically and politically potent force as the baby boom cohort moves into the retirement years. Given that fertility levels are likely to remain constant and at historically low levels, the major instrument of social change in the future, yet the most uncertain, is migration, especially foreign immigration. The latter component is uncertain precisely because it is subject to the whims of politics; to pressures from established socio-cultural and immigrant groups; and to shifting economic, political, and environmental conditions in the rest of the world. At the same time, tighter labour markets in the United States and in some of the traditional immigrant source countries, notably in Europe and Asia, could lead to much higher levels of emigration and return migration. Competition for skilled immigrants will be particularly intense. Moreover, estimates also suggest that even an age-selective (i.e., youth-oriented) immigration policy will not change the aging process or the labour market situation very much (Denton et al., 1998).

Equally uncertain is where, and how well, these people will live. We know that immigration levels of at least 250,000 a year are considered necessary to prevent population decline after 2020. But is this high level of immigration, on a sustained basis, especially given its non-traditional origins and geographic concentration, administratively practical, economically necessary, socially acceptable, and politically feasible? There is presently a broader social consensus in Quebec about the need for further increases in immigration than in the rest of Canada, but will this level be sustained if the pool of potential French-speaking immigrants and those thought to be "francisable" shrinks? How will the rest of the country view Toronto and Vancouver when the new ethnocultural minorities in those cities and their suburbs become the majorities, which is set to happen in the near future? The social face of these places will indeed be different—a rainbow of diversity. Can we guarantee that the resources and opportunities will be available to accommodate and retain these populations, and to take full advantage of the new cultures and skills that they bring?

● ●

CRITICAL THINKING QUESTIONS

1. Canada is becoming remarkably diverse, as influenced by cultures and nationalities from all over the world, yet this is not true of all parts of Canada as some regions remain relatively homogeneous. How can this be explained in terms of Canada's uneven geography of growth? Provide examples.
2. As Canada has become more culturally diverse, it has also become more diverse in terms of living arrangements and familial relations. Elaborate on some of the most salient changes to have influenced the family over recent decades.
3. In your opinion, is this uneven geography of growth and social change a problem in Canada? Why or why not?

● ●

CHAPTER 19

CHANGES IN CONJUGAL LIFE IN CANADA: IS COHABITATION PROGRESSIVELY REPLACING MARRIAGE?

Céline Le Bourdais and Évelyne Lapierre-Adamcyk

● ●

IN THE LAST 30 YEARS, most Western countries have witnessed formidable changes in the foundation of the family institution. Demographic indicators point to a postponement of marriage and to a decline in the proportion of individuals who are likely to marry during their lifetime. Marriage has also been characterized by growing levels of instability, with divorce rates showing that it is not that uncommon among these countries to find that one marriage out of two is likely to dissolve. The dramatic increase in cohabiting unions over the last 30 years—first as a way for young adults to start their conjugal life and, more recently, as an environment in which to start and raise a family—further led researchers to question the "future of marriage." Currently, the recognition of same-sex marriage has prompted debates about the meaning of marriage. How has the institution of marriage changed in recent decades, and how do these changes vary across cultures and across countries?

One of the ways to document the weakening of marriage and its change in meaning is to look more closely at the progression of cohabitation over time. In this chapter, we first describe the demographic trends of marriage and cohabitation in Canada, and, second, assess whether cohabitation constitutes a new stage in the progression to marriage or an alternative to marriage altogether. After addressing these issues, we close by discussing possible explanations underlying the observed changes. By contrasting the evolution of demographic behaviours adopted across the different regions in Canada, we show that cohabitation has reached different stages of development in Quebec as opposed to elsewhere in Canada, as formulated by Kiernan (2001). In the former, cohabitation seems now to be nearly indistinguishable from marriage, as it is in Sweden, whereas in the latter, cohabitation is still accepted predominantly as a childless phase of conjugal life, as is the case in the United States.

Profound changes have transformed the conjugal life of Canadians in recent decades. Figure 19.1 presents the evolution of total female marriage rates, calculated by combining marriage vital statistics and Census population counts, and exemplifies the fall of marriage over the last 30 years. These rates show the proportions of women within synthetic cohorts who would marry at least once if the behaviours observed in any given year were to last.

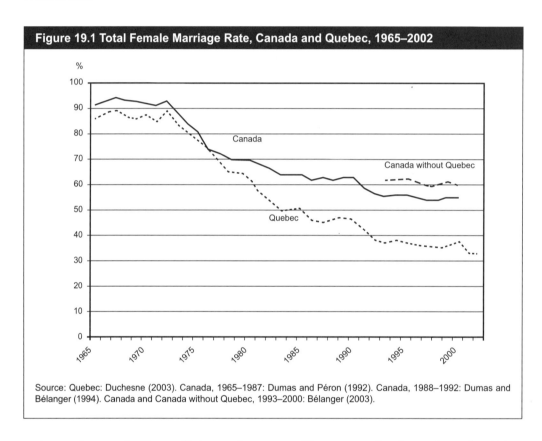

Figure 19.1 Total Female Marriage Rate, Canada and Quebec, 1965–2002

Source: Quebec: Duchesne (2003). Canada, 1965–1987: Dumas and Péron (1992). Canada, 1988–1992: Dumas and Bélanger (1994). Canada and Canada without Quebec, 1993–2000: Bélanger (2003).

As can be seen in Figure 19.1, marriage was still very popular throughout the 1960s; more than nine women out of 10 would marry over the course of their life. In the mid-1970s, marriage started to lose ground progressively, and by the turn of the century, just slightly over half of women were expected to marry in Canada. In Quebec, the fall was far more drastic: From nearly 90 early in the 1960s, the proportion of women who would marry at least once in their life fell to 50 percent in 1984, and only one woman in three is now expected to marry according to most recent data. The gap separating Quebec's women from their counterparts living elsewhere in Canada widened throughout the period studied as Quebecers deserted marriage. By 2000, 60 percent of women living outside Quebec were expected to marry at least once, compared with less than 40 percent of those living in Quebec. When measured for men, total marriage rates are generally slightly lower but follow similar trends.

The decline of marriage has also been accompanied by a postponement of the age at first marriage. When marriage was widespread, it was relatively precocious, with an average age of 25.4 years among men and 22.5 years among women in Canada in 1960 (26.0 and 23.5 in Quebec, respectively; Duchesne, 2003; Dumas and Péron, 1992). Now that marriage has become less popular, individuals marry approximately five years later. In 2001, the age at first marriage was 30.2 and 28.2 years, respectively, for men and women in Canada (30.6 and 28.8 years in Quebec in 2002; Duchesne, 2003; Statistics Canada, 2003a).

Not only has marriage become less popular but it has also become more unstable since the adoption of the Divorce Law by the Canadian Parliament in 1968. In 1970, the total divorce rate was approximately 10 percent, indicating that one marriage in 10 would eventually end in divorce. Although fluctuating depending on the courts' availability and because of modifications to the Divorce Law introduced in 1985, the divorce rate increased steadily in the following years until it reached a plateau in the 1990s. Thirty years after divorce became more easily accessible, the rate has multiplied by four. In Canada as a whole, nearly 40 percent of couples are expected to divorce. Interestingly, in Quebec, where marriage is least popular, it is most fragile, with nearly one couple out of two likely to divorce (Lapierre-Adamcyk and Le Bourdais, 2004). Although marriage is on the decline and divorce is on the rise, one cannot conclude that conjugal life has receded to the same extent. From survey data, we know that the majority of Canadian men and women wish "to have a lasting relationship as a couple" (Lapierre-Adamcyk, Le Bourdais, and Marcil-Gratton, 1999). Hence, the decline of marriage has been mostly offset by the growth of cohabiting unions.

THE GROWTH OF COHABITING UNIONS AS A FORM OF CONJUGAL LIFE

Because of its informal and unstable nature, the importance of cohabitation is often difficult to measure and varies depending on point of view. In Canada, cohabiting unions were recognized as an alternative form of conjugal life from the beginning. As early as the 1971 Census, long before cohabitation had become commonplace, cohabiting couples were instructed to consider themselves as "married"; they were thus counted as *couples*, but they remained invisible among the larger number of married couples (Le Bourdais and Juby, 2001). In 1981, Statistics Canada maintained this instruction on marital status, but included *common-law partner* as a category to describe the relationship of individuals with the household, permitting estimation of the number of cohabiting unions for heads of household. Figure 19.2 presents the percentages of couples who were identified as cohabiting across Canada in three different Censuses. In 1981, 6 percent of couples were cohabiting in Canada. The proportion varied from 3.4 percent in the Atlantic region to roughly 7 percent in the provinces of Quebec and British Columbia. In the 1970s, cohabitation was still a relatively new phenomenon. Consensual unions were usually short-lived; after a few years, cohabitors had either married or separated, explaining the relatively low percentage in the 1981 Census.

From that point on, the evolution of cohabitation took a very different course in Quebec from the rest of Canada. During the 1980s, the percentage of couples who were cohabiting in Quebec more than doubled to 19 percent in 1991. The increase continued unabatedly throughout the 1990s. In 20 years, the proportion of couples who were cohabiting was multiplied by more than four in Quebec, but only by 1.9 in British Columbia. Consequently, although both provinces began at a similar level, the percentage of cohabiting couples is now nearly 2.5 times higher in the former than in the latter. As of 2001, the popularity of cohabitation in Quebec is as widespread as it is in Sweden, where 30 percent of couples are cohabiting, and clearly greater than in France (17.5 percent) or the United States (8.2 percent; Statistics Canada, 2002b). The percentage in Canada outside Quebec (12 percent) falls between these two countries.

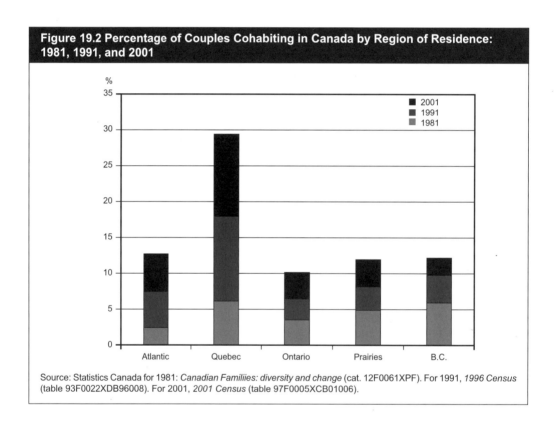

Figure 19.2 Percentage of Couples Cohabiting in Canada by Region of Residence: 1981, 1991, and 2001

Source: Statistics Canada for 1981: *Canadian Familiies: diversity and change* (cat. 12F0061XPF). For 1991, *1996 Census* (table 93F0022XDB96008). For 2001, *2001 Census* (table 97F0005XCB01006).

Census data give an idea of the percentage of individuals who are cohabiting at a given point in time. In large part, these percentages are composed of young individuals who chose cohabitation to start their conjugal life, but they underestimate the extent to which this phenomenon occurs because cohabitating individuals can marry or separate before the Census date. Moreover, as divorce rose, Census data also increasingly included proportions of individuals who opted for a consensual union after a first marriage dissolved.

Figure 19.3 presents the cumulative probabilities (derived from life table estimates) that women experience a first union, through marriage or cohabitation, in five different cohorts. This figure first shows that the vast majority of individuals across all cohorts still form conjugal unions: Well above 90 percent of women born in the 1960s or earlier had

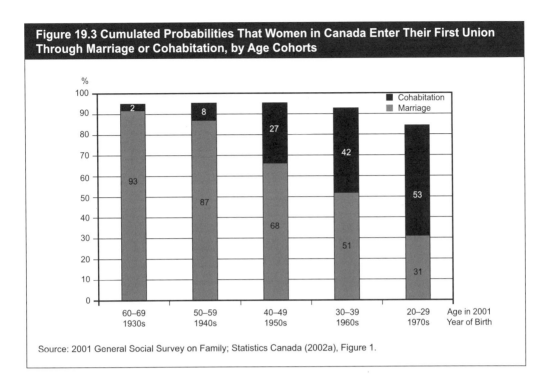

Figure 19.3 Cumulated Probabilities That Women in Canada Enter Their First Union Through Marriage or Cohabitation, by Age Cohorts

Source: 2001 General Social Survey on Family; Statistics Canada (2002a), Figure 1.

formed a union at least once in their life, and 84 percent of those born in the 1970s had already done so by age 29.

How women started their conjugal life changed drastically across cohorts, however. In the oldest cohort born in the 1930s (ages 60–69 in 2001), 93 percent of women married directly, and only 2 percent began by living with a cohabiting partner. The percentage of women cohabiting in their first union throughout the 1970s rose to 27 percent among those born in the 1950s, and to 42 percent among those born in the 1960s. Among the youngest cohorts who entered their first union during the 1990s, cohabitation has become the favoured way to start conjugal life. By age 29, 53 percent of women had formed a consensual union, as compared with only 31 percent who had married directly. The percentage of women who will eventually marry directly in the youngest cohorts should be slightly higher as they get older, however, because age at first marriage is increasing as individuals postpone marriage. The figures presented for Canada as a whole are similar to those observed in the United States, where 43 percent of the first unions concluded by women in the early 1980s and 54 percent of those formed in the early 1990s began with cohabitation (Bumpass and Lu, 2000).

The trends observed in Canada vary tremendously across the country. As can be seen in Figure 19.4, marriage was the typical way to start a first union in the early 1970s. It characterized 85 percent of first unions in Canada outside Quebec, and 80 percent of those in Quebec. Twenty years later, the situation has totally reversed in Quebec. Four times out of five, Quebec women opted for cohabitation to start their first union in the early 1990s, compared with one in two for their counterparts living elsewhere in Canada. Quebec women now increasingly resemble their Swedish counterparts who, nine times out of 10, choose cohabitation to start conjugal life (Kiernan, 2001), whereas other Canadian women have similar behaviours to those of their southern neighbours.

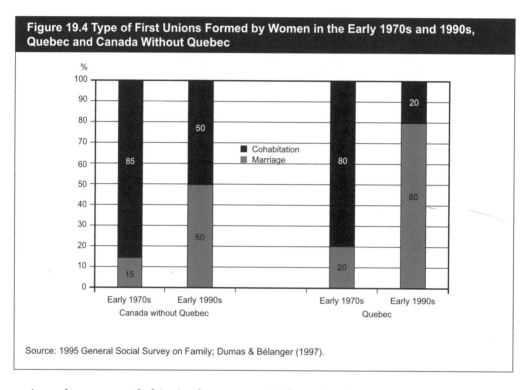

Figure 19.4 Type of First Unions Formed by Women in the Early 1970s and 1990s, Quebec and Canada Without Quebec

Source: 1995 General Social Survey on Family; Dumas & Bélanger (1997).

As we have seen, cohabitation has progressively replaced marriage, at least in Quebec, as a way to start conjugal life. We know from various studies, however, that cohabiting unions are more short-lived than marriages, and that they have become even less stable over time (Bumpass and Lu, 2000; Dumas and Bélanger, 1997; Statistics Canada, 2002a). A partial explanation for the rising instability of cohabiting unions can perhaps be found in the wide diversity of existing unions. For a significant proportion of couples, cohabitation has replaced "going steady" relationships, which do not necessarily involve any long-term engagement. For another group, cohabiting unions constitute a "prelude to marriage" or a "trial marriage"—that is, a period in which to test the solidity of the relationship while completing schooling and attaining professional achievement (Villeneuve-Gokalp, 1991). As cohabitation has become more socially acceptable, it seems to have attracted larger numbers of less committed couples. As a result, the proportion of cohabiters who married their partners within three to five years of the beginning of the union has decreased, while the proportion of those who separated has increased (Bumpass and Lu, 2000; Turcotte and Bélanger, 1997; for a review, see Smock and Gupta, 2001). Concomitantly, the percentage of cohabiting unions that endured longer than three to five years has increased, both in Canada and in the United States, partly countervailing the trend toward rising instability. Again, the situation in Quebec differs from that observed elsewhere in Canada. Cohabitations are of longer duration in Quebec, and they are less likely to transform into marriage (Le Bourdais and Marcil-Gratton, 1996; Turcotte and Bélanger, 1997).

Transitions outside cohabiting unions tend to occur relatively early after the union starts. Hence, two years after the beginning of the union, the likelihood of experiencing separation or marriage falls quite abruptly (Brown, 2000). These results tend to suggest that cohabitation, in Canada as in the United States, has successfully completed its second phase; it is "either a prelude to or a probationary period where the strength of the relationship may be tested prior to committing to marriage and is predominantly a childless phase" (Kiernan, 2001:5). The passage to the next stage requires cohabitation to become an alternative to marriage, allowing individuals to fulfill both conjugal and parental roles.

THE GROWTH OF COHABITING UNIONS AS A FORM OF FAMILY LIFE

The percentage of non-marital births has increased sharply over the last 20 years. In the early 1980s, approximately one birth in six occurred outside marriage in Canada (Marcil-Gratton, 1998). By 2000, nearly one child in three was born to an unmarried mother (Statistics Canada, 2003b). These figures roughly compare to those observed in the United States (Cherlin, 2004), but increasingly differ from the situation experienced in Quebec, where nearly 60 percent of all registered births in 2000 were to unmarried mothers (Duchesne, 2003). Clearly, marriage no longer constitutes the sole acceptable way to become a parent, and non-marital pregnancies do not automatically bring social reprobation, forcing young mothers to either rapidly marry the child's father or place the child for adoption.

To be born outside marriage does not necessarily mean to be born to a single mother. In fact, the percentage of children born to an unknown or non-declared father was only 3.4 percent in 2002 in Quebec, a slight decrease from previous years (Duchesne, 2003). This suggests that non-marital births are more closely associated with the decline of marriage and the progression of cohabitation than with an increase of formerly "illegitimate" births.

Survey data rather than vital statistics allow a better description of the family environment in which children are born. Figure 19.5 presents the distribution (in percentages) of various cohorts of children according to type of parents' union at the time of their birth. First, this figure shows that the vast majority (over 85 percent) of children born in 1971–1973 were born to married parents who had not previously cohabited; this was the case in Quebec and elsewhere in Canada. Yet by 1997–1998, nearly half (46 percent) of all births in Quebec were to cohabiting parents, and well beyond 50 percent of first-born children. An equivalent proportion (45 percent) of children were born to married parents who, most often, had previously cohabited; only 19 percent were born to parents who had married directly. On the other hand, elsewhere in Canada, three-quarters of births still occurred within marriage. Among those, approximately half (39 percent) were born to parents who married directly without first cohabiting.

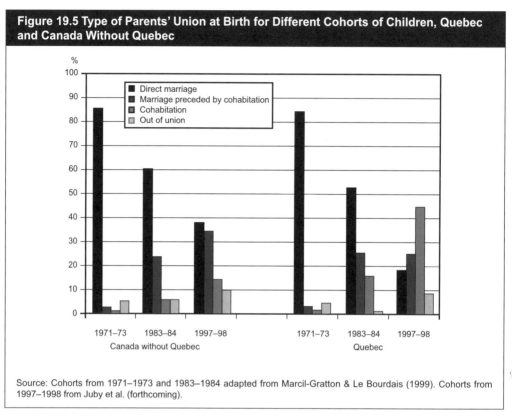

Figure 19.5 Type of Parents' Union at Birth for Different Cohorts of Children, Quebec and Canada Without Quebec

Source: Cohorts from 1971–1973 and 1983–1984 adapted from Marcil-Gratton & Le Bourdais (1999). Cohorts from 1997–1998 from Juby et al. (forthcoming).

In Kiernan's (2001:5) third stage of the partnership transition, cohabitation is socially acceptable, and "becoming a parent is no longer restricted to marriage." In Quebec, now that cohabitation has become the modal way in which to give birth, the transition to this third stage seems to have been successfully achieved. Elsewhere in Canada, however, if half of children born in the late 1990s were born to parents who had cohabited, only 30 percent (15 percent out of 51 percent) were born within a cohabiting union (Figure 19.4). This suggests that cohabiting unions have not yet become an alternative setting in which to become a parent, and that women who become pregnant while living with a cohabiting partner will tend to legalize their union before the birth of the child. In a way, the evolution of family life in Canada outside Quebec parallels that observed in the United States, where only a small fraction of the increase in non-marital births was due to a decline in the likelihood that pregnant cohabiting mothers will marry before the birth of their child (Raley, 2001). The greatest portion of the increase seems to be attributable to rising percentages of women cohabiting, and to the greater likelihood that single pregnant women start cohabiting (rather than marry). These results led Raley to conclude, along with Manning (1993), that cohabitation was perhaps becoming a trial marriage among singles, but that it was still too early to conclude that it had become a substitute for marriage.

If cohabitation is to be considered a substitute for marriage, it needs to provide not only a family setting in which to give birth but also a lasting arrangement in which to raise children. Previous studies have shown that cohabiting couples giving birth to a child appear to be more stable than childless unions (Wu and Balakrishnan, 1995). But are these couples as solid as married couples with children? Can we expect the risk of family disruption to vary according to historical context—that is, in relation to the importance and acceptance of cohabitation as a way to start family life? Can we expect the gap in family disruptions between marriages and cohabitations to narrow as cohabitation has become the modal way in which to form a family in Quebec?

The distribution of children according to the family setting in which they live at a given moment provides an indirect indication of the duration of families across the country, depending upon the type of parental union. In 2001 in Canada, over 80 percent of children aged zero to 14 years were living with two parents who were either their biological parents, adoptive parents, or step-parents. Census data do not allow distinction among biological families, adoptive families, and stepfamilies because respondents are instructed to declare as "son" or "daughter" their biological children, adopted children, or stepchildren. Between 17 percent and 20 percent were living with a single parent, usually the mother (eight times out of 10). Outside Quebec, the percentage of children living with cohabiting parents was relatively low, ranging between 7 percent in Ontario and 11 percent in the Atlantic provinces. It was clearly higher in Quebec, where it reached 30 percent, reflecting the longer duration of cohabiting unions in this province (Statistics Canada, 2002c). Some of the higher percentage of children living in a non-married two-parent family in Quebec is also probably due to the greater propensity of couples to choose cohabitation rather than marriage when they form a union after having seen their first family collapse. Hence, according to the 2001 General Social Survey, nearly 75 percent of Quebec stepfamilies were headed by a cohabiting couple, whereas this percentage was slightly below 50 percent elsewhere in Canada (Statistics Canada, 2002a).

The only way to directly compare the stability of marriages and cohabiting unions with children is to use longitudinal data and to begin at the moment a child is born. This is precisely the approach we took in two studies of family disruption in Canada (Desrosiers and Le Bourdais, 1996; Le Bourdais, Neill, and Marcil-Gratton, 2000). The most recent study was based on retrospective information collected from respondents to the 1995 General Social Survey, who had become mothers for the first time in an intact family (i.e., within a union with their child's father) between 1970 and 1995. We examined the relative risks of family disruption faced by these women, according to their conjugal situation at the time of first birth and their region of residence (Quebec vs. elsewhere in Canada).

Compared with the families formed directly through marriage in Canada outside Quebec, married couples who lived together before marriage appeared to have a 1.66 greater chance of separating following the birth of their first child. In other words, starting conjugal life through cohabitation rather than marriage increased by two-thirds the risk of separation among parents who had already married by the time their first child was born. Conjugal instability was much greater among cohabiting-couple families. For those who were still cohabiting at the birth of the child, the risk of disruption was nearly five times higher than that observed for those who had married directly, even after controlling for mothers' socio-demographic characteristics (i.e., highest level of education completed at the time of the survey; pre-conjugal conception; age and school enrolment status at the beginning of the union; period of family formation; employment status; cumulated duration of employment; and cumulated number of work interruptions through the family episode).

Compared with their counterparts living elsewhere in Canada, Quebec families formed within direct marriage appeared more unstable, with a risk of separation that is 45 percent greater. In Quebec, however, married couples who lived together before marriage formed equally stable families as those who did not. Cohabiting families in Quebec appeared to be more fragile than those whose parents had married by the time the first child was born, but the difference between the two groups was not nearly as large as that observed elsewhere in Canada. In Quebec, cohabiting-couple families were 2.5 times (relative risk of 3.47 compared with 1.45) more likely to separate than those married directly, whereas they were five times more likely to do so in the rest of Canada.

As the context in which families are formed changed—that is, as cohabitation became progressively more acceptable and widespread—the risk of separation associated with the different types of unions also changed. We cannot assume the risks of separation across unions to remain invariant over time, as the nature of both cohabitation and marriage is also changing over time (Manting, 1996). The comparison of the relative risks of family disruption among parents who married directly without first cohabiting in Quebec and elsewhere in Canada is instructive, as is the comparison between married and cohabiting parents within each given region. Both comparisons show that, as direct marriage becomes increasingly unusual, it no longer provides a guarantee of stability, and as cohabitation becomes more widespread, it becomes more stable. For these reasons, the promotion of marriage as the only way to raise a family may have little value and, of greater importance, could well result in the opposite—that is, in a desertion of family life altogether, as seems to have occurred in countries such as Italy or Japan, where fertility has fallen to a very low level (Livi-Bacci and Salvini, 2000).

COHABITING UNIONS IN CANADA: RIGHTS AND BENEFITS FOR ADULTS AND CHILDREN

Canada adopted a very pragmatic approach in relation to the growth of cohabitation. Just as the statistical agency was prone to recognizing cohabiting couples as the equivalent of married couples from the beginning, cohabitors rapidly gained access to social programs and benefits. In the absence of a contract or ceremony to clearly mark the start of the union, a criterion of duration (usually one to three years) of living together is usually used before cohabiting couples can access benefits, but this criterion is often waived if the couple has a child. As long as they live together, cohabiting couples now seem to have the same benefits and advantages as married couples: They have a right to equality of treatment, a right that was confirmed by the Supreme Court of Canada in 1995 (Goubau, 2004).

Many areas of family law, however, such as laws governing union dissolution and child support, remain under provincial jurisdiction. Some differences exist across provinces, mostly the way that cohabiting couples are treated at separation. Some provinces, such as Alberta and Quebec, have been reluctant to provide total equality for married and cohabiting couples in terms of sharing assets at separation, but for opposite reasons. On the one hand, in Alberta, where marriage was judged the ideal family context, it was felt that additional recognition of cohabitation would undermine marriage. In Quebec, on the other hand, the justification for not assimilating cohabitation to marriage was based on the respect of the freedom of choice of cohabiting partners, who deliberately preferred cohabitation to marriage in order to avoid the rights and obligations attached to the latter (Le Bourdais and Juby, 2001). In December 2002, the Supreme Court of Canada reinforced this latter interpretation by overruling a provincial decision rendered earlier in Nova Scotia. The Supreme Court argued that if cohabiting partners had not previously signed a contract or written agreement, upon separation, they could not ask for alimony, nor count on sharing equally most assets accumulated through the union, as married spouses do. At separation, the legal system thus respects the private nature of the arrangements made by cohabitors, but during the union, it invokes the right of equality of treatment to justify that cohabiting and married couples be treated in the same way when dealing with a third party.

Although respecting the conjugal choices of adults, the courts and governments have aimed to ensure the protection of children irrespective of their parents' situation. In Canada, children now have the same rights and privileges, no matter the family circumstances of their birth, and birth statistics no longer classify as "illegitimate" births that occurred outside marriage. Parents, whether married or cohabiting, together or separated, have the same responsibilities and obligations toward their children. As much as possible, policies and laws have aimed to reduce the effect of parental separation on children's well-being. In December 2002, a new initiative, the Child-Centred Family Justice Strategy, was developed, aimed at the needs of children and at the reduction of the level of conflict between parents. It eliminated the terms "access" and "custody" included in the Divorce Act and replaced them with the less conflicting notions of "parental responsibilities" and "parental time," and developed services (mediation, parental education courses) to ease the process of separation (Le Bourdais, Marcil-Gratton, and Juby, 2003).

Officially, children are entitled to the same rights and benefits, irrespective of the conjugal status of their parents. Interestingly, though, the reality appears to be slightly different. Because cohabiting parents are not required, at separation, to share the assets accumulated through the union, children are likely to suffer more difficult economic conditions following parental separation if they were living in a cohabiting rather than married family (Dubreuil, 1999). Moreover, cohabiting fathers are less likely to maintain frequent contact with their children or provide child support on a regular basis following separation (Marcil-Gratton and Le Bourdais, 1999). Sole custody to the mother, rather than joint custody, has also been shown to be more frequent after the dissolution of a cohabiting union. Consequently, children and adults are likely to experience different living conditions following family disruption, depending on whether the parents were married or cohabiting.

THE DIVERGENT EVOLUTION OF COHABITATION IN QUEBEC AND ELSEWHERE IN CANADA

The data presented here have revealed profound changes in the processes of union and family formation and dissolution in Canada, and show how institutions such as the law and the national statistical agency have adapted to these transformations. Our analysis has contrasted the evolution of the demographic behaviours adopted in Quebec with that elsewhere in Canada, and led us to conclude that cohabitation has reached different stages of development across the country.

Outside Quebec, cohabitation seems to have successfully achieved the second stage of Kiernan's (2001) model of partnership transition, but to have not yet attained the third: It has become widely accepted as a form of conjugal life—that is, as a prelude or probationary period in which to test the strength of the relationship before marrying—but not yet as an environment in which to become a parent. In that respect, Canada without Quebec closely resembles the United States, where cohabitation still predominantly remains a childless phase of conjugal life.

In Quebec, though, the progression of cohabitation is far more advanced. Now that cohabitation has become the modal way in which to give birth in Quebec (i.e., an alternative to marriage in order to have children), clearly the transition to the third stage of development appears to have been fully completed. Has Quebec also achieved the transition to the fourth stage of Kiernan's (2001:5) model in which "cohabitation and marriage become indistinguishable with children being born and reared within both"? To help distinguish between these two stages, Heuveline and Timberlake (2004) have introduced a further criterion to those advanced by Kiernan: Unlike unmarried couples who, in the previous stage, opted for cohabitation as an *alternative* to marriage, those formed in the latter stage would be *indifferent* to marrying, because of the widespread acceptability of cohabitation and the provision of institutional supports that discriminate little between married and cohabiting families.

Some of the evidence presented here tends to suggest that the transition to this last stage of development is well underway in Quebec. Except for the sharing of assets and the right to alimony after separation, cohabiting families are entitled to the same rights and benefits as married families, and they do not suffer from discrimination. Moreover, the number of cohabiting families is steadily progressing as a result of the increasing duration of these family episodes and the declining likelihood of cohabiting couples marrying following the birth of a child. As the propensity of cohabiting couples with children to marry becomes closer to that of childless couples, cohabiters can be seen as being indifferent to marriage in the sense that the timing of marriage is not closely linked to the presence of children. Yet, in spite of these developments, we cannot conclude that cohabitation is indistinguishable from or a substitute for marriage. As we have seen above, cohabitation still leads to different outcomes from marriage concerning custody and child support following a family disruption. Thus, cohabitation is still, to a certain extent, "selective" of individuals with given characteristics.

We cannot end this chapter without raising some hypotheses to explain the divergent evolution of cohabitation in Quebec as compared with elsewhere in Canada. Part of the answer probably lies in the different religious and cultural backgrounds of the two societies (for a similar argument, see Laplante, 2004; Pollard and Wu, 1998). Up to the 1960s, Quebec society was under the yoke of the Catholic Church, which controlled most aspects of Quebecers' lives. During the 1960s, a vast movement of secularization, known as the Quiet Revolution, touched all aspects of society, including health, education, and social services, and led to the development of a modern state. Individuals rapidly embraced this revolution and progressively deserted the Church and abandoned its precepts. In the wake of this movement, Quebec women, who had maintained traditional behaviours in terms of contraception and family life, enthusiastically adopted the pill as a contraceptive method, and couples progressively did away not only with religious marriage but also with the institution of marriage altogether. Consequently, the total fertility rate and the total marriage rate plunged rapidly in Quebec, as it did in other Catholic societies, such as Spain, Italy, and, to a lesser degree, France (Le Bourdais and Marcil-Gratton, 1996). Elsewhere in Canada, the Protestant Church exerted less control over civil society and adapted more easily to the changes observed in family behaviours. Non-Catholic Canadians thus did not feel that they had to break away from their church to fulfill their personal aspirations for conjugal and family life.

This cultural difference partly explains the divergent trends in cohabitation observed in Quebec and in the rest of Canada, but cannot account for the fact that Quebecers now closely resemble their Swedish counterparts, who were not influenced by the Catholic Church. We argue that much of the evolution observed in Quebec has to do with changes in men's and women's roles. As Théry (1993) argued, the principal motor of recent conjugal changes is to be found in the redefinition of men's and women's roles in society and in conjugal relationships. Families remain, to this day, the last places where equality between men and women does not seem to be fully recognized. As societies are promoting greater equality within families, deep changes are likely to occur and lead to ongoing family transformations. Interestingly, the few studies that aimed to document existing differences between marriage and cohabitation have found that the organization of daily life is more egalitarian within the latter than in the former. Cohabiting partners are more prone than married couples to sharing domestic work (Shelton and John, 1993). They are also more likely to share paid work, as cohabiting women are more involved in the labour market (Le Bourdais and Sauriol, 1998). By contrast, married couples are more inclined than cohabiting partners to pool their financial resources (for a review, see Seltzer, 2000). These studies suggest that cohabitation and marriage constitute two different forms of conjugal engagement, each characterized by different forms of relationships. Cohabitation is based on a greater equality and professional autonomy of partners, whereas marriage rests on greater specialization and complementarity between spouses (Villeneuve-Gokalp, 1991). This interpretation is further supported by Brines and Joyner's (1999) study that showed that similar levels of earnings were associated with greater stability among cohabiting couples, whereas marital stability was more closely linked to specialization of labour and thus to unequal earnings.

In Quebec, we argue that the tremendous progression of cohabitation has to do with profound changes in men's and women's roles and expectations brought about in large part by the feminist movement, which is stronger and more deeply rooted than elsewhere in Canada. Quebec couples strive for greater equality between men and women, and cohabitation perhaps offers them the best opportunity in this regard. In that sense, cohabitation is probably here to stay because both Quebec men and women express attitudes more favourable to a redefinition of conjugal unions than other Canadians (Lapierre-Adamcyk et al., 1999). As long as cohabitation and marriage represent two different models of conjugal and family life, however, cohabitation remains an alternative to rather than a true substitute for marriage.

● ●

CRITICAL THINKING QUESTIONS

1. Cohabitation is more common in some parts of Canada than others. Elaborate on this statement. Why do you think this is the case?
2. What are some of the differences between cohabiting unions and legal marriages? Do you think that cohabitation will someday come to replace legal marriage as an institution in Canada? Why or why not?
3. Common-law unions and legal marriages are not quite one and the same under the law. Elaborate on some of the similarities and differences. What do you think are some of the implications of this for both adults and their children?

● ●

Chapter 20

Shifts in Ethnic Origins Among the Offspring of Immigrants: Is Ethnic Mobility a Measurable Phenomenon?

Gustave Goldmann

● ●

INTRODUCTION

Ethnic mobility is not a new phenomenon. Early studies in acculturation focused on the impact or consequences of contact between people of different cultures (Boas, 1966; Holmes, 1886, McGee, 1898; Spicer 1968:21). From relatively early on, there was a recognition of the existence of the concept of ethnic mobility, although that specific term was not used. History is replete with examples of the birth of new groups out of the fusion of two or more ethnic groups, e.g., the English, the French, the Iranians, the Métis of North America, the Latinos of South America, and the Mulattos of Brazil. Although we know of its existence, few (if any) studies focus on the measurement of ethnic mobility as a component of demographic flow.

The purpose of this article is to examine the issue of ethnic mobility in Canadian society from an empirical perspective, using data from the national Censuses of population. The emergence of new ethnic groups, such as the Métis, cannot be explained by the usual components of demographic flow. Ethnic mobility may be observed in the introduction of new response categories to the questions dealing with ancestry and identity. It may also be observed in either altered distributions of responses for identity or ancestry or in apparent inconsistencies between the respondents' declared origins and their reported identity.

This chapter begins with definitions of the basic concepts that are key to the analysis, including a very brief overview of the demographic principles that are germane to the study. The empirical section of the chapter provides evidence of demographic flows that serve to illustrate that the phenomenon of ethnic mobility can be observed. The conclusion of the chapter raises a series of questions that may serve to form a research agenda on this topic.

POPULATION DYNAMICS: DEMOGRAPHIC AND SOCIOLOGICAL
PERSPECTIVES

Demography has been defined as the "science of population" (Shryrock, Siegal, and associates, 1976:1). In its broadest terms, a population is defined as "the totality of the persons inhabiting a given location" (Jary and Jary, 1991:482). A given population has three basic dimensions: its stock, which includes characteristics such as age, sex, size, and composition; its location, which generally corresponds to an area defined by some geopolitical boundaries; and its flow, which is the result of fertility, mortality, and migration. The definition given above focuses primarily on geographic or geopolitical boundaries, such as the population of Canada or of Quebec, and does not take into account other dimensions that may serve to define a population, such as socio-cultural characteristics. Populations may be further subdivided into groups based on selected socio-demographic and/or economic characteristics of the stock. For instance, it is possible to define population groups on the basis of age (the elderly aged 65 and over) on the basis of ancestral origins (the population of Ukrainian descent), or some combination of characteristics (Chinese women). The three dimensions of populations referred to above generally apply to population groups as well.

Ethnic groups are a specific instance of population groups. They may be defined as "a community-type group of people who share the same culture or to descendants of such people who may not share this culture but who identify themselves with this ancestral group" (Isajiw 1993:411). Before proceeding too far with these definitions, it is important to note that the meaning and interpretation of ethnicity may not be entirely clear and agreed upon by all researchers in the field. For instance, Schermerhorn (1970:12) bases his definition of ethnicity on "real or putative common ancestry." This clearly locates ethnicity as a characteristic describing the ancestral origins of the individual. Other authors, such as Breton, et al. (1990:10), view ethnicity as a more subjective attribute that is based on factors such as identity and cultural behaviour. Since the focus of this study is ethnic mobility, ethnicity is considered in the context of the affiliation of individuals to groups, which locates it in the domain of a subjective attribute.

Boundaries are conceptually defined as "any sociocultural, political, economic or sociological feature that is observably distinctive for constituent groups in a plural society" (Cohen and Middleton, 1970). This definition raises two key points. First, boundaries must be visible, which, in turn, implies that they are measurable. Secondly, the use of the term "plural society" implies the coexistence of more than one group in a given locality. Clearly, in a population in which there is only one group, ethnicity is not a salient delineation. However, there are very few instances in which this condition holds true (Cohen 1993:367). Certainly, given the importance of immigration as a component of demographic growth in Canada and the resulting ethnic mosaic that is Canadian society, the opportunity is present for contact between members of different ethnic groups.

Furthermore, according to Frederik Barth's (1969) subjectivist approach, a given ethnic group is described by its boundaries in relation to other groups at a given point in time. By adding a temporal dimension to the definition, Barth opens the door to the possibility of change in boundaries, a point that is central to the discussion on ethnic mobility.

If one examines the delineation of ethnic groups over time in a multicultural society such as Canada, two crucial points become apparent. First, the definition of ethnic groups may be externally or internally generated. In some cases, the characteristics that define the group are ascribed by others—externally imposed boundaries—such as the broad classification of "visible minority" that is used in anti-discrimination legislation in Canada. In other cases the boundaries are defined on the basis of how the individuals who make up the group perceive themselves—boundaries based on self-identification—such as the Métis people. Both types of definitions are subject to change overtime, although the externally imposed boundaries may be more volatile since the conditions under which they are imposed are often subject to socio-political considerations.

This leads to the second point. The boundaries describing ethnic groups are permeable and malleable since they are generally based on characteristics of the stock and on relations within a given society. Since membership in an ethnic group is based on presumed identity (Weber, 1978), it is reasonable to assume that the criteria on which the identity is based may change overtime. Boundaries may change as a result of one or more of the following factors: demographic shifts in the population caused by natural population increase and decrease; migration and changing marital patterns; changes in the means of observing and measuring the boundaries; changes in the socio-political context and environment; and changes in attitudes and perceptions of people toward their origins (Goldmann, 1994:15).

In classic demographic analyses, the change in size of a population group occurs through natural processes such as births and deaths and through geographic migration. If we accept the notion that the boundaries defining ethnic groups within a given society are permeable and subject to change, we may add ethnic mobility as a component of flow.

ETHNIC MOBILITY DESCRIBED

Ethnic mobility is defined as the virtual movements of people through changes in their group affiliation. This may be either self-imposed as a result of shifts in how people declare the group with which they identify—voluntary ethnic mobility, or it may be externally imposed by changing the definition of a group thereby moving the boundaries to include a different subset of people—imposed ethnic mobility. Ethnicity, the boundaries defining ethnic groups, and the flows of people between groups are fundamental components of the concept of ethnic mobility. The first two have already been dealt with. The following discussion deals with the third component.

Certain conditions must exist in order for mobility to occur and to be observed. First, movement occurs between a point of origin (the source) and a destination (the target). In the case of ethnic mobility it is not necessary for the source and target groups to be geographically distinct. However, they need to be identifiable in some sense in order to be able to observe the results of the movement.

Second, the movement must result in an observable difference in the target population. Malinowsky (1945) and his colleagues at the London School of Economics called attention to the fact that contact between members of different groups inevitably resulted in change. In other words, prolonged contact between different ethnic groups will result in some degree of mobility, as manifested in changes in identity either at the individual or collective level. At a minimum, there will be observable changes in the respective sizes of the source and destination groups. It may also result in an observable change in the characteristics of one or both groups.

Third, the socio-political and economic context in which the target and source population groups exist must support such a movement. It may, in fact, be the catalyst for this type of movement (Bromlei, 1974:69). For instance, in a society where exogamous marriages are acceptable, some form of ethnic mobility will be observed among the offspring of such unions (Bromlei, 1984:54–64). The process of acculturation may also result in ethnic mobility. John Berry (1991) and Berry and Sam (1997) describes four strategies of acculturation—assimilation, integration, separation, and marginalization—each of which implies some degree of ethnic mobility. Assimilation and marginalization imply a radical ethnic mobility, one in which the members of one group make a complete transition to another group. For example, after many generations in Canada the members of some ethnic groups like the British, French, or Germans now declare themselves to be ethnically Canadian in the Census, signalling a movement of their declared identity from their ancestral group. Integration and separation may or may not result in ethnic mobility. It may be argued that the presence of hyphenated ethnicities that are symbolic of either integration or assimilation, such as African-American or Jewish-Canadian, is an example of ethnic mobility since it results in the forming of new groups.

Fourth, the movement or flow must be measurable. Ideally ethnic mobility is best measured though a longitudinal survey. However, the Census and related cross-sectional surveys provide an indication of changes in declared origins and/or identities. They also measure changes in the sizes of either the target population group when there is an inflow or the source population group in the event of an outflow. Finally, it is possible to determine whether group boundaries and definitions have changed as a result of the movement by analyzing the characteristics of the declared origins and/or identities.

METHODOLOGY

THE STUDY POPULATION

The rationale for selecting the four ethnic groups for this study includes their history with respect to immigration to Canada, the characteristics by which they are defined, their respective attitudes toward exogamy, and their representation in the total population. It is important that the groups selected represent "old" migrants with a long history in Canada, such as the Germans and the Ukrainians, and relatively newer migrants such as the Jews and the Chinese. The terms "new" and "old" are relative in this context as, for example, there is evidence of Jewish migration to Canada before Confederation. However, the bulk of Jewish migration occurred in this century. Similarly, although they were employed as migrant workers in the construction of the national railway, most of the Chinese population living in Canada arrived in the second half of the 20th century. By contrast, German and Ukrainian migration to Canada occurred in the middle to the end of the 19th century.

Data Sources and Extraction Criteria

It is important to note that the characteristics by which the groups are defined (i.e., their boundaries) contribute a great deal to the potential for ethnic mobility. For instance, people belonging to a group that is defined largely on phenotypical characteristics, such as the Chinese, are less likely to identify solely with another group. Furthermore, it is unlikely that someone without the phenotypical features will identify with the group. A similar argument may be made for a group that is defined in part on religious characteristics, such as the Jewish population. However, the argument isn't as strong since it is possible for people to convert to Judaism and to adopt the corresponding identity and culture. It is also possible for members of this group to leave by identifying with another group such as Canadian.

Exogamy is probably one of the major catalysts for ethnic mobility. Intermarriage, especially when it occurs over a number of generations, results in multiple identities. It is possible that as the number of identities increases the salience of a particular group to the individual concerned diminishes. This may result in one of two conditions: the individual will either select one identity on the basis of cultural attachment or rational choice or he or she will simply adopt the identity of the majority—i.e., he or she will assimilate. In either case, this represents ethnic mobility.

The data for this study were extracted from the 1971, 1981, 1986, 1991, and 1996 Censuses of population. Since the focus of this study is on non-immigrants, respondents who declared that they were immigrants are removed for the analysis. This includes people who were non-permanent residents as well as people living in institutions. The data on ethnic origin served as the key for selecting the members of the populations under study. All non-immigrants who responded that they were a member of one of the four designated ethnic groups were selected for the sample. The selection criteria included respondents who reported both single and multiple origins in the 1986, 1991, and 1996 Censuses.

Selection of Birth Cohorts

True longitudinal analysis requires that data for the same population are available for a series of time points. Since no form of personal identification is included in the Census data, it is necessary to simulate longitudinal analysis by selecting cohorts of respondents according to criteria that minimize the impact of change in their definition over time. Such an approach may be further refined by controlling for exogenous factors that can affect the composition of the cohorts, such as immigration and emigration. The cohorts for this study (Table 20.1) were selected on the basis of year of birth.

The lower and upper bounds of the cohorts eliminate the effect of births and minimize the effect of deaths. It is a demographic fact that in a closed population group (one in which there is no inflow from births and immigration and no outflow due to factors other than natural causes—mortality) the size of the group will decrease over time. The intensity of that decrease is a function of the survival rates for this group. According to the survival rates calculated from the standard life tables for the Canadian population mortality is not a significant factor for these cohorts over the time period covered in the analysis. In any event, the projections described below effectively control for mortality, thereby minimizing its impact on the results.

Table 20.1 Birth Cohorts for the Study Population, Canada

Cohort	Years of Birth	Ages in 1971	Ages in 1981	Ages in 1986	Ages in 1991	Ages in 1996
1	1952–1956	15–19	25–29	30–34	35–39	40–44
2	1947–1951	24–29	20–34	35–39	40–44	45–49
3	1942–1946	25–29	35–39	40–44	45–49	50–54
4	1937–1941	30–34	40–44	45–49	50–54	55–59
5	1932–1936	35–39	45–49	50–54	55–59	60–64

PROJECTIONS BY COHORT

Two series of projections are presented in this chapter. The first is based on 1971 population data and the second is based on 1986 data. It is important to note that these two Census years represent major milestones in changes in the methodology used to collect the data that are germane to this study. Census data were collected using self-enumeration for the first time in 1971. The 1986 Census represents a major departure from previous Censuses with respect to collecting data on ethnic origin. Whereas the question on ethnic origin in previous Censuses encouraged the respondents to provide only one origin, in 1986 the question included plurals for the word "origin" and respondents were encouraged to mark as many as applied. Therefore, the second set of projections includes values for both single and total origins.

The projections were calculated by surviving the population by sex in each cohort for each ethnic group to the subsequent period using survival rates derived from the standard life tables. Ratios of observed to projected populations provide an indication of the impact of factors other than mortality on the actual counts for each cohort. If the ratios remain equal to 1 over time, the only factor affecting the size of the cohorts is mortality. A significant increase in the ratio beyond one between two time periods is an indication that the size of the cohort has increased, taking into account the standard survival rates for the people it includes. A significant decrease below one between two time periods indicates that factors other than death are affecting the size of the cohort. The three most likely possibilities are emigration, undercount, and ethnic mobility.

EMPIRICAL EVIDENCE

GENERAL OBSERVATIONS

It is an acknowledged and well-documented fact that the Census questions that were used to collect the data on ethnic origin during the period covered by this study changed significantly (see Goldmann, 1993; Kralt, 1990). It is also an acknowledged fact that changes in the design of the survey vehicle will generally have an impact on response patterns (Goldmann, 1993:436). Therefore, the challenge in this analysis is to select time periods that minimize the impact of changes in the measurement vehicle.

The impact of the changes introduced in the 1986 Census is clearly visible in the data. First, there are significant increases in the counts of total ethnic origin for each of the

Table 20.2 Projections by Ethnic Origin, Non-immigrants, Canada

Cohort	Base Year = 1971		Base Year = 1986			Base Year = 1986		
				Single Origins			Total Origins	
	1971	1981	1986	1991	1996	1986	1991	1996
Chinese								
1	3,820	3,802	3,325	3,307	3,283	4,730	4,704	4,670
2	2,115	2,105	1,460	1,449	1,435	2,440	2,422	2,397
3	1,555	1,548	945	935	920	1,550	1,533	1,509
4	1,340	1,337	675	663	645	990	972	947
5	1,145	1,135	815	792	760	1,060	1,030	988
German								
1	102,915	102,451	60,670	60,339	59,903	184,545	183,568	182,276
2	83,740	83,348	44,880	44,555	44,097	140,245	139,244	137,827
3	71,860	71,518	40,740	40,298	39,660	105,660	104,524	102,882
4	61,200	60,847	39,470	38,780	37,784	85,550	84,059	81,908
5	58,600	58,099	39,310	38,179	36,574	75,855	73,684	70,600
Jewish								
1	22,800	22,697	14,670	14,591	14,487	21,130	21,017	20,869
2	19,960	19,864	13,255	13,160	13,025	18,310	18,180	17,995
3	14,715	14,643	9,950	9,843	9,689	13,325	13,093	12,887
4	9,920	9,863	7,295	7,167	6,983	9,290	9,128	8,895
5	9,650	9,568	7,410	7,200	6,901	8,855	8,603	8,246
Ukranian								
1	51,845	51,612	33,915	33,732	33,491	80,480	80,052	79,486
2	41,450	41,256	29,900	29,684	29,380	62,385	61,940	61,311
3	34,880	34,715	27,080	26,789	26,368	46,635	46,134	45,410
4	30,925	30,748	25,780	25,328	24,676	37,755	37,094	36,140
5	32,570	32,294	27,780	26,990	25,868	36,395	35,360	33,889

groups in the study population between 1981 and 1986. Second, counts are reported for both single and multiple origins. This is why the analysis focuses on the following two time periods: from 1971 to 1981 and from 1986 to 1996. This is not to suggest that no changes in the questions were introduced within these two periods—only that the impact of the changes on the analysis is considered minimal.

FROM 1971 TO 1981

In 1971, the Census question on ethnic origin asked respondents to report to which ethnic or cultural group their ancestors on the male side belonged on first coming to this continent. The qualifier "on the male side" was removed in 1981, thereby changing the underlying philosophy of the question from one dealing with patrilineal descent to one concerned with ambilineal descent. This allowed respondents to report their ancestry in the manner that was most appropriate in their particular circumstances (either patrilineal or matrilineal). Although one would anticipate that this would result in no change for ethnic groups that are defined along patrilineal lines and an increase for groups that follow a matrilineal tradition, this proved not to be the case. There was a decline in the counts in the following table for each of the four groups that comprise the study population. Emigration may be a factor, but it is unlikely to explain population declines of the scope indicated. Nor can the decline be explained by a shift to multiple responses. Although multiple origins were collected in 1981, they were not encouraged. Hence the incidence of multiple responses for ethnic origin was quite small. This leaves only three possible explanations—mortality, differential undercount, and ethnic mobility.

The results in Table 20.4 show that the ratio of the actual population to the projected counts is less than one in 1981 for each of the four groups of the study population, indicating that factors other than observed mortality rates contributed to the decrease in these groups. This suggests that undercount and ethnic mobility had a relatively high impact on the Jewish group (0.765), a moderate impact on the German and Chinese groups (ratios of 0.818 and 0.807 respectively), and a relatively low impact on the Ukrainian group (0.934).

An analysis of the distribution of ratios by cohort adds an interesting dimension to these results. For the Jewish and Ukrainian groups the ratio tends to increase for the older cohorts. This shows that the contribution of undercount and ethnic mobility to the

Table 20.3 Ethnic Origins, Projected and Actual, Canada, 1971 and 1981

	Chinese		German		Jewish		Ukranian	
	Projected	Actual	Projected	Actual	Projected	Actual	Projected	Actual
1971	9,975	9,975	378,315	378,315	77,045	77,045	191,670	191,670
1981	9,992	8,005	376,263	307,770	76,638	58,595	190,625	178,000
AAGR	-0.0536	-2.2002	-0.0544	-2.0637	-0.0530	-2,7374	-0.0547	-0.7399

Table 20.4 Ratio of Actual to Projected Ethnic Origins, Canada, 1981

Cohort	Chinese	German	Jewish	Ukranian
1	0.847	0.864	0.750	0.892
2	0.777	0.795	0.725	0.935
3	0.717	0.783	0.765	0.941
4	0.755	0.808	0.807	0.952
5	0.912	0.823	0.838	0.975
Total	0.807	0.818	0.765	0.934

decreases in size is greater for the younger cohorts. In the case of the Chinese and German groups, the potential contribution of these factors appears to peak in the middle cohort.

The result for the Jewish and Ukrainian groups is consistent with current knowledge of the impact of undercount on populations and with the conceptual notion that younger cohorts are more likely to change their ethnic affiliation, either as a result of intermarriage or as a result of changes in their outlook. More in-depth analysis is required to explain the results for the Chinese and German groups.

Undercount in Census data is the result of missing households and individuals during the enumeration process. It is age and sex dependent and it is correlated to some extent to socio-economic status. For instance, unemployed males between the ages of 20 to 24 tend to have the highest rates of undercount. The following table summarizes the respective rates of undercount for each cohort between 1971 and 1996.

Table 20.5 Rates of Undercount by Age Group and Census Year, Canada

1971		1981		1986		1991		1996	
Age	U/C	Age	U/C	Age	U/C	Age	U/C	Age	U/C
15–19	2.60	25–29	} 2.31	30–34	4.51	35–39	} 2.84	40–44	1.79
20–24	4.49	30–34		35–39	} 2.32	40–44		45–49	1.73
25–29	} 2.50	35–39	} 2.29	40–44		45–49	} 1.61	50–54	1.04
30–34		40–44		45–49	} 1.58	50–54		55–59	2.03
35–39		45–49	0.81	50–54		55–59	1.69	60–64	1.38

The key issue to consider in this analysis is the change in the differential undercount. If the rate remains unchanged or similar, then undercount is not a contributing factor to the change in the size of a cohort. Similarly, if the rate decreases between two successive Censuses undercount is not a contributing factor to the population decline. By examining the rates in Table 20.5 it is evident that no such changes occurred in undercoverage over this period (in fact, the rates have decreased for all cohorts between 1971 and 1981). Therefore, the decline in the population groups between 1971 and 1981 cannot be explained by differential undercount.

Emigration must be considered as a possible explanation for part, if not all, of the decrease in these groups. Unfortunately, no convenient or reliable sources of data on emigration by age and ethnic group exist for Canada. In absolute terms over this period, the rates of decrease range from a low of 7 percent for the Ukrainian group to a high of 24 percent for the Jewish group. Although it is possible for 7 percent of a particular population to emigrate over a 10-year period without drawing too much attention, it is unlikely that the emigration of 24 percent of a specific group would go unnoticed. In fact, there is very little anecdotal evidence to support any argument that suggests that emigration accounts for these decreases.

By a process of elimination this leaves only one possible explanation for the decline: People changed how they declared their origins from 1971 to 1981. It is not possible to empirically determine the exact direction of the ethnic mobility since we cannot trace a given respondent's data over time. However, given that only non-immigrants were selected for the study population, it is feasible that some of the respondents declared themselves as Canadian rather than their ancestral origins. It is also possible that some respondents of mixed ancestry selected a different origin in 1981. For example, someone of mixed Jewish and British ancestry may have declared himself or herself to be Jewish in 1971 and British in 1981. One other possibility, which was true in the past for the German group (de Vries, 1985; Ryder, 1955), is that the respondents selected an origin that they felt to be more acceptable given the socio-political climate of the day. The data do not allow us to pursue this line of analysis empirically.

THE MULTIPLE RESPONSE ERA: FROM 1986 TO 1996

The introduction of multiple origins as a standard component of the total responses to the question on ethnic origin in the 1986 Census represents the next major transition in collecting these data. Including both multiple and single ethnic origins presents an opportunity as well as a challenge in analyzing these data. It is now possible to examine the impact of multiple origins, which is one of the major indicators of ethnic mobility, on the growth and decline of each cohort.

The form and structure of the Census question on ethnic origin was essentially the same in 1986 and 1991. Both referred to "origin(s)" and both included more than one space to enter write in responses, thereby alerting respondents to the fact that multiple origins were acceptable. In fact, both included an instruction for respondents to mark as many responses as applicable. In 1996 Statistics Canada introduced an open question in which respondents were given the opportunity to write in their ancestry or ancestries. The text of the question was essentially the same as in the previous two Censuses. However, the question included four spaces instead of the list of check boxes and respondents were instructed to enter as many origins as applicable. Furthermore, Canadian was included in the list of examples.

In absolute terms the incidence of reporting multiple origins increased most dramatically for the Jewish and Chinese, with average annual growth rates (AAGR) of 3.6528 and 3.5758 respectively between 1986 and 1991. Since the growth rate in single responses was also positive for the Chinese group (1.1439), this represents a net influx of people. The situation is slightly different for the Jewish group. There was a decline in single origins between 1986 and 1991, which opens the possibility of a shift of responses from single to multiple origins. It is interesting to note that the decrease in the population declaring single Jewish origins (4,540) is greater than the increase in the number of people declaring multiple Jewish origins (3,655). This is reflected in the net decline of the total of all cohorts over this period—an outflow from this group. The German group remained relatively stable over this period—a slight increase in multiple origins (0.5959) and a slight decrease in single origins (–0.3804) resulting in a net influx of 0.2315. The Ukrainian group experienced a slight loss in both single and multiple origins over this period (–0.8189 and –0.1170 respectively) resulting in a net loss for this population.

Table 20.6 Counts and Average Annual Growth Rates by Origin, Canada, 1986 to 1996

	Chinese					German				
	Census			AAGR		Census			AAGR	
	1986	1991	1996	1986–91	1991–96	1986	1991	1996	1986–91	1991–96
Projected-single	7,220	7,147	7,044	-0.2045	-0.2901	225,070	222,151	218,018	-0.2610	-0.3756
Projected-total	10,779	10,662	10,512	-0.2007	-0.2846	591,855	585,080	575,494	-0.2303	-0.3304
Actual-single	7,220	7,645	7,290	1.1439	-0.9510	225,070	220,830	162,505	-0.3804	-0.1337
Actual-multiple	3,550	4,245	3,365	3.5759	-4.6463	366,785	377,915	395,745	0.5979	0.9220
Actual-total	10,770	11,890	10,665	1.9787	-2.1934	591,885	998,745	558,250	0.2315	-1.4006

	Jewish					Ukranian				
	Census			AAGR		Census			AAGR	
	1986	1991	1996	1986–91	1991–96	1986	1991	1996	1986–91	1991–96
Projected-single	52,580	51,981	51,085	-0.2368	-0.3401	144,455	142,500	139,782	-0.2693	-0.3884
Projected-total	70,820	70,021	68,891	-0.2269	-0.3255	263,650	260,581	256,237	-0.2342	-0.3362
Actual-single	52,580	48,040	34,445	-1.8060	-6.6534	144,455	138,660	116,700	-0.8189	-3.4484
Actual-multiple	18,240	21,895	25,995	3.6528	3.4329	119,195	118,500	120,485	-0.1170	0.3322
Actual-total	70,820	69,935	60,440	-0.2515	-2.9183	263,650	257,160	237,185	-0.4985	-1.6172

All four groups experienced a net loss in total reported origins between 1991 and 1996. When examining the components of total origin, we see that there were increases in multiple origins among the Jewish, German, and Ukrainian groups. This indicates that the growth in multiple origins was not sufficient to compensate for the decline in single origins for these three groups. By contrast there was a decrease in both single and multiple origins for the Chinese group.

The fluctuations in response patterns for both the German and Ukrainian groups between 1986 and 1991 were relatively modest. The AAGRs for single, multiple, and total origins ranged between –1 and +1. This is not surprising given that they are both relatively old groups with respect to their immigration history with a stronger tendency towards assimilation than either the Jewish or Chinese populations. A different pattern emerges between 1991 and 1996. There were significant rates of decrease in single origins and modest increases in multiple origins. This pattern is also consistent with the immigration history of these two population groups.

Three points surface when examining the ratios for both single and total origins for the total of all cohorts shown in Table 20.7. First, the ratios of single and total origins are greater than 1 for the Chinese group for 1991 and 1996. This indicates a growth in the group rather than the expected decrease due to natural factors for a closed population. By the logic presented in the analysis of the period between 1971 and 1981, we know that undercount is not a factor. Therefore, since the counts are for non-immigrants, the only explanation for this increase is ethnic mobility into the group. In other words, people who were not reporting themselves as Chinese in 1986 did so in 1991 and 1996.

Table 20.7 Ratios by Ethnic Group by Cohort, 1986 to 1996

	Cohort	Single/Projected Single		Single/Total			Total/Projected Total	
		1991	1996	1986	1991	1996	1991	1996
Chinese Origin	Total	1.070	1.035	0.670	0.643	0.694	1.115	1.014
	1	0.984	1.004	0.703	0.690	0.725	1.003	0.973
	2	1.076	0.896	0.598	0.612	0.587	1.053	0.914
	3	1.080	0.994	0.610	0.529	0.606	1.246	1.001
	4	1.305	1.309	0.682	0.636	0.725	1.399	1.230
	5	1.205	1.249	0.769	0.707	0.763	1.310	1.260
German Origin	Total	0.994	0.745	0.380	0.369	0.291	1.023	0.970
	1	0.975	0.710	0.329	0.312	0.243	1.026	0.961
	2	1.001	0.718	0.320	0.311	0.236	1.031	0.972
	3	1.012	0.750	0.386	0.383	0.299	1.017	0.967
	4	0.989	0.769	0.461	0.447	0.362	1.021	0.979
	5	1.004	0.807	0.518	0.513	0.426	1.013	0.983
Jewish Origin	Total	0.925	0.674	0.742	0.687	0.570	0.999	0.877
	1	0.929	0.664	0.694	0.637	0.529	1.013	0.871
	2	0.907	0.634	0.724	0.657	0.530	0.999	0.866
	3	0.938	0.663	0.752	0.712	0.571	0.990	0.873
	4	0.915	0.722	0.785	0.735	0.635	0.978	0.893
	5	0.939	0.739	0.837	0.787	0.681	0.999	0.908
Ukranian Origin	Total	0.973	0.835	0.548	0.539	0.492	0.987	0.926
	1	0.970	0.804	0.421	0.412	0.364	0.994	0.929
	2	0.955	0.788	0.479	0.466	0.415	0.982	0.910
	3	0.973	0.831	0.583	0.575	0.530	0.981	0.911
	4	0.978	0.870	0.683	0.684	0.633	0.976	0.938
	5	0.992	0.899	0.763	0.757	0.721	1.000	0.951

Second, the ratio for single origins for the German group does not vary significantly from 1 in 1991 and drops substantially in 1996 (0.745). If we accept that undercount is not a contributing factor, this leaves a shift to multiple origins and ethnic mobility, which are essentially the same phenomenon, as possible explanations. For total origins the ratio is 1.023 in 1991 and it drops to 0.970 in 1996. This tells us that the German group experienced a definite net inflow in 1991 and a net outflow in 1996 with respect to the expected pattern of population growth/decline. The net inflow in 1991 can only be the result of ethnic mobility. We cannot draw the same conclusion from the ratio for 1996 since it is only slightly below 1. Therefore, it is possible that emigration and ethnic mobility may be contributing factors.

Third, the ratios for single and total origins were less than 1 for both the Jewish and Ukrainian groups in 1991 and they declined further in 1996. As with the German group, the significant decrease in the ratio for single origins in 1996 indicates ethnic mobility either entirely to other groups or to multiple origins, including Jewish or Ukrainian. The decrease in ratios for total origins indicates a net outflow of people from these groups due to factors other than mortality. Since the ratios are substantially less than 1 in both cases, it is reasonable to conclude that ethnic mobility is a contributing factor to the decline in the size of these groups.

Since differential undercount is not a contributing factor, this leaves only emigration and ethnic mobility. Once again, emigration cannot be entirely dismissed, although it is unlikely to account for the observed declines in these groups. Given the observed shift of respondents to declare Canadian origins in the 1996 Census (Boyd and Norris, 1998), it is reasonable to assume that this phenomenon applies to these population groups.

CONCLUSION

An examination of the Census data for the respective ethnic groups that were part of the study population has shown that net growths and declines were observed that cannot be explained by natural population increases (births and deaths), by migration processes (immigration and emigration) or by variations in undercount. We have also seen that sociological and anthropological theory support the notion of ethnic mobility. Given the observed trends, and the theoretical foundation for this concept, it is reasonable to conclude that ethnic mobility exists and that it can be measured.

However, there are many questions left unanswered by this analysis. For instance, is ethnic mobility an artifact of the data-collection vehicle? Have changes in the measurement instrument resulted in ethnic mobility or were the instruments changed in response to the perception that ethnic mobility exists in the population? What is the impact of ethnic mobility on the socio-economic characteristics of the source and target populations? Can the results of this study be generalized to other, or to all, ethnic groups? Are there other factors, such as language transfer and socio-economic status, that should be considered as independent variables in future analyses? What additional data are required to adequately measure this phenomenon?

Understanding ethnic mobility, both as a phenomenon and as an event, will shed light on the dynamics of the relations between the groups that form the Canadian mosaic. This, in turn, will serve to overcome some of the barriers that currently exist in our society.

● ●

CRITICAL THINKING QUESTIONS

1. While ethnicity, at first glance, might be thought of as a fixed, ascribed characteristic to be easily measured through a Census, in reality this is far from the case. What evidence does Goldmann use to demonstrate this point? What is his explanation for this?
2. What is your ethnicity? Is their any uncertainty associated with the way in which you self-identify? Why or why not?
3. In societies like Canada, with a long history of immigration and intermarriage, racial and ethnic identities are far from stable. How might this be problematic in studying the socio-economic characteristics of distinct ethnic groups over time?

● ●

CHAPTER 21

FROM PRE-CONTACT TO THE PRESENT: THE DEMOGRAPHY OF THE ABORIGINAL PEOPLES OF CANADA

Donna Maynard and Don Kerr

● ●

INTRODUCTION

Even a brief demographic assessment of Canada's Aboriginal population should consider both "demographic processes" (fertility, mortality, and migration) and "demographic states" (size, distribution, and structure). For current purposes, we begin by considering the demographic dynamics of this population prior to first European contact in North America. We then move on to review some of the limited historical evidence on the demography of First Nations over the last several hundred years. The Aboriginal population in North America moved from a state of relative population stability prior to European contact through to almost three centuries of severe population decline (with excessive mortality). More recently we have witnessed a period of demographic recovery and rapid population growth, with many reasons for optimism.

This chapter on Canadian Aboriginal demography outlines some of the most salient changes to characterize this population by providing a brief sketch of the historical record. What sort of evidence is currently available on the demography of North America before European contact? How did the timing of their demographic transition differ relative to other Canadians? What sort of methodological and data problems limit the scope of research in this area? In addressing these issues, we will demonstrate how the Aboriginal population in Canada continues to be relatively unique in terms of its demographic development, with important implications for cultural continuity, public policy, and socio-economic development.

THE PRE-CONTACT POPULATION

POPULATION DISTRIBUTION

Most accounts of Canada's demographic history begin with European contact. Historical research is highly reliant upon the survival of historical records and documents, and

297

for that reason, there have been large obstacles to research into the early history of the peoples of the Americas. Nonetheless, the evidence that is available on the demography of North American before European contact has been pieced together through the efforts of archaeologists, physical anthropologists, and ethnohistorians. Physical anthropologists make estimates of the living conditions, diet, fertility, morbidity, and mortality of pre-contact peoples through the systematic study of skeletal remains and burial sites. Archaeologists can inform demographers about settlement patterns and technology use before contact. Ethnohistorians attempt to make sense of the scattered and incomplete documents left behind by the first Europeans who came into contact with the Aboriginal population. In combination, this information makes possible a number of inferences about the demography of the original inhabitants of Canada before and after contact with Europeans.

The distribution of population prior to European settlement in North America resembled its modern population distribution to a certain extent. Density was highest in the south of the country and diminished in moving further to the north, with the lowest population densities in Canada's Arctic regions. The coast of British Columbia and the Great Lakes/St. Lawrence river area had the highest population densities, with lower densities across the Prairies and in Atlantic Canada. Like today, the pre-contact population lived in greatest numbers in the most habitable areas of the country. Highly heterogeneous cultures existed between regions in which many unique languages and cultural attributes flourished (see Figure 21.1). In fact, a conservative estimate places the number of relatively well-documented and classified pre-contact languages at around 50 (Goddard, 1996). Historians have divided these languages into fully 11 distinct language groups, indicative of the very high level of linguistic and cultural diversity that existed in pre-contact Canada (Grimes, 2000).

British Columbia had the highest levels of population density before European contact. One half of the 50 languages recorded were found in this area. The peoples of this area were largely aquatic foragers, whalers, and fisherman who were able to take advantage of the mild climate and abundance and diversity of food sources, including salmon runs. These sedentary peoples are among the most densely populated non-agricultural peoples ever documented by anthropologists (Boyd, 1990). The Iroquoian nations of the St. Lawrence River and Great Lakes (the second densest region) lived an entirely different way of life. These farmer-hunters generally practised slash-and-burn agriculture quite extensively, which necessitated a semi-nomadic way of life as villages had to be abandoned every few decades when the land was exhausted, but were generally occupied year round (Saunders et al., 1992).

In the Prairies, many peoples lived nomadic lifestyles in small bands, with communal big game (bison) hunting as a primary source of food and other resources. As one moved further north, population density declined in Canada's northern boreal forests, which have limited resources and long severe winters. Population densities were limited by the carrying capacity of the land, i.e., the number of people a region could support, given the current state of technology, or the way people use resources (Boserup, 1965; Harris and Ross, 1987). In northern Quebec and Ontario, for example, there is little evidence of

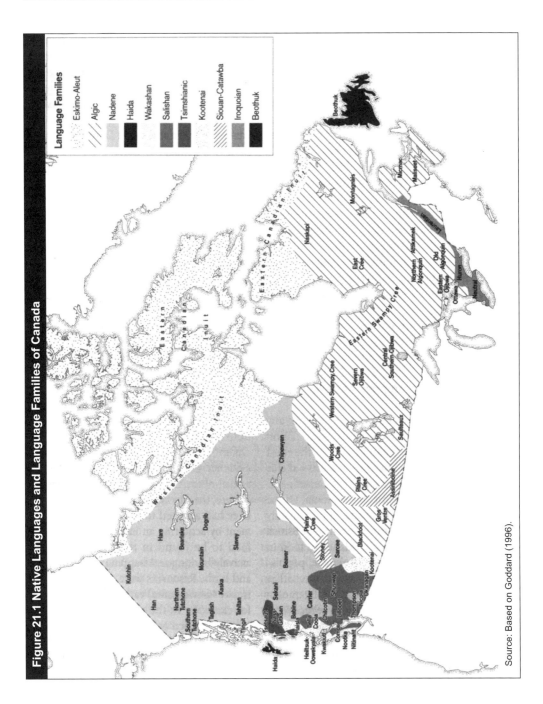

Figure 21.1 Native Languages and Language Families of Canada

Source: Based on Goddard (1996).

permanent settlements before contact and the people there survived by having a very intimate knowledge of the limited flora and fauna available. Canada's Arctic regions (often called the far North) were characterized by extremely low population densities distributed across a huge land mass from Greenland to Alaska. Many of the small communities were so isolated that bands of Copper and Netsilik Inuit were unknown to the Canadian government as recently as the 1920s (Morrison, 1984).

POPULATION PROCESSES

The pre-contact stage in Canada may be thought of as a quasi-stationary demographic state, with high mortality largely offset by high fertility. The net effect was likely population stability and, at times, slow growth (Romaniuc, 2000). This state existed until the arrival of Europeans, which initiated three centuries of disturbingly high levels of mortality and population decline.

MORTALITY

Prior to contact, mortality in North America appears to have paralleled the European mortality situation at this time. In fact, throughout most of human history and in most areas of the world, life expectancy at birth probably fluctuated between 20 and 30 years (Weiss, 1973). Excavations by anthropologists show that (like their European counterparts) pre-contact peoples had particularly high levels of infant and child mortality (Ubelaker, 2000). It has been estimated that the chances of dying before one's first birthday was about 25 percent, and that roughly 40 percent of all children died before reaching adulthood. Skeletal records suggest that much of this mortality was due to a variety of contagious/parasitic diseases, including tuberculosis, hepatitis, respiratory infections, gastrointestinal illness, and a variety of parasites (Ubelaker, 2000).

FERTILITY

Fertility levels in pre-contact Canada were probably universally high, which appear to have served to counteract high mortality. Despite a relatively high death rate, high fertility maintained population numbers, and even allowed for slow growth at times. Child-bearing started at a young age for women and continued until menopause, encouraging high fertility (Charbonneau, 1984). At the same time, involuntary sterility due to lack of nutrition or untreated disease was much more common than today, serving to limit fertility to some extent (Romaniuc, 2000). Breast-feeding, which temporarily suppresses fertility, was probably practised by many peoples for as long as two years. This had the effect of increasing the spacing of births, and thus lowered the total number of births for each woman (Jain and Bongaarts, 1981).

CONTACT

Contact with Europeans led to three centuries of population decline before population stabilization and recovery in the late 19th century. The actual number lost is open to debate, but this decline was certainly an enormous disaster in human and cultural terms. Exposure to Old World diseases is generally considered the most important of a variety of factors affecting this population decline. Mortality climbed (often dramatically) starting in eastern Canada, with first contact, and moving west in a piecemeal fashion after that. These Old World diseases had a dramatic impact under what have been described as "virgin soil conditions," as the population of North America had no natural immunity to diseases that originated in Europe. Many diseases had a devastating impact, including smallpox, measles, cholera, typhoid, diphtheria, scarlet fever, whooping cough, pneumonia, malaria, and yellow fever, among others (Thornton, 2000).

Records from priests, soldiers, traders, and early settlers contain many examples of epidemics decimating entire peoples (Dickason, 1992; Jenness, 1977). Although the effects of earliest of the epidemics are of unknown magnitude, some later ones into the 1800s were relatively well documented. For example, Boyd (1990) describes the events surrounding a major smallpox epidemic that hit the Queen Charlotte Islands in the 1860s, between Indian Censuses as conducted by the Hudson's Bay Company. When a ship infected by smallpox landed at Victoria, the disease quickly spread into a nearby Indian trading camp. Instead of being quarantined, the British authorities decided to send the members of this camp back to their various villages. Predictably, the populations of numerous settlements across the island were subsequently infected, with excessively high mortality. The subsequent Indian Census documented a dramatic drop in the enumerated population across the Queen Charlottes, which most obviously was a direct by-product of this pandemic. This was not an isolated event, but rather the fifth known outbreak of smallpox in this region since initial contact; depopulation continued through to the late 19th and early 20th century.

Romaniuc (2000) emphasizes that in addition to such pandemics, intensification of warfare and fighting (largely the result of French and British attempts to secure control over contested territory) also had its impact, as did the forced removals and destruction of traditional economies. A clear example of genocide exists in Canada, as the Beothuk people of Newfoundland were completely wiped out due to disease and constant feuding with early European settlers. The opening of the West to farming, which often involved the forced removals of the original inhabitants, caused the near extinction of the buffalo, the destruction of the traditional economic base of the region. The early history of Canada was particularly catastrophic from the point of view of the First Nations who originally inhabited the territories that were to eventually become Canada, with excessive mortality and resultant social disorganization.

ESTIMATING THE SIZE OF THE PRE-CONTACT POPULATION

As mentioned, the impact of the earliest epidemics is unknown, and is limited largely to reports of empty villages by early traders and officials. Information compiled by priests, soldiers, traders, and government officials were gathered many years after contact. This, some argue, makes it impossible to assess the impact of virgin soil epidemics or the extent of depopulation (Thornton, 2000; Ubelaker, 2000). Estimates on the size of the Canadian population before contact, then, vary widely and boil down to disagreements as to the accuracy of the earliest population figures recorded by early colonial administrators (Daniels, 1992).

When recordings began, some villages had already experienced pandemics, whereas others had been left largely unscathed. In addition, historical demographers have long recognized the shortcoming of these sorts of administrative records as colonial authorities were obviously not well trained as Census takers and were largely unfamiliar with the population they were attempting to enumerate. All demographic reconstruction, then, may be considered speculative. A low estimate of the pre-contact population (Mooney, 1928) used a systematic review of the earliest records available, with virtually no adjustments. This figure was around 200,000. Other conservative estimates include Ubelaker's (1976) estimate of 270,000, and Charbonneau's (1984) upward adjustment of Mooney's work, which estimated the population at 300,000. Yet perhaps one of the most widely referenced estimates was that of Dickason (1992:63), who estimated a pre-contact population of about 500,000, as based on informed judgment and considerable knowledge on the history of Aboriginal Canadians. In many ways, this might be considered a mid-range estimate, as there are other estimates several times higher than Dickason's figure (Dobyns, 1983; Thornton, 1987). The truth of the matter is that the exact scale of this depopulation will never be known, as pandemics often preceded European settlement, and as diseases followed trade routes with initial contact with priests, soldiers, and traders alike.

DEMOGRAPHIC RECOVERY: A CENTURY OF POPULATION STABILITY AND RAPID GROWTH

The late 19th and early 20th centuries saw the beginning of demographic stability and recovery for Canada's Aboriginal population after three centuries of population decline. The growth rate went from negative to moderately positive, with a nadir of 100,000 people increasing to 166,000 by 1951 (Goldmann and Siggner, 1995). Mortality was still high at this time, but the waning influence of epidemics in conjunction with consistently high fertility meant that births began to outnumber deaths and the population began to grow. At the time of contact, European and Aboriginal mortality were similarly high. By the 1900s Aboriginal mortality conditions resembled those of Europeans 100 years earlier (Romaniuc, 2000). There is little evidence that Aboriginal fertility at this time was anything but natural (i.e., no obvious intentional control) and remained high well into the 20th century. Major reductions to both mortality and fertility have since occurred in this population, but the timing and pace of decline has been significantly different than that of other Canadians (Trovato, 2000, 2001; Young, 1994).

DEFINITIONAL ISSUES

Measuring the demographic states and processes of the Aboriginal population in Canada has never been easy, and in certain ways has become more difficult. Aboriginal peoples are spread across Canada, living in urban and rural areas, on reserves, and in the far North. There are no residency rules, and no clear objective legal status with which to define this population. Several centuries of cultural exchange and assimilation, intermarriage, and mixed-ancestry child-bearing make identifying what constitutes the modern Aboriginal population and how it has changed particularly elusive.

A number of different strategies have been employed, which take into account ancestry as well as perceived ethnic identity and treaty status. These include Canadian Census questions about ancestry and, more recently, identity. Other data problems, however, also manifest themselves in terms of inconsistencies in data collection over time, leading to problems with establishing quality time-series. The data is often also limited to particular subgroups of the Canadian Aboriginal population (as, for example, exclusively the status Indian population). This inhibits research attempts to put together a more complete national demographic picture of this population, as a significant proportion of Canadians with Aboriginal origins do not have legal status under the Indian Act.

Despite the difficulties, data from a variety of sources, measuring this population in a number of ways show clear demographic and socio-demographic patterns. This includes the fact that the Aboriginal population has undergone a period of stabilization and rapid growth beginning in the late 19th century. Over recent decades, the number of Canadians who report Aboriginal ancestry has grown very rapidly as, for example, about 1.3 million Canadians did so in the 2001 Census. Most Aboriginal demographic characteristics and patterns of change deviate from those of the Canadian population as a whole. The population is younger on average, and both mortality (including infant mortality) and fertility have been consistently higher than that of other Canadians, up to and including the present. Health and other socio-demographic and economic inequalities related to various forms of marginalization have been widely associated with this difference in mortality and, to a lesser extent, fertility.

DECLINING MORTALITY

In an overview of mortality patterns among Aboriginal peoples in both Canada and the United States, Trovato (2001) points to common problems that emerge out of recent research. While there have clearly been long-term gains in terms of both life expectancy and infant mortality, Aboriginal North Americans continue to experience mortality conditions that are significantly worse than in their respective national populations. Whereas Canadian society overall is among the world leaders in terms of its level of population health, current features of Aboriginal mortality and morbidity clearly indicate epidemiological patterns that are very much at odds with this overall situation.

In examining past trends, unfortunately, the information as currently available on mortality is far from complete and can only provide for a partial picture. Part of the reason for this is that Canada's system of vital statistics, which is mandated to document all births and deaths in this country (including cause of death), has never allowed for the identification of Canadians on the basis of race, ancestry, or cultural origins. In examining the historical record, probably the best source of information currently available on the mortality of Aboriginal peoples is the Indian Register, a population register that is maintained by Indian and Northern Affairs Canada (Indian and Northern Affairs Canada, 1998). This register, which includes exclusively status Indians, has been continuously updated in documenting births and deaths as far back as the 19th century. In addition, there is also the lesser-known population register on the Inuit of northern Quebec, which has documented births and deaths as far back as the 1940s (Robitaille and Choinière, 1985). For both the Métis and non-status Indians, there is currently an absence of direct data on mortality, although some limited efforts have been made in terms of indirect estimation (Norris et al., 1995).

For the country as a whole, Canada has witnessed some rather dramatic gains in terms of mortality reduction, gains that can be well summarized by merely comparing overall life expectancy at the beginning and end of the 20th century. For example, average life expectancy for Canadians overall at the end of the 20th century has been documented as being about 30 years longer than at its beginning, which is suggestive of some rather important changes in the pattern of disease dominance. In 1901, male life expectancy at birth was only about 47 years whereas female life expectancy was only about 50 years (Statistics Canada, 1999). Yet while mortality was relatively high among Canadians in general, it appears to have particularly high among Canada's Aboriginal population (see Table 21.1). For example, in working with data from the Indian Register, Romaniuc (1981) has estimated a life expectancy at birth in 1900 for registered Indians of only 33 years, more than 15 years less than what has been documented for all Canadians at this time.

Among the Inuit, the earliest direct empirical evidence available was collected in the 1940s, and indicates a life expectancy at birth of only about 35 years (Robitaille and Choinière, 1985). Again, even by the standards of the day, such mortality can be considered as excessive. For example, Canadian life expectancy at the time was almost 30 years greater (at 66 years for females and 63 years for males). Among registered Indians, the situation was not much better, with little evidence of improvement throughout the first several decades of the century. By 1941 registered Indians in Canada had an estimated life expectancy of only 38 years. To put this into some sort of perspective, Aboriginal mortality in the 1940s appears to have been comparable if not worse than mortality levels currently documented in some of the most troubled regions of contemporary Africa, such as Zambia, Angola, or Sierra Leone (Population Reference Bureau, 2001).

Particularly important to explaining recent gains in life expectancy are significant reductions in infant and child mortality. Using data from the Indian Register, Romaniuc (2000) found that status Indians in the 1940s had an infant mortality rate of 200 infant deaths per 1,000 live births. By the 1970s, that figure had fallen to 40, more recently dropping to about 12 (Loh et al., 1998). The Inuit had even higher levels initially, but were down to a rate of 28 per 1,000 in the early 1990s (Frideres, 1998). These figures might be compared to Canada as a whole in the 1990s, where the infant mortality rate was about six deaths per 1,000. In other words, status Indians are twice as likely to die before their first birthday compared to other Canadians, whereas Inuit are four to five times as likely. In terms of overall life expectancy, the Inuit in the 1990s continued to experience mortality levels comparable to the Canadian population overall in the 1930s. While not nearly as high, the mortality of status Indians was comparable to what other Canadians were experiencing during the 1960s (see Table 21.1).

HEALTH AND CAUSES OF DEATH

This reduction in mortality as witnessed throughout the 20th century suggests a level of success in reducing the risk of premature death. The shift in mortality to older ages is itself a result of better nutrition and hygiene, higher standards of living, medical intervention, and antibiotics. Yet while there has been this decline in premature death for all Canadians, again this is true to a lesser extent for the Aboriginal population. Residents of many First Nations communities in Canada continue to witness higher risk of contagious and parasitic disease as well as a variety of non-communicable chronic health problems (Health and Welfare Canada, 1999).

A higher incidence of infectious and parasitic diseases is generally associated with poverty and difficult living conditions, which may involve inadequate housing, water

Table 21.1 Estimated Life Expectancy at Birth for Registered Indians, Inuit and Total Canadian Populations, for Selected Periods and Years, Canada, 1900–1995

Year or Period	Registered Indians Both Sexes		Inuit Northern Quebec	Inuit Northwest Territories	Total Canadians Year	Males	Females
1900	33				1901	47.0	50.0
					1921	58.8	60.6
1940	38		1941–51 35	29	1941	63.0	66.3
			1951–61 39	37			
1960	56		1961–71 59	51	1961	68.4	74.2
			1971–81 62				
	Males	Females					
1960–4	59.7	63.5			1966	68.7	75.2
1965–8	60.5	65.6			1976	70.2	77.5
1976	59.8	66.3			1981	71.9	79.0
1981	62.4	68.9			1984–6	73.0	79.8
1982–5	64.0	72.8					
1991	66.9	74.0	1991 58M/69F		1991	74.6	80.9
1995	68.0	75.7			1995	75.2	81.4

Sources: Registered Indian life expectancy: 1900, 1940, 1960 from A. Romaniuc (1981); 1960–4, 1982–5 from Medical Services Branch, Health and Welfare Canada; 1976, 1981 from G. Rowe and M.J. Norris (1985); 1991 from F. Nault et al. (1993); 1995 from Loh et. al. (1998). Inuit: N. Robitaille and R. Choinière (1985). Norris; (2000). Canadian: Statistics Canada, 1998. 'Canadian Life Tables', Vital Statistics.

supply, and sanitation (Indian and Northern Affairs Canada, 1999; Romaniuc, 2000). The largest differences of this kind of preventable mortality between Aboriginal and other Canadians are witnessed among infants. Differences are highest for post-neonatal mortality (beyond 28 days), which has been associated with socio-economic and lifestyle factors (Indian and Northern Affairs Canada, 1999). The First Nations and Inuit Regional Health Survey (Health and Welfare Canada, 1999) also notes that the Aboriginal population is more likely to report a range of chronic health conditions, including high blood pressure and diabetes, which tends to be the non-insulin-dependent type, having earlier age of onset and complications such as kidney disease and increased cardiovascular risks. Romaniuc (2000:119) emphasized that many of these difficulties are widely considered to be "poor men's afflictions."

Among Canadians as a whole, cardiovascular disease is the most common cause of death followed closely by cancer and other forms of degenerative disease. For status Indians, the most common cause of death is actually injury and poisonings, followed by cardiovascular disease, cancer, and respiratory illnesses (Bobet and Dardick, 1995; Indian and Northern Affairs Canada, 1999; Ponting, 1997). Frideres (1998) estimates that deaths due to accidents, injuries, and/or poisoning represent about one-third of all deaths on Indian reserves, while for the Canadian population overall, this cause represents only 6 percent of deaths. As the risk of accidents and degenerative disease vary strongly by age group (the former for younger people, the latter for older people), it may be suggested that part of this difference is due to the relatively younger age structure of the Aboriginal population (discussed further in the chapter). To some extent this is true as, for example, after standardizing (controlling for) the age structure, Harris and McCullough (1988) found that the differences due to accidental death were not quite as large, although status Indians continued to be three times as likely to die of injuries and poisonings than other Canadians.

FERTILITY

The fertility of Aboriginal Canadians through much of the 19th and early 20th century remained relatively high. Aboriginal levels of fertility at this point in time appear to have been largely limited by such determinants as involuntary sterility, age of entry into a sexual union, or whether or not a mother was breast-feeding her infant, rather than any deliberate use of fertility control methods (Romaniuc, 2000). Norris (2000) estimated that the crude birth rate (CBR) for status Indians from 1900 through the 1940s fluctuated at around 40 live births per 1,000 people, while Robitaille and Choinière (1085) estimated a CBR for the Inuit at around 30 to 35. Yet instead of a steady downturn trend in fertility analogous to what was experienced by the Canadian population overall (following major mortality decline), there is evidence to suggest that the CBR actually rose slightly in the 1950s for status Indians and the Inuit before stabilizing at levels higher than indicated above (Romaniuc, 2000). Although highly accurate data are not available, evidence suggests that fertility peaked during the 1950s, and then began a downward trend that has continued through to the present. For example, by the 1990s, the CBR of status Indians had fallen to only 22 live births per 1000 population. While this reduction is dramatic, it is still quite high compared to the Canadian population as a whole, which had an estimated CBR of 11 live births per 1000 persons at this same point in time (Bélanger, 2002).

It was during the postwar period and onward that most Canadians gained access to comprehensive health care and social assistance programs. Increased care decreased the risk of maternal and neonatal mortality and lowered the likelihood of stillbirths and spontaneous abortions (Romaniuc, 1984). Although fertility has been declining since the 1960s for the Aboriginal population, available time-series data on the status Indian and Inuit populations show that it has not fallen to the below-replacement level characteristic of Canada overall (see Figure 21.2). However, the timing and levels of child-bearing in the Aboriginal population increasingly resemble that of other Canadians.

DEMOGRAPHIC DIFFERENCES BY ABORIGINAL GROUP

At one point in Canada's history, the Aboriginal population could be defined easily on the basis of ancestry and way of life. In spite of the great variety among Aboriginal languages, customs, and material culture, there were recognizable common elements of culture and biology. Today, the situation has become far more complicated owing to several

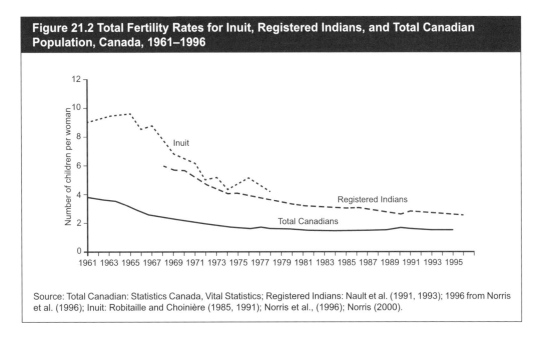

Figure 21.2 Total Fertility Rates for Inuit, Registered Indians, and Total Canadian Population, Canada, 1961–1996

Source: Total Canadian: Statistics Canada, Vital Statistics; Registered Indians: Nault et al. (1991, 1993); 1996 from Norris et al. (1996); Inuit: Robitaille and Choinière (1985, 1991); Norris et al., (1996); Norris (2000).

centuries of cultural exchange, assimilation, intermarriage, and births of mixed ancestry. Though it may have been obvious to the 17th- or 18th-century observer who was Cree or Micmac, as opposed to British or French, today it is often far from obvious.

As an example of some of the difficulties involved, the question must be addressed as to how one classifies people of mixed ancestry. This issue is not of minor consequence, since the majority of Canadians who currently report Aboriginal ancestry do so as part of a reported mixed ancestry. Of the 1,319,890 people who reported Aboriginal ancestry in the 2001 Census (or about 4.4 percent of Canada's population), well over half (754,845) also reported other, non- Aboriginal origins (Statistics Canada, 2003). Similarly, some people of Aboriginal ancestry report no particular affiliation or identification with their Aboriginal ancestry or culture (Siggner et al., 2001). Is it enough to rely upon the reported ancestry in delineating this population, and if not, what are some of the other criteria that have been proposed?

According to the Canadian Constitution, there are three major groups of Aboriginal peoples in Canada: North American Indians, the Métis, and the Inuit. While some might suggest that such a classification obscures a virtual "kaleidoscope of cultures and traditions" (Frideres, 1998), this classification has had wide circulation among social scientists and has certainly had a strong influence on the character of most demographic research. Yet although the Constitution recognizes these three broadly defined Aboriginal groups, it does not actually define what constitutes their populations. As a result, many researchers have merely relied upon information collected through the Census on ancestry or cultural origins in classifying people into one of the above categories.

A further subdivision of this population into two additional groups is provided for in the Indian Act (first passed in 1867): North American Indians who hold legal Indian status (status Indians) and those who do not (non-status Indians). By virtue of the Indian Act, status Indians have certain specified entitlements, including the right to elect representatives to negotiate with the federal government over land claim settlements and many other rights under treaties concluded with the Crown. According to the 2001 Census, which also asked Canadians whether they are "registered under the Indian Act," over one-half of the population with North American Indian ancestry are in fact status Indians (558,175 people out of 1,000, 890). This Census count of the status Indian population is widely considered an understatement of the true size of this sub-population owing to constraints on the quality of Census data. A number of reserves and settlements refused to participate in the Canadian Census, while even among those participating, the rate of coverage error (undercount) remains high.

In general, it may be said that the mortality and fertility conditions described are experienced to varying extents within these different groups. While status Indians and Inuit share the core Aboriginal demographic experience, that of non-status Indians and Métis more closely resemble the Canadian population as a whole. There are various reasons for this division. Non-status Indians and Métis experience higher levels of intermarriage, so it is expected that their fertility behaviour would more closely match that of the rest of the Canadian population. There are also greater similarities in certain socio-economic variables such as labour force participation, education, home language, and place of residence. Non-status Indians experience less of the social and geographic isolation that has continued to characterize many Inuit and reserve communities.

Indirect estimates show that both mortality and fertility are highest among the Inuit, followed by status Indians, Métis, and non-status Indians. Norris et al. (1995) estimated fertility rates of 3.4 births per woman in the Inuit population, 2.8 for status Indians, 2.4 for Métis, and 2.0 for non-status Indians. Likewise, life expectancy at birth has been estimated at 63 for Inuit, 72 for status Indians, 73 for Métis, and 74 for non-status Indians (Loh et al., 1998; Norris et al., 1995). In terms of overall population health, the rankings are similar with Inuit and status Indians more likely to be suffering from an illness or chronic disease (Indian and Northern Affairs Canada, 1999). There are also certainly demographic differences within each population, although this is particularly difficult to document. Census data show that Inuit living in southern Canada, for example, have lower fertility than those living in the far North (Robitaille and Choinière, 1985). In another example, mortality and fertility among status Indians are higher for those living on reserve than off reserve (Loh et al., 1998).

POPULATION STRUCTURE

As a by-product of higher fertility and mortality, the Aboriginal population is younger than the Canadian population as a whole. Median age for the total Canadian population in 2001 was 37.7 compared to 24.7 for the Aboriginal Identity population, 24 for status Indians, and 20.6 for Inuit (Statistics Canada, 2003). According to the 2001 Census, the percentage of the Canadian population as a whole under the age of 15 was about 20 percent, which compares to 33.2 percent for the Identity population and 39 percent for the Inuit. Similarly, a population is younger if it lacks significant numbers of people at the oldest ages. For all Canadians, one in eight people are age 65+; while for the Identity

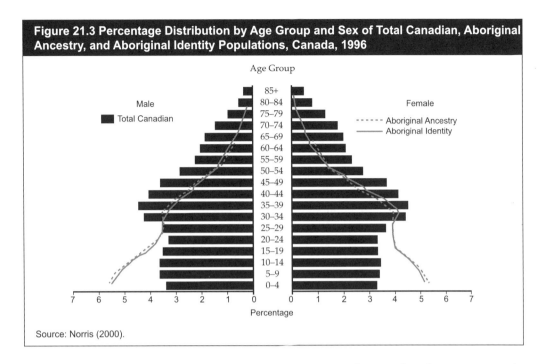

Figure 21.3 Percentage Distribution by Age Group and Sex of Total Canadian, Aboriginal Ancestry, and Aboriginal Identity Populations, Canada, 1996

Source: Norris (2000).

population this figure is one in 20. For the Inuit, it is even less, with only approximately one in every 30 people aged 65+ (Statistics Canada, 2003).

Age/sex structure influences societal working to the degree that roles and expectations are defined by gender and stage of the life cycle. Aboriginal peoples, then, have a distinctive set of challenges and priorities that are at odds with the current Canadian policy focus on population aging. This policy focus has tended to emphasize a redirection of resources away from the young and toward the old. This may be considered one of the ways in which broad public issues may be completely out of line with the needs and experiences of Aboriginal peoples. Priorities of young populations, for example, might include meeting young people's educational needs, assistance for those first establishing themselves in the labour market, and provisions for young families, including affordable housing. The role of the welfare state itself is different depending on the age structure of the population.

CONCLUSION

The demographic history of Aboriginal peoples shows clear patterns of stability and change. General population stability typified the pre-contact stage of Canadian history, followed by three centuries of severe population decline during early contact and colonization. The Aboriginal population stabilized again briefly in the late 19th century before beginning a period of rapid growth. This period was characterized by significant gains in life expectancy, although these gains continue to be lesser for Aboriginals than other Canadians. Fertility also declined during this period, but has yet to reach the below-replacement level of Canada as a whole.

In presenting a very general overview of recent trends, there are reasons for both optimism and pessimism. As alluded to throughout, the demographic conditions of Aboriginal peoples have been associated with various forms of marginalization, most importantly socio-economic. Indeed, Aboriginal peoples do not share equally in Canada's affluence. Substandard housing and health care, inadequate education, high unemployment, and low wages are all conditions that are particularly prevalent in many Aboriginal communities (Frideres, 1998; Ponting, 1997). On the other hand, in taking the longer-term view, the last half-century might be best labelled as a period of demographic recovery as Aboriginal peoples experienced major gains in terms of reducing mortality (with corresponding gains through natural increase). The age structure of Aboriginal peoples is also dramatically different from that of other Canadians (i.e., much younger), suggesting a distinctive set of challenges and priorities.

A growing proportion of Canadians currently identify with the Aboriginal ancestry, as official statistics suggest a phenomenal growth in number across North America. In reference to this situation in the United States, Passel (1997) speaks of a newfound political awareness and self-confidence that have contributed to a raising of North American Indian consciousness in a population that had heretofore not identified with this culture. The demographic future of Aboriginal peoples holds much uncertainty, depending not only on demographic trends but also on various non-conventional growth factors (such as intermarriage and the degree to which cultural continuity is maintained from one generation to the next). Various socio-economic, cultural, and political unknowns will have a direct impact upon how people identify in the future, perhaps even a larger impact than strictly demographic factors.

• •

CRITICAL THINKING QUESTIONS

1. Provide a sketch of the history of Aboriginal peoples from pre-contact through to the present. How did the timing of their demographic transition differ relative to other Canadians?

2. The Aboriginal population in Canada continues to be relatively unique in terms of its demographic development. What are some of the implications of current demographic trends? What are some of the more salient implications for public policy and socio-economic development?

3. Why do you think that both mortality and fertility continues to remain higher among Canada's Aboriginal population? Do you have any ideas as to what could be done to reduce excessive mortality? Do you consider higher fertility rates among Aboriginal peoples problematic? Why or why not?

• •

CHAPTER 22

SPATIAL RESIDENTIAL PATTERNS OF SELECTED ETHNIC GROUPS: SIGNIFICANCE AND POLICY IMPLICATIONS

T.R. Balakrishnan and Stephen Gyimah

• •

INTRODUCTION

One of the striking features of contemporary Canadian population is its remarkable ethnic diversity. There are more than 200 ethnic groups identified in the Census who have their origins in the migration of peoples from all over the world to Canada. The removal of discriminatory clauses in the immigration laws in the early 1960s, combined with the changing "push" factors in the countries of origin and the selection criteria used, resulted in an ethnic composition of Canada that is very different from what it was before World War II. While western Europeans predominated before 1960, in the 1960s and 1970s most immigrants were primarily from southern and eastern Europe. Since then, however, the majority of immigrants are from Third World countries. More than half of the immigrants since 1980 were the so-called "visible minorities": Blacks, South Asians, Chinese, Latinos, and Central Americans. For example, of the 1.8 million immigrants who arrived between 1991 and 2001, 58 percent came from Asia (including the Middle East), 20 percent from Europe; 11.5 percent from the Caribbean, Central and South America; 8 percent from Africa; and 3 percent from the United States (Statistics Canada, 2003).

The importance of immigrants and their composition on the Canadian population is further accentuated by the fact that their numbers now account for greater population growth than natural increase. Canadian fertility rates have been below replacement level for two decades, which affects not only entrants to the labour force but the proportion of the elderly in the total population. The proportion of foreign born in 2001 is 18.4 percent, the highest in 70 years. Only Australia, with a foreign-born population of 22 percent, is ahead of Canada in the industrialized world. Because the immigrants are usually in the more productive, younger age groups, their positive impact on fertility and labour force participation is significant.

The increased number of immigrants and their diversity poses challenging problems for the host society. Among the recent immigrants (1991–2001), 73.4 percent are visible minorities with very different cultural backgrounds. There was very little migration of visible minorities before 1961, much of the increase happening after 1971 (Table 22.1). About half of the visible minority population in Canada came between 1981–2001, and if we include the children born to these immigrants in Canada, their impact is even higher. An interesting observation in the table is that the number of immigrants during 1991–2001 was more than double those in 1981–1991. The only exception is Blacks, whose rate of immigration seems to have lessened compared to that of the Asian populations. Given present immigration policies, there is reason to believe these trends will continue for some time.

What is the best way to integrate minority groups into Canadian society and protect their rights and privileges? Integration can be perceived at various levels: spatial, economic, political, cultural, etc. Spatial integration would mean that the geographic distribution of various ethnic groups is similar to one another or, in other words, they are distributed as evenly as the total population across the country. Similarly, economic integration would mean that when education, training, etc., are properly controlled for, the income and occupation of the ethnic groups are similar to each other. Canada's multiculturalism policies are meant to achieve integration of various minorities while enabling them to preserve their heritage. This chapter investigates only one aspect of integration, namely, the spatial aspect.

SPATIAL INTEGRATION OF ETHNIC GROUPS

An examination of the geographical distribution of ethnic groups in Canada shows a wide diversity by regions, provinces, cities, and areas within cities. Many of these

Table 22.1 Selected Visible Minority Groups by Immigration Status, Canada, 2001

	Chinese	South Asian	Blacks	Filipino	All Visible Minorities
	%	%	%	%	%
Canadian Born	24.5	28.9	45.0	25.7	29.7
Foreign Born	73.3	69.0	52.0	72.3	67.2
Immigrated Pre-1961	1.6	0.3	0.7	0.1	0.7
Between 1961–1970	3.5	3.6	5.5	2.9	3.6
1971–1980	11.5	13.4	12.5	13.9	12.1
1981–1990	17.7	15.0	12.2	17.0	17.1
1991–2001	38.9	36.7	21.1	38.4	33.7
Non-permanent Residents	2.2	2.1	3.0	2.1	3.1
Total	100	100	100	100	100
Percentage Increase in Immigration Between 1981–1990 & 1991–2001	120.4	144.2	73.3	125.4	97.9
Number	1029395	917075	662210	308575	3983845

differences have historical roots in past immigration and settlement patterns. People of British Isles and French heritage predominate in the four Atlantic provinces. The French dominate in Quebec. Ontario is the most diverse of all with all European groups and Asians and Blacks represented. Germans, Ukrainians, Poles, and the Dutch are overrepresented in the Prairies, while English is most often reported in British Columbia (along with Chinese and East Indian). Internal migration due to various causes has reduced some of these regional ethnic differences over time. Recent immigrants who are largely visible minorities have their own distinct pattern of settlement. They are overwhelmingly attracted to the large metropolitan areas. In 2001, 94 percent of immigrants who arrived during the 1990s were living in Canada's Census metropolitan areas (CMAs), compared with 64 percent of the total population who lived in these areas. Nearly three-quarters (73 percent) of the immigrants who came in the 1990s lived in Montreal, Toronto, or Vancouver (Statistics Canada, 2003). This trend is not surprising. Employment opportunities and the presence of large numbers of the same ethnic group predict such a pattern. New immigrants choose to live near their previously established immigrant friends and relatives, a process referred to as chain immigration.

Two caveats should be underscored in the interpretation of the data on ethnic origin presented here and throughout the rest of the chapter. The first is the case of multiple reporting on ethnic ancestries. Mostly due to intermarriage, multiple reporting has become common, especially among the early immigrants to Canada, such as the British, German, and western European groups, but is less prevalent among recent immigrants. In 2001, 38 percent of the population reported more than one ethnic ancestry, an increase from 36 percent in 1996. Owing to double counting, the numbers will add to more than the total, a caution to be kept in mind when interpreting the data.

The second caveat has to do with the reporting of "Canadian." Changes to the ethnic origin question in the 1996 and 2001 Censuses resulted in an increase in the number of people reporting Canadian or Canadien as part of their ethnic heritage in both 1996 and 2001. In the 2001 Census, 39 percent of the total population reported Canadian as their ethnic origin, either alone or in combination with other origins, up from 31 percent in 1996 (Statistics Canada, 2003). Of these, 23 percent reported Canadian as their only ethnic origin while the rest (16 percent) reported Canadian along with other origins. Most individuals who reported Canadian in 2001 had English or French as a mother tongue were born in Canada, and had both parents born in Canada (Statistics Canada, 2003).

Both the incidence of multiple reporting and reporting Canadian occur much less often among recent immigrants, who are largely visible minorities. Most give only single responses, hence the analyses and their interpretation, which is of greater interest, for these groups are less ambiguous compared to the early European groups.

The ethnic composition of the populations in the three largest metropolitan areas of Canada in 1996 and 2001 show that the members of the charter British and French groups have decreased in all of them (Table 22.2). In Montreal, people who gave a British origin declined from 10.96 percent in 1996 to 9.3 percent in 2001. Similarly those who gave a French origin response decreased from 34.8 percent to 20.5 percent. It should be emphasized that these figures are deceptive, especially for the French, because of the Canadian response. In Quebec the number giving a Canadian response was very high. Many of French origin gave Canadian origin either singly or in combination with French. Therefore, the decrease in French response is compensated for by a corresponding increase in the Canadian response. In Toronto, those of British origins decreased from 31.9 percent in 1996 to 27.4 percent in 2001, and in Vancouver from 41.2 percent to 36.8 percent. Though there were less French-origin people in these two cities, they also showed a modest decrease.

Western and eastern Europeans who came to Canada earlier also show declines in their proportions in all three metropolitan areas. Italians and Portuguese (more recent immigrants coming mainly in the 1960s and 1970s) also show slight declines. Small declines can also be noticed in the Jewish case. In contrast, the visible minority groups increased substantially during the last five years under review here. In Canada as a whole, the proportion of the visible minority population increased from 11.2 percent to 13.4 percent (Statistics Canada, 2003). While the proportions in Montreal were similar to the national figures, the attraction of Toronto and Vancouver was overwhelming.

In Toronto the proportion of visible minorities, which was already high at 31.6 percent in 1996, increased substantially to 38.7 percent, and in Vancouver from 31.1 percent to 38.7 percent. About two-thirds of the minority population are made up of South Asians, Chinese, and Blacks, and all substantially increased their proportions in the three largest metropolitan areas, more so in Toronto and Vancouver than in Montreal. People of South Asian origin now form one-tenth of Toronto's population, the proportion increasing from 8.4 percent in 1996 to 10.8 percent in 2001. In Vancouver, the percentage of South Asians increased from 6.8 percent in 1996 to 8.3 percent in 2001. The increase in the proportion of Chinese was similar to that of the South Asians in Toronto. Vancouver's largest minority group increased proportionally from 15.8 percent to 17.6 percent in 2001. One person in six in Vancouver is presently of Chinese descent.

CONCENTRATION OF ETHNIC GROUPS WITHIN CITIES

Just as ethnic populations are unevenly distributed across the regions, provinces, and metropolitan areas, they are also non-randomly distributed within cities. Spatial residential patterns of ethnic and racial groups have been a long-standing area of interest for social scientists, urban planners, and political policy makers, which explains the interest in Chinatowns, Little Italys, and Portuguese, Greek, and Black neighbourhoods. In American cities, Blacks and Hispanics are often found to be highly segregated, which is a cause for concern for policy makers. One of the reasons for the interest in residential segregation is that it is often seen as a measure of how well or how poorly a group has integrated into the society at large. The assumption is that a group isolated in a particular area is probably not participating in the housing and labour markets to the fullest extent. It is further argued that living in close proximity to others of the same ethnic or racial background, while increasing interaction within groups, reduces interaction outside the group. Thus, while residential segregation maintains ethnic identity, it reduces integration into the wider society economically, socially, and politically.

Three hypotheses have been advanced and tested to explain the trends and changes in residential segregation. The first can be called the "social class hypothesis." According

Table 22.2 Percentage of Population by Selected Ethnic Groups in Montreal, Toronto, and Vancouver, 1996 and 2001						
	Montreal		Toronto		Vancouver	
Origins	1996	2001	1996	2001	1996	2001
Canadian	38.37	57.07	16.67	18.63	17.01	19.31
British	10.96	9.34	31.86	27.40	41.16	36.83
French	34.77	20.55	5.56	4.46	7.20	6.24
German	1.83	1.59	5.27	4.74	10.21	9.53
Dutch	0.36	0.33	2.00	1.85	3.58	3.42
Polish	1.15	1.14	3.78	3.59	2.73	2.61
Ukranian	0.60	0.59	2.25	2.25	4.00	3.89
Italian	6.64	6.65	9.72	9.25	3.51	3.51
Portuguese	1.18	1.21	3.79	3.69	0.86	0.85
Jewish	2.70	2.38	3.67	3.47	1.21	1.12
South Asian	1.45	1.79	8.43	10.84	6.84	8.30
Chinese	1.54	1.73	8.43	9.35	15.77	17.63
African	0.81	2.72	2.32	2.97	0.73	0.97
Caribbean	3.03	3.00	5.72	6.05	0.55	0.55
Aboriginal	1.33	1.46	0.93	0.96	2.58	2.66
All Visible Minorities	12.21	13.86	31.61	38.67	31.13	38.71

Based on total responses (those who gave single or multiple).

to this hypothesis, ethnic segregation is largely a reflection of social-class differences among the ethnic groups. Ethnic groups in Canada migrated at different points in time and vary considerably in terms of their socio-economic background, language proficiency, and educational and occupational skills. Lack of economic and social capital forces recent immigrant groups to live in the poorer areas of the city, often in the city core. As their conditions improve, they are able to disperse to more desirable neighbourhoods. With increased integration in the country's occupational and industrial structure, ethnic residential segregation should decrease. This basically human ecological perspective, which goes back to studies of Chicago (Burgess, 1925; Park, 1926), stresses the economic dimension and puts less emphasis, if any, on cultural and psychological factors in settlement patterns (Clark, 1986). While many studies have shown the importance of social class in residential segregation patterns, others have conclusively proven that much residential segregation remains even after one controls for social class, and alternative explanations must be explored (Balakrishnan, 1982; Balakrishnan and Hou, 1999a; Balakrishnan and Kralt, 1987; Darroch and Marston, 1971; Dunn, 1998; Fairbarn and Khatun, 1989; Massey and Denton, 1988; Ray, 1994). The continued high segregation of Blacks, Native peoples, Chinese, and South Asians in both Canada and the United States, in spite of their socio-economic advancement over the decades, supports this theory.

The second hypothesis states that ethnic residential segregation is due to social distance among ethnic groups. Social distance can be measured by such factors as acceptance of a particular ethnic group as work colleagues, neighbours, close friends, or spouses. Greater social distance should be reflected in higher levels of residential segregation. Prejudice and discrimination, strong indices of social distance, can be expected to correlate to residential segregation. Not surprisingly, many studies have found a parallel between social distance and residential segregation (Balakrishnan, 1982; Balakrishnan and Hou, 1999a; Bauder and Sharpe, 2002; Kalbach, 1990; Lieberson, 1970; Lieberson and Waters, 1988; Massey and Denton, 1987).

A third hypothesis explaining ethnic residential segregation may be called the "ethnic identity" hypothesis. This is fundamentally different from the two earlier hypotheses, which are based on the premise that residential segregation is due to involuntary causes (one's social class and social status determines residential choices) and hence are intrinsically bad. In contrast, the ethnic-identity hypothesis postulates that people of the same ethnic ancestry choose to live in proximity so that social interaction can be maximized and group norms and values maintained (Balakrishnan and Selvanathan, 1990; Driedger and Church, 1974). Size and concentration provide distinct advantages. Many institutions such as ethnic clubs, churches, heritage language newspapers, stores specializing in ethnic food, clothing, etc., require threshold populations concentrated in space. Thus, ethnic residential segregation has certain merits whether or not it is perceived as such by the ethnic group. According to this hypothesis, the greater the self-identity of an ethnic group, the more likely they will be residentially segregated. The level of self-identity among the ethnic groups may vary for several reasons. Apart from historical and political causes, it could be due to the strength of commonly held beliefs and values, kinship networks, and feelings of solidarity.

With the type of macro-level Census data we are examining, it is hardly possible to test these hypotheses rigorously. The data do, however, provide a theoretical framework for interpretation. While one cannot separate the effects of social class, social distance, or self-identity on residential segregation levels, it is possible to observe the relationship between residential segregation and these underlying factors.

Our analysis will be restricted largely to the three largest metropolitan areas of Montreal, Toronto, and Vancouver. They attract most of the immigrants and are very ethnically diverse metropolitan areas. The data used here are from the Canadian Censuses at the Census tract (CT) level. We will largely deal with the responses to the ethnic origin questions, classified in 10 broad categories. One should always be aware of the differential impact of multiple origin responses in these categories. One simple way of assessing the extent of spatial concentration is by seeing whether a particular ethnic group is over- or underrepresented in an area. As the CTs are supposed to be fairly comparable in overall population size, an idea of concentration can be obtained by comparing the cumulative proportion of CTs with the cumulative proportion of the ethnic population in those tracts. Census tracts in the three CMAs were arranged in decreasing order of ethnic population in 2001, and the cumulative proportions calculated. Table 22.3 shows the extent of concentration by examining the proportion of tracts in which 50 percent and 90 percent of an ethnic-group population is found.

There is a low concentration of people of British and French origins in all three cities. Though the British are a minority in Montreal, they do not show a high level of concentration. About a fifth of the tracts have to be covered to account for half of the British origin population, and more than two-thirds to account for 90 percent of the population. Although the French are a much smaller group in Toronto and Vancouver, they show very little concentration. In fact, they are as dispersed as they are in Montreal. Earlier studies on previous Census data have also shown that there is little French concentration in the CMAs outside of Quebec (Balakrishnan, 2000). Concentration is also low for the western, central, and eastern European groups, though slightly more than for the British. Italians are somewhat more concentrated than the other European groups, probably a function of their more recent migration to Canada. Half the Italians in Montreal live in 12.3 percent of the CTs, and in Toronto in 13.6 percent of the tracts.

Table 22.3 Percentage of Census Tracts in which 50 Percent and 90 Percent of Ethnic Populations are Concentrated, Montreal, Toronto, and Vancouver, 2001

Ethnic Group	Montreal	Toronto	Vancouver	Montreal	Toronto	Vancouver
		50%			90%	
British	19.7	25.4	29.3	71.4	70.0	73.3
French	29.8	25.3	28.5	74.7	68.7	72.8
Western Europe	21.0	24.5	29.3	68.1	68.7	73.6
Central and Eastern Europe	17.8	26.0	32.4	60.4	72.4	76.7
Italian	12.3	13.6	23.1	55.9	60.6	68.7
Jewish	2.4	3.8	14.3	13.6	26.2	51.0
South Asian	4.6	13.7	10.4	27.2	50.1	50.0
Chinese	9.1	10.2	10.6	42.4	50.6	50.3
African	14.15	15.9	22.5	50.2	57.4	63.0
Caribbean	11.5	17.4	20.2	44.7	57.5	57.5
Number of Tracts	**846**	**924**	**386**	**846**	**924**	**386**

The most residentially concentrated minority group in Canada are the Jews. In 2001, half the Jewish population in Montreal lived in 2.4 percent of the CTs, and 90 percent in 13.6 percent of the tracts. Their concentrations show little change over the years. In 1991, the corresponding figures were 2.0 percent and 9.0 percent respectively (Balakrishnan and Hou, 1999a). They are also highly concentrated in Toronto, the corresponding figures being 3.8 percent and 26.2 percent respectively. They are somewhat more dispersed in Vancouver, with half the Jews living in 14.3 percent of the CTs. It is interesting to note that the two CMAs where two-thirds of all Jews in Canada live, Montreal and Toronto, are also where they are most concentrated (they are less concentrated in other CMAs; figures not shown here). It seems size has a positive effect on concentration for the Jews even though they are not recent immigrants, nor are they in the lower socio-economic classes. Their concentration is probably more a function of a strong cultural bond.

After the Jewish population, visible minorities are the most concentrated groups in the three cities. In Montreal, half the South Asians lived in 4.6 percent of the CTs, and 90 percent in 27.2 percent of the CTs. They show little change from the situation 10 years ago in 1991, when the corresponding figures were 5.1 percent and 21.3 percent respectively. Among the visible minorities, they were the most concentrated. They are less concentrated in Toronto and Vancouver, where most of them live. Half the South Asians live in 13.7 percent of the CTs in Toronto and 10.4 percent in Vancouver. Chinese show somewhat lower concentration than do South Asians in Montreal, but in Toronto and Vancouver, their concentration is about the same. Half the Chinese live in about a tenth of the CTs in all three CMAs. The Black population, whether of African or Caribbean origin, show significantly lower concentration than the other two major visible minorities of Chinese or South Asians, a striking difference from the U.S. residential patterns (Massey and Denton, 1987). This is surprising given their lower socio-economic position compared to the Asian population and their not too different position in the social distance scale. One may surmise that the greater cultural diversity among the Black population may have something to do with this pattern.

A summary measure, the Gini Index, was constructed to investigate the extent of spatial concentration of a minority group in a city. It is derived from concentration curves, also known as Lorenz curves. The vertical axis shows the cumulative percentage of the population in a particular ethnic group, and the horizontal axis shows the CTs arranged in decreasing order of the ethnic population. A curve that coincides with the diagonal line indicates that the ethnic population is distributed equally among the CTs, implying no spatial concentration. The farther the curve is from the diagonal, the greater the concentration. The Gini Index is the ratio of the area between the curve and the diagonal to the area of the triangle above the diagonal. Thus, the range is from 0 to 1, where 0 indicates no concentration and 1 indicates complete concentration.

The Gini indices for the three CMAs for 1986–2001 are shown in Table 22.4. The figures for 2001 are not strictly comparable to the earlier years; 2001 figures are calculated using total responses (single as well as multiple) while the earlier figures are calculated based only on single responses. Some categories for 2001 are grouped and hence cannot be constructed for earlier years. Subject to these limitations, we can make some interesting observations. The Gini indices of concentration are uniformly high in Montreal for the various ethnic groups. Earlier studies have all shown high concentrations in comparison to the rest of the metropolitan areas in Canada (Balakrishnan, 1982; Balakrishnan and Hou, 1999a). Obviously the ability to speak French plays a large part in the choice of residential location in Montreal. Language facility among the ethnic groups varies a great deal depending on the place of origin, date of immigration, etc. As mentioned earlier, the European groups are less concentrated. There seems to be a decline in the concentration of Italians over the time period 1986–2001 in all three CMAs. Gini indices are very high for the Jewish population and continue to be so, except in Vancouver where they are lower and seemed to decline in recent years. South Asians and Chinese have high concentration indices throughout the 1986–2001 period. High immigration during the recent decade does not seem to have increased the concentration indices.

Table 22.4 Gini Indices of Concentration by Ethnic Group for Montreal, Toronto, and Vancouver, 1986 to 2001

Origin	Montreal				Toronto				Vancouver			
	1986	1991	1996	2001	1986	1991	1996	2001	1986	1991	1996	2001
British	0.533	0.538	0.650	0.442	0.287	0.323	0.357	0.375	0.255	0.262	0.299	0.315
French	0.365	0.405	0.404	0.304	0.341	0.387	0.433	0.380	0.357	0.356	0.400	0.330
Western Europe				0.421				0.388				0.319
Central & E. Europe				0.502				0.360				0.264
Italian	0.715	0.688	0.691	0.580	0.638	0.627	0.625	0.550	0.610	0.579	0.547	0.411
Jewish	0.922	0.924	0.927	0.895	0.861	0.880	0.887	0.814	0.732	0.740	0.725	0.586
South Asian	0.804	0.834	0.803	0.809	0.650	0.630	0.623	0.593	0.585	0.624	0.653	0.629
Chinese	0.770	0.731	0.704	0.675	0.672	0.668	0.676	0.635	0.654	0.608	0.564	0.569
Black	0.715	0.703	0.624		0.632	0.624	0.581		0.637	0.618	0.488	
African				0.587				0.541				0.444
Caribbean				0.646				0.518				0.494

1986–1996 are based on single responses only.
2001 are based on total responses.

The case of Blacks is interesting given their very different patterns from the U.S. In America, Blacks are highly concentrated. The indices for the Blacks are almost twice that for the Asians, whereas in Canada, they are less concentrated than the Asian groups. Unlike Blacks in the U.S., Blacks in Canada are more recent immigrants with a wide diversity in terms of places of origin, historical past, and cultural background. There is a mix of African Blacks, French-speaking Haitians, and English-speaking Caribbeans, as well as a sizable number of native-born Blacks. This lack of homogeneity may explain their greater dispersion in Canadian cities.

In summary, concentration on the whole is highest in Montreal and lowest in Vancouver, with Toronto in the middle. While the generally high indices in Montreal can be attributed to the distinctness of French culture and language to the immigrant groups, it is problematic to explain why Vancouver has lower indices than Toronto. Our earlier studies have also noticed this difference between Toronto and Vancouver (Balakrishnan, 1982; Balakrishnan and Hou, 1999a). Our explanation then was that the western CMAs, such as Calgary, Edmonton, and Vancouver, attracted a large number of immigrants simultaneously rather than in sequence as in Toronto, and hence did not have time to develop distinct ethnic enclaves. Whether there is also a greater tolerance and acceptance of ethnic diversity in the West and whether this has resulted in lower residential segregation is open to empirical investigation. Among the ethnic groups, concentrations are lower for European groups and higher for visible minorities. Concentrations over the time period 1986–2001 have remained stable or declined for most of the ethnic groups.

SEGREGATION OF ETHNIC GROUPS

In the previous section, we calculated Gini indices, which measured the spatial concentration of a minority group. The indices would be high if the minority group lived in a small portion of the total area of a city. In contrast, when the group is distributed widely in a city, the indices would be low. Segregation, on the other hand, measures the degree to which two or more groups live apart from one another. Thus, the two are different conceptually and methodologically. However, they are often found to be highly correlated. When a minority group is concentrated in space, it is also more likely to be segregated from other groups. In this section, we will focus on the extent of segregation between ethnic groups, measured by the Index of Dissimilarity (ID). The Index of Dissimilarity compares the distribution of two different populations over the same set of spatial units (CTs in our case) in a metropolitan area. It is the sum of either the positive or negative differences between the proportional distributions of two populations. The index has a range from 0 (no segregation) to 1 (complete segregation). An associated index is the Index of Segregation (IS), which compares the distribution of a given population with all other populations minus itself.

The ISs for selected ethnic groups in Montreal, Toronto, and Vancouver are presented in Table 22.5. They are based on total responses, in other words, singly or in combination with another ethnic ancestry response. Due to changes in the categories used, some comparisons between 1996 and 2001 were not possible. As observed earlier, segregation indices in general seem to be highest in Montreal and lowest in Vancouver. In Montreal, it is not surprising that the French are the least segregated. Their substantial majority in the city and dispersion across the city would explain this phenomenon. The British and western Europeans show relatively low segregation. The British seem to actually show a decline. Central and eastern European groups and Italians show moderate segregation (around .4). Jewish segregation has always been high in Montreal and continues to be so. The index of .777 in 2001 for the Jews is high and reaches the level found for Blacks in many U.S. cities. The visible minorities also exhibit high segregation, but show considerable differences among themselves. The IS for South Asians is .636 compared to .520 for Chinese. Blacks show lower segregation than Asian groups; .426 for African origins and .464 for Caribbean origins. The pattern of lower levels of segregation for Blacks compared to Asians is a clear departure from the U.S. patterns, where Black segregation is almost double that of the Asian groups (Massey and Denton, 1987, 1993).

Segregation indices are somewhat lower in Toronto than in Montreal, but show the same pattern. Certain observations can still be made. The French, though a minority in Toronto, show low segregation, the index being only .272, even lower than the British at .364. As a matter of fact, it is remarkable how well the French are spatially integrated outside of Quebec. The other European groups also have low levels of segregation, except Italians, who have a moderate index of .402. Jews continue to be the most highly segregated group in Toronto with a IS of .696, almost the same as in 1996. Visible minorities are more segregated than European ethnic groups. Unlike in Montreal, South Asians in Toronto are less segregated than the Chinese, and Blacks are noticeably less segregated than either the Chinese or South Asians.

Table 22.5 Segregation Indices for Selected Ethnic Groups in Montreal, Toronto, and Vancouver, 1996 and 2001

Ethnic Group	Montreal		Toronto		Vancouver	
	1996	2001	1996	2001	1996	2001
British	0.422	0.316	0.298	0.364	0.221	0.290
French	0.213	0.184	0.238	0.272	0.167	0.206
Other Western Europeans		0.282		0.292		0.216
Central and Eastern Europeans		0.409		0.303		0.142
Italians	0.437	0.432	0.396	0.402	0.237	0.257
Jewish	0.793	0.777	0.703	0.696	0.437	0.427
South Asian	0.632	0.636	0.432	0.440	0.489	0.517
Chinese	0.542	0.520	0.524	0.509	0.493	0.494
Black	0.470		0.388		0.311	
African		0.426		0.360		0.293
Caribbean		0.464		0.356		0.325

Based on total responses (single and multiple)

Vancouver is the least segregated of the three gateway cities in Canada. Earlier studies have consistently found this to be so, and the latest figures confirm this. The Charter groups of British and French and the European groups all show a level of only around .2. Even the Jewish population is less segregated with an index of .427, much less than in Montreal or Toronto. South Asians and Chinese, who form the two largest visible minority groups in Vancouver, show fairly high segregation with indices around .5. The reasons for this are to be found in the historical development of these groups in the city and their social cohesion. Blacks, who form a small minority in Vancouver, are fairly dispersed over the city as shown by the indices, which are around .3.

ETHNIC SEGREGATION AND SOCIAL DISTANCE

We hypothesized that one of the many factors that cause segregation among the ethnic groups is social distance (Balakrishnan and Selvanathan, 1990; Driedger and Church, 1974; Guest and Weed, 1976; Kantrowitz, 1973). While economic resources influence residential location, social distance is also important in explaining ethnic segregation in Canadian cities. For example, a survey done in Toronto in 1978–1979 showed that British Canadians expressed a preference not to live next door to people of other specific ethnic groups, the proportion varying according to the prestige of these groups (Reitz, 1988). It may well be that some of these attitudes will be reflected in their behaviour when it comes to residential choice. Ethnic groups that are culturally similar to each other are less likely to be segregated among themselves compared to other ethnic groups. A few Canadian studies have measured social distance between the ethnic groups in Canada and found them to be similar to the patterns found in the U.S. (Driedger and Peters, 1977; Pineo,

1977). In Pineo's study of a measure of social standing, the visible minorities formed the bottom of the scale. Though we do not have a well-tested social distance scale of recent construction, based on earlier studies done by others, we venture to classify our ethnic groups in order of increasing distance from the British as follows: British; northern and western Europe (French, German, Dutch, Scandinavian, etc.); central and eastern Europe (Polish, Hungarian, Ukrainian, Czech, etc.); southern Europe (Italian, Portuguese, etc.); and visible minorities (South Asians, Chinese, Blacks, etc.). Though Jews show high segregation, we are not able to place them in the social distance scale. They probably are close to the central or eastern European category. Earlier studies done in Canada specifically examining the relationship between ethnic segregation and social distance have shown that residential segregation increased with social distance in Canadian metropolitan areas (Balakrishnan, 1982; Balakrishnan and Kralt, 1987; Kalbach, 1990). Asian groups who had the highest social distance from the western European groups were the most segregated. The relationship between social distance and segregation holds even when social class is controlled (Balakrishnan and Kralt, 1987; Balakrishnan and Selvanathan, 1990).

The relationship between social distance and residential segregation is examined here with the 2001 data for the three largest metropolitan cities of Canada. Indices of dissimilarity between the ethnic groups are presented in Table 22.6. There seems to be support for the social distance hypothesis. The ISs between the British and the French and other western European groups are generally low, below .2. Even in Montreal, where the British are a clear minority, the index between British and French is only .3, and in Toronto and Vancouver they are .118 and .113 respectively. The indices from the other western European groups are also low: .180 in Montreal, .099 in Toronto, and .087 in Vancouver. They are somewhat higher between the British and central and eastern European groups, the index being .395 in Montreal and .349 in Toronto. Vancouver has consistently lower ISs for all ethnic groups. The index between British and central and eastern European groups was only .140. Italians show somewhat higher segregation from the British, the indices being .479 in Montreal, .466 in Toronto, and again lower in Vancouver at .265. The visible minorities show much higher segregation from the British in all three cities. Among them, South Asians and Chinese exhibit greater segregation from the British than the Blacks, a finding of considerable significance when compared to the U.S. patterns.

The pattern for the French is very similar to that of the British: low segregation from the western European groups, medium segregation from the central and eastern European groups, and high segregation from the visible minority groups. Their own size seems to make no difference for the French as the patterns are similar in all three cities. Given the cultural affinity of western European groups to the British, it is not surprising that their segregation patterns are also similar as far as other ethnic groups are concerned. Central and eastern European groups and Italians are moderately segregated from the charter groups of British and French and somewhat more segregated from the Jews and visible minorities. The Jewish population is the most segregated ethnic group in Canada. They show high segregation from all the other groups irrespective of their origin. Their ISs from the other groups are in the range of .7 to .8 both in Montreal and Toronto. It is interesting to note that their segregation from the visible minorities is the same as it is from the British or French. They do not fall in the social distance scale. As observed earlier, the ISs are lower in Vancouver. The ID between Jews and other ethnic groups are only in the range of .4 to .5.

Table 22.6 Indices of Dissimilarity between the Ethnic Groups, Montreal, Toronto, and Vancouver, 2001

	British	French	W. Eur.	Central & E.Eur	Italian	Jewish	South Asian	Chinese	African	Caribbean
Montreal										
British	—	0.300	0.180	0.395	0.479	0.728	0.629	0.524	0.489	0.543
French		—	0.287	0.448	0.474	0.800	0.694	0.579	0.509	0.537
Western European			—	0.473	0.484	0.695	0.520	0.518	0.474	0.539
Central & Eastern European				—	0.289	0.608	0.561	0.467	0.347	0.411
Italian					—	0.810	0.673	0.562	0.473	0.417
Jewish						—	0.718	0.718	0.692	0.794
South Asian							—	0.515	0.474	0.579
Chinese								—	0.422	0.533
African									—	0.385
Caribbean										—
Toronto										
British	—	0.118	0.099	0.349	0.466	0.695	0.563	0.593	0.510	0.495
French		—	0.144	0.345	0.464	0.700	0.546	0.586	0.492	0.471
Western European			—	0.341	0.462	0.686	0.570	0.591	0.522	0.510
Central & Eastern European				—	0.273	0.621	0.512	0.542	0.446	0.449
Italian					—	0.741	0.560	0.626	0.520	0.500
Jewish						—	0.821	0.713	0.752	0.793
South Asian							—	0.514	0.381	0.294
Chinese								—	0.530	0.535
African									—	0.277
Caribbean										—
Vancouver										
British	—	0.113	0.087	0.140	0.265	0.431	0.570	0.551	0.350	0.359
French		—	0.119	0.143	0.266	0.441	0.561	0.556	0.337	0.337
Western European			—	0.155	0.272	0.464	0.548	0.561	0.349	0.358
Central & Eastern European				—	0.207	0.420	0.537	0.458	0.297	0.325
Italian					—	0.505	0.582	0.473	0.380	0.417
Jewish						—	0.698	0.500	0.493	0.518
South Asian							—	0.581	0.521	0.549
Chinese								—	0.485	0.527
African									—	0.373
Caribbean										—

Among the visible minorities, a significant finding is that the ISs are relatively high. One would have expected that, given their shared experiences of relative deprivation, discrimination, and prejudice, perceived or otherwise, the segregation among themselves would be low. In other words, we would expect ethnic groups such as the Chinese, South Asians, and Blacks to reside in the same areas of the city. Though slightly lower than from the European groups, the ISs among the visible minority groups are still high, around .5. The ID between South Asians and Chinese is .515 in Montreal, .514 in Toronto, and .581 in Vancouver. The indices between South Asians and Black groups are also in the same range except in Toronto, where the ID between South Asians and Africans is only .381, and .294 between South Asians and Caribbeans. The indices between the Chinese and Black groups also hover around .5. This would mean that while the visible minority groups are more concentrated, they do not necessarily live in the same neighbourhoods, but rather have their own favoured locations within the cities. The cultural differences among the visible minorities are probably significant enough not to make physical proximity particularly advantageous, in spite of their similar social distance from the European groups. However, though not living in the same CTs, they are often found in nearby tracts.

SUMMARY, CONCLUSIONS, AND POLICY IMPLICATIONS

In the last two decades Canada has witnessed not only high rates of immigration but also a substantial change in the ethnic composition of migrants. This has been a consequence of a liberalization of immigration laws in terms of discriminatory clauses and of policy directions taken in light of below-replacement fertility rates, an aging population, and labour force needs. More than half the immigrants now are visible minorities, mainly from Asian countries. Canada has never been more ethnically diverse than at present. The spatial aspect of this ethnic diversity, especially in the three largest metropolitan areas of Montreal, Toronto, and Vancouver, was the focus of this study.

Within the three metropolitan areas, the rank order of the concentration of the selected ethnic origin groups has remained basically the same when compared to studies done for earlier periods. British, French, and western European groups are least concentrated, other European groups somewhat more concentrated, and the visible minority groups most concentrated. As ISs are highly correlated with concentration indices, it is not surprising that they exhibit the same trends. British, French, and other western European groups are least segregated, central and eastern Europeans and Italians are moderately segregated, while the visible minorities of Chinese, South Asians, and Blacks are most segregated. The persistence of this pattern of the relationship of segregation to social prestige of the ethnic groups is an important observation of considerable social significance. Is it due to differences in social class, social distance, or cultural cohesion? Because of their interrelationship, it is not possible to differentiate the effects of all causal factors in segregation, but some general observations can be made. Long-established groups of European origins in the higher socio-economic class seem to be least segregated. Here again, Jews are an exception. They have the highest segregation rates, which is clearly the powerful influence of cultural factors in their desire to live in close proximity to each other.

One cannot also make generalizations across societies easily. For example, Asian groups enjoy a greater social status than Blacks in the U.S., and this clearly shows in the concentration and segregation indices there. Blacks in America continue to have very high ISs, around .8 to .9 in most U.S. cities, more than double that of the Asian groups, a situation quite different from that in Canada. Massey and Denton emphasize this Black-Asian difference, commenting that it is the Black race in particular, rather than race per se, that is important in residential segregation in the America (Massey and Denton, 1987). Black migration to American cities and settlement patterns within them reveal a long history of discrimination in housing. Slavery and its consequences were instrumental in Black settlement in the central core of cities in the northern U.S., and subsequent movements within cities were dominated by the racial factor. These factors are largely irrelevant to Canadian urban growth.

There is strong support for the social distance hypothesis: British, French, and western European groups are least segregated from each other, more segregated from other groups, and most segregated from the visible minority groups. Central and eastern European groups are moderately segregated from the British and French and more segregated from the visible minority groups. A rather surprising finding is that the visible minorities are not only highly segregated from the White ethnic groups, but they are also highly segregated among themselves. Some of this segregation is due to social class differences between the visible minorities and the European groups. One needs to control for social class differences and then look at segregation among ethnic groups, which can then be attributed to other causes. At this time we are not able to do this owing to a lack of socio-economic data by ethnicity at the small area level. But past studies have abundantly shown that substantial segregation exists between the visible minorities and European groups even after controlling for social class (Balakrishnan, 1982; Balakrishnan and Kralt, 1987; Darroch and Marston, 1971).

The fact that certain ethnic groups are highly concentrated and segregated from other ethnic groups needs further investigation. Is high concentration a characteristic of poor neighbourhoods? This is clearly the case of Blacks in many U.S. cities, but it is less evident in Canadian cities. Jewish neighbourhoods are not poor, nor are some Chinese neighbourhoods in Scarborough. At the same time there are many poor neighbourhoods showing high concentrations of Blacks, Portuguese, Vietnamese, etc. The crucial policy question is whether the concentration of an ethnic group can lead to neighbourhood poverty. American studies have shown that as the concentration of Blacks increases in an area, the overall socio-economic status of the area goes down (Massey and Denton, 1993). In Canada, Kazemipur and Halli report that some studies have suggested that as the Aboriginal population of a neighbourhood increases, the real estate prices fall, and so does the desirability of the neighbourhood. Some real estate agents may direct Natives to certain neighbourhoods and not to others. This can lead to high concentrations of Natives in a small number of neighbourhoods in many Canadian cities (Kazemipur and Halli, 2000). Whether such discriminatory practices have affected the concentration of other visible minority groups such as the Chinese, South Asians, or Blacks is not known, but should be explored.

It is possible that a great deal of the concentration and segregation of many minority groups in Canada is due to voluntary causes rather than class differences or social distance. A certain threshold population size may enable a minority group to establish an ethnic neighbourhood with many advantages. Specialized social institutions such as an ethnic community club, ethnic food stores and restaurants, entertainment venues, and religious institutions such as an ethnic church or temple, synagogue, etc., become viable in an ethnic enclave. Canada's multiculturalism policy supports such social institutions and encourages citizens to maintain their cultural heritage. Policy-oriented research should examine whether ethnic enclaves enable their inhabitants to develop and enjoy a culturally and socially rich life rather than degenerate into a ghetto with all the attendant negative images of poverty and crime. One way of looking at this is to compare members of an ethnic group who live inside or outside of an ethnic enclave.

Another important policy concern is whether residential segregation is a reflection of occupational segregation. New immigrant groups may often be concentrated in certain occupations such as construction, manufacturing, garment making, etc. This may be due to their limited skills on arrival, official language facility, etc. It is expected that they will be able to move into other occupations with time. In a study done in Toronto in 1977, Reitz found that this was indeed so for the second generation of immigrants, though the extent of assimilation in the occupational structure varied for the different ethnic groups (Reitz, 1990). Balakrishnan and Hou compared Census data for the 1981, 1986, and 1991 years and found that, while residential segregation remained about the same during the decade of 1981–1991 for almost all the ethnic groups, occupational segregation decreased significantly (Balakrishnan and Hou, 1999b). This would imply that residential segregation has not adversely affected the socio-economic integration of ethnic groups in Canadian society. Our findings for 2001 show that residential segregation continues at about the same level as in 1991. This was also a period of high immigration, but many immigrants now come to Canada with higher education and job skills than earlier arrivals. With increased economic assimilation, one would expect residential segregation to decline. This has not happened to date in the case of the visible minority groups to any significant degree. However, with longer stays in Canada and increased social mobility, it is possible that residential segregation will decrease among minority groups, though some level of segregation will remain, if only because of discrimination and prejudice and the desire for some ethnic groups to live in proximity.

The future of ethnic residential segregation is hard to predict. The high level of segregation among some ethnic groups such as the visible minorities has been sustained by many factors, such as their size and recency of immigration, lack of official language facility, and cultural differences. It may also have been influenced by discrimination and prejudice, actual or perceived, experienced by them in their interaction with the largely White host society. With time the impact of these factors on residential location should decrease. Intermarriage between White European groups and the visible minority groups will be a powerful factor in reducing segregation. There is evidence that there is a greater acceptance of ethnically diverse groups by the host society, especially among young people.

Though the Canadian government's multiculturalism policies may help preserve ethnic identity, over time there is bound to be an erosion of the cultural heritage of many groups. As we try to understand the dynamics of ethnic diversity in Canada, it is clear that their spatial dimension is an integral part of the overall picture.

● ●

CRITICAL THINKING QUESTIONS

1. Are ethnic groups in Canada characterized by a high level of residential segregation and concentration (relative, for example, to the situation in the United States)? Describe the patterns that currently exist.

2. Elaborate on some of the most fundamental explanations put forth by Balakrishnan and Gyimah in explaining current ethnic residential patterns in Canada. Which explanations do you think hold greatest relevance in explaining the current situation?

3. In light of the evidence put forth in this chapter, do you think Canada's multiculturalism policy is working? Why or why not?

● ●

CHAPTER 23

POPULATION CHANGE
AND POLICY IMPLICATIONS

Roderic Beaujot and Don Kerr

● ●

POPULATION CHANGE HAS VARIOUS IMPLICATIONS for the well-being of individuals and societies. When Censuses were first conducted, in Roman times, it was mostly to determine the potential size of armies, or the taxes that could be raised from a given population. In the modern era of welfare states, Censuses are used to find out more about the population groups whose welfare is at stake.

In effect, much attention is paid to demographics by governments, the media, and the public because of the implications of change in these fundamental characteristics of societies. Much of the attention focuses on differences across population groups. At this stage of human history, we especially pay attention to the "demographic divide" that separates the rapidly growing and younger populations of developing societies compared to the slower growing and rapidly aging more developed countries. In their Population Bulletin entitled "Global Demographic Divide," Kent and Haub (2005) write about "poverty and population," then they treat "policy responses to high fertility" for the less developed countries, along with "policy responses to low fertility" for the more developed countries, and "international migration" for countries on both sides of the divide. While the demographic transition and globalization are bringing the world together, there remain important differences, partly due to past demographic trends and their associated causes.

POPULATION CHANGE: THE BIG PICTURE

As the chapters of this book have demonstrated, the patterns within Canada are no less striking. The release of census and other demographic data receive much public attention. For instance, the first release from the 2001 Census prompted concern that the population was increasing very slowly, that some areas were declining, and that the population was increasingly concentrated in four major urban regions: Ontario's Golden Horseshoe, Montreal and the adjacent region, British Columbia's lower mainland and southern Vancouver Island, and the Calgary–Edmonton corridor. While the population of Canada increased by 4.0 percent between 2001 and 2005, other than Manitoba (which grew by 2.7 percent), the provinces that did not have one of these cities either declined or grew by less than 1 percent over the 2001–2005 period. As international migration comprises a larger proportion of population change, and with the uneven geographic distribution of immigrants, there is the implication of demographic variability over space.

When the Census released the data on age distribution, much attention was given to the aging population as the baby boom inevitably ages. For years, young people have been looking forward to the retirement of the baby boom, with the expectation that this would open up opportunities in the labour market. At the time of the 2001 Census, there were still 40 percent more people at ages for labour force entry (15–24), compared to those at ages for labour force exit (55–64). However, by 2006, this ratio of 15–24/55–64 is down to 1.2, and by 2011 there will be basically the same number of people at ages for labour force entry compared to labour force exit. These changes have implications both for the opportunities of individuals and for the functioning of labour markets.

The data on ethnicity, visible minority status, immigration status, and language indicate that Canada is also changing on these dimensions. Even with a broad definition of "Aboriginal status," there are three times as many people with "visible minority status" (non-White, non-Caucasian, non-Aboriginal). The projections of the visible minority population indicate that by 2017—that is, 150 years after Confederation—about one in five people will be a visible minority person (Statistics Canada, 2005a). Already in 2001, those with a mother tongue other than English or French comprised 18 percent of the population, compared to 23 percent French and 59 percent English.

The data on families and households indicate that the diversification continues, with growth especially in lone-parent families, cohabiting couples, blended and stepfamilies, dual-income couples, and single-person households. With families having become very "nucleated" in residence patterns, there is much interest to know about the exchanges and flows of resources across households within broader "extended" family networks.

These patterns of population change, including slower growth, large urban concentrations, rapid aging, growth in visible minorities, and family diversification, are producing rather different demographic patterns than were present when Canada's welfare state was being established in the 1960s. This welfare state took its strongest form for the elderly, who were small in numbers but represented a significant pocket of poverty. Transfers were established toward the retirement-age population, anticipating that continued high fertility would mean that the elderly would remain a relatively small proportion of the total, and continued economic growth would ensure that the working-age population could well afford these transfers.

Since most families in the 1960s were of the breadwinner type, the concern was to establish supports for people who became widows or orphans due to the death of breadwinners. The problems now relate much less to these mortality considerations, and much more to the economic disadvantages produced by lone parenthood. While the problems of the 1960s were related to forming a bilingual country where the French would have equal opportunities, the issues of the current century relate to integration in a multicultural society. These changes are putting pressures not only on the parameters of the welfare state, but also on the basis for the federation, including the differentiation across regions, and the opportunities of the populations of Aboriginal origin.

In "Vulnerability to Persistent Low Income," Hatfield (2004) identifies five groups that have significant disadvantages: lone parents, people with work-limiting disabilities, unattached 45–64, recent immigrants, and Aboriginals living off-reserve. It is interesting to note that each of these groups is growing in relative size. Lone-parent families and the number of unattached are growing as a function of family change. Recent immigrants are more numerous because of high immigration. With an older labour force, there are more people with work-related disabilities. The Aboriginal population is growing as a function of being at a later stage of the demographic transition, and those who are off-reserve are often disadvantaged compared to other recent migrants to metropolitan areas.

MORTALITY, FERTILITY, AND MIGRATION: PAST AND FUTURE

Over the 20th century, life expectancy at birth increased from under 50 years to almost 80 years. As seen in chapters 6 and 7, this has been a function of various factors, from nutrition and standards of living, to public health and medical developments. The reductions in mortality rates first benefited infants and children, but since the 1970s there have been significant improvements for adults and elderly people. Canadian life expectancy has come to surpass that of the United States, in part because there is less inequality in access to health services in Canada (see Chapter 9). While the gender differences increased over the period 1901–1976, they have since declined due probably to greater similarities in lifestyles, especially smoking behaviour (see Chapter 10).

There is potential for further changes along these lines. Medical developments are hardest to predict, but there is much room for optimism as the health field attracts some of the best talent, and there is strong public willingness to invest further in health. There are concerns about deteriorating lifestyles, relating especially to obesity and environmental problems, but the research and information on the lifestyle and environmental factors that influence health can make for greater consciousness on the associated risk factors, with possible change in personal behaviour and social control over environmental conditions. In effect, the projections in mortality anticipate a continuation of the trends since 1970, with life expectancy rising from 79.7 in 2002 to high, medium, and low projections for 2031 of 84.6, 84.0, and 83.2 respectively (Bélanger et al., 2005:23).

While the anticipated change is in a positive direction, it will not happen by itself. There is need for policy attention to the factors that influence public health, and for continued access to health benefits. As the associated costs increase, there is pressure on health budgets at both provincial and federal levels. In some areas of public policy, greater expenditures can reduce the problems, but in the health domain improvements lead to further costs in looking after the health of survivors. With greater numbers of frail elderly, there are increased costs in a range of health and social services (Keefe et al., 2005; Légaré et al., 2006).

The trends in fertility are harder to interpret and more difficult to project. The puzzling difference between fertility in Canada and the United States is an example of the difficulty in understanding trends and differences (see Chapter 3). With the advantage of hindsight, the baby boom is now interpreted as a deviation from a long-term trend, with this trend best understood through the concept of two demographic transitions. The first transition involved economic changes that reduced the economic value and increased the economic cost of children, and cultural changes that justified the deliberate control over child-bearing and that promoted the appropriateness of small families (see in particular Chapters 2 and 4). The second transition involved family changes that brought greater flexibility in the entry and exit from unions, along with the associated greater variability and diversity of family trajectories, and an overall delay in adult transitions into labour force and family roles (see Chapter 19). The patterns of the second transition are justified by a culture that promotes the value of individualism and diversity, where each person is free to form the kinds of family relationships that he or she desires.

With these two transitions, the total fertility rate declined from 4.8 in 1901 to 1.5 in the period 2000–2003. But if these two transitions are helpful in interpreting the past, what can we say regarding the future? We can probably say that cultural considerations operate in terms of a desire to have children while economic considerations are more relevant to the constraints on child-bearing (Beaujot and Muhammad, 2006). There appears to be a persistent desire to have children; for instance, at ages 20–34, 90.4 percent of childless married or cohabiting people expect to have children, and 81.2 percent see children as important or very important to their happiness (Moyser, 2006). In the context of patterns that have been relatively stable, the projections by Statistics Canada use fertility levels of 1.3, 1.5, and 1.7 for the low, medium, and high assumptions (Bélanger et al., 2005:21).

It is generally agreed that there is limited leeway for deliberate policy to sustain fertility, but fertility tends to be higher in societies where a variety of policies support families in the context of gender equality and family diversity (MacDonald, 2006). There is considerable disagreement on the best policy approach, in part because the needs of families differ over the family life course (Beaujot and Ravanera, 2005). Given the difficulties of young families, the support should probably concentrate on both access to daycare and direct transfers to parents, along with parental leave and flexibility for part-time and full-time work.

Compared to mortality and fertility, it is most difficult to theorize in the area of migration. Some people move all the time, others live and die in the same place, and still others return to their place of origin. There are clearly economic and social factors at stake, and we might argue that social factors especially influence whether or not people move. That is, people move at life course stages where they are less integrated in their current residence. However, economic questions play a large role in the "push" and "pull" factors across areas of origin and destination.

Focusing on international migration, there are factors associated with lack of opportunities at places of origin, but also the extent of the potential to integrate at places of destination, and the relations across places of origin and destination. These relations across nations can be described in terms of periods of globalization that increased international migration after the turn of the 20th century, with a period of interruption including two world wars and the economic Depression of the 1930s, and a subsequent period of globalization in the second half of the 20th century (see Chapters 10 and 11). The continued globalization, along with the strong economic and demographic differentials across countries, would imply a continuation of high immigration. Canada is particularly well placed in this regard, with policies for the admission and integration of various types of immigrants (see Chapter 12). At the same time, it is hard to predict possible difficulties in integrating populations from diverse countries of origin, and it is equally difficult to predict possible resentment on the part of those who are already in the country. The difficulties faced by recent immigrants (see Chapters 12 and 13) might be a function of numbers that are in excess of the absorptive capacity. There are also different interests at stake, with certain sectors seeking to have access to cheap labour, others seeking to retain advantages for people with Canadian training, and the strongest interests among people who are themselves recent immigrants.

The average levels of international migration over the period 1951–1991 have seen 145,000 annual arrivals and 57,000 departures per year (Beaujot and Kerr, 2004:107). The period 1991–2005 has seen annual averages of 225,000 arrivals and 42,000 departures (Bélanger, 2006:18; Bélanger et al., 2005:28). Per 1,000 population, the figures show 7.0 arrivals in 1951–1991, and 7.5 in 1991–2005. The higher numbers in the more recent period are clearly deliberate, especially in not reducing immigration during the economic recession of the early 1990s. The projections from Statistics Canada use low, medium, and high rates of immigration at 5.5, 7.0, and 8.5 per 1,000 population, with emigration at 1.5 per 1,000 population in all three projections scenarios (Bélanger et al., 2005:37). This implies annual levels reaching 204,000, 280,000, and 364,000 immigrants in 2031.

There are several policy concerns in immigration, thus the requirement that the Minister of Immigration and Citizenship make an annual statement to Parliament on the government's plans and priorities. While immigration is often justified in economic and demographic terms, it is best seen in a social and political context in terms of building a pluralist and multicultural society. The policies relate to the admission and integration of immigrants. Here again there are a variety of views across the country. The regions that receive more immigrants typically argue that they need more assistance in integrating the new arrivals, while other regions complain that they need more help to become more attractive to immigration.

POPULATION SIZE, DISTRIBUTION, AND COMPOSITION: PAST AND FUTURE

While world population has grown rapidly in the 20th century, increasing from 1.6 to 6.1 billion, or a 3.7-fold multiplication, the Canadian population increased from 5.3 to 30.7 million, or a 5.8-fold multiplication. In the last half-century, growth has been strongest in the period 1951–1971, due to both the baby boom and relatively high immigration. In the period 1971–2001, the annual growth amounts to 1.15 percent per year.

Looking at the potential futures, Statistics Canada highlights three scenarios that differentiate the projections at the national level (Bélanger et al., 2005:37–38). Using the assumptions as defined above, these scenarios are as follows:

Scenario 1: Low growth with low fertility (1.3 births per woman), low life expectancy (83.2 years), and low immigration (5.5 per 1,000 population).

Scenario 3: Medium growth with medium fertility (1.5), medium life expectancy (84.0), and medium immigration (7.0).

Scenario 6: High growth with high fertility (1.7), high life expectancy (84.6), and high immigration (8.5).

Based on existing theory and evidence, each of these is a legitimate projection. Nonetheless, we would argue that Scenario 1 uses a rather low level of fertility, while Scenario 6 uses a rather high level of immigration. Scenario 3 is easiest to defend.

In 2005, the total population of Canada amounted to 32.3 million people. Using the assumptions for the future, by 2051, the Canadian population would reach 36.2 million in the low projection, 41.9 in the medium projection, and 48.2 million in the high projection (see Appendix A). In the 50 years from 1951 to 2001, the population of Canada increased by 122 percent. In comparison, the next 50 years would see increases of 17 percent, 35 percent, and 55 percent respectively. In the low scenario, the population reaches a maximum of 36.6 million in 2039, then declines to 36.2 million in 2051. In the medium scenario, the growth declines over time, but it remains positive at 0.3 percent in 2051. In the high scenario, the growth rate declines from 0.9 percent in 2005–2006 to 0.6 percent in 2050–2051.

The natural increase—that is, births minus deaths—become negative in 2020, 2030, and 2046 in the low, medium, and high scenarios respectively. After these dates, all population growth is due to net international migration. As we anticipate negative natural increase, it is important to appreciate that this situation still includes population renewal through births, but there are more deaths than births (see Chapter 1). For instance, in the medium projection, the number of births exceeds the number of immigrants throughout the projection period. When natural increase is expected to become negative in this medium projection, in 2030, there are still 346,000 births compared to 280,000 immigrants. In effect, rather than speaking of the net change brought about by births minus deaths and immigrants minus emigrants, it is equally important to compare births and immigrants in population renewal. While natural increase is negative after 2030 in the medium projection, making net migration the only source of population growth, the births continue to outnumber immigrants by 28 percent in 2051.

Dating back more than a century, the population aging will continue due to persistent low fertility and declining mortality (see Chapter 15). This aging will be especially accelerated over the period 2011–2031 as baby boomers move into retirement ages. In 1951, 7.8 percent of the population was aged 65+ compared to 10 percent in 1981 and 13 percent in 2005. By 2031, this figure will be in the range of 23 percent to 25 percent, according to the high, medium, and low projections. In 2051, the figures would be in the range of 24.7 to 28.5. The acceleration applies especially to the population aged 80 and above, which will increase from 1.1 million in 2005 to a figure ranging from 2.3 to 2.6 million in 2031, and 3.8 to 4.5 million in 2051.

Other populations are worth following, including the working-age population, taken here as people aged 15 to 64 (Bélanger et al., 2005:48–49). In 2005, this population numbered 22.4 million, or 70 percent of the population. According to the medium scenario, the working-age population will increase until 2021, reaching 24.2 million, then decline slightly for a decade and rise again to 25.2 million in 2051. In the low scenario the decline starts in 2017, but in the high scenario there is continued growth to 29.0 million in 2051. As a proportion of the total population, all scenarios show a decline from 70 percent in 2005 to some 62 percent in the early 2030s, then stable levels close to 60 percent. All scenarios also show a slight aging of the working-age population. It is of interest to compare the population aged 15–24 to that aged 55–64 as these are the typical ages for entry into and exit from the labour force. At the time of the 2001 Census, the ratio of 15–24 to 55–64 was 1.4, by 2006 this is 1.2, and by 2011 it will be 1.0, reaching a figure of 0.8 to 0.9 in 2031. That is, after 2011, regardless of the projection scenario, there will be fewer people at ages for labour force entry compared to those at ages for labour force exit.

With the 17 percent decline in total births, from 405,500 in 1990 to 335,200 in 2003, there has followed a reduction in the size of the population at elementary school ages. After 2006, the population of secondary school ages will begin to decline, reaching a point of stability around 2016 in the medium projection (Beaujot and Kerr, 2004:168). The population subject to post-secondary education, taken here as ages 18–24, will increase to about 2011, then decline to reach a point of stability after the early 2020s, according to the medium projections.

The projections at the provincial level are more uncertain since they are affected by trends in interprovincial migration. Thus, three additional scenarios are considered (each using the medium projections), and projections are made only to 2031 (Bélanger et al., 2005:52–58). In the high-growth scenario, each province has a higher population in 2031 than in 2005. At least under some scenarios, Newfoundland/Labrador, New Brunswick, Saskatchewan, Northwest Territories, and Yukon would have smaller populations in 2031 than in 2005. Taking the medium scenario (see Appendix A), Ontario will increase from 38.9 percent of Canada in 2005 to 41.3 percent in 2031. Quebec will remain the second province, with 23.5 percent in 2005 and 21.5 percent in 2031. Alberta and British Columbia together will increase from 23.3 percent to 24.7 percent, while Manitoba and Saskatchewan together will decline from 6.7 percent to 6.0 percent of the national population. The Atlantic provinces will decline from 7.2 percent to 6.2 percent, and the three territories together will remain at 0.3 percent of the total population. That is, Ontario, Alberta, and British Columbia will increase in their relative share of the total population, while all other provinces will decline in relative size.

IMPLICATIONS: POPULATION CHANGE AND POLICY ISSUES

Several of the policy challenges facing the country have their demographic components: unequal size of provinces, slow labour force growth, high health costs, difficulties for young people to establish themselves and form families, diversity across family structures, disadvantages of unattached older adults, integration of recent immigrants, opportunities for people of Aboriginal origins, disadvantages of people with work-related disabilities, and care of the frail elderly.

In this context, it is useful to discuss the influence that population processes are likely to have on human resources. In drawing comparisons over the longer term, Livi-Bacci (2000) proposes that we cannot expect to have the kinds of economic benefits from demographic change as we have seen in the previous century. He observes that the huge reductions in mortality in the 20th century especially benefited children, and then younger adults, thus reducing the wastage of human resources and increasing the health of the working-age population. However, the future gains in mortality will benefit mostly the older population, who are beyond ages for the labour force. Similarly, the past reductions in fertility have permitted greater labour force activity on the part of adults, but now this low fertility is reducing the numbers of young adults at ages to enter the labour market. For migration, the benefits, at least from internal migration, are less likely to be repeated in the future as the population is already living in areas of concentration, and the changes in distribution are likely to see depopulation of major regions, with associated loss of value of the capital infrastructure. International migration has contributed in the past to the settlement of western Canada, to industrialization, and to postwar economic growth. While there will also be benefits from international migration in the future, the Canadian labour force is well educated, implying fewer gains from importing skilled labour, and there will be competition among receiving countries.

Discussions of problems facing the Canadian population, especially slower growth, slower labour force growth, and aging, often think of immigration as a way of fixing the problem. This idea has become known as "replacement migration"; that is, using immigration to replace births and to return to earlier population dynamics. The United Nations (2000) publication on this concept uses three possible definitions of replacement migration. In the first definition migration is used to prevent the population from declining in the long term. As seen from the population projections from Statistics Canada, the medium scenario qualifies in this regard. Other simulations suggest that even an immigration of some 200,000 per year would avoid this decline (Beaujot and Kerr, 2004:168–170). The second definition is to use immigration to prevent the labour force population from declining. Here again, Canada is in good position, even with immigration levels slightly below those of the medium scenario.

Of course, there are other ways of preventing the labour force from declining in the longer term, such as slightly higher fertility, and higher labour force participation rates. In their review of 16 countries, McDonald and Kippen (2001) observe that Canada is well placed in this regard, and that compared to the other countries, Canada has high immigration, moderate fertility, and low labour force participation. That is, there is potential for improvement in labour force participation, relative to other countries, in order to prevent the labour force from declining. The third meaning of replacement migration is to use migration to maintain the relative size of the population aged 15–64 compared to that aged 65 and over. As is seen by the population projections, this is essentially an impossibility. Population aging is inevitable, and immigration cannot be used to stop this process.

While we have focused on challenges from the point of view of human resources and "population as producers" to ensure that demographic trends do not undermine economic production, it is also useful to consider some of the challenges from the point of view of "population as consumers", and the associated pressures. In *An Essay on the Principle of Population*, Malthus ([1798] 1965) observed a tendency for populations to grow faster than available food. While he underestimated the potential to produce more food, population pressures can be observed in other areas. Increased population size, along with high levels of consumption, are the means through which human activity is having a significant effect on the environment of the planet, especially through global warming. In the discussions of the Kyoto targets for carbon-dioxide concentration, much attention is paid to reducing emissions, but little attention is paid to the multiplier of population size.

These questions associated with "population as consumers" are very difficult to bring into discussions that focus on population as human resources. In particular, the focus on economic production leaves out questions relating to the capacity of the environment to absorb the consequences of this production. The difficulties of bringing these things together present some of the most significant challenges facing not only Canada but humanity as a whole.

● ●

CRITICAL THINKING QUESTIONS

1. Explain how the demographic dynamics of the Canadian population are expected to be different over the period 2001–2051 compared to 1951–2001. What are the implications of these differences?
2. Explain the role of demographic processes (fertility, mortality, migration) in population growth and population aging in Canada over the period 1951–2051.
3. Elaborate on policy questions that might influence fertility, mortality, and migration. Secondly, what are some of the policy implications of the changing size, growth, and age structure of the Canadian population?

● ●

CANADIAN POPULATION ESTIMATES (1971–2005) AND PROJECTIONS (2005–2031)

● ●

THIS APPENDIX WILL CONSIDER (1) intercensal population estimates, (2) postcensal population estimates, and (3) population projections. Intercensal population estimates can provide figures on the size of Canada's population between past Censuses while postcensal estimates can provide reasonably accurate and timely estimates as to population size through to the present day. Population projections focus exclusively on the future. This appendix provides a brief introduction as to the methods and utility of these estimates and projections by Statistics Canada.

POPULATION ESTIMATES

While Censuses can provide a wealth of information on the size, distribution, and characteristics of a population, they are not without their limitations. For example, the Canadian Census, which is conducted once every five years, does not provide information on the size and distribution of Canada's population between Censuses, nor does it provide information on the years that have passed since the previous Census. In addition, population counts based on a Census are inaccurate because of Census coverage error. That is, some people are completely missed in the Census, just as some are counted more than once. These two errors are known respectively as Census undercount and Census overcount. The coverage error in combination are referred to as net undercount (undercount minus overcount).

In light of these problems with the Census, most countries generate population estimates that not only correct for coverage error but also produce population data for non-Census years. This is true of Canada, the United States, Australia, and Britain, and most other OECD countries. Beginning with the 1971 Census, reasonably precise estimates of coverage error are available, with the net undercount usually being between 2 and 3 percent at the national level (Statistics Canada, 1994; 2005). With the availability of these estimates, a time series of population data (fully adjusted for Census coverage error) has been generated from 1971 to the present. In reference to these estimates, it is possible to distinguish between intercensal population estimates and postcensal population estimates. Intercensal estimates apply to the years between Censuses (1971–2001), whereas postcensal estimates apply to non-Census years after the most recent Census (2001–2005). At the time of writing, the 2006 Census results have not yet been released.

When one is working with these demographic data, postcensal estimates are more timely (as there is no need to wait until the release of the next Census), although less accurate. On the other hand, intercensal estimates involve the retroactive adjustment of past figures with new Census data. Both types of estimates (intercensal and postcensal) involve data on all relevant components of demographic change, including births, deaths, immigration, and emigration, as well as interprovincial migration. In keeping with Canada's system of demographic accounts, all of those components are either documented directly on the basis of vital statistics and/or administrative data or estimated indirectly on the basis of administrative data sets. A number of federal and provincial government departments (including Citizenship and Immigration Canada, the Canada Revenue Agency, as well as the many provincial ministries of Health) collaborate with Statistics Canada in the compilation of reasonably accurate estimates on these demographic components.

POSTCENSAL ESTIMATES

In developing postcensal population estimates (by province and territory), Statistics Canada uses the following equation, which is a slightly revised version of the basic demographic balancing equation presented in Chapter 1. For each province and territory, it is possible to estimate total population by accounting for all relevant demographic change since the most current Census. For example, for postcensal estimates, the following equation applies directly only to those years that follow the most recent Census.

$$P(t+a) = Pt + B(t,t+a) - D(t,t+a) + I(t,t+a) - E(t,t+a) + NPR(t,t+a) + In(t,t+a) - Out(t,t+a)$$

where:

$P(t + a)$ = postcensal estimate of the population at time $t + a$

Pt = base population at time t (most recent Census adjusted for coverage error)

$B(t,t + a)$ = number of births between time t and time $t + a$

$D (t,t + a)$ = number of deaths between time t and time $t + a$

$I(t,t + a)$ = number of immigrants between time t and time $t + a$

$E(t,t + a)$ = number of emigrants between time t and time $t + a$

$NPR(t,t + a)$ = net change in the number of non-permanent residents between time t and time $t + a$ (i.e., people on work permits, student visas, refugee claimants, etc.)

$In(t,t + a)$ = number of in-migrants (from other provinces) between time t and time $t + a$

$Out(t,t + a)$ = number of out-migrants (to other provinces) between time t and time $t + a$

As an initial step, the base population Pt is adjusted to reflect Canada's population on July 1 rather than Census day (in mid-May) and is also adjusted for coverage error. All component data are for the reference year July 1 to June 30 rather than specific calendar years. When population estimates are developed by age and sex, the same basic equation is applied to each age and sex cohort; the component data used are organized by birth cohort and sex. This is referred to as the cohort component approach to generating population estimates.

INTERCENSAL ESTIMATES

Shortly after each Census, intercensal estimates are also published, in an effort to reconcile previous estimates with the new Census-based information. The production of intercensal estimates involves two further steps beyond the generation of postcensal estimates: (1) the calculation of the error of closure; and (2) the distribution of the error of closure by intercensal year. The error of closure can be defined as the difference between the enumerated population of the most recent Census (after adjustments for Census coverage error) and the most current set of postcensal population estimates for this same date (that is, Census day). On the assumption that the coverage studies that follow each enumeration are unbiased, the adjusted Census figures are accepted as true. Assuming that this error of closure can then be distributed uniformly over the corresponding intercensal period, some relatively simple arithmetic functions can be used to adjust the previous postcensal estimates.

This generation of intercensal estimates by age and sex is analogous to the above in first identifying the respective closure errors and then revising past estimates accordingly to correct for closure error. Similarly, analogous adjustments are made at the national level for provinces and territories. In working with provincial/territorial data, and then working up to the national level, this method is referred to by Statistics Canada as a regional cohort component approach to creating population estimates, with adjustments for closure error.

Table A.1 includes the full series of intercensal estimates currently available, for Canada and the provinces (1971–2001) as well as the most current set of postcensal estimates (2001–2005). For this same time series, detailed population estimates by single years of age and sex are also available for all provinces/territories with Table A.2 providing these estimates at the national level for 2005. At the time of writing, the 2006 Census is not released, nor have the corresponding Census coverage studies been completed, a necessary step before the creation of the 2001–2006 intercensal estimates. All of the population figures in Tables A.1 and A.2 have been adjusted for coverage error (both undercount and overcount), beginning with the 1971 Census.

POPULATION PROJECTIONS

While intercensal population estimates provide figures on the size of Canada's population between past Censuses and postcensal estimates provide reasonably accurate and timely estimates as to population size through to the present day, population projections focus exclusively on the future. Rather than stopping with the most up-to-date information as available from vital statistics and/or administrative data, population projections make assumptions as to future fertility, mortality, and migration. A population projection is essentially a calculation of the number of people that a population might have at some future date, given what we know about the current population size as well reasonable assumptions as to future fertility, mortality, and migration.

Table A.3 provides population projections for Canada, the provinces, and territories, using a medium-growth scenario produced by Statistics Canada in their last official 2005–2031 round of projections (Bélanger, Martel, and Malenfant, 2005). Statistics Canada has produced several other scenarios (not reproduced in Table A.3), some of which project

Table A.1 Annual Population Estimates, July 1977 to July 2005, Canada, Provinces; Intercensal Estimates, 1971–2001; Postcensal Estimates, 2001–2005

Year	Canada	N.L	P.E.I.	N.S.	N.B.	Que.	Ont.	Man.	Sask.	Alta.	B.C.
Intercensal Estimates											
1971	21,961,999	530,851	112,591	797,291	642,469	6,137,306	7,849,002	998,874	932,037	1,665,717	2,240,472
1972	22,218,475	539,125	113,461	802,257	648,770	6,174,216	7,963,125	1,001,653	920,780	1,694,090	2,302,085
1973	22,491,757	545,560	114,620	812,384	656,719	6,213,149	8,075,533	1,007,356	911,936	1,725,327	2,367,272
1974	22,807,918	549,599	115,961	818,745	664,741	6,268,572	8,204,240	1,018,202	908,455	1,754,622	2,442,581
1975	23,143,192	556,488	117,723	826,540	677,003	6,330,304	8,319,738	1,024,969	917,411	1,808,690	2,499,569
1976	23,449,791	562,640	118,647	835,172	689,494	6,396,767	8,413,806	1,031,763	931,619	1,869,301	2,533,791
1977	23,725,921	565,300	120,031	839,728	695,782	6,431,717	8,505,692	1,038,008	944,801	1,947,657	2,569,702
1978	23,963,370	567,700	121,714	844,549	699,534	6,440,203	8,591,725	1,041,243	951,918	2,021,771	2,613,998
1979	24,201,801	570,124	122,998	849,219	703,182	6,466,439	8,662,661	1,037,389	959,519	2,097,565	2,662,990
1980	24,516,071	572,891	123,726	852,860	706,078	6,507,000	8,745,256	1,034,646	967,356	2,192,409	2,743,224
1981	24,820,393	574,775	123,741	854,646	706,325	6,547,705	8,811,312	1,036,433	975,867	2,294,198	2,823,933
1982	25,117,442	574,597	123,859	859,965	708,230	6,579,290	8,922,284	1,046,780	987,274	2,368,258	2,872,920
1983	25,366,969	579,581	125,446	869,155	715,358	6,602,318	9,041,672	1,061,075	1,001,872	2,390,376	2,905,476
1984	25,607,651	580,181	126,614	877,150	721,020	6,631,212	9,171,902	1,071,865	1,015,494	2,390,102	2,945,635
1985	25,842,736	579,297	127,664	885,094	723,693	6,665,702	9,297,550	1,082,270	1,025,469	2,402,956	2,974,277
1986	26,101,155	576,495	128,413	889,326	725,154	6,708,468	9,438,132	1,091,682	1,029,270	2,430,935	3,004,104
1987	26,448,855	575,158	128,573	893,457	727,880	6,782,537	9,644,258	1,098,024	1,032,745	2,435,326	3,050,160
1988	26,795,383	574,989	129,279	897,386	730,358	6,839,030	9,842,215	1,102,035	1,028,012	2,454,427	3,115,357
1989	27,281,795	576,388	130,077	903,852	735,222	6,928,690	10,107,519	1,103,560	1,019,222	2,495,247	3,197,880
1990	27,697,530	578,037	130,539	909,637	740,120	7,003,876	10,297,875	1,105,668	1,007,114	2,547,166	3,290,814
1991	28,031,394	579,518	130,306	915,102	745,528	7,064,586	10,428,132	1,109,614	1,002,686	2,592,626	3,373,464

Table A.1 Annual Population Estimates, July 1977 to July 2005, Canada, Provinces; Intercensal Estimates, 1971–2001; Postcensal Estimates, 2001–2005 (continued)

Year	Canada	N.L	P.E.I.	N.S.	N.B.	Que.	Ont.	Man.	Sask.	Alta.	B.C.
1992	28,366,737	580,029	130,778	919,571	748,103	7,108,000	10,569,806	1,112,696	1,003,956	2,632,907	3,468,445
1993	28,681,676	579,939	132,142	924,029	748,812	7,155,273	10,688,391	1,117,621	1,006,854	2,667,448	3,567,406
1994	28,999,006	574,469	133,416	926,959	750,203	7,191,884	10,818,251	1,123,229	1,009,521	2,700,682	3,675,699
1995	29,302,091	567,442	134,407	928,193	750,979	7,219,446	10,949,976	1,129,146	1,014,126	2,734,515	3,777,004
1996	29,610,757	559,807	135,751	931,413	752,312	7,246,896	11,083,052	1,134,188	1,019,100	2,775,163	3,874,276
1997	29,907,172	551,011	136,109	932,481	752,543	7,274,630	11,228,284	1,136,137	1,018,067	2,830,056	3,948,544
1998	30,157,082	539,932	135,819	931,907	750,551	7,295,973	11,367,018	1,137,515	1,017,506	2,899,452	3,983,077
1999	30,403,878	533,409	136,296	933,847	750,611	7,323,308	11,506,359	1,142,491	1,014,707	2,953,255	4,011,342
2000	30,689,035	528,043	136,486	933,881	750,518	7,357,029	11,685,380	1,147,373	1,007,767	3,004,940	4,039,198
2001	31,021,251	521,986	136,672	932,389	749,890	7,396,990	11,897,647	1,151,285	1,000,134	3,056,739	4,078,447
Postcensal Estimates											
2002	31,372,587	519,449	136,934	934,507	750,327	7,445,745	12,102,045	1,155,584	995,886	3,116,332	4,115,413
2003	31,669,150	518,469	137,300	936,302	751,215	7,493,958	12,259,568	1,161,626	994,519	3,159,620	4,154,591
2004	31,974,363	517,284	137,861	937,509	752,078	7,547,728	12,407,347	1,170,229	994,300	3,204,780	4,201,867
2005	32,270,507	515,961	138,113	937,889	752,006	7,598,146	12,541,410	1,177,556	994,126	3,256,816	4,254,522

Notes:
The postcensal estimates from 2001 onward will eventually be adjusted with the release of the 2006 census and coverage studies
Nunavut, previously part of the Northwest Territories, was established as a separate territory on 1 April 1999.
Sources: Adapted from Statistics Canada, 2006. Annual Demographic Statistics. Catalogue no. 91-213-XPB.

Table A.2 Age/Sex Distribution (in the 1,000's) of the 2005 Population of Canada

Age	Male	Female	Both Sexes
0	172.5	164.6	337.1
1	173.4	165.8	339.2
2	172.7	165.4	338.0
3	172.6	165.1	337.7
4	177.2	169.2	346.3
0-4	868.4	830.0	1,698.4
5	183.9	175.5	359.5
6	185.7	177.2	362.9
7	190.3	182.2	372.5
8	197.7	187.8	385.6
9	205.3	196.5	401.8
5-9	963.0	919.3	1,882.3
10	210.1	199.2	409.3
11	211.3	200.2	411.4
12	214.9	204.4	419.3
13	219.2	209.7	428.9
14	223.7	212.1	435.8
10-14	1,079.1	1,025.7	2,104.8
15	224.9	213.7	438.6
16	218.5	207.8	426.4
17	213.7	203.7	417.4
18	217.2	207.3	424.5
19	225.3	213.6	438.9
15-19	1,099.7	1,046.2	2,145.8
20	229.4	216.8	446.2
21	230.2	219.2	449.4
22	230.1	219.4	449.4
23	228.7	219.3	448.0
24	229.2	221.2	450.4
20-24	1,147.5	1,095.8	2,243.3
25	228.0	220.2	448.2
26	222.1	216.9	439.0
27	219.0	213.8	432.8
28	220.0	216.3	436.3
29	221.4	216.6	437.9
25-29	1,110.5	1,083.8	2,194.3
30	222.2	217.7	439.9
31	217.8	214.9	432.6
32	221.0	217.0	437.9
33	226.1	221.5	447.6
34	235.3	231.4	466.8
30-34	1,122.4	1,102.4	2,224.8
35	236.3	232.0	468.3
36	233.7	230.9	464.6
37	233.0	231.0	463.9
38	236.4	234.5	471.0
39	250.4	247.6	498.0
35-39	1,189.8	1,175.9	2,365.8
40	268.4	265.6	534.0
41	278.3	274.7	552.9
42	281.4	277.4	558.8
43	275.4	272.6	547.9
44	276.6	275.6	552.2
40-44	1,380.1	1,365.8	2,745.9
45	272.8	272.3	545.0
46	265.3	266.6	531.9
47	263.4	263.4	526.7
48	257.0	259.0	516.0
49	248.5	251.2	499.7
45-49	1,307.0	1,312.5	2,619.5
50	245.9	249.6	495.5
51	236.1	241.5	477.5
52	225.5	230.8	456.2
53	218.0	222.4	440.4
54	213.7	218.3	432.0
50-54	1,139.1	1,162.6	2,301.8
55	208.8	213.0	421.8
56	204.5	209.3	413.8
57	204.5	208.5	413.0
58	203.0	207.5	410.5
59	174.1	178.4	352.4
55-59	994.9	1,016.6	2,011.5
60	162.0	165.9	328.0
61	156.9	161.9	318.8
62	151.6	156.3	308.0
63	140.2	146.1	286.2
64	133.0	140.7	273.7
60-64	743.8	770.9	1,514.6
65	124.2	132.2	256.4
66	119.8	128.0	247.8
67	114.4	123.0	237.3
68	108.7	118.2	226.8
69	107.4	117.7	225.1
65-69	574.4	619.1	1,193.5
70	102.7	114.0	216.7
71	98.8	110.1	208.9
72	98.3	111.1	209.4
73	96.2	110.0	206.3
74	92.6	108.8	201.5
70-74	488.6	554.0	1,042.6
75	87.2	105.3	192.5
76	80.1	99.8	179.9
77	76.0	97.4	173.4
78	69.5	93.2	162.7
79	65.0	90.8	155.8
75-79	377.7	486.5	864.3
80	59.1	86.4	145.5
81	53.2	82.3	135.5
82	48.1	76.7	124.8
83	43.4	72.5	115.9
84	37.9	65.8	103.7
80-84	241.7	383.6	625.3
85	31.7	58.3	90.0
86	24.5	47.7	72.2
87	20.3	41.1	61.4
88	16.6	36.4	53.0
89	14.1	31.9	46.0
85-89	107.1	215.4	322.5
90+	44.6	125.0	169.5
0-14	2,910.6	2,774.9	5,685.5
0-17	3,567.7	3,400.1	6,967.9
18-64	10,577.6	10,507.3	21,084.9
65+	1,834.1	2,383.7	4,217.8
median age			39
total population			32,270.5

Sources: Statistics Canada, 2006. Annual Demographic Statistics. Catalogue no. 91-213-XPB. CD-Rom.

Table A.3 Annual Population Projections, July 2005 to July 2030, Canada, Provinces and Territories; Medium Growth Scenario

Year	Canada	Nfld	P.E.I.	N.S.	N.B.	Que.	Ont.	Man.	Sask.	Alta.	B.C.	Yukon	N.W.T.	Nvt.
2005	32,270.5	516.0	138.1	937.9	752.0	7,598.1	12,541.4	1,177.6	994.1	3,256.8	4,254.5	31.0	43.0	30.0
2006	32,547.2	515.2	138.7	939.6	752.9	7,641.6	12,682.0	1,183.1	991.5	3,295.0	4,302.9	31.1	43.6	30.2
2007	32,821.6	514.6	139.2	941.3	753.8	7,683.9	12,821.6	1,188.8	989.0	3,332.8	4,350.9	31.2	44.2	30.4
2008	33,095.0	513.9	139.7	943.1	754.7	7,725.1	12,960.5	1,194.9	986.9	3,370.6	4,399.0	31.3	44.8	30.6
2009	33,367.5	513.4	140.2	944.8	755.5	7,765.2	13,099.0	1,201.2	985.0	3,408.3	4,447.5	31.4	45.3	30.7
2010	33,639.4	512.9	140.7	946.6	756.5	7,804.0	13,237.1	1,207.8	983.4	3,445.8	4,496.3	31.5	45.9	30.9
2011	33,909.7	512.5	141.2	948.5	757.4	7,841.4	13,374.7	1,214.8	982.0	3,483.2	4,545.0	31.6	46.4	31.1
2012	34,180.7	512.2	141.7	950.4	758.3	7,878.3	13,512.9	1,221.8	980.8	3,520.4	4,594.0	31.7	46.9	31.3
2013	34,452.1	511.9	142.2	952.3	759.3	7,914.6	13,651.7	1,229.0	979.9	3,557.4	4,643.2	31.8	47.5	31.4
2014	34,723.8	511.7	142.7	954.3	760.3	7,950.0	13,791.1	1,236.2	979.1	3,594.3	4,692.6	31.9	48.0	31.6
2015	34,995.4	511.5	143.2	956.3	761.2	7,984.8	13,931.0	1,243.5	978.6	3,630.9	4,742.2	32.0	48.5	31.8
2016	35,266.8	511.3	143.7	958.4	762.2	8,018.7	14,071.4	1,250.9	978.2	3,667.1	4,792.0	32.1	48.9	31.9
2017	35,537.6	511.2	144.2	960.4	763.1	8,052.0	14,212.1	1,258.3	977.9	3,703.0	4,841.7	32.2	49.4	32.1
2018	35,807.6	511.1	144.7	962.4	764.0	8,084.5	14,353.1	1,265.8	977.7	3,738.4	4,891.5	32.3	49.9	32.2
2019	36,076.4	511.0	145.2	964.4	764.8	8,116.2	14,494.3	1,273.3	977.5	3,773.4	4,941.2	32.5	50.3	32.3
2020	36,343.5	510.8	145.6	966.4	765.6	8,147.0	14,635.5	1,280.7	977.4	3,807.9	4,990.7	32.6	50.7	32.4
2021	36,608.5	510.7	146.1	968.2	766.4	8,176.8	14,776.6	1,288.1	977.4	3,841.9	5,040.0	32.7	51.1	32.5
2022	36,870.9	510.5	146.6	970.0	767.0	8,205.6	14,917.3	1,295.4	977.3	3,875.2	5,089.0	32.9	51.5	32.6
2023	37,130.1	510.2	147.0	971.7	767.6	8,233.1	15,057.4	1,302.6	977.3	3,908.0	5,137.6	33.0	51.9	32.7
2024	37,385.4	509.9	147.4	973.2	768.0	8,259.2	15,196.7	1,309.8	977.2	3,940.1	5,185.6	33.2	52.2	32.8
2025	37,636.4	509.5	147.8	974.6	768.3	8,283.8	15,335.0	1,316.8	977.1	3,971.5	5,233.1	33.3	52.6	32.9
2026	37,882.7	509.1	148.2	975.8	768.5	8,306.8	15,472.0	1,323.7	977.0	4,002.2	5,280.0	33.4	52.9	33.0
2027	38,123.6	508.5	148.5	976.9	768.6	8,328.1	15,607.5	1,330.4	976.9	4,032.2	5,326.1	33.6	53.2	33.1
2028	38,359.0	507.9	148.8	977.8	768.5	8,347.7	15,741.3	1,337.0	976.7	4,061.5	5,371.5	33.7	53.5	33.1
2029	38,588.5	507.2	149.1	978.5	768.2	8,365.6	15,873.1	1,343.4	976.4	4,090.0	5,416.2	33.8	53.8	33.2
2030	38,812.1	506.5	149.3	979.0	767.8	8,381.8	16,002.9	1,349.6	976.1	4,117.8	5,460.0	33.9	54.1	33.2

Note: These projections are from Statistics Canada's Scenario 3, which is a medium growth scenario (and largely reflects a continuation of current trends).
Sources: Bélanger, Martel and Malenfant, 2006. Population Projections for Canada, Provinces and Territories, 2005–2031. Catalogue no. 91-520-XIE, CD-Rom.

higher growth and others with less growth. At the core of its projection methodology is the same regional cohort component approach as relied upon in the aforementioned population estimates (with some minor modifications).

Population projections essentially involve what can best be considered carefully conceived assumptions on the future course of all of the relevant demographic components of population change, including at the national level fertility, mortality, immigration, and emigration, and at the provincial level, the additional component of interprovincial migration. These projections also consider possible changes in the number of non-permanent residents in Canada (i.e., people on work visas, student visas, refugee claimants, etc.). The projection in Table A.3 largely assumes a continuation of current fertility, immigration and emigration rates, modest gains in terms of life expectancy, and no change in the number of non-permanent residents in Canada. By the end of this projection period, the total fertility rate is assumed to have remained at its current level of about 1.5 births per woman, whereas life expectancy at birth is expected to increase to 81.9 and 86 years for men and women respectively. Immigration levels are projected to gradually increase from about 240,000 in 2005–2006 to about 280,000 in 2030–2031. In terms of interprovincial migration, this projection more or less assumes a continuation of patterns observed over the last 25 years, with greater emphasis placed on the last few years of this period.

According to Statistics Canada's medium growth projection scenario, total population size will reach the 39 million mark in about 25 years, while the overall rate of population growth is expected to slow (from about 1 percent in 2005 to about half this rate 0.5 percent by 2031). All provinces (with the exception of Newfoundland and Saskatchewan) are projected to increase in size, although the most pronounced growth is projected for Ontario (due largely to international migration), as well as Alberta and B.C. (due to both international and internal migration). Canada's eastern-most provinces are expected to experience an ongoing decline in terms of their relative demographic weight in Canada, a generalization that is also true of Quebec to a lesser extent. As Canada's population growth has been quite uneven over the last several decades, it is quite likely that this continue well into the future. Those regions of the country with the most buoyant economies are expected to experience considerably more population growth than others, predominantly since migrants (both internal and international) tend to seek out economic opportunities.

ALTERNATE SCENARIOS AS TO FUTURE POPULATION

It is understood that the demographic characteristics obtained from projections are those observed only if specified assumptions on fertility, mortality, and migration prevail. Yet there is clearly a lack of certainty as to future trends on these components, and for this reason, demographers typically rely upon several alternate scenarios. In fact, the medium growth scenario reproduced in Table A.3 is only one of several projections that Statistics Canada produced in its most recent round or population projections. Three of these projections are included in Figure A.1, for Canada overall (with a low- and high-growth scenario supplementing the medium-growth scenario already discussed above).

Very briefly, the high-growth scenario assumes somewhat of a rebound in fertility (up to about 1.7) whereas the low-growth scenario assumes further fertility decline (down to about 1.3). The high-growth scenario assumes significantly higher immigration (up to levels above 350,000) whereas the low-growth scenario assumes slightly reduced immigration (at levels hovering around 200,000). In terms of mortality, the slow-growth scenario involves a slightly more conservative forecast (with male and female life expectancies rising to only about 81.1 and 85.3 years respectively) whereas the high-growth scenario is more optimistic (with expectancies of 82.6 and 86.6 years by the end of the projection period). The reader might consider the possibility of change in demographic components beyond what entered into these alternate scenarios (as, for example, a return to above-replacement fertility or greater gains in terms of reducing mortality). These in turn could widen the range of projections observed in Figure A.1.

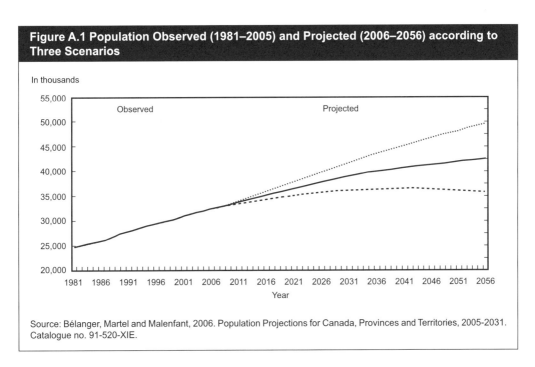

Figure A.1 Population Observed (1981–2005) and Projected (2006–2056) according to Three Scenarios

Source: Bélanger, Martel and Malenfant, 2006. Population Projections for Canada, Provinces and Territories, 2005-2031. Catalogue no. 91-520-XIE.

According to these projections, even with further fertility decline and reduced immigration (low-growth scenario), Canada's population is quite likely to continue to grow for at least another 25 to 30 years before stabilizing in the third decade of the current century. With a fertility upturn and continued strong immigration levels (high-growth scenario), Canada's population could very well reach the 40 million mark by 2030 and perhaps 50 million by mid-century. The difference between the high- and low-growth scenarios by mid-century is rather large, at fully 15 million people. The fact that Statistics Canada's official population projections differ so noticeably only serves to once again highlight the uncertainty as associated with Canada's demographic future.

PROJECTIONS BY AGE AND SEX

As Statistics Canada projects total population size, it also produces refined projections, broken down by age/sex and province/territory. Again, the detailed results, as well as the methodology that entered into these projections, are available elsewhere (Bélanger et al., 2005). As with its population estimates, Statistics Canada works with a slightly revised cohort component approach with all relevant components projected into the future, delineated by age and sex. Table A.4 provides the results from these projections, with detailed age sex data for Canada, as of 2031 (medium growth scenario).

Canada's population is projected to age considerably over the next several decades, particularly as the sizable baby boom generation ages. Figure A.2 demonstrates this by representing Table A.2 (2005 postcensal estimate) and Table A.4 (2031 population projection, medium growth) in terms of two population pyramids. In inspecting the 2031 age pyramid, the baby boom will be aged 65–85 and will be less visible because some of them will have died. Children (aged 0 to 14) will be outnumbered by seniors (65 years and older), as in fact, this is projected by Statistics Canada to occur as early as 2015. For the first time in Canada's history, Canada's children will be outnumbered by elderly people with all the corresponding adjustments this will necessitate. All projection scenarios produced by Statistics Canada suggest major population aging, as median age (39 years in 2005) is expected to climb to a level between 43 and 46 years in 2031 and between 45 and 50 years in 2056, depending upon scenario. According to the medium-growth scenarios, half the Canadian population would be over 47 years of age in 2056. The high-growth scenario is associated with slightly less population aging (as fertility rates recover somewhat) whereas the low-growth scenario is associated with slightly greater population aging.

Table A.4 Age/Sex Distribution (in the 1,000's) of the Projected 2031 Population of Canada, Medium Growth Scenario

Age	Male	Female	Both Sexes	Age	Male	Female	Both Sexes	Age	Male	Female	Both Sexes	Age	Male	Female	Both Sexes
0	177.8	168.4	346.2	25	218.1	212.1	430.2	50	264.7	264.5	529.2	75	190.4	218.0	408.4
1	179.6	170.6	350.2	26	220.7	217.4	438.1	51	262.3	261.4	523.7	76	182.4	212.5	394.9
2	182.6	173.9	356.5	27	222.0	220.3	442.3	52	255.7	255.8	511.5	77	169.2	201.2	370.4
3	185.2	176.3	361.5	28	221.6	221.0	442.6	53	250.7	250.0	500.7	78	155.3	188.0	343.3
4	188.1	179.0	367.1	29	222.9	222.7	445.6	54	249.0	249.0	498.0	79	143.9	176.4	320.3
0-4	913.3	868.2	1,781.5	25-29	1,105.3	1,093.5	2,198.8	50-54	1,282.4	1,280.7	2,563.1	75-79	841.2	996.1	1,837.3
5	190.9	181.7	372.6	30	228.7	228.3	457.0	55	247.0	246.0	493.0	80	134.3	167.9	302.2
6	193.6	184.2	377.8	31	236.5	236.2	472.7	56	243.9	243.9	487.8	81	124.2	158.3	282.5
7	196.1	186.6	382.7	32	239.3	239.0	478.3	57	236.2	237.8	474.0	82	114.7	149.6	264.3
8	198.4	188.6	387.0	33	244.8	245.1	489.9	58	235.6	236.8	472.4	83	107.3	142.5	249.8
9	200.5	190.4	390.9	34	253.1	251.6	504.7	59	236.4	237.8	474.2	84	98.6	134.6	233.2
5-9	979.5	931.5	1,911.0	30-34	1,202.4	1,200.2	2,402.6	55-59	1,199.1	1,202.3	2,401.4	80-84	579.1	752.9	1,332.0
10	202.4	192.1	394.5	35	260.9	260.7	521.6	60	241.0	244.2	485.2	85	77.6	109.6	187.2
11	204.1	193.6	397.7	36	265.6	263.8	529.4	61	238.5	242.0	480.5	86	65.5	95.5	161.0
12	205.5	194.8	400.3	37	266.7	265.1	531.8	62	233.0	238.4	471.4	87	57.0	86.2	143.2
13	206.5	195.9	402.4	38	270.2	269.3	539.5	63	229.1	235.9	465.0	88	48.6	76.2	124.8
14	207.6	196.8	404.4	39	274.4	274.4	548.8	64	228.8	236.8	465.6	89	39.0	64.5	103.5
10-14	1,026.1	973.2	1,999.3	35-39	1,337.8	1,333.3	2,671.1	60-64	1,170.4	1,197.3	2,367.7	85-89	287.7	432.0	719.7
15	208.8	197.7	406.5	40	278.1	276.5	554.6	65	237.4	246.1	483.5	90+	129.8	270.9	400.7
16	209.9	198.9	408.8	41	278.5	277.6	556.1	66	249.4	259.8	509.2				
17	211.0	199.9	410.9	42	271.2	270.8	542.0	67	253.7	264.9	518.6	0-14	2,918.9	2,772.9	5,691.8
18	212.4	201.2	413.6	43	265.3	265.3	530.6	68	252.2	264.4	516.6	0-17	3,548.6	3,369.4	6,918.0
19	214.9	203.6	418.5	44	266.6	267.1	533.7	69	242.6	257.1	499.7	18-64	11,522.3	11,452.8	22,975.1
15-19	1,057.0	1,001.3	2,058.3	40-44	1,359.7	1,357.3	2,717.0	65-69	1,235.3	1,292.3	2,527.6	65+	4,177.9	4,957.6	9,135.5
20	216.7	206.0	422.7	45	270.8	269.9	540.7	70	238.9	256.6	495.5				
21	218.1	208.4	426.5	46	272.1	269.4	541.5	71	230.8	250.3	481.1				
22	219.4	209.9	429.3	47	270.3	268.4	538.7	72	219.7	242.2	461.9				
23	219.6	210.7	430.3	48	267.7	266.0	533.7	73	213.0	235.9	448.9				
24	218.5	210.8	429.3	49	264.7	263.9	528.6	74	202.4	228.4	430.8				
20-24	1,092.3	1,045.8	2,138.1	45-49	1,345.6	1,337.6	2,683.2	70-74	1,104.8	1,213.4	2,318.2				

Source: Bélanger, Martel and Malenfant, 2006. Population Projections for Canada, Provinces and Territories, 2005–2031. Catalogue no. 91-520-XIE, CD-Rom.

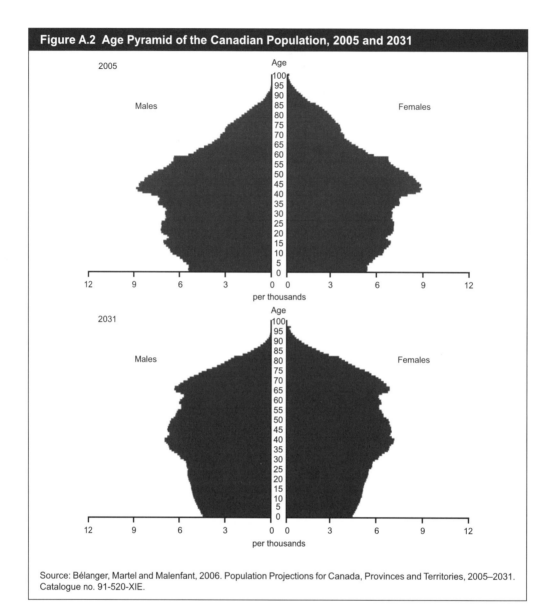

Figure A.2 Age Pyramid of the Canadian Population, 2005 and 2031

Source: Bélanger, Martel and Malenfant, 2006. Population Projections for Canada, Provinces and Territories, 2005–2031. Catalogue no. 91-520-XIE.

REFERENCES

CHAPTER 1

Abbott, Michael G., and. Charles M. Beach. (1993). "Immigrant Earnings Differentials and Birthyear Effects for Men in Canada: Post-war-1972." *Canadian Journal of Economics* 25:505–524.

Baker, Michael and Dwayne Benjamin. (1994). "The Performance of Immigrants in the Canadian Labor Market." *Journal of Labor Economics* 12: 369–405.

Baker, Michael, and Dwayne Benjamin. (1997). "Ethnicity, Foreign Birth and Earnings: A Canada/ U.S. Comparison." In Michael G. Abbot, Charles M. Beach, and Richard P. Chaykowski (eds.), *Transition and Structural Change in the North American Labour Market*. Kingston: John Deutsch Institute and Industrial Relations Centre, Queen's University.

Beaujot, Roderic, Suzanne Shiel, and Lorraine Schoel. (1989). *Immigration and the Population of Canada*. Ottawa: Report prepared for Immigration Policy Branch, Employment and Immigration. Ottawa: Employment and Immigration Canada.

Bélanger, Alain. (2002). *Report on the Demographic Situation in Canada 2001*. Cat. no. 91-209. Ottawa: Statistics Canada.

Bélanger, Alain, Laurent Martel and Eric Caron-Malenfant. (2005). *Population Projections for Canada, the Provinces and Territories, 2005–2031*. Statistics Canada Cat. no. 91-520 XIE.

Chesnais, Jean-Claude. (1989). "L'inversion de la pyramide des âges en Europe: Perspectives et problèmes." *International Population Conference* 3:53–68. Liège: IUSSP.

Citizenship and Immigration Canada. (2002). *Facts and Figures: Immigration Overview*. Ottawa: Strategic Policy, Planning and Research. Citizenship and Immigration Canada.

Dumas, Jean. (1990). *Report on the Demographic Situation in Canada 1990*. Ottawa: Statistics Canada, Cat. No. 91-209.

Lesthaeghe, Ronald. (1995). "The Second Demographic Transition in Western Countries: An Interpretation." In Karen Oppenheim and Ann-Magritt Jensen (eds.), *Gender and Family Change in Industrialized Countries*. Oxford: Clarendon Press.

Li, Peter S. (2003). *Destination Canada: Immigration Debates and Issues*. Toronto: Oxford University Press.

Oeppen, Jim, and James W. Vaupel. (2002). "Demography: Broken Limits to Life Expectancy." *Science* 296:1029–1031.

Statistics Canada. (2002). *Profile of the Canadian Population: Where We Live*. Cat. no. 96F0030. Ottawa: Statistics Canada.

_____. (2003a). *Canada's Ethnocultural Portrait: A Changing Mosaic*. Cat. no. 96F0030XIE2001008. Ottawa: Statistics Canada.

_____. (2003b). *Annual Demographic Statistics 2002*. Cat. no. 91-213. Ottawa: Statistics Canada.

_____. (2004). *Births*. Cat. no. 84F0210XPB. Ottawa: Statistics Canada.

_____. (2006). *Annual Demographic Statistics 2005*. Cat. no. 91-213. Ottawa: Statistics Canada.

United Nations. (2006). United Nations Population Information Network. Online at http://www.
    un.org/popin/data.html#Global%20Data.

U.S. Census Bureau. (2004). "The Foreign-Born Population of the United States." *Current Population
    Reports P20-534*. Bureau of the Census: International database, International Programs Centre.

Van de Kaa, Dirk. (1987). "Europe's Second Demographic Transition." *Population Bulletin* 42:1–58.

CHAPTER 2

Bogue, Donald J. (1967). "The End of the Population Explosion." *The Public Interest* (Spring):5-15.

Census Bureau. (2005). International Database, Population Division. Online at http://www.census.
    gov/ipc/www/idbprint.html.

Citizenship and Immigration Canada. (2005). *Citizenship and Immigration Statistics*. Online at http://
    www.cic.gc.ca/english/pub/index-2.html#statistics.

Council of Europe. (1997). *Recent Demographic Developments in Europe*. Strasbourg, UNECE

Eberstadt, Nicolas. (1997). "World Population Implosion?" *The Public Interest* 129:3–22.

Espenshade, Thomas J. (1986) "Population Dynamics with Immigration and Low Fertility." *Population
    and Development Review* 12 (Supplement):2048–2261.

George, M.V., François Nault, and Anatole Romaniuc. (1991). "Effects of Fertility and International
    Migration on Changing Age Composition in Canada." *Statistical Journal of the United Nations*
    ECE 8:13–24.

International Data Base. (2005). Census Bureau, Population Division. Online at http://www.census.
    gov/ipc/www/idbprint.html.

Jones, Gavin W. (1993). "Consequences of Rapid Fertility Decline for Old-Age Security." In Richard
    Leete and Iqbal Alam (eds.), *The Revolution in Asian Fertility: Dimensions, Causes, and Implications*.
    Oxford: Clarendon Press.

Keyfitz, Nathan. (1986). "The Family That Does Not Reproduce Itself." *Population and Development
    Review* 12 (Supplement):139–154.

Kono, Shigemi. (1994) "Ageing and the Family in the Developed Countries and Areas of Asia:
    Continuities and Transitions" in United Nations, *Ageing and the Family*. United Nations
    publication No. E.94. XIII 4).

Lachapelle, Réjean. (1990) "Changes in Fertility among Canada's Linguistic Groups." In Craig
    McKie and Keith Thompson (eds.), *Canadian Social Trends*. Toronto: Thompson Educational
    Publishing.

Lee, Yean-Ju, and Alberto Palloni. (1992). "Changes in the Family Status of Elderly Women in
    Korea." *Demography* 29:69–92.

Martin, Linda G. (1989). "The Greying of Japan." *Population Bulletin* 44, Population Reference
    Bureau.

_____. (1991). "Population Aging Policies in East Asia and the United States." *Science* 251:527–
    531.

McIntosh, C. Alison. (1981). "Low Fertility and Liberal Democracy in Western Europe." *Population
    and Development Review* 7:181–207.

McNeill, William H. (1998). "The Politics of Declining Populations." In Paul Demeny and Geoffrey
    McNicoll (eds.), *The Earthscan Reader in Population and Development*. London: Earthscan
    Publications.

Morgan, S. Philip. (1991). "Late Nineteenth- and Early Twentieth-Century Childlessness." *American Journal of Sociology* 97:779–807.

_____. (1996). "Characteristic Features of Modern American Fertility." *Population and Development Review* 22 (Supplement):19–63.

Ntozi, James P.M. (2002). "Impact of HIV/AIDS on Fertility in Sub-Saharan Africa." Fourth meeting of the follow-up committee on the implementation of the DND and ICPD-PA, Yaounde, Cameroon, January 2002.

Peterson, Peter G. (1999). "Gray Dawn: The Global Aging Crisis." *Foreign Affairs* 78:42–55.

Prinz, Christopher, and Wolfgang Lutz. (1993). "Alternative Demographic Scenarios for 20 Large Member States of the Council of Europe, 1990–2050." In Robert Cliquet (ed.), *The Future of Europe's Population*. Strasbourg: Council of Europe.

Ram, Bali. (2000). "Current Issues in Family Demography: Canadian Examples." *Canadian Studies in Population* 27:1–41.

Teitelbaum, Michael and Jay Winter. (1985). *The Fear of Population Decline.* Orlando: Academic Press.

Teitelbaum, Michael, and Jay Winter. (1998). *A Question of Numbers: High Migration, Low Fertility, and the Politics of National Identity.* New York: Hill and Wang.

United Nations. (1992). *Patterns of Fertility in Low-Fertility Settings.* New York: United Nations.

_____. (1994). "Overview of Recent Research Findings on Population Ageing and the Family." *Aging of the Family.* New York: United Nations.

_____. (1998). *World Population Monitoring 1996.* New York: United Nations.

_____. (1999). *World Population Prospects: The 1998 Revisions.* New York: United Nations.

_____. (2004). *World Population Prospects: The 2002 Revisions.* New York: United Nations.

_____. (2005). *World Population Prospects: The 2004 Revisions.* New York: United Nations.

UNECE.org. (2005). *Economic Commission for Europe.* Demographic database of the Population Activities unit. Geneva, Switzerland.

Wilmoth, John R. (1998). "The Future of Human Longevity: A Demographer's Perspective." *Science* 280:395–397.

CHAPTER 3

Adams, Michael. (2003). *Fire and Ice, the United States, Canada, and the Myth of Converging Values.* Toronto: Penguin.

Bélanger, Alain. (2002). *Report on the Demographic Situation in Canada, 2001.* Ottawa: Statistics Canada Cat. No. 91-209.

Bélanger, Alain, and Cathy Oikawa. (1999). "Who Has a Third Child?" *Canadian Social Trends* 53:23-26. Ottawa: Statistics Canada.

_____, and Genevieve Ouellet. (2002). "A Comparative Study of Recent Trends in Canadian and American Fertility, 1980–1999," *Report on the Demographic Situation in Canada 2001.* Ottawa: Statistics Canada.

Bongaarts, John, and Griffith Feeney. (1998). "On the Quantum and Tempo of Fertility." *Population and Development Review* 24 (2):271–291.

Brewster, Karin L., and Ronald R. Rindfruss. (2000). "Fertility and Women's Employment in Industrialized Nations." *Annual Review of Sociology* 26:271–296.

Bumpass, Larry and Hsien-Hen Lu. (2000). "Trends in Cohabitation and Implications for Children's Family Contexts in the United States." *Population Studies* 54: 29-41.

Bumpass, Larry L., and Kelly R. Raley. (1995). "Redefining Single Parent Families: Cohabitation and Changing Family Reality." *Demography* 32 (1):97–109.

Butz, William P., and Michael P. Ward. (1979). "The Emergence of Countercyclical U.S. Fertility." *American Economic Review* 69 (1):318–328.

Canton, Erik, Casper von Ewijk, and T.G. Paul Tang. (2004). "Aging and International Capital Flows." CPB Netherlands Bureau for Economic Policy Analysis.

Chiuri, Maria Concetta, and Tullio Jappelli. (2000). "Financial Markets, Judicial Constraints and Housing Tenure: An International Comparison." Working Paper #230. Luxembourg: Luxembourg Income Study.

Dumas, Jean. (1984). *Report on the Demographic Situation in Canada*. Ottawa: Statistics Canada Cat. No. 91-209.

Dumas, Jean, and Alan Bélanger. (1997). "Common-Law Unions in Canada at the End of the 20th Century." Report on the Demographic Situation in Canada, 1996. Ottawa: Statistics Canada.

Easterlin, Richard A. (1978). "What Will 1984 Be Like? Socioeconomic Implications of Recent Twists in Age Structure." *Demography* 15 (3):397–432.

Fields, Jason and Lynne Casper. (2001). *America's Families and Living Arrangements*. Current Population Reports P-20-537. Washington: U.S. Census Bureau.

Fortin, Pierre. (2003). "Differences in Annual Work Hours Per Capita between the United States and Canada." *International Productivity Monitor* 6:38–46.

Heisz, Andrew. (2002). "The Evolution of Job Stability in Canada: Trends and Comparisons to U.S. Results." Research paper. Ottawa: Statistics Canada.

Le Bourdais, Céline, et al. (2000). "The Changing Face of Conjugal Relationships." *Canadian Social Trends*. Ottawa: Statistics Canada.

Lesthaeghe, Ronald. (1991). "The Second Demographic Transition in Western Countries: An Interpretation." Working Paper 31. Interuniversity program in Demography. Brussels: Vrije Universiteit Brussel.

Macunovich, Diane. (2002). *Birth Quake: The Baby Boom and Its Aftershocks*. Chicago: University of Chicago Press.

Simmons, John. (1995). "Fertility and Values in 15 Western Countries during the 1980's." In Ruud De Moor (ed.), *Values in Western Societies*. Tilberg: Tilburg University Press.

Sorrentino, Constance. (2000). "International Unemployment Rates: How Comparable Are They?" *Monthly Labor Review* 123 (6):3–20.

Statistics Canada. (2003). "Benefiting from Extended Parental Leave." *Perspectives on Labour and Income* 4 (3). Statistics Canada Cat. No. 75-001-XIE.

U.S. Census Bureau. (2005). *International Data Base Projections*. Online at http://www.census.gov/ipc/www/idbprint.html.

U.S. National Vital Statistics (2002). *Report on Vital Statistics* 51:2.

Ventura, Stephanie and Christine Bachrach. (2000). *Nonmarital Childbearing in the United States, 1940-99*. National Vital Statistics Report 48. Washington: Center for Disease Control and Prevention.

World Bank. (2003). *World Development Indicators 2005*. Washington: The World Bank Group.

CHAPTER 4

Baillargeon, Jacques, and Hélène Pelletier-Baillargeon. (1963). *La régulation des naissances. Précis de la méthode sympto-thermique*. Montréal.

Beaujot, Roderic. (2000). "Les deux transitions démographiques du Québec." *Cahiers québécois de démographie* XXIX:201–230.

Breault, Rita. (1975). *Les idées nouvelles nous viennent de la base*. Montréal: Seréna Quebec Archives.

Charbonneau, Paul-Eugène. (1966). "Lettre ouverte aux théologiens sur un problème du monde moderne: la limitation des naissances." *Perspectives sociales* 21 :35-41.

d'Anjou, Joseph. (1964). "Pilule ou maîtrise de soi?" *Relations* 12 : 5-9.

Dumas, Paul, and Charles Chaput. (1935). "La méthode Ogino-Knauss." *Journal de l'hôtel-Dieu* IV:7–54.

Forest, M. Ceslas. (1934). "La théorie Ogino-Knauss. Un remède contre le néo-malthusianisme." *Revue dominicaine* XL:67–69.

Gagnieux, Christian. (1975). "Le médecin face à la contraception." Unpublished Ph.d. dissertation. Lyon: Université Claude Bernard.

Gauvreau, Danielle, and Peter Gossage. (1997). "Empêcher la famille." *Canadian Historical Review* 78: 478-510.

Gervais, Diane. (2002) "Morale catholique et détresse conjugale au Québec. La réponse du Service de régulation des naissances Seréna, 1955–1970." *Revue d'histoire de l'Amérique française* LV:185–215.

Health and Welfare Canada. (1978). *Report 1978: Oral Contraceptives*. Montréal: Health and Welfare Canada.

Henripin, Jacques. (1968). *Le Coût de la Croissance Démographique*. Montréal: Les Presses de l'Université de Montréal.

Hudon, Louis-Émile. (1936). *Questions de morale matrimoniale*. Quebec City: Laval University.

Laberge, Huguette. (1965). "20 médecins canadien-français ont répondu à la question 'Prescrivez-vous la pilule contraceptive?'" *Photo-Journal* 3:6–13.

Lancet II. (1977). "Editorial: Mortality Associated with the Pill," *The Lancet II* 5: 747–748.

Mayrand, Benoît. (1934). *Un problème moral: La continence périodique dans le mariage suivant la méthode Ogino*. Coublivie, Isère.

McInnis, Marvin. (2000). "Canada's Population in the Twentieth Century." In Michael R. Haines and Richard H. Steckel (eds.), *A Population History of North America*. Cambridge: Cambridge University Press.

Paquin, Jules. (1960). *Morale et médicine*. Montréal: L'Immaculee Conception.

Sevegrand, Martine. (1995). *Les enfants du bon Dieu. Les catholiques français et la procréation au XXe siècle*. Paris : Albin Michel.

Statistics Canada. (1983). *Births and Deaths*. Statistics Canada Catalogue 84-204,

Statistics Canada. (1993). *Births and Deaths*. Statistics Canada Catalogue 94-204.

CHAPTER 5

Abbasi-Shavazi, M.J., and P. McDonald. (2000). "Fertility and Multiculturalism: Immigrant Fertility in Australia, 1977–1991." *International Migration Review* 34 (1):215–242.

Balakrishnan, T.R., G.E. Ebanks, and C.F. Grindstaff. (1979). *Patterns of Fertility in Canada, 1971*. Ottawa: Statistics Canada.

Beaujot, Roderic. (1991). *Population Change in Canada: The Challenges of Policy Adaptation*. Toronto: McClelland & Steward.

Bélanger, Alain. (2000). "Reflections on the Evolution of Components of Demographic Growth in Canada in the Context of the Triennial Review of the Canadian Pension Plan." *Seminar, Demographic, and Economic Perspectives of Canada*. Ottawa: Office of the Chief Actuary. Online at http://www.osfi-bsif.gc.ca/.

_____, and Stéphane Gilbert. (2003). *Report on the Demographic Situation in Canada 2003*. Ottawa: Statistics Canada.

Boyd, Monica, and E. Grieco. (1998). "Triumphant Transitions: Socioeconomic Achievements of the Second Generation in Canada." *International Immigration Review* 32:857–876.

Cho, Lee-Jay, Robert D. Retherford, and Minja Kim Choe. (1986). *The Own-Children Method of Fertility Estimation*. Honolulu: University of Hawaii Press.

Citizenship and Immigration Canada. (2001). *Le Canada se réaffirme en faveur de l'immigration: La ministre Caplan dépose les nivaux d'immigration de 2002*. Ottawa: Citizenship and Immigration Canada. Online at http://www.cic.gc.ca.

Desplanques, Guy. (1993). "Mesurer les disparités de fécondité à l'aide du seul recensement." *Population* 48 (6):2011–2024.

Dumas, Jean, and Alain Bélanger. (1994). *Report on the Demographic Situation in Canada, 1994*. Ottawa: Statistics Canada.

Goldstein, S., and A. Goldstein. (1981). "The Impact of Migration on Fertility: An 'Own Children' Analysis for Thailand." *Population Studies* (July):265–284.

Henripin, Jacques. (1972). "Trends and Factors of Fertility in Canada." *1961 Census Monograph*. Ottawa: Dominion Bureau of Statistics.

Hervitz, H.M. (1985). "Selectivity, Adaptation, or Disruption? A Comparison of Alternative Hypothesis on the Effect of Migration on Fertility: The Case of Brazil." *International Migration Review* 19 (2):293–317.

Kalbach, Warren. (1970). "The Impact of Immigration on Canada's Population." 1961 Census Monograph. Ottawa: Dominion Bureau of Statistics.

Massey, Douglas. (1981). "Dimensions of the New immigration to the United States and the Prospects for Assimilation." *Annual Review of Sociology* 7(1)::57–85.

Ng, Edward, and François Nault. (1997). "Fertility among Recent Immigrant Women to Canada, 1991: An Examination of the Disruption Hypothesis." *International Migration* 35 (4):559–580.

Ram, Bali, and M.V. George. (1990). "Immigrant Fertility Patterns in Canada, 1961–1986." *International Migration* 28 (4):413–426.

Statistics Canada. (2001). *Population Projections for Canada, Provinces and Territories, 2000–2026*. Cat. no. 91-520. Ottawa: Statistics Canada.

CHAPTER 6

Briggs, Elizabeth, and Colin Briggs. (1998). *Before Modern Medicine: Diseases and Yesterday's Remedies*. Winnipeg: Westgarth.

Chen, Jiajian, and Wayne J. Millar. (1999). "Birth Outcome, the Social Environment, and Child Health." *Health Reports* 10 (4):57–67.

_____ and Wayne J. Millar. (2000). "Are Recent Cohorts Healthier Than Their Predecessors?" *Health Reports* 11 (4):9–23.

Dominion Bureau of Statistics. (1967). *Canada: One hundred, 1867–1967*. Ottawa: Ministry of Trade and Commerce.

Health Canada. (2000). *HIV and AIDS in Canada: Surveillance Report to December 31, 1999*. Ottawa: Health Canada.

_____, Statistics Canada, and Canadian Institute for Health Information. (1999). *Statistical Report on the Health of Canadians*. Ottawa: Statistics Canada and the Canadian Institute for Health Information.

Heart and Stroke Foundation of Canada. (1999). *The Changing Face of Heart Disease and Stroke in Canada 2000*. Ottawa: Heart and Stroke Foundation of Canada.

Leacy, F.H. (ed.). (1983). *Historical Statistics of Canada*, 2nd ed. Cat. no. 11-516. Ottawa: Social Science Federation and Statistics Canada.

Millar, Wayne J., and Gerry B. Hill. (1998). "Childhood Asthma." *Health Reports* 10 (3):9–21.

National Cancer Institute of Canada. (2000). *Canadian Cancer Statistics 2000.* Toronto: Division of HIV/AIDS Surveillance.

Porter, Roy. (1997). *The Greatest Benefit to Mankind: A Medical History of Humanity from Antiquity to the Present.* London: HarperCollins.

Statistics Canada. (1999). *Statistical Report on the Health of Canadians.* Cat. no. 82-570-XIE. Ottawa: Statistics Canada.

_____. (1999a). *Health Statistics at a Glance.* Prod. no. 82F0075XCB. Ottawa: Statistics Canada.

_____. (2000). *Vital Statistics Compendium.* Cat. no. 84-214. Ottawa: Statistics Canada.

Trottier, Helen, Laurent Martel, Christian Houle, Jean-Marie Berthelot, and Jacques Légaré. (2000). "Living at Home or in an Institution: What Makes the Difference for Seniors?" *Health Reports* 11 (4):49–61.

CHAPTER 7

Base de donneés sur la longgévité Canadienne. (2003). Université de Montréal, Départment de démographie. Disponible sur le site web: http://www.demo.umontreal.ca/bdlc.

Bourbeau, Robert, Bernard Desjardins, et Jacques Légaré. (2002). *Pensées longitudinales dans l'étude de la mortalité, du vieillissement et do la longévité.* Communication présentée à la Chaire Quetelet, 2002, Louvain-la-Neuve, Belgique, octobre 22–25, 2002.

Bourbeau, Robert, Jacques Légaré and Valérie Emond. (1997). *New Birth Cohort Life Tables for Canada and Quebec, 1801-1991.* Statistics Canada Cat. No. 91F0015MPE1997003.

_____, and André Lebel. (2000). "Mortality Statistics of the Oldest-Old: An Evaluation of Canadian Data." *Demographic Research* 2:np.

Choinière, Robert. (2003). *La mortalité au Québec: Une comparaison international.* Quebec City: Institut national de sante publique.

Duchesne, Louis. (2000). "Chapitre 1: Rétrospective du XXe siècle." Dans *La situation demographique au Quebec-Bilan 1999. Rètrospective du XXe siècle.* Québec City: Institut de la statistique du Québec.

Institut National d'Études Démographiques. (2002). Online at http://www.ined.fr/population-en-chiffes/pays-developpes/index.html.

Légaré, Jacques, Robert Bourbeau, Bertrand Desgardins, and Claude Deblois. (2003). "Variation de la taille des cohortes et diminution de la mortalité aux âges avancés: Implications pour le financement par répartition des systèmes de santé." Communication présentée au Congres de l'Association internationale de la sécurité sociale, Anvers, Belgique, mai 5–7, 2003.

Martel, Sylvie and Robert Bourbeau. (2003) «Compression de la mortalité et rectangularisation de la courbe de survie au Québec au cours du XXe siècle". *Cahiers québécois de démographie*, 32, 1 : 43-76.

Ministère de la Santé et des Services Sociaux. (2001). *Surveillance de la mortalité au Québec: 1977–1998.* Government du Québec, Collection 14—Analyses et surveillance.

Nizard, Alfred. (1997) "Les trois révolutions de la mortalité depuis 1950." Population et sociétés bulletin mensuel d'information de l'Institut national d'études démographiques 327.

Oeppen, Jim, and James W. Vaupel. (2002). "Demography: Broken Limits to Life Expectancy." *Science* 296:1029–1031.

Olshansky, S. Jay, and Brian Ault. (1986). "The Fourth Stage of the Epidemiologic Transition: The Age of Delayed Degenerative Diseases." *Millbank Quarterly* 64 (3):355–391.

Omran, Abdel R. (1971). "The Epidemiologic Transition: A Theory of the Epidemiology of Population Change." *Millbank Memorial Fund Quarterly* 49 (4):509–538.

Robine, Jean-Marie. (2001). "Redéfinir les phases de la transition épidémiologique à travers l'étude de la dispersion des durées de vie: Le cas de France." *Population* 56 (1–2) :199–222.

Smuga, Mélanie. (2002). *La mortalité infantile et périnatale au Québec: Évolution depuis 1926 et disparités regionales de 1980 à 1997*. Montréal: Université de Montréal, Département de démographie, mémoire de maîtrise.

Statistics Canada. (1926-1971). Database on Mortality by Cause, Health Statistics Division. Statistics Canada.

Statistics Canada. (2002). *Rapport sur l'état de la population du Canada 2001*. Cat. no. 91-209-XPF. Ottawa: Statistics Canada.

Vallin, Jacques, et France Meslé. (2001). *Tables de mortalité françaises pour les XIXe et XXe siècles et projections pur le XXIe siècle*. Paris: Institut national d'études démographiques, collection données statistiques 4.

CHAPTER 8

Anderson, Robert, Arialdi Minino, Donna Hoyert, and Harry Rosenberg. "Comparability of Cause of Death between ICD-9 and ICD-10: Preliminary Estimates." *National Vital Statistics Reports* 49 (2):1–9.

Cairney, John, and T. Joel Wade. (1998). "Correlates of Body Weight in the 1994 National Population Health Survey." *International Journal of Obesity* 22 (6):584–591.

Calle, Eugenia E., Carmen Rodriguez, Kimberly Walker-Thurmond, and Michael J. Thun. (2003). "Overweight, Obesity, and Mortality from Cancer in a Prospectively Studied Cohort of U.S. Adults." *New England Journal of Medicine* 348:1623–1638.

Congressional Budget Office. 2003. "How Many People Lack Health Insurance and for How Long?" *A Congressional Budget Office Paper*. Washington, DC, 1–22.

Flegal, Katherine M., Margaret D. Carroll, Cynthia L. Ogden, and Clifford L. Johnson. (2002). "Prevalence and Trends in Obesity among U.S. Adults, 1999–2000." *Journal of the American Medical Association* 288:1723–1727.

Gilmore, Jason. (1999). "Body Mass Index and Health." *Health Reports*. Ottawa: Statistics Canada 11:31–43.

Joffres, Michel R., Pavel Hamet, David R. MacLean, Gilbert J. L'italien, and George Fodor. (2001). "Distribution of Blood Pressure and Hypertension in Canada and the United States." *American Journal of Hypertension* 14:1099–1105.

Manuel, Douglas G., and Yang Mao. (2002). "Avoidable Mortality in the United States and Canada, 1980–1996." *American Journal of Public Health* 92:1481–1484.

McGinnis, J. Michael, and William H. Foege. (1993). "Actual Causes of Death in the United States." *Journal of the American Medical Association* 270:2207–2212.

National Center for Health Statistics. (1998). «Death Rates for 282 Selected Causes by 5-Year Age Groups, Race, and Sex: United States, 1979–1998». Hyattsville: NCHS.

National Center for Health Statistics. (2002). *Health, U.S., 2002, with Chartbook on Trends in the Health of Americans*. Hyattsville: NHCS.

_____. (2004). "Death Rates for 282 Selected Causes by 5 Year Age Groups, Race, and Sex: United States 1979–1998." No. GMWK292A. Online at www.cdc.gov/nchs/datawk/statab/unpubd/mortabs/gmwk292.htm.

Peeters, Anna, Jan J. Barendregt, Frans Willekens, Johan P. Mackenback, Abdullah Al Mumun, and Luc Bonneux. (2003). "Obesity in Adulthood and Its Consequences for Life Expectancy: A Life-Table Analysis." *Annals of Internal Medicine* 138:24–32.

Ross, Nancy A., Michael C. Wolfson, James R. Dunn, Jean-Marie Berthelot, George A. Kaplan, and John W. Lynch. (2000). "Relation between Income Inequality and Mortality in Canada and in the United States: Cross-sectional Assessment Using Census Data and Vital Statistics." *British Medical Journal* 320:898–902.

Schoenborn, Charlotte A. (1993). "Trends in Health Status and Practices in Canada and the United States." *Canadian Social Trends.* Ottawa: Statistics Canada.

Statistics Canada. (2001). *Mortality — Summary List of Causes, Shelf Tables: 1998,* 1–188. Ottawa: Statistics Canada.

Tanguay, M. Serge, B. Phyllis Will, and Karla Nobrega. (2003). "Smoking Patterns in the 20th Century." *… au courant.* Cat. no. 82-005. Ottawa: Statistics Canada.

U.S. Census Bureau. (1998). U.S. 1998 mid-year population, unpublished file NESTV 98. Washington, D.C.

White, Kevin M. (2002). "Longevity Advances in High-Income Countries, 1955–96." *Population and Development Review* 28:59–76.

Wolf-Maier, Katharina, Richard S. Cooper, Jose R. Banegas, Simona Giampaoli, Hans-Werner Hense, et al. (2003). "Hypertension Prevalence and Blood Pressure Levels in 6 European Countries, Canada, and the United States." *Journal of the American Medical Association* 289:2363–2869.

CHAPTER 9

Andreev, Kirill F. (2000). "Sex Differentials in Survival in the Canadian Population, 1921–1997: A Descriptive Analysis with Focus on Age-Specific Structure, Descriptive Findings." *Demographic Research* 3 (12). Online at http://www.demographic research.org/Volumes/Vol13/12.

Arriaga, Eduardo E. (1984). "Measuring and Explaining the Change in Life Expectancies." *Demography* 21 (1):83–96.

Bartecchi, Carl F., Thomas D. MacKenzie, and Robert W. Schrier. (1994). "The Human Costs of Tobacco Use, Part I." *New England Journal of Medicine* 330 (13):907–912.

Bélanger, Alain. (2003). *Report on the Demographic Situation in Canada 2002: Current Demographic Analysis.* Cat. no. 91-209-XPE. Ottawa: Minister of Industries.

Bombard, J., A. Malarcher, M. Schooley, and A. MacNeil. (2004). "State-Specific Prevalence of Current Cigarette Smoking among Adults — United States, 2003." *Journal of the American Medical Association* 292 (24):2966–2967.

Boyle, P., A. d'Onofrio, P. Maisonneuve, G. Severi, C. Robertson, M. Tubiana, and U. Veronesi. (2003). "Measuring Progress against Cancer in Europe: Has the 15% Decline Targeted for 2000 Come about?" *Annals of Oncology* 14:1312–1325.

Coale, Ansley. (2003). "Increases in Expectation of Life and Population Growth." *Population and Development Review* 29 (1):113–120.

Das Gupta, Partha. (1993). *Standardization and Decomposition of Rates: A User's Manual.* U.S. Bureau of the Census, Current Population Reports. Washington: U.S. Government Printing Office.

Davis, Kingsley. (1984). "Wives and Work: Consequences of the Sex Role Revolution." *Population and Development Review* 10 (3):397–417.

Doll, Richard, and Richard Peto. (1981). "The Causes of Cancer: Quantitative Estimates of Avoidable Risks of Cancer in the United States Today." *Journal of the National Cancer Institute* 66:1191–1308.

Fries, James F. (1980). "Aging, Natural Death, and Compression of Mortality." *New England Journal of Medicine* 303:130–135.

Hegmann, K.T., A. Fraser, R.P. Keaney, S.E. Moser, D.S. Nilasena, M. Sedlars, L. Higham-Gren, and J.L. Lyon. (1993). "The Effect of Age at Smoking Initiation on Lung Cancer Risk." *Epidemiology* 4:444–448.

Kannisto, Väinö, Jens Lauritsen, A. Robert Thatcher, and James W. Vaupel. (1994). "Reductions in Mortality at Advanced Ages: Several Decades of Evidence from 27 Countries." *Population and Development Review* 20 (4):793–810.

Lesthaeghe, Ronald, and Johan Surkyn. (1988). "Cultural Dynamics and Economic Theories of Fertility Change." *Population and Development Review* 14:1–45.

Lopez, Alan D. (1983). "The Sex Differential in Mortality in Developed countries." In Alan D. Lopez and Lado T. Ruzicka (eds.), *Sex Differentials in Mortality: Trends, Determinants, and Consequences.* Canberra: Department of Demography, Australian National University Printing Press.

_____. (1995). "The Lung Cancer Epidemic in Developed Countries." In Alan D. Lopez, Graziella Caselli, and Tapani Valkonen (eds.) *Adult Mortality in Developed Countries: From Description to Explanation.* Oxford: Oxford University Press.

Luy, Marc. (2003). "Causes of Male Excess Mortality: Insights from Cloistered Populations." *Population and Development Review* 29 (4):647–676.

Manton, Kenneth. G. (1982). "Changing Concepts of Morbidity and Mortality in the Elderly Population." *Millbank Memorial Fund Quarterly/Health and Society* 60:183–244.

McDonald, Peter. (2000). "Gender Equity in Theories of Fertility Transition." *Population and Development Review* 26 (3):427–440.

McGinnis, J. Michael, and William H. Foege. (1993). "Actual Causes of Death in the United States." *Journal of the American Medical Association* 270 (10):2207–2212.

Mokdad, Ali H., James S. Marks, Donna F. Stroup, and Julie L. Gerberding. (2004). "Actual Causes of Death in the United States, 2000." *Journal of the American Medical Association* 291 (10):1238–1245.

Murthy, P.K. (2005). "A Comparison of Different Methods for Decomposition of Changes in Expectation of Life at Birth and Differentials in Life Expectancy at Birth." *Demographic Research* 12 (7). Online at http://www.demographic-research.org.

Nagnur, D. (1986). *Longevity and Historical Life Tables, 1921–1981 (Abridged): Canada and the Provinces.* Cat. no. 89-506. Ottawa: Minister of Supply and Services Canada.

Nathanson, Constance A. (1984). "Sex Differences in Mortality." *Annual Review of Sociology* 10:191–213.

_____. (1995). "The Position of Women and Mortality in Developed Countries." In Alan Lopez, Graziella Caselli, and Tampani Valkonen (eds.), *Adult Mortality in Developed Countries: From Description to Explanation.* Oxford: Oxford University Press.

Olshansky, S. Jay, and Brian A. Ault. (1986). "The Fourth Stage of Epidemiologic Transition: The Age of Delayed Degenerative Diseases." *Millbank Quarterly* 46 (3):355–391.

Omran, Abdel. R. (1971). "The Epidemiological Transition: A Theory of Epidemiology of Population Change." *Millbank Memorial Fund Quarterly* 49:509–538.

Owens, Ian P.F. (2002). "Sex Differences in Mortality Rate." *Science* 297:2008–2009.

Pampel, Fred C. (2001). "Gender Equality and the Sex Differential in Mortality from Accidents in High-Income Nations." *Population Research and Policy Review* 20:397–421.

_____. (2002). "Cigarette Use and the Narrowing Sex Differential in Mortality." *Population and Development Review* 28 (1):77–104.

_____. (2003). "Declining Sex Differences in Mortality from Lung Cancer in High-Income Nations." *Demography* 40 (1):45–65.

Perls, Thomas T., and Ruth C. Fretts. (1998). "Why Women Live Longer Than Men." *Scientific American Presents* 9:100–104.

Peron, Yves, and Claude Strohmenger. (1985). *Demographic and Health Indicators: Presentation and Interpretation.* Cat. no. 83-543E. Ottawa: Minister of Supply and Services Canada.

Peto, Richard, Alan D. Lopez, Jillian Boreham, Michael Thun, and Clark Heath, Jr. (1992). "Mortality from Tobacco in Developed Countries: Indirect Estimation from National Vital Statistics." *Lancet* 339:1268–1278.

_____, Alan D. Lopez, Jillian Boreham, Michael Thun, and Clark Heath, Jr. (2000). *Mortality from Smoking in Developed Countries 1950–2000: Indirect Estimates from National Vital Statistics.* Oxford: Oxford University Press.

Population Reference Bureau. (2003, 2004). *World Population Data Sheet.* Washington: Population Reference Bureau.

Preston, Samuel H. (1976). *Mortality Patterns in National Populations.* New York: Academic Press.

Ravenholt, R.T. (1990). "Tobacco's Global Death March." *Population and Development Review* 16 (2):213–240.

Riley, James C. (2001). *Rising Life Expectancy: A Global History.* Cambridge: Cambridge University Press.

Rogers, Richard G., and Robert A. Hackenberg. (1987). "Extending Epidemiologic Transition Theory: A New Stage." *Social Biology* 34 (3/4):234–243.

_____., Robert A. Hummer, and Charles B. Nam. (2000). *Living and Dying in the U.S.A.: Behavioral, Health, and Social Differentials of Adult Mortality.* San Diego: Academic Press.

Salomon, Joshua A., and Christopher J.L. Murray. (2002). "The Epidemiologic Transition Revisited: Causes of Death by Age and Sex." *Population and Development Review* 28 (2):205–228.

Smith, David W.E. (1993). *Human Longevity.* New York: Oxford University Press.

Stack, Steven. (2000a). "Suicide: A 15-Year Review of the Sociological Literature, Part I: Cultural and Economic Factors." *Suicide and Life-Threatening Behavior* 30 (2):145–162.

_____. (2000b). "Suicide: A 15-Year Review of the Sociological Literature, Part II: Modernization and Social Integration Perspectives." *Suicide and Life-Threatening Behavior* 30 (2):163–176.

Trovato, Frank, and N.M. Lalu. (1996a). "Narrowing Sex Differences in Life Expectancy in the Industrialized World: Early 1970s to Early 1990s." *Social Biology* 43 (1/2):20–37.

_____, and N.M. Lalu. (1996b). "Causes of Death Responsible for the Changing Sex Differential in Life Expectancy between 1970 and 1990 in Thirty Industrialized Countries." *Canadian Studies in Population* 23 (2):99–126.

_____, and N.M. Lalu. (1998). "Contribution of Cause-Specific Mortality to Changing Sex Differences in Life Expectancy: Seven Nation Case Study." *Social Biology* 45 (1/2):1–20.

Tuljapurkar, Shripad, Nan Li, and Carl Boe. (2000). "A Universal Pattern of Mortality Decline in the G7 Countries." *Nature* 405:789–792.

Van de Kaa, Dirk J. (1987). "Europe's Second Demographic Transition." *Population Bulletin* 42. Washington: Population Reference Bureau.

_____. (1999). "Europe and Its Population: The Long View." In D. Van de Kaa, H. Leridon, G. Gesano, and M. Okolski (eds.), *European Populations: Unity in Diversity.* Dordrecht: Kluwer Publishers.

_____. (2004). "Is the Second Demographic Transition a Useful Research Concept: Questions and Answers." *Vienna Yearbook of Population Research 2004.* Vienna: Austrian Academy of Sciences.

Vaupel, James W., and Romo V. Canudas. (2003). "Decomposing Change in Life Expectancy: A Bouquet of Formulas in Honor of Nathan Keyfitz's 90th Birthday." *Demography* 40 (2):201–216.

Verbrugge, Lois M. (1976). "Sex Differentials in Morbidity and Mortality in the United States." *Social Biology* 23 (4):275–296.

Waldron, Ingrid. (1976). "Why Do Women Live Longer Than Men?" *Social Science and Medicine* 10:349–362.

_____. (1986). "The Contribution of Smoking to Sex Differences in Mortality." *Public Health Reports* 101 (2):163–173.

_____. (1993). "Recent Trends in Sex Mortality Ratios for Adults in Developed Countries." *Social Science and Medicine* 36 (4):451–462.

_____. (1995). "Contributions of Biological and Behavioral Factors to Changing Sex Differences in Ischaemic Heart Disease Mortality." In A.D. Lopez, G. Caselli, and T. Valkonen (eds.), *Adult Mortality in Developed Countries: From Description to Explanation.* Oxford: Oxford University Press.

_____. (2000). "Trends in Gender Differences in Mortality: Relationships to Changing Gender Differences in Behavior and Other Causal Factors." In E. Annandale and K. Hung, *Gender Inequalities in Health.* Buckingham: Open University Press.

White, Kevin M. (2002). "Longevity Advances in High-Income Countries, 1955–96." *Population and Development Review* 28 (1):59–76.

_____, and Samuel H. Preston. (1996). "How Many Americans Are Alive Because of Twentieth-Century Improvements in Mortality?" *Population and Development Review* 22 (3):415–429.

Wilmoth, John R. (1998). "The Future of Human Longevity: A Demographer's Perspective." *Science* 280:395–397.

Wingard, Deborah. L. (1984). "The Sex Differential in Mortality Rates: Demographic and Behavioral Factors." *American Journal of Epidemiology* 115 (2):205–216.

World Health Organization. (1998). *World Health Statistics Annual 1996.* Geneva: World Health Organization.

_____. (2003). *Mortality Data Base.* Geneva. Online at www.who.org.

CHAPTER 10

Abella, Irving, and Harold Troper. (1982). *None Is Too Many: Canada and the Jews of Europe, 1933–1948.* New York: Random House.

Avery, Donald H. (2000). "Immigration: Peopling Canada." *The Beaver* 80 (1):28–38.

Badets, Jan, and Linda Howatson-Leo. (1999). "Recent Immigrants in the Labour Force." *Canadian Social Trends* 52 (Spring):16–22.

Calliste, Agnes. (1993). "Race, Gender and Canadian Immigration Policy." *Journal of Canadian Studies* 28 (4):131–148.

Census of Population. (1901). *Bulletin VIII.* Ottawa: Government of Canada.

Citizenship and Immigration. (1999). *Facts and Figures, 1998: Immigration Overview.* Strategic Policy, Planning and Research. Ottawa: CIC Communications Branch.

Hawkins, Freda. (1972). *Canada and Immigration: Public Policy and Public Concern.* Montréal: McGill-Queen's University Press.

Kalbach, Warren. (1970). "The Impact of Immigration on Canada's Population." 1961 Census Monograph. Ottawa: Dominion Bureau of Statistics.

Kelley, Ninette, and Michael Trebilcock. (1998). *The Making of the Mosaic: A History of Canadian Immigration Policy.* Toronto: University of Toronto Press.

Knowles, Valerie. (1997). *Strangers at Our Gates: Canadian Immigration and Immigration Policy, 1540–1997.* Toronto: Dundurn Press.

McKie, Craig. (1994). "Temporary Residents of Canada." *Canadian Social Trends* 32 (Spring):12–15.

Michalowski, Margaret. (1996). "Visitors and Visa Workers: Old Wine in New Bottles?" In Alan Simmons (ed.), *International Migration, Refugee Flows and Human Rights in North America: The Impact of Free Trade and Restructuring.* New York: Center for Migration Studies.

Picot, Garnett, and Andrew Heisz. (2000). *The Performance of the 1990s Canadian Labour Market.* Cat. no. 11F0019MIE-148. Ottawa: Statistics Canada.

Statistics Canada. (1990) *Immigrants in Canada: Selected Highlights.* Ottawa: Statistics Canada.

Statistics Canada. (1997). *1996 Census: Immigration and Citizenship.* The Nation Series. Cat. No. 93F0023XDB96000 and Cat. No. 99-936.

Statistics Canada. (1997). Catalogue nos. 99-517 (Vol. VII. Part 1), 92-727 (Vol. I, Part 3), 92-913.

Statistics Canada. (2000). *Canada Year Book.* Statistics Canada Cat. No. 11-402-XPE.

Troper, Harold. (1972). *Only Farmers Need Apply.* Toronto: Griffin House.

Urquhart, M.C., and K.A.H. Buckley (eds.). (1965). *Historical Statistics of Canada.* Toronto and Cambridge: Cambridge University Press.

CHAPTER 11

Brettel, Caroline B., and James F. Hollifield (eds.). (2000). *Migration Theory: Talking across Disciplines.* New York: Routledge.

Castles, Stephen. (2003). «Migration and Community Formation under Conditions of Globalization.» In Raymond Breton and Jeffrey Reitz (eds.) *Globalization and Society: Processes of Differentiation Examined.* Westport: Praeger.

_____, and Mark J. Miller. (1998). *The Age of Migration: International Population Movements in the Modern World,* 2nd ed. New York: Guilford.

Li, Peter. (2000). «Earning Disparities between Immigrants and Native-Born Canadians.» *Canadian Review of Sociology and Anthropology* 37 (3):289–311.

Massey, Douglas S., Joaquin Arango, Graeme Hugo, Ali Kouaouchi, Adela Pellegrino, and J.E. Taylor. (1998). *Worlds in Motion: Understanding International Migration at the End of the Millennium.* Oxford: Clarendon Press.

Reitz, Jeffrey. (2001). "Immigrant Success in the Knowledge Economy: Institutional Changes and the Immigrant Experience in Canada, 1970–1995." *Journal of Social Issues* 57:579–613.

Salt, John (ed.). (2001). *Perspectives on Trafficking of Migrants.* Geneva: IOM.

Simmons, Alan. (1989). "Explaining Migration: Theory at the Crossroads." In Josiane Duchene (ed.), *Explanation in the Social Sciences: The Search for Causes in Demography.* Louvaine-la-neuve: Institut de Demographie, Universite Catholique de Louvain.

_____. (1999). «Canadian Immigration Policy: An Analysis of Imagined Futures.» In Shiva Hailli and Leo Driedger (eds.), *Immigrant Canada.* Toronto: University of Toronto Press.

Stalker, Peter. (2000). *Workers without Frontiers: The Impact of Globalization on International Migration.* Boulder: Lynn Rienner.

Wanner, Richard A. (1998). «Prejudice, Profit or Productivity: Explaining Returns to Human Capital among Male Immigrants to Canada.» *Canadian Ethnic Studies* 30 (3):24–55.

World Bank. (1997). *The State in a Changing World: World Development Report 1997.* New York: Oxford University Press.

UNHCR. (2000). *The State of the World's Refugees: 50 Years of Humanitarian Action.* New York: UNHCR's Division of Communication and Information.

Zlotnik, H. (1999) "Trends of International Migration Since 1965: What Existing Data Reveal." *International Migration* 37 (1):21–62.

Zolberg, Aristide, Astri Sukhrke, and Sergio Aguayo. (1989). *Escape from Violence: Conflict and the Refugee Crisis in the Developing World.* New York: Oxford University Press.

CHAPTER 12

Abbott, Michael G., and Charles M. Beach. (1993). "Immigrant Earnings Differentials and Birth Year Effects for Men in Canada: Post-war-1972." *Canadian Journal of Economics* 26:505–524.

Andras, R. (1975). "Highlights from the Green Paper on Immigration and Population." Tabled in the House of Commons, February 3, 1975.

Beach, Charles M., and Alan G. Green (eds.). (1988). *The Role of Immigration in Canada's Future.* Kingston: John Deutsch Institute, Queen's University.

Borjas, George J. (1999). *Heaven's Door: Immigration Policy and the American Economy.* Princeton: Princeton University Press.

Canada. (1961). *Report of the Special Committee of the Senate on Manpower and Immigration.* Ottawa: Supply and Services Canada.

Collacott, Martin. (2002). "Canada's Immigration Policy: The Need for Reform." Occasional Paper 64. Vancouver: Fraser Institute.

Economic Council of Canada. (1991). *New Faces in the Crowd: Economic and Social Impact of Immigration.* Ottawa: Supply and Services Canada.

Foot, David. (2000). *Boom, Bust and Echo.* Toronto: Macfarlane, Walter & Ross.

Francis, Diane. (2002). *Immigration: The Economic Case.* Toronto: Key Porter Books.

Green, Alan G. (2000). "Twentieth-Century Canadian Economic History." In R. Gallman and S. Engerman (eds.), *The Cambridge Economic History of the United States,* vol. III. Cambridge: Cambridge University Press.

_____, and David Green. (1998). "Structural Change and the Mobility of Immigrants: Canada, 1921–1961." Paper prepared for the conference on regions in Canadian growth, Queen's University, Kingston.

_____, and David Green. (1999). "The Economic Goals of Canada's Immigration Policy." *Canadian Public Policy* 25 (4):425–451.

_____, and G.R. Sparks. (1999). "Population Growth and the Dynamics of Canadian Development: A Multivariate Time Series Approach." *Explorations in Economic History* 36:56–76.

Green, David. (1999). "Immigrant Occupational Attainment: Assimilation and Adjustment over Time." *Journal of Labor Economics* 17 (1):49–79.

Health and Welfare Canada. (1994). *Canada's Future: A Report of the Demographic Review Committee.* Ottawa: Supply and Services Canada.

Henripin, Jacques. (1988). "Panel Discussion on Canadian Immigration Objectives: Levels, Composition, and Directions." In Charles M. Beach and Alan G. Green (eds.), *The Role of Immigration in Canada's Future.* Kingston: John Deutsch Institute, Queen's University.

Kent, Tom. (1988). "Immigration Issues: A Personal Perspective." In Charles M. Beach and Alan G. Green (eds.), *The Role of Immigration in Canada's Future.* Kingston: John Deutsch Institute, Queen's University.

Lew, B. (2000). "European Immigration to Canada During the 1920s: The Impact of United States Quotas and Canadian Restrictions." Unpublished. Peterborough: Department of Economics, Trent University.

Reder, M. (1963). "The Economic Consequences of Increased Immigration." *Review of Economics and Statistics* 35:221–230.

Stoffman, Daniel. (2002). *Who Gets in? What's Wrong with Canada's Immigration Program and How to Fix It.* Toronto: Macfarlane, Walter & Ross.

Wilson, Stuart. (2003). "Immigration and Capital Accumulation in Canada: a Long-run Perspective." In Charles Beach, Alan Green and Jeffrey Reitz (eds.), *Canadian Immigration Policy for the 21st Century.* Kingston: John Deutsch Institute, McGill-Queens University Press.

CHAPTER 13

Abbott, Michael G., and Charles M. Beach. (1993). "Immigrant Earnings Differentials and Birth Year Effects for Men in Canada: Post-war-1972." *Canadian Journal of Economics* 25:505–524.

Aydemir, Abdurrahman, and Mikal Skuterud. (2004). "Explaining the Deteriorating Entry Earnings of Canada's Immigrant Cohorts: 1966–2000." Cat. no. 11F0019MIE2004225. Analytical Studies Research Paper Series. Ottawa: Statistics Canada.

_____, and Mikal Skuterud. (2005). "Explaining the Deteriorating Entry Earnings of Canada's Immigrant Cohorts: 1966–2000." *Canadian Journal of Economics* 38:641–672.

Baker, Michael, and Dwayne Benjamin. (1994). "The Performance of Immigrants in the Canadian Labour Market." *Journal of Labor Economic* 12:369–405.

Beaudry, Paul, and David Green. (2000). "Cohort Patterns in Canadian Earnings: Assessing the Role of Skill Premia in Inequality Trends." *Canadian Journal of Economics* 33:907–936.

Bloom, David E., and Morley Gunderson. (1991). "An Analysis of the Earnings of Canadian Immigrants." In John M. Abowd and Richard B. Freeman (eds.), *Immigration, Trade and the Labour Market*. Chicago: University of Chicago Press.

Borjas, George J. (1985). "Assimilation, Changes in Cohort Quality, and the Earnings of Immigrants." *Journal of Labor Economics* 3:463–489.

Burbidge, John B., Lonnie S. Magee, and A. Leslie Robb. (2002). "The Education Premium in Canada and the United States." *Canadian Public Policy* 28 (2):203–217.

Carliner, Geoffrey. (1981). "Wage Differences by Language Group and the Market for Language Skills in Canada." *Journal of Human Resources* 16:384–399.

Chiswick, Barry R. (1978). "The Effect of Americanization on the Earnings of Foreign-Born Men." *Journal of Political Economy* 86:897–921.

Ferrer, Ana, David Green, and Craig Riddell. (2003). "The Effect of Literacy on Immigrant Earnings." Vancouver: Department of Economics, University of British Columbia.

Freeman, Richard B., and Karen Needels. (1993). "Skill Differentials in Canada in an Era of Rising Labor Market Inequality." In David Card and Richard B. Freeman (eds.), *Small Differences That Matter: Labor Markets and Income Maintenance in Canada and the United States*. Chicago: University of Chicago Press.

Frenette, Marc, and René Morissette. (2003). "Will They Ever Converge? Earnings of Immigrant and Canadian-Born Workers over the Last Two Decades." Cat. no. 11F0019MIE2003215. *Analytical studies research paper series*. Ottawa: Statistics Canada.

Grant, Mary L. (1999). "Evidence of New Immigrant Assimilation in Canada." *Canadian Journal of Economics* 32:930–955.

Green, David A., and Christopher Worswick. (2002). "Earnings of Immigrant Men in Canada: The Roles of Labour Market Entry Effects and Returns to Foreign Experience." Paper prepared for Citizenship and Immigration Canada. Vancouver: Department of Economics, University of British Columbia.

Hum, Derek, and Wayne Simpson. (2003). "Reinterpreting the Performance of Immigrant Wages from Panel Data." Winnipeg: Department of Economics, University of Manitoba.

Li, Peter S. (2003). "Initial Earnings and Catch-up Capacity of Immigrants." *Canadian Public Policy* 29 (3):319–327.

McBride, Stephan, and Arthur Sweetman. (2004). "Post-secondary Field of Study and the Canadian Outcomes of Immigrants and Non-immigrants." Analytical Research Paper Series. Cat. no. 11F0019MIE2004234. Ottawa: Statistics Canada.

McDonald, James Ted, and Christopher Worswick. (1997). "Unemployment Incidence of Immigrant Men in Canada." *Canadian Public Policy* 23 (4):353–373.

_____, and Christopher Worswick. (1998). "The Earnings of Immigrant Men in Canada: Job Tenure, Cohort, and Macroeconomic Conditions." *Industrial and Labour Relations Review* 51:465–482.

Meng, Ronald. (1987). "The Earnings of Canadian Immigrant and Native-Born Males." *Applied Economics* 19:1107–1119.

Murphy, Kevin M., Paul Romer, and Craig Riddell. (1998). "Wages, Skills and Technology in the United States and Canada." NBER Working Paper Series 6638. National Bureau of Economic Research.

Picot, Garnett. (1998). "What Is Happening to Earnings Inequality and Youth Wages in the 1990s?" Cat. no. 11F0019MIE1998116. Analytical Studies Research Paper Series. Ottawa: Statistics Canada.

_____, and Feng Hou. (2003). "The Rise in Low-Income among Immigrants in Canada." Cat. no. 11F0019MIE2003198.Analytical Studies Research Paper Series. Ottawa: Statistics Canada.

Reitz, Jeffrey. (2001). "Immigrant Success in the Knowledge Economy: Institutional Changes and the Immigrant Experience in Canada, 1970–1995." *Journal of Social Issues* 57:579–613.

Schaafsma, J., and Arthur Sweetman. (2001). "Immigrant Earnings: Age at Immigration Matters." *Canadian Journal of Economics* 34 (4):1066–1099.

Sweetman, Arthur. (2004). "Immigrant Source Country School Quality and Canadian Labour Market Outcomes." Cat. no. 11F0019MIE2004234. Analytical Studies Research Paper Series. Ottawa: Statistics Canada.

CHAPTER 14

Badets, Jan. (2003). "The Changing Diversity of Canada: The 2001 Census." Conference paper, Sixth Annual Canadian Metropolis Conference, Edmonton.

Chiu, Tina, And Danielle Zietsma. (2003). "Earnings of Immigrants in the 1990s." *Canadian Social Trends* 70:24–28.

Collacott, Martin. (2002). "Canada's Immigration Policy: The Need for Major Reform." Occasional Paper 64. Vancouver: The Fraser Institute.

Francis, Diane. (2002). *Immigration: The Economic Case*. Toronto: Key Porter Books.

Germain, Annick. (2002). "The Social Sustainability of Multicultural Cities: A Neighborhood Affair?" *BELGEO, revue belge de géographie* 4:377–386.

Hiebert, Daniel. (1999). "Immigration and the Changing Social Geography of Greater Vancouver." *BC Studies* 121:35–82.

_____. (2003). "Are Immigrants Welcome? Introducing the Vancouver Community Studies Survey." Working Paper Series 03-06. Vancouver: Centre of Excellence Research on Immigration and Integration in the Metropolis.

IPSOS-Public Affairs. (2004). *Globus: International Affairs Poll*. Associated Press.

Ley, David. (2003). "Offsetting Immigration and Domestic Migration in Gateway Cities: Canadian and Australian Reflections on an 'American Dilemma,'" Working Paper Series 03-01. Vancouver: Centre of Excellence Research on Immigration and Integration in the Metropolis.

Li, Peter S. (2000). "Earning Disparities between Immigrants and Native-Born Canadians." *Canadian Review of Sociology and Anthropology* 37:289–311.

Peach, Ceri. (1996). "Good Segregation, Bad Segregation." *Planning Perspectives* 11:1–20.

Pendakur, Krishna, and Ravi Pendakur. (2004). "Colour My World: Has the Majority-Minority Earnings Gap Changed over Time?" Working Paper Series 04-11. Vancouver: Centre of Excellence Research on Immigration and Integration in the Metropolis.

Pew Global Attitudes Project. (2002). *What the World Thinks in 2002*. Washington, D.C.: The Pew Research Center for the People and the Press.

Picot, Garrett, and Feng Hou. (2003). "The Rise in Low-Income Rates among Immigrants in Canada." Analytical Research Paper Series. Ottawa: Statistics Canada.

Reitz, Jeffery. (2001). "Immigrant Skill Utilization in the Canadian Labour Market: Implications of Human Capital Research." *Journal of International Migration and Integration* 2:347–378.

_____. (2004). "Canada: Immigration and Nation-Building in the Transition to a Knowledge Economy." In Wayne A. Cornelius, Takeyuki Tsuda, Philip L. Martin, and James F. Hollifield (eds.), *Controlling Immigration: A Global Perspective*. Stanford: Stanford University Press.

Rose, Damaris. (2004). "Immigrant Settlement Strategies and Support Needs in Canada's Major Cities: Some Policy Issues." Research paper, Conference on "What Makes Good Public Policy in Canadian Municipalities?" Ottawa.

Sandercock, Leonie. (2003). "Integrating Immigrants: The Challenge for Cities, City Governments, and the City-Building Professions." RIIM Working Paper 03-20. Online at www.riim.metropolis.net

Smith, Craig S. (2005). "Fear of Islamists Drives Growth of Far Right in Belgium." *New York Times* (February12, 2005):5.

Stoffman, Daniel. (2002). *Who Gets in? What's Wrong with Canada's Immigration Program and How to Fix It*. Toronto: Macfarland Walter & Ross.

Statistics Canada. (2004). Metropolis Core Tables, Part 3, Table 2. CERIS Data. Toronto: Ryerson University.

Statistics Canada. (2005). *Population Projections of Visible Minority Groups, Canada, Provinces and Regions, 2001–2017*. Cat. no. 91-541-XIE. Ottawa: Statistics Canada.

United Way and Canadian Council on Social Development. (2003). *Poverty by Postal Code: The Geography of Neighbourhood Poverty, 1981–2001*. Toronto: United Way and Canadian Council on Social Development.

CHAPTER 15

Barer, Morris L., Robert G. Evans, and Clyde Hertzman. (1995). "Avalanche or Glacier? Health Care and the Demographic Rhetoric." *Canadian Journal of Aging* 14 (2):193–224.

Bourbeau, Robert, Jacques Légaré, and Valérie Émond. (1997). "New Birth Cohort Life Table for Canada and Quebec, 1801–1991." Demographic document no. 3. Ottawa: Statistics Canada.

Fellegi, Ivan P. (1988). "Can We Afford an Aging Society?" *Canadian Economic Observer* 1 (10):4.1–4.34.

George, M.V., François Nault, and Anatole Romaniuc. (1991). "Effects of Fertility and International Migration on the Changing Age Composition in Canada." *Statistical Journal of the United Nations Economic Commission for Europe* 8 (1):13–24.

Hourriez, Jean-Michel. (1993). "La consommation médicale à l'horizon 2010." In *Économie et statistique* 265:17–30.

International Social Security Association. (1998). *Restructuring Public Pension Programs*. Geneva: International Social Security Association.

Le Bras, H. (1990). "Faut-il faire des enfants ou des économies?" *Population âgées et révolution grise: Les hommes et les sociétés face à leurs vieillissements*. Louvain-la-neuve: Éditions ciaco.

Légaré, Jacques, and Yves Carrière. (1999), "Dying Healthy or Living Longer: A Society's Choice." In Jean-Marie Robine et al. (eds.), *The Paradoxes of Longevity*. New York: Springer.

_____, Madeleine Rochon, and Yves Carrière. (2000). "Évolutions possibles de la mortalité: impacts sur les coûts de santé." In Christine Wattelar and Josianne Duchêne (eds.), *Le défi de l'incertitude: Nouvelles approches en perspectives et prospectives démographiques*. Louvain-la-neuve: Academia-Bruylant et l'Harmattan.

Marcil-Gratton, Nicole, and Jacques Légaré. (1987). "Being Old Today and Tomorrow: A Different Proposition." *Canadian Studies in Population* 14 (2):23–41.

Martel, Laurent, and Alain Bélanger. (1999) "An Analysis of the Change in Dependence-Free Life Expectancy in Canada between 1986 and 1996." *Report of the Demographic Situation in Canada, 1998–1999*. Ottawa: Statistics Canada.

Nault, François. (1997). "Narrowing Mortality Gaps, 1978–1995." Cat. no. 82–003, 35–41. Health Reports. Ottawa: Statistics Canada.

Prinz, Christopher. (1997). "Report of the Seminar on Revisiting the Ageing Process, Montreal, Canada, October 2–4, 1996." *IUSSP Newsletter* 57:24–32.

Robine, Jean-Marie, Isabelle Romieu. (1998). "Healthy Active Ageing: Health Expectancies at Age 65 in the Different Parts of the World." Montpellier reves/inserm, papers no. 318.

UNECE. (2005). United Nations Economic Commission for Europe. Online at: http://www.unece.org.

United Nations. (1999). *World Population Prospects: The 1998 Revisions*. New York: United Nations.

Zweifel, Peter, Stefan Felder, and Markus Meiers. (1999). "Ageing of Population and Health Care Expenditures: A Red Herring?" *Health Economics* 8 (6):485–498.

CHAPTER 16

Graff, Thomas O., and Robert F. Wiseman. (1978). "Changing Concentrations of Older Americans." *Geographical Review* 68 (4):379–393.

McCarthy, Kevin F. (1983). *The Elderly Population's Changing Spatial Distribution: Patterns of Change Since 1960*. Santa Monica: Rand Corporation.

McDaniel, Susan A. (1986). *Canada's Aging Population*. Toronto: Butterworths.

Mitra, S. (1992). "Can Immigration Affect Age Composition When Fertility Is below Replacement?" *Canadian Studies in Population* 19 (2): 163-174.

Moore, Eric G. (1993). "What Questions Should We Ask? Data Availability and Analytic Strategies in Population Geography." Annual lecture, "New Directions in Population Geography." Atlanta: Association of American Geographers.

_____, and David McGuinness. (1999). "Geographic Dimensions of Aging: The Canadian Experience 1986–1996." In Kavita Pandit and Suzanne Davies Withers (eds.), *Migration and Restructuring in the United States: A Geographic Perspective*. Lanham: Rowman & Littlefield.

_____, Donald McGuinness, Michael A. Pacey, and Mark W. Rosenberg. (2000). "Geographical Dimensions of Aging: The Canadian Experience 1991–1996." Research paper 23, Program for Research on Social and Economic Dimensions of an Aging Population. Hamilton: McMaster University.

_____, Mark W. Rosenberg, and Donald McGuinness. (1997). *Growing Old in Canada: Demographic and Geographic Perspectives*. Toronto: Nelson; Statistics Canada.

Morrison, Peter A. (1992). "Is 'Aging in Place' a Blueprint for the Future?" Address, "Major Directions in Population Geography." San Diego: Association of American Geographers.

Newbold, K. Bruce. (1993). "Characterization and Explanation of Primary, Return and Onward Interprovincial Migration: Canada 1976–1986." Unpublished doctoral dissertation, Department of Geography, McMaster University.

Northcott, Herbert C. (1988). *Changing Residence: The Geographic Mobility of Elderly Canadians*. Toronto: Butterworths.

Rogers, Aandrei. (1992). "Elderly Migration and Population Redistribution in the United States." In Aandrei Rogers (ed.), *Elderly Migration and Population Redistribution*. London: Belhaven Press.

_____. (1995). *Multiregional Demography: Principles, Methods and Extensions*. New York: John Wiley.

_____, and James Raymer. (2001). "Immigration and the Regional Demographics of the Elderly Population in the United States." *Journal of Gerontology (B-psychological and Social Sciences)* 56 (1):S44–S55.

Rogerson, Peter A. (1996). "Geographic Perspectives on Elderly Population Growth." *Growth and Change* 27:75–95.

Romaniuc, Anatole. (1994). "Fertility in Canada: Retrospective and Prospective." In Frank Trovato and Carl F. Grindstaff (eds.), *Perspectives on Canada's Population: An Introduction to Concepts and Issues*. Toronto: Oxford University Press.

Serow, William J. (1987). "Determinants of Interstate Migration: Differences between Elderly and Non-elderly Movers." *Journal of Gerontology* 42 (1):95–100.

Shaw, R. Paul. (1985). *Intermetropolitan Migration in Canada: Changing Determinants over Three Decades*. Toronto: NC Press.

Statistics Canada. (2002a). *1991 Census of Population (Provinces, Census Divisions, Municipalities); 1991 Census of Population (46 Large Urban Centres, Census Tracts (Neighbourhoods)*. Online at http://estat.statcan.ca/Estat/data.htm.

_____. (2002b). *1996 Census of Population (Provinces, Census Divisions, Municipalities); 1996 Census of Population (46 Large Urban Centres, Census Tracts (Neighbourhoods)*. Online at http://estat.statcan.ca/Estat/data.htm.

_____. (2002c). *2001 Census of Population (Provinces, Census Divisions, Municipalities); 2001 Census of Population 46 Large Urban Centres, Census Tracts (Neighbourhoods)*. Online at http://estat.statcan.ca/Estat/data.htm.

_____. (2003a). *Estimates of Population, by Age Group and Sex, Canada, Provinces and Territories, Annual (Persons)* (Table 051-0001); *Estimates of Population, by Sex and Age Group, Census Divisions and Census Metropolitan Areas, 1996 Census Boundaries, Annual (Persons) Terminated* (Table 051-0016). Online at http://estat.statcan.ca/Estat/data.htm.

_____. (2003b). *Total Population, Census Divisions and Census Metropolitan Areas, 1996 Census Boundaries, Annual (Persons)* (Table 051-0014). Online at http://estat.statcan.ca/Estat/data.htm.

Stone, Leroy O., and Susan Fletcher. (1986). *The Seniors Boom: Dramatic Increases in Longevity and Prospects for Better Health*. Cat. no. 89–515.

Ottawa: Statistics Canada, Minister of Supply and Services.

CHAPTER 17

Barer, Morris L., Robert G. Evans, and Clyde Hertzman. (1995). "Avalanche or Glacier? Health Care and the Demographic Rhetoric." *Canadian Journal of Aging* 14:193–224.

_____, Robert G. Evans, Clyde Hertzman, and M. Johri. (1998). "Lies, Damned Lies, and Health Care Zombies: Discredited Ideas That Will Not Die." HPI Discussion Paper 10. Houston: University of Texas-Houston Health Science Center.

_____, Robert G. Evans, Clyde Hertzman, and Johnathan Lomas. (1987). "Aging and Health Care Utilization: New Evidence on Old Fallacies." *Social Science and Medicine* 24:851–862.

_____, Kimberlyn M. McGrail, K. Cardiff, L. Wood, and C.J. Green (eds.). (2000). *Tales from the Other Drug Wars*. Vancouver: University of British Columbia Centre for Health Services and Policy Research.

Binstock, Robert H. (1994). "Changing Criteria in Old-Age Programs: The Introduction of Economic Status and Need for Services." *Gerontologist* 34:726–730.

Carrière, Yves. (2000). "The Impact of Population Aging and Hospital Days: Will There Be a Problem?" In Ellen M. Gee and Gloria M. Gutman (eds.), *The Overselling of Population Aging: Apocalyptic Demography, Intergenerational Challenges, and Social Policy*. Toronto: Oxford University Press.

Clark, Robert L., and Joseph J. Spengler. (1980). "Dependency Ratios: Their Use in Economic Analyses." In Julian L. Simon, and Julie daVanzo (eds.), *Research in Population Economics*, vol. 2. Greenwich: JAI Press.

Conference Board of Canada. (2000). *The Future Cost of Health Care in Canada, 2000–2002*. Ottawa: Conference Board of Canada.

Denton, Frank T., Christine H. Feaver, and Byron G. Spencer. (1998). "The Future Population of Canada, Its Age Distribution and Dependency Relations." *Canadian Journal of Aging* 17:83–109.

Evans, Robert G., Kimberlyn M. McGrail, Steve G. Morgan, Morris L. Barer, and Clyde Hertzman. (2001). "Apocalypse No: Population Aging and the Future of Health Care Systems." *Canadian Journal of Aging* 20:160–191.

Foot, David K. (1989). "Public Expenditure, Population Aging and Economic Dependency in Canada, 1921–2021." *Population Research Policy Review* 8:97–117.

Gee, Ellen M. (1997). "Pensions and Population Aging: Reframing the Challenge of the 'Baby Boom.'" Invited plenary address, Canadian Association on Gerontology, Ottawa.

———. (2000). "Population and Politics: Voodoo Demography, Population Aging, and Canadian Social Policy." In Ellen M. Gee and Gloria M. Gutman (eds.), *The Overselling of Population Aging: Apocalyptic Demography, Intergenerational Challenges, and Social Policy*. Toronto: Oxford University Press.

Gee, Ellen M., and Gloria M. Gutman (eds.). (2000). *The Overselling of Population Aging: Apocalyptic Demography, Intergenerational Challenges, and Social Policy*. Toronto: Oxford University Press.

Kotlikoff, Laurence J. (1993). *Generational Accounting: Knowing Who Pays, and When, and What We Spend*. New York: Free Press.

Longman, Phillip. (1987). *Born to Pay: The New Politics of Aging in America*. Boston: Houghton Mifflin.

Manton, Kenneth G., Larry Corder, and Eric Stallard. (1997). "Chronic Disability Trends in Elderly in the United States." *The National Academy of Sciences of the United States* 94:2593–2598.

McDaniel, Susan A. (1987). "Demographic Aging as a Guiding Paradigm in Canada's Welfare State." *Canadian Public Policy* 13:330–336.

———. (1997). "Intergenerational Transfers, Social Solidarity, and Social Policy: Unanswered Questions and Policy changes." *Canadian Public Policy/Canadian Journal of Aging* (Joint Supplementary Issue):1–21.

McDonald, L. (2000). "Alarmist Economics and Women's Pensions: A Case of 'Semanticide.'" In Ellen M. Gee and Gloria M. Gutman (eds.), *The Overselling of Population Aging: Apocalyptic Demography, Intergenerational Challenges, and Social Policy*. Toronto: Oxford University Press.

McLaren, Angus. (1990). *Our Own Master Race: Eugenics in Canada, 1845–1945*. Toronto: McClelland & Stewart.

Mullan, Phil. (2000). *The Imaginary Time Bomb: Why an Ageing Population Is Not a Social Problem*. London: IB Tauris & Co.

National Academy on an Aging Society. (1999). *Demography Is Not Destiny*. Washington: National Academy on an Aging Society.

Northcott, Herbert C. (1994). "Public Perceptions of the Population Aging 'Crisis.'" *Canadian Public Policy* 20:66–77.

Preston, Samuel H. (1984). "Children and the Elderly: Divergent Paths for America's Dependants." *Demography* 21:435–457.

Prince, Michael J., and Neena L. Chappell. (1994). *Voluntary Action by Seniors in Canada*. Victoria: Centre on Aging, University of Victoria.

Robertson, Ann. (1997). "Beyond Apocalyptic Demography: Towards a Moral Economy of Interdependence." *Ageing and Society* 17:425–446.

Schwartz, William B. (1998). Life without Disease: The Pursuit of Medical Utopia. Berkeley: University of California Press.

CHAPTER 18

Armstrong, R. (1999). "Profile of the Situation of First Nations Communities." *Canadian Social Trends* 55:14–16. Cat. no. 11008. Ottawa: Statistics Canada.

Bakker, I., and K. Scott. (1997). "From the Post-war to the Post-liberal Keynesian Welfare State." In W. Clement (ed.), *Understanding Canada: Building on the New Canadian Political Economy*. Montreal and Kingston: McGill-Queen's University Press.

Beach, Charles, and G. Slotsve. (1996). *Are We Becoming Two Societies*? Toronto: C.D. Howe Institute.

Beaujot, Roderic. (1991). *Population Change in Canada: The Challenges of Policy Adaptation*. Toronto: Oxford University Press.

_____, and Deb Mathews. (2000). "Immigration and the Future of Canada's Population." Discussion paper 00-1. Population Studies Centre. London: University of Western Ontario.

Blomley, N. (1992). "The Business of Mobility: Geography, Liberalism and the Charter of Rights." *Canadian Geographer* 36:236–253.

Bourne, Larry S., and M. Flowers. (1999). "Changing Urban Places: Mobility, Migration and Immigration in Canada." Research paper 193. Centre for Urban and Community Studies. Toronto: University of Toronto.

Brodie, J. (1997). "The New Political Economy of Regions." In W. Clement (ed.), *Understanding Canada: Building on the New Canadian Political Economy*. Montreal: McGill-Queen's.

Brotman, S. (1999). "Incidence of Poverty among Seniors in Canada: Exploring the Impact of Gender, Ethnicity and Race." *Canadian Journal on Aging* 17:166–185.

Bunting, T., and P. Filion (eds.). (2000). *Canadian Cities in Transition*, 2nd ed. Toronto: Oxford University Press.

Canadian Council on Social Development. (2000). *Urban Poverty in Canada*. Ottawa: Canadian Council on Social Development.

Canadian Journal of Regional Science. (1997). Special Issue: Metropolis Project, Immigration and Settlement. *Canadian Journal of Regional Science* 20:1/2.

Denton, Frank T., Christine H. Feaver, and Byron G. Spencer. (1998). "The Future Population of Canada, Its Age Distribution and Dependency Relations." *Canadian Journal of Aging* 17:83–109.

Evenden, L., and G. Walker. (1993). "From Periphery to Centre: The Changing Geography of the Suburbs." In Larry S. Bourne and D. Ley (eds.), *The Changing Social Geography of Canadian Cities*. Montreal and Kingston: McGill-Queen's University Press.

Foot, David, and Daniel Stoffman. (1996). *Boom, Bust and Echo: How to Profit from the Coming Demographic Shift*. Toronto: Macfarlane Walter & Ross.

Germain, A. and D. Rose. (2000). *Montréal: The Quest for a Metropolis*. Chichester, U.K.: John Wiley and Sons.

Halli, Shiva S., and Leo Driedger (eds.). (1999). *Immigrant Canada*. Toronto: University of Toronto Press.

Isajiw, Wsevolod (1999). *Understanding Diversity: Ethnicity and Race in the Canadian Context.* Toronto: Thompson Educational.

Kazemipur, Abdie, and Shiva S. Halli. (2000). *The New Poverty in Canada: Ethnic Groups and Ghetto Neighbourhoods.* Toronto: Thompson Educational Publishing.

Le Bourdais, Céline, et al. (2000). "The Changing Face of Conjugal Relationships." *Canadian Social Trends.* Cat. no. 11-008. Ottawa: Statistics Canada.

Myles, John, Garrett Picot, and Wendy Pyper. (2000). *Neighbourhood Inequality in Canadian Cities.* Cat. no. 11F0019MPE-160. Ottawa: Statistics Canada.

Péron, Yves, et al. (1999). *Canadian Families at the Approach of the Year 2000.* Cat. no. 96-321-MPE-4. Ottawa: Statistics Canada.

Polèse, Mario, and Richard Stren (eds.). (2000). *The Social Sustainability of Cities: Diversity and the Management of Change.* Toronto: University of Toronto Press.

Statistics Canada. (1994). *Population Projections for Canada, the Provinces and Territories.* Cat. no. 91-520. Ottawa: Statistics Canada, Demography Division.

_____. (1999). *Annual Demographic Statistics 1998.* Ottawa: Statistics Canada and Industry Canada.

Villeneuve, Paul, and Valerie Preston. (2001). "La mondialisation vue d'en bas: Une perspective feministe." *Canadian Geographer* 45 (1):42.

Yalnizyan, Armine. (1998). *The Growing Gap: A Report on the Growing Inequality between Rich and Poor in Canada.* Toronto: Centre for Social Justice.

CHAPTER 19

Bélanger, Alain. (2003). *Report on the Demographic Situation in Canada, 2002.* Cat. no. 91-209-XPE. Ottawa: Statistics Canada.

Brines, Julie, and Kara Joyner. (1999). "The Ties That Bind: Principles of Cohesion in Cohabitation and Marriage." *American Journal of Sociology* 64:333–355.

Brown, Susan L. (2000). "Union Transitions among Cohabitors: The Significance of Relationship Assessments and Expectations." *Journal of Marriage and the Family* 62:833–846.

Bumpass, Larry L., and Hsien-Hen Lu. (2000). "Trends in Cohabitation and Implications for Children's Family Contexts in the United States." *Population Studies* 54:29–41.

Cherlin, Andrew J. (2004). "The Deinstitutionalization of American Marriage." *Journal of Marriage and the Family* 66:848–861.

Desrosiers, Hélène, and Céline Le Bourdais. (1996). "Progression des unions libres et avenir des familles biparentales." *Recherches feministes* 9:65–83.

Dubreuil, Christianne. (1999). "L'union de fait au Quebec: Inexistence dans le Code civil." *Cahiers quebecois de demographie* 28:229–236.

Duchesne, Louis. (2003). *La situation demographique au Quebec, bilan 2003.* Quebec: Institut de la statistique du Quebec.

Dumas, Jean, and Alain Bélanger. (1994). *Report on the Demographic Situation in Canada 1994.* Cat. no. 91–209E. Ottawa: Statistics Canada.

_____, and Alain Bélanger. (1997). *Report on the Demographic Situation in Canada 1996.* Cat. no. 91–209E. Ottawa: Statistics Canada.

_____, and Yves Péron. (1992). *Marriage and Conjugal Life in Canada.* Cat. no. 91–534F. Ottawa: Statistics Canada.

Goubau, Dominique. (2004). "La notion de conjoint: La loi et la societe avancent-elles au meme pas?" In *Actes de la XVIe conference des juristes de l'E tat.* Cowansville:Editions Yvon Blais.

Heuveline, Patrick, and Jeffery M. Timberlake. (2004). "The Role of Cohabitation in Family Formation: The United States in Comparative Perspective." *Journal of Marriage and the Family* 66:1214–1230.

Juby, Heather, Nicole Marcil-Gratton, and Céline Le Bourdais. (2005). *When Parents Separate: Further Findings from the National Longitudinal Survey of Children and Youth.* Phase 2 research report of the project, "The Impact of Parents' Family Transitions on Children's Family Environment and Economic Well-being: A Longitudinal Assessment." Ottawa: Department of Justice Canada, Child Support Team.

Kiernan, Kathleen. (2001). "Cohabitation in Western Europe: Trends, Issues, and Implications." In Alan Booth and Ann C. Crouter (eds.), *Just Living Together: Implications of Cohabitation on Families, Children, and Social Policy.* Mahwah: Erlbaum.

Lapierre-Adamcyk, Évelyn, and Céline Le Bourdais. (2004). "Couples et familles: Une réalité sociologique et demographique en constante évolution." In *Actes de la XVIe conferrence des juristes de l'Etat.* Cowansville: Editions Yvon Blais.

_____, Céline Le Bourdais, and Nicole Marcil-Gratton. (1999). "La signification du choix de l'union libre au Quebec et en Ontario." *Cahiers québécois de demographie* 28:199–227.

Laplante, Benôit. (2004). *The Diffusion of Cohabitation in Quebec and Ontario and the Power of Norms in Religion.* Montreal: Institut national de la recherche scientifique (INRS)-Urbanisation, Culture, et Societe.

Le Bourdais, Céline, and Heather Juby. (2001). "The Impact of Cohabitation on the Family Life Course in Contemporary North America: Insights from across the Border." In Alan Booth and Ann C. Crouter (eds.), *Just Living Together: Implications of Cohabitation on Families, Children, and Social Policy.* Mahwah: Erlbaum.

_____, and Nicole Marcil-Gratton. (1996). "Family Transformations across the Canadian/American Border: When the Laggard Becomes the Leader." *Journal of Comparative Family Studies* 27:415–436.

_____, and Nicole Marcil-Gratton, and Heather Juby. (2003). "Family Life in a Changing World: The Evolution of the Canadian Family in a Context of Marital and Economic Instability." In Mark J. Kasoffand Christine Drennen (Eds.), *Family, Work, and Health Policy in Canada: Proceedings from the 16th Annual Reddin Symposium.* Bowling Green: Canadian Studies Center, Bowling Green State University.

_____, Chislaine Neil, and Nicole Marcil-Gratton. (2000). "L'effet du type d'union sur la stabilite des familles dites 'intactes.'" *Recherches sociographiques* 41:53–74.

_____, and Annie Sauriol. (1998). "La part des peres dans la division du travail domestique au sein des familles canadiennes." *Etudes et Documents No. 69.* Montreal: INRS-Urbanisation.

Livi-Bacci, Massimo, and Silvana Salvini. (2000). "Trop de famille et trop peu d'enfants: La fecondite en Italie depuis 1960." *Cahiers quebecois de demographie* 29:231–254.

Manning, Wendy D. (1993). "Marriage and Cohabitation Following Premarital Conception." *Journal of Marriage and the Family* 55:839–850.

Manting, Dorien. (1996). "The Changing Meaning of Cohabitation and Marriage." *European Sociological Review* 12:53–65.

Marcil-Gratton, Nicole. (1998). *Growing up with Mom and Dad? The Intricate Family Life Courses of Canadian Children.* Cat. no. 89-566-XIE.

Ottawa: Statistics Canada.

_____, and Céline Le Bourdais. (1999). *Custody, Access and Child Support: Findings from the National Longitudinal Survey of Children and Youth.* Department of Justice Canada, Child Support Team. Online at http://canada.justice.gc.ca/en/ps/pad/reports/index.html#res.

Pollard, Michael S., and Zheng Wu. (1998). "Divergence of Marriage Patterns in Quebec and Elsewhere in Canada." *Population Development Review* 24:329–356.

Raley, R. Kelly. (2001). "Increasing Fertility in Cohabiting Unions: Evidence for the Second Demographic Transition in the United States?" *Demography* 38:59–66.

Seltzer, Judith A. (2000). "Families Formed outside of Marriage." *Journal of Marriage and the Family* 62:1247–1268.

Shelton, Beth Anne, and Daphne John. (1993). "Does Marital Status Make a Difference?" *Journal of Family Issues* 14:401–420.

Smock, Pamela J., and Sanjiv Gupta. (2001). "Cohabitation in Contemporary North America." In Alan Booth and Ann C. Crouter (eds.), *Just Living Together: Implications of Cohabitation on Families, Children, and Social Policy*. Mahwah: Erlbaum.

Statistics Canada. (1984). *Canadian Families: Diversity and Change*. Cat. No. 12F0061XPF.

_____. (1995) 1995 General Social Survey. Ottawa: Statistics Canada.

_____. (1997). 1996 Census (Table 93F0022XDB96008). Ottawa: Statistics Canada.

_____. (2002a). *Changing Conjugal Life in Canada*. Cat. no. 89-576-XIE. Ottawa: Statistics Canada.

_____. (2002b). Profile of Canadian Families and Households: Diversification Continues. Cat. no. 96F0030XIE2001003. Ottawa: Statistics Canada.

_____. (2002c). *2001 Census*. Table 97F0005XCB01002. Ottawa: Statistics Canada.

_____. (2002d). 2001 Census (Table 97F0005XCB01006. Ottawa: Statistics Canada.

_____. (2003a). "Marriages." *The Daily*. Cat. no. 11-001-XIE, November 20. Ottawa: Statistics Canada.

_____. (2003b). *Annual Demographic Statistics 2002*. Cat. no. 91-213-XIB. Ottawa: Statistics Canada.

Thery, I. (1993). *Le demariage*. Paris: Odile Jacob.

Turcotte, Pierre, and Alain Bélanger. (1997). *The Dynamics of Formation and Dissolution of First Common-Law Unions in Canada*. Ottawa: Statistics Canada.

Villeneuve-Gokalp, Catherine. (1991). "From Marriage to Informal Union: Recent Changes in the Behavior of French Couples." *Population: An English Selection* 3:81–111.

Wu, Zheng, and T.R. Balakrishnan. (1995). "Dissolution of Premarital Cohabitation in Canada." *Demography* 32:521–532.

CHAPTER 20

Barth, Fredrik. (1969). *Ethnic Groups and Boundaries*. Boston: Little, Brown.

Berry, John W. (1991). "Sociopsychological Costs and Benefits of Multiculturalism." Working Paper No. 24. Ottawa: Economic Council of Canada.

_____, and David L. Sam. (1997). "Acculturation and Adaptation." In John W. Berry, Marshall H. Segall, and Cigdem Kagitcibasi (eds.), *Handbook of Cross Cultural Psychology*. Toronto: Allyn and Bacon.

Boas, Franz. (1966). *Race, Language, and Culture*. New York: Free Press.

Boyd, Monica, and Doug Norris. (1998). "Becoming Canadian: Temporal Shifts in Ethnic Origins." Unpublished paper. Tallahassee: Florida State University.

Breton, Raymond, Wsevolod W. Isajiw, Warren E. Kalbach, and Jeffrey G. Reitz. (1990). *Ethnic Identity and Equality: Varieties of Experience in a Canadian City*. Toronto: University of Toronto Press.

Bromlei, Iulian. (1974). "The Term Ethnos and Its Definition." In Iulian Bromlei (ed.), *Soviet Ethnology and Anthropology Today*. The Hague: Mouton.

_____. (1984). *Theoretical Ethnography*. Translated by V. Epsteinand E. Khazanov. Moscow: Nauka.

Census of Canada. (1876). *Statistics of Canada (1665 to 1871)*, vol. IV. Ottawa: I.B. Taylor.

Cohen, Ronald. (1993). "Ethnicity, the State, and Moral Order." In Gustave Goldmann and Nampeo McKenney (eds.), *Statistics Canada and U.S. Bureau of the Census: Challenges of Measuring an Ethnic World: Science, Politics, and Reality*. Washington: U.S. Government Printing Office.

_____, and John Middleton. (1970). *From Tribe to Nation in Africa: Studies in Incorporation Processes*. Scranton, Pa.: Chandler Publishing Company.

de Vries, John. (1985). "Some Methodological Aspect of Self-Report Questions on Language and Ethnicity." *Journal of Multilingual and Multicultural Development* 6 (5):347–368.

Goldmann, Gustave J. (1993). "Canadian Data on Ethnic Origin: Who Needs It and Why?" In Gustave Goldmann and Nampeo McKenney (eds.), *Statistics Canada and U.S. Bureau of the Census: Challenges of Measuring an Ethnic World: Science, Politics, and Reality*. Washington: U.S. Government Printing Office.

_____. (1994). "The Shifting of Ethnic Boundaries: Causes, Factors, and Effects." MA thesis. Ottawa: Carleton University.

Holmes, William H. (1886). "Pottery of the Ancient Pueblos." In *U.S. Bureau of American Ethnology, Fourth Annual Report, 1882–1883*. Washington: Smithsonian Institution.

Isajiw, Wsevolod W. (1993). "Definition and Dimensions of Ethnicity: A Theoretical Framework." In Gustave Goldmann and Nampeo McKenney (eds.), *Statistics Canada and U.S. Bureau of the Census: Challenges of Measuring an Ethnic World: Science, Politics, and Reality*. Washington: U.S. Government Printing Office.

Jary, David, and Julia Jary. (1991). *Collins Dictionary of Sociology*. Glascow: Harper-Collins.

Kralt, John. (1990). "Ethnic Origins in the Canadian Census, 1871–1986." In Shiva S. Halli, Frank Trovato, and Leo Driedger (eds.), *Ethnic Demography: Canadian Immigrant, Racial, and Cultural Variations*. Ottawa: Carleton University Press.

Malinowski, Bronislaw. (1945). *The Dynamics of Culture Change: Inquiry into Race Relations in Africa*. New Haven: Yale University Press.

McGee, W.J. (1898). "Piratical Acculturation." *American Anthropologist* 11 (August):243–249.

Ryder, Norman B. (1955). "The Interpretation of Origin Statistics." *Canadian Journal of Economics and Political Science* 21:466–479.

Schermerhorn, Richard A. (1970). *Comparative Ethnic Relations: A Framework for Theory and Research*. New York: Random House.

Shryock, Henry S., Jacob S. Siegal, and associates. (1976). *The Methods and Materials of Demography*. San Diego: Harcourt Brace Jovanovich.

Spicer, Edward H. (1968). "Acculturation." *International Encyclopedia of the Social Sciences*. New York: Free Press.

Statistics Canada. 1994. *Revised Intercensal Population and Family Estimates, July 1, 1971-1991*. Ottawa: Statistics Canada Cat. No. 84-537.

_____. (1999). *Annual Demographic Statistics, 1998*. Ottawa: Statistics Canada Cat. No. 91-213 XIB.

Weber, Max. (1978). "Ethnic Groups." In G. Roth and C. Wittich (eds.), *Economy and Society*, vol. 1. Los Angeles: University of California Press.

CHAPTER 21

Barsh, Russel. (1994). "Canada's Aboriginal Peoples: Social Integration or Disintegration?" *The Canadian Journal of Native Studies* 14:1–46.

Bélanger, Alain. (2002). *Report on the Demographic Situation in Canada 2001*. Cat. no. 91-209. Ottawa: Statistics Canada,

Bobet, E., and S. Dardick. (1995). "Overview of 1992 Indian Health Data." Working document. Ottawa: Health and Welfare Canada, Medical Services Branch.

Bongaarts, John. (1978). "A Framework for Analyzing the Proximate Determinants of Fertility." *Population and Development Review* 4 (1):105–132.

Boserup, Ester. (1965). *The Conditions of Agricultural Growth*. Chicago: Aldine.

Boxhill, W. (1984). "Limitations of the Use of Ethnic Origin Data to Quantify Visible Minorities in Canada." Working paper. Prepared for Statistics Canada, Housing Family and Social Statistics Division.

Boyd, Robert. (1990). "Demographic History, 1774–1874." In W. Sturtevant (ed.), *Handbook of North American Indians*, vol. 7: *Northwest Coast*. Washington: Smithsonian Institution Press.

Charbonneau, Hubert. (1984). *Trois siècles de dépopulation amérindienne et inuit du Canada. In* Louise Normandeau and Victor Piché (eds.) Montréal: Les Presses de l'Université de Montréal.

Daniels, J. (1992). "The Indian Population of North America in 1492." *William and Mary Quarterly* 49:298–320.

Dickason, O. (1992). *Canada's First Nations: A History of Founding Peoples from Earliest Times*. Toronto: Oxford University Press.

Dobyns, H. (1983). *Their Number Became Thinned: Native American Population Dynamics in Eastern North America*. Knoxville: University of Tennessee Press.

Escbach, Karl. (1995). "The Enduring and Vanishing American Indian Population: Growth and Intermarriage in 1990." *Ethnic and Racial Studies* 18:89–108.

Frideres, James S. (1998). *Aboriginal Populations in Canada: Contemporary Conflicts*. Scarborough: Prentice Hall and Allyn and Bacon Canada.

Goddard, I. (1996). *Languages: Handbook of North American Indians*. Washington: Smithsonian Institution.

Goldman, Gustave. (1989). "Shifts in Ethnic Origins among the Offspring of Immigrants: Is Ethnic Mobility a Measurable Phenomenon?" *Canadian Ethnic Studies* 30:121–148.

_____, and Andy Siggner. (1995). "Statistical Concepts of the Aboriginal Peoples Survey." In *Towards the Twenty-first Century: Emerging Socio-demographic Trends and Policy Issues in Canada*. Ottawa: Federation of Canadian Demography.

Grimes, B.F. (2000). *Ethnologue: Languages of the World*, 14th ed. Dallas: SIL International.

Guimond, Eric. (1999). "Ethnic Mobility and Demographic Growth of Canada's Aboriginal Populations from 1986 to 1996." In Alain Bélanger (ed.), *Report on the Demographic Situation in Canada 1998–1999*. Cat. no. 91-209. Ottawa: Statistics Canada.

Harris, J., and R. McCullough. (1988). *Health Indicators Derived from Vital Statistics for the Status Indian and Canadian Population, 1978–1986*. Ottawa: Health and Welfare Canada.

Harris, M., and E. Ross. (1987). *Death, Sex, and Fertility: Population Regulation in Preindustrial and Developing Societies*. New York: Columbia University Press.

Health and Welfare Canada. (1999). *First Nations and Inuit Regional Health Survey*. Ottawa: Health and Welfare Canada.

Hout, Michael, and Joshua Goldstein. (1994). "How 4.5 Million Irish Immigrants Became 40 Million Irish Americans: Demographic and Subjective Aspects of Ethnic Composition of White Americans." *American Sociological Review* 59:64–82.

Indian and Northern Affairs Canada. (1998). *Registered Indian Population by Sex and Residence 1997*. Ottawa: Indian Affairs and Northern Development.

_____. (1999). *A Second Diagnostic on the Health of First Nations and Inuit People in Canada.* Ottawa: Indian and Northern Affairs Canada.

_____. (2000). *Registered Indian Population Projections for Canada and Regions, 1998–2008.* Ottawa: Indian and Northern Affairs Canada.

Jain, A., and John Bongaarts. (1981). "Breastfeeding: Patterns, Correlates, and Fertility Effects." *Studies in Family Planning* 12:79–99.

Jenness, D. (1977). *The Indians of Canada.* Toronto: University of Toronto Press.

Krotki, Karol J. (1995). "The Eight Million Artificial Canadians, Their Future and Related Policies. In *Toward the Twenty-first Century: Emerging Socio-demographic Trends and Policy Issues in Canada.* Ottawa: Proceedings of the 1995 symposium organized by the Federation of Canadian Demographers.

Lieberson, Stanley, and Mary C. Waters. (1988). *From Many Strands: Ethnic and Racial Groups in Contemporary America.* New York: Russell Sage Foundation.

_____, and Mary C. Waters. (1993). "The Ethnic Responses of Whites: What Causes Their Instability, Simplification, and Inconsistency." *Social Forces* 72:421–450.

Loh, Shirley, Ravi Verma, Edward Ng, Mary Jane Norris, M.V. George, and Jeanine Perreault. (1998). "Population Projections of Registered Indians, 1996 to 2021." Working paper. Ottawa: Statistics Canada.

Mooney, J. (1928). *The Aboriginal Population of America North of Mexico.* Washington: Smithsonian Miscellaneous Collections 80:1–40.

Morrison, W. (1984). *Under One Flag: Canadian Sovereignty and the Native People of Northern Canada.* Ottawa: Treaties and Historical Research Centre.

Nault, François, J. Chen, M.V. George, and Mary Jane Norris. (1993). *Population Projections of Registered Indians, 1991–2016.* Ottawa: Statistics Canada.

Norris, Mary Jane. (2000). "Contemporary Demography of Aboriginal Peoples in Canada." In D. Long and O.P. Dickason (eds.), *Visions of the Heart: Canadian Aboriginal Issues.* Toronto: Harcourt Canada.

_____, Don Kerr, and François Nault. (1995). *Technical Report Projections of the Population with Aboriginal Identity, Canada, 1991–2016.* Report prepared by the Population Projections Section, Demography Division, Statistics Canada, for the Royal Commission on Aboriginal Peoples. Ottawa: Statistics Canada.

_____, Don Kerr, and Francois Nault. (1996). *Royal Commission on Aboriginal Peoples, Projections of the Population with Aboriginal Identity,* Canada, 1991–2016; Summary Report. Ottawa: Canada Mortgage and Housing Corporation.

Passel, Jeffrey. (1997). "The Growing American Indian Population: 1960–1990: Beyond Demography." *Population Research and Policy Review* 16:11–31.

Ponting, Rick J. (1997). *First Nations in Canada: Perspectives on Opportunity, Empowerment, and Self-Determination.* Toronto: McGraw-Hill Ryerson.

Population Reference Bureau. (2001).*World Population Data Sheet.* Washington: Population Reference Bureau.

Robitaille, Norman and Robert Choinière. (1985). *An Overview of Demographic and Socioeconomic Conditions of the Inuit in Canada.* Ottawa: Department of Indian and Northern Affairs.

Robitaille, Norman and Eric Guimond. (1994) "La situation démographique des groupes autochtones du Québec". *Recherches Sociographiques* 35(3): 433-454.

Romaniuc, Anatole. (1981). "Increase in Natural Fertility During the Early Stages of Modernization: Canadian Indian Case Study." *Demography* 18:157–172.

_____. (1984). *Fertility in Canada: From Baby-Boom to Baby-Bust.* Cat. no. 91-524. Ottawa: Statistics Canada.

_____. (2000). "The Aboriginal Population of Canada: Growth Dynamics under Conditions of Encounter of Civilizations." *Canadian Journal of Native Studies* 20:99–137.

Rowe, Geoff and Mary Jane Norris. (1985). *Mortality Projections of Registered Indians, 1982 to 1996.* Ottawa: Indian and Northern Affairs Canada.

Saunders, S., P. Ramsden, and D. Herring. (1992). "Transformation and Disease: Precontact Ontario Iroquoians." In J. Verano and D. Ubelaker (eds.), *Disease and Demography in the Americas.* Washington: Smithsonian Institution Press.

Siggner, Andy, Annette Vermaeten, Chris Durham, Jeremy Hull, Eric Guimond, and Mary Jane Norris. (2001). *New Developments in Aboriginal Definitions and Measures.* Presented at the Canadian Population Society Meetings, Quebec City, June.

Statistics Canada. (1998). *Annual Demographic Statistics 1997.* Cat. no. 91-213. Ottawa: Statistics Canada.

_____. (1999). "Life Expectancy." *Health Reports* 11 (3):9–24.

_____. (2003). *Aboriginal Peoples of Canada: A Demographic Profile.* Cat. no. 96F0030XIE2001007. Ottawa: Statistics Canada.

Thornton, Russell. (1987). *American Indian Holocaust and Survival: A Population History Since 1492.* Norman: University of Oklahoma Press.

_____. (2000). "Population of Native Americans." In Michael M. Haines and Richard H. Steckel (eds.), *A Population History of North America.* Cambridge: Cambridge University Press.

Trovato, Frank. (2000). "Canadian Indian Mortality During the 1980's." *Social Biology* 47:135–145.

_____. (2001). "Aboriginal Mortality in Canada, the United States, and New Zealand." *Journal of Biosocial Science* 33:67–86.

Ubelaker, D.H. (1976). "Prehistoric New World Population Size: Historical Review and Current Appraisals of North American Estimates." *American Journal of Physical Anthropology* 45:661–666.

_____. (2000). "Patterns of Disease in Early American Populations." In Michael M. Haines and Richard H. Steckel (eds.), *A Population History of North America.* Cambridge: Cambridge University Press.

Weiss, K. (1973). "Demographic Models for Anthropology." *Memoirs of the Society for American Anthropology,* no. 27. Washington: American Antiquity.

Young, K.T. (1994). *The Health of Native Americans: Towards a Biocultural Epidemiology.* New York: Oxford University Press.

CHAPTER 22

Balakrishnan, T.R. (1982). "Changing Patterns of Ethnic Residential Segregation in the Metropolitan Areas of Canada." *Canadian Review of Sociology and Anthropology* 19 (1):92–100.

_____. (2000). "Residential Segregation and Canada's Ethnic Groups." In M. Kalbach and Warren Kalbach (eds.), *Perspectives on Ethnicity in Canada.* Toronto: Harcourt Canada.

_____, and Feng Hou. (1999a). "Residential Patterns in Cities." In Shiva S. Halli and Leo Driedger (eds.), *Immigrant Canada.* Toronto: University of Toronto Press.

_____, and Feng Hou. (1999b). "Socio-economic Integration and Spatial Residential Patterns of Immigrant Groups in Canada." *Population Research and Policy Review* 18 (6):201–217.

_____, and John Kralt. (1987). "Segregation of Visible Minorities in Montreal, Toronto, and Vancouver." In Leo Driedger (ed.), *Ethnic Canada: Identities and Inequalities.* Toronto: Copp Clark Pitman.

_____, and E. Selvanathan. (1990). "Ethnic Segregation in Metropolitan Canada." In Shiva S. Halli, Frank Trovato, and Leo Driedger (eds.), *Ethnic Demography*. Ottawa: Carleton University Press.

Bauder, Harald, and Bob Sharpe. (2002). "Residential Segregation of Visible Minorities in Canada's Gateway Cities." *Canadian Geographer* 46 (3):204–222.

Burgess, Ernest W. (1925). "The Growth of the City: An Introduction to a Research Project." In Robert E. Park, Ernest W. Burgess, and R.E. McKenzie (eds.), *The City*. Chicago: University of Chicago Press.

Clark, William. (1986). "Residential Segregation in American Cities: A Review and Interpretation." *Population Research and Policy Review* 5:95–127.

Darroch, A. Gordon, and Wilfred G. Marston. (1971). "The Social Class Basis of Ethnic Residential Segregation: The Canadian Case." *American Journal of Sociology* 77:491–510.

Driedger, Leo, and Glenn Church. (1974). "Residential Segregation and Institutional Completeness: A Comparison of Ethnic Minorities." *Canadian Review of Sociology and Anthropology* 11:30–52.

_____, and Jacob Peters. (1977). "Identity and Social Distance: Towards Simmel's 'The Stranger.'" *Canadian Review of Sociology and Anthropology* 14:158–173.

Dunn, Kevin M. (1998). "Rethinking Ethnic Concentration: The Case of Cabramatta, Sydney." *Urban Studies* 35 (3):503–527.

Fairbarn, Kenneth J., and Hafiza Khatun. (1989). "Residential Segregation and the Intra-urban Migration of South Asians in Edmonton." *Canadian Ethnic Studies* 21 (1):45–64.

Guest, Avery M., and James A. Weed. (1976). "Ethnic Residential Segregation: Patterns of Change." *American Journal of Sociology* 81:1088–1108.

Kalbach, Warren. (1990). "Ethnic Residential Segregation and Its Significance for the Individual in an Urban Setting." In Raymond Breton, Wsevolod Isajiw, Warren Kalbach, and Jeffrey G. Reitz (eds.), *Ethnic Identity and Equality: Varieties of Experiences in a Canadian City*. Toronto: University of Toronto Press.

Kantrowitz, Nathan. (1973). *Ethnic and Racial Segregation in the New York Metropolis*. New York: Praeger.

Kazemipur, Abdie, and Shiva S. Halli. (2000). *The New Poverty in Canada: Ethnic Groups and Ghetto Neighbourhoods*. Toronto: Thompson Educational Publishing.

Lieberson, Stanley. (1970). *Language and Ethnic Relations in Canada*. New York: John Wiley & Sons.

_____, and Mary Waters. (1988). *From Many Strands*. New York: Russell Sage Foundation.

Massey, Douglas, and Nancy Denton. (1987). "Trends in the Residential Segregation of Blacks, Hispanics, and Asians: 1970–1980." *American Sociological Review* 52:802–825.

_____, and Nancy Denton. (1988). "The Dimension of Residential Segregation." *Social Forces* 67:281–315.

_____, and Nancy Denton. (1993). *American Apartheid*. Cambridge: Harvard University Press.

Park, Robert E. (1926). "The Urban Community as a Spatial Pattern and a Moral Order." In Ernest W. Burgess (ed.), *The Urban Community*. Chicago: University of Chicago Press.

Pineo, Peter C. (1977). "The Social Standing of Ethnic and Racial Groupings." *Canadian Review of Sociology and Anthropology* 14:147–157.

Ray, Brian. (1994). "Immigrant Settlement and Housing in Metropolitan Toronto." *Canadian Geographer* 38 (3):262–265.

Reitz, Jeffrey. (1988). "Less Racial Discrimination in Canada or Simply Less Racial Conflict? Implications of Comparisons with Britain." *Canadian Public Policy* 14:424–441.

_____. (1990). "Ethnic Concentrations in Labour Markets and Their Implications for Ethnic Inequality." In Raymond Breton et al. (eds.), *Ethnic Identity and Equality*. Toronto. University of Toronto Press.

Statistics Canada. (2003). "Canada's Ethno-cultural Portrait: The Changing Mosaic." 2001 Census: Analysis Series. Cat. no. 96F0030XIE2001008. Ottawa: Statistics Canada.

CHAPTER 23

Beaujot, Roderic, and Don Kerr. (2004). *Population Change in Canada*. Toronto: Oxford University Press.

_____, and Ali Muhammad. (2006). "Transformed Families and the Basis for Childbearing." In Kevin McQuillan and Zenaida Ravanera (eds.), *Canada's Changing Families: Implications for Individuals and Society*. Toronto: University of Toronto Press.

_____, and Zenaida Ravanera. (2005). "Family Models of Earning and Caring: Implications for Child Care." Paper presented at the Third Conference of the Canadian Research Data Centre Network, Montreal, May 19–20. Online at http://sociology.uwo.ca/popstudies/dp/dp05_01.pdf.

Bélanger, Alain. (2006). *Report on the Demographic Situation in Canada 2003*. Cat. no. 91-209-XIE. Ottawa: Statistics Canada.

_____, Laurent Martel, and Eric Caron-Malenfant. (2005). *Population Projections for Canada, Provinces and Territories, 2005–2031*. Cat. no. 91-520-XPE. Ottawa: Statistics Canada.

Hatfield, Michael. (2004). "Vulnerability to Persistent Low Income." Policy research initiative. *Horizons* 7 (2):19–26.

Keefe, Janice, Yves Carrière, and Jacques Légaré. (2005). "Developing New Strategies to Support Future Caregivers of the Aged in Canada: Projections of Need and Their Policy Implications." Paper presented at the meetings of the International Union for the Scientific Study of Population, Tours, France, July 18–23. Available as SEDAP Research Paper No. 140: http://socserv.socsci. mcmaster.ca/sedap/.

Kent, Mary M., and Carl Haub. (2005). "Global Demographic Divide." *Population Bulletin* 60 (4):1–24.

Légaré, Jacques, Robert Bourbeau, Bertrand Desjardins, and Claude Deblois. (2006). "Variation on Cohort Size and Lower Mortality in the Elderly: Implications for Pay-as-You-Go Healthcare Systems." In Yi Zeng et al. (eds.), *Longer Life and Healthy Aging*. Dordrecht: Springer.

Livi-Bacci, Massimo. (2000). "An Additional Person: Increasing or Diminishing Returns?" Paper presented at the meetings of the Population Association of America, March, Los Angeles.

Malthus, Thomas R. [1798]. (1965). *An Essay on the Principle of Population*. New York: Angustus Kelley.

McDonald, Peter. (2006). "Fertility and the State: The Efficacy of Policy." *Population and Development Review* (forthcoming).

_____, and Rebecca Kippen. (2001). "Labour Supply Prospects in 16 Developed Countries: 2000–2050." *Population and Development Review* 27 (1):1–32.

Moyser, Melissa. (2006). "Why Are Canadians Having Children?" Paper presented at meetings of the Canadian Population Society, Toronto, June 1–3.

Statistics Canada. (2005a). *Population Projections of Visible Minority Groups, Canada, Provinces and Regions, 2001–2017*. Cat. no. 91-541-XIE.

Ottawa: Statistics Canada.

_____. (2005b). *Projections of the Aboriginal Populations, Canada, Provinces and Territories, 2001–2017*. Cat. no. 91-547-XIE. Ottawa: Statistics Canada.

United Nations. (2000). *Replacement Migration: Is It a Solution to Declining and Aging Populations?* New York: United Nations, Population Division.

APPENDIX

Bélanger, Alain, Laurent Martel and Eric Caron-Malenfant. 2005. *Population Projections for Canada, the Provinces and Territories, 2005-2031.* Statistics Canada Cat. no. 91-520 XIE.

Statistics Canada. 1994. *Revised Intercensal Population and Family Estimates, July 1, 1971-1991.* Ottawa: Statistics Canada Cat. No. 84-537.

Statistics Canada. 2005. *Annual Demographic Statistics 2004.* Ottawa: Statistics Canada Cat. No. 91-213.

Statistics Canada. 2006. *CD-ROM Annual Demographic Statistics 2005.* Ottawa: Statistics Canada Cat. No. 91-213 XPB.

COPYRIGHT ACKNOWLEDGMENTS

Chapter 9 by Frank Trovato, "Narrowing Sex Differential in Life Expectancy in Canada," adapted from "Narrowing Sex Differential in Life Expectancy in Canada and Austria: Comparative Analysis," *Vienna Yearbook of Population Research* (2005): 17-52. Reprinted by permission of Frank Trovato.

Chapter 10 by Monica Boyd and Michael Vickers, excerpts from "100 Years of Immigration in Canada," published in the Statistics Canada publication *Canadian Social Trends,* Catalogue 11-008, No. 58 (Fall 2000): 2-12. Reprinted by permission of Statistics Canada.

Chapter 11 by Alan Simmons, "Globalization, Undocumented Migration and Unwanted Refugees: Trends, Explanations, and Solutions," from *Demographic Futures in the Context of Globalization: Public Police Issues,* May 2004. Reprinted by permission of Alan Simmons.

Chapter 12 by Alan G. Green, "What is the Role of Immigration in Canada's Future?," from *Canadian Immigration Policy for the 21st Century,* Charles Beach, Alan Green, and Jeffrey Reitz, eds., (Kingston: John Deutsch Institute, 2003): 33-44. Copyright © John Deutsch Institute, 2003. Reprinted by permission of the John Deutsch Institute.

Chapter 13 by Garnett Picot and Arthur Sweetman, excerpts from "The Deteriorating Economic Welfare of Immigrants and Possible Causes: Update 2005," published in the Statistics Canada publication *Analytical Studies Branch Research Paper Series,* Catalogue 11F00019MIE, No. 262, (June 27, 2005). Reprinted by permission of Statistics Canada.

Chapter 14 by Daniel Hiebert, "Migration and the Demographic Transformation of Canadian Cities: The Social Geography of Canada's Major Metropolitan Centres in 2017," from *The Department of Canadian Heritage.* Reprinted by permission of the Minister of Public Works and Government Services Canada.

Chapter 15 by Jacques Légaré, "Aging and Social Security Program Reforms: Canada in International Perspective" from *Volunteering, Isuma* Volume 2 No. 2. (Ottawa: Policy Research Initiative, 1991). Available at http://isuma.net/v02n02/legare/legare_e.shtml. Reprinted by permission of the Policy Research Initiative and Jacques Légaré.

Chapter 16 by Eric Moore and Michael Pacey, "Geographic Dimensions of Aging in Canada, 1991-2001," from *Canadian Journal on Aging Supplement S5-S21, Volume 23* (2004): S7-S19. Copyright © Canadian Association of Gerontology, 2004. Reprinted by permission of University of Toronto Press Inc., www.utpjournals.com.

Chapter 17 by Ellen Gee, "Misconceptions and Misapprehensions about Population Aging," from *International Journal of Epidemiology 31*(4) (2002): 750-753. Copyright © Oxford University Press Journals, 2002.

Chapter 18 by Larry S. Bourne and Demaris Rose, "The Changing Face of Canada: The Uneven Geographies of Population and Social Change," from *Canadian Geographer 45*(1) (Spring 2001): 106-119. Reprinted by permission of Blackwell Publishing.

Chapter 19 by Céline Le Bourdais and Évelyn Lapierre-Adamcyk, "Changes in Conjugal Life in Canada: Is Cohabitation Progressively Replacing Marriage?," from *Journal of Marriage and Family 66*(4) (November 2004): 929-942.

Chapter 20 by Gustave Goldmann, "Shifts in Ethnic Origins among the Offspring of Immigrants: Is Ethnic Mobility a Measurable Phenomenon?," from *Canadian Ethnic Studies 30* (3) (Fall 1998): 3-13, 5-35. Reprinted by permission of the Canadian Ethnic Studies Association.

Chapter 22 by T.R. Balakrishnan and Stephan Gyimah, "Spatial Residential Patterns of Selected Ethnic Groups: Significance and Policy Implications," from *Canadian Ethnic Studies 35* (2003): 33-52. Reprinted by permission of Canadian Ethnic Studies Association.

FIGURES

Figure 1.1: "Birth's and Deaths, 2005-2056, Statistics Canada's Medium Projection," adapted from Statistics Canada publication *Population Projections for Canada, Provinces and Territories — 2000 to 2003,"* Catalogue 91-520, (Ottawa: Statistics Canada, March 13, 2001), 62. Reprinted by permission of Statistics Canada.

Figure 1.3: "Age Pyramid of the Population of Canada, July 1, 1985, 1995, and 2005," adapted from Statistics Canada, *Annual Demographic Statistics, 2005*, Catalogue 91-213, (Ottawa: Statistics Canada, April 4, 2006) and *Canada's Ethnocultural Portrait: A Changing Mosaic, 2001 Census,* Catalogue 96F0030XIE2001008, (Ottawa: Statistics Canada, January 23, 2001). Reprinted by permission of Statistics Canada.

Figure 2.1: United Nations, "Total Fertility Rates by Continent, 1950-55 to 1990," from *World Population Prospects: The 2004 Revision,* (2005).

Figure 2.2: "Total Fertility Rates for Selected Countries, 1950 to 1998," from *International Data Base, Census Bureau, Population Division*. Reprinted by permission of U.S. Census Bureau.

Figure 3.1: "Total Fertility Rates for Canada, the U.S. and Quebec, 1975 to 2001," from *Report on Vital Statistics 51:2*, 2002 and adapted in part from Statistics Canada publication *Report on the Demographic Situation in Canada, 2002*, Catalogue 91-209, (Ottawa: Statistics Canada, December 22, 2003). Reprinted by permission of Statistics Canada.

Figure 3.4: "GNI per Capita versus Total Fertility Rate for Canada, 1975 to 2001," from The World Bank, *World Development Indicators CD Rom*, 2003; and U.S. Census International Data Base, *International Data Base Projections, 2005*. Reprinted by permission of U.S. Census Bureau.

Figure 3.5: "GNI per Capita versus Total Fertility Rate for U.S. 1975 to 2001," from The World Bank, *World Development Indicators CD Rom*, 2003; and U.S. Census International Data Base, *International Data Base Projections, 2005*. Reprinted by permission of U.S. Census Bureau.

Figure 3.6: "Total Abortion Rate per Woman for Canada and the U.S., 1975 to 2000," from *Report on Vital Statistics 51:2*, 2002; and data calculated in part from Statistics Canada Web site *Induced abortions by age group http://www40.statcan.ca/l01/cst01/health43.htm?sdi=induced%20abortion*. Reprinted by permission of Statistics Canada.

Figure 5.1: "Change in the Proportion of Children Under Five Years of Age with an Immigrant Mother, by Mother's Place of Birth, Canada, 1981-2001," adapted from Statistics Canada publication *Report on the Demographic Situation in Canada — 2002*, Catalogue 91-209, (Ottawa: Statistics Canada, December 22, 2003), 135. Reprinted by permission of Statistics Canada.

Figure 5.2: "Change in the Proportion of Foreign-born Women Aged 15 to 54 by Place of Birth, Canada, 1981-2001," adapted from Statistics Canada publication *Report on the Demographic Situation in Canada — 2002*, Catalogue 91-209, (Ottawa: Statistics Canada, December 22, 2003), 136. Reprinted by permission of Statistics Canada.

Figure 5.3: "Total Fertility Rate of Women Born Abroad by Period of Immigration, Canada, 1981-2001," adapted from Statistics Canada publication *Report on the Demographic Situation in Canada —2002*, Catalogue 91-209, (Ottawa: Statistics Canada, December 22, 2003), 143. Reprinted by permission of Statistics Canada.

Figure 5.4, Part 1: "Total Fertility Rate of Women Born Abroad Since Immigration and Region of Origin, Canada, 1996-2001," adapted from Statistics Canada publication *Report on the Demographic Situation in Canada —2002*, Catalogue 91-209, (Ottawa: Statistics Canada, December 22, 2003), 144. Reprinted by permission of Statistics Canada.

Figure 5.4, Part 2: "Age Specific Fertility Rates of Immigrant Women Since Immigration, Canada, 1996-2001," adapted from Statistics Canada publication *Report on the Demographic Situation in*

The Changing Face of Canada

Canada —*2002*, Catalogue 91-209, (Ottawa: Statistics Canada, December 22, 2003), 144. Reprinted by permission of Statistics Canada.

Figure 6.1: "Age Specific Mortality Rates (per 100 000) for Selected Causes of Death, Canada, 1997," adapted from Statistics Canada *Canadian Social Trends,* Catalogue 11-008, No. 59, (Ottawa: Statistics Canada, Winter 2000), 15. Reprinted by permission of Statistics Canada.

Figure 6.2: National Cancer Institute of Canada, "Percentage Probabilities of Developing Cancer in the Next Ten Years, by Age and Sex, Canada, 2000," Reprinted by permission of National Cancer Institute of Canada.

Figure 7.1: "Number of Deaths and Crude Death Rate by Sex, Quebec, 1921-1999," Data is adapted in part from Statistics Canada, Health Statistics Division, Vital Statistics — Death Database. Reprinted by permission of Statistics Canada.

Figure 7.2: Robert Bourbeau, et al., "Life Expectancy at Birth by Sex, Quebec, 1901-1999" from *Base de donnees sur la longevite canadienne.* Reprinted by permission of Dr. Robert Bourbeau.

Figure 7.3: Mélanie Smuga, "Infant Mortality Rate, Neonatal and Post-neonatal, Quebec, 1926-1999," from *La mortalité infantile et périnatale au Québec: Évolution depuis 1926 et disparités régionales de 1980 à 1997.*

Figure 7.4: Sylvie Martel and Robert Bourbeau, "Percentage Distribution of Deaths by Age, Quebec, 1921-24, 1955-59 and 1995-99," from *Compression de la mortalité et rectangularisation de la courbe de survie au Québec au cours du XXe siècle, Cahiers québécois de démographie, 32*(1), 2003. Reprinted by permission of Dr. Robert Bourbeau.

Figure 7.5: Sylvie Martel and Robert Bourbeau, "Survival Curves by Sex, Quebec, 1921-24, 1955-59 and 1995-99," from *Compression de la mortalité et rectangularisation de la courbe de survie au Québec au cours du XXe siècle. Cahiers québécois de démographie, 32*(1), 2003. Reprinted by permission of Dr. Robert Bourbeau.

Figure 7.6: "Distribution of Deaths by Cause, Quebec, 1926-1998," data adapted in part from Statistics Canada, Health Statistics Division, Vital Statistics — Death Database. Reprinted by permission of Statistics Canada.

Figure 10.1: "Number of Immigrants per Year, Canada, 1901-1998," adapted from Statistics Canada *Canadian Social Trends,* Catalogue 11-008, No. 58, (Ottawa: Statistics Canada, Fall 2000), 4. Reprinted by permission of Statistics Canada.

Figure 10.2: "Immigration as a Percentage of Total Population Growth, Canada, 1901-11 to 1991-96," adapted from Statistics Canada *Canadian Social Trends,* Catalogue 11-008, No. 58, (Ottawa: Statistics Canada, Fall 2000), 4. Reprinted by permission of Statistics Canada.

Figure 10.4: "Number of Men per 100 Women, Immigrants and Non-immigrants, Canada, 1911-1996," adapted from Statistics Canada *Canadian Social Trends,* Catalogue 11-008, No. 58, (Ottawa: Statistics Canada, Fall 2000), 6. Reprinted by permission of Statistics Canada.

Figure 10.5: "Settlement Patterns of the Immigrant Population for Provinces and Territories, Canada, 1901-1996," adapted from Statistics Canada *Canadian Social Trends,* Catalogue 11-008, No. 58, (Ottawa: Statistics Canada, Fall 2000), 9. Reprinted by permission of Statistics Canada.

Figure 11.1: H. Zlotnik, "Percentage of International Migrants Originating in Less Developed Countries, 1960-64 to 1995-95," from *Trends of International Migration Since 1965: What Existing Data Reveal. International Migration 37*(1), 1999. Reprinted by permission of Blackwell Publishing.

Figure 11.2: H. Zlotnik, "Number of Countries of Origin Constituting 75% of All Immigrants, 1965-69 and 1990-94," from *Trends of International Migration Since 1965: What Existing Data Reveal.* Copyright © *International Migration 37*(1), 1999. Reprinted by permission of Blackwell Publishing.

Figure 11.3: United Nations High Commissioner for Refugees, "Refugee Populations over Time, 1975-2000," from *The State of the World's Refugees: 50 Years of Humanitarian Action*, (2000).

Figure 13.1: "Earnings of Immigrants as a Proportion of Those Canadian-born, No Controls for Differences between the Two Populations," adapted from Statistics Canada publication *Will They Ever Converge? Earnings of Immigrants and Canadian-born Workers over the Last Two Decades*, Catalogue 11F0019MIE2003215, (Ottawa: Statistics Canada, October 8, 2003). Reprinted by permission of Statistics Canada.

Figure 13.2: "Earnings Ratio: Earnings of Immigrants Compared to Those of Comparable Canadian-born," adapted from Statistics Canada publication *Will They Ever Converge? Earnings of Immigrants and Canadian-born Workers over the Last Two Decades*, Catalogue 11F0019MIE2003215, (Ottawa: Statistics Canada, October 8, 2003). Reprinted by permission of Statistics Canada.

Figure 18.1: Larry S. Bourne and Demaris Rose, "The Canadian Urban System," from *The Changing Face of Canada: The Uneven Geographies of Population and Social Change. Canadian Geographer*, Spring 2001: 45, 1. Reprinted by permission of Blackwell Publishing.

Figure 18.2: A. Germain and D. Rose, "Annual International Migration Flows to Canada, 1860-1998," from *Montréal: The Quest for a Metropolis*. Reprinted by permission of John Wiley and Sons.

Figure 18.3: Figure 18.3: "Components of Population Growth and Change in Canada, 1961-1998," adapted from the Statistics Canada publication *Annual Demographic Statistics, 2005*, Catalogue 91-213, (Ottawa: Statistics Canada, April 4, 2006). Reprinted by permission of Statistics Canada.

Figure 19.2: "Percentage of Couples Cohabiting in Canada by Region of Residence: 1981, 1991, and 2001 (Figure 1)," adapted from the Statistics Canada publication *Changing Conjugal Life in Canada*, Catalogue 89-576, (Ottawa: Statistics Canada, July 11, 2002). Reprinted by permission of Statistics Canada.

Figure 19.4: "Type of First Unions Formed by Women in the Early 1970s and 1990s, Quebec and Canada Without Quebec, 1995 General Social Survey on Family," adapted from the Statistics Canada publication *Report on the Demographic Situation in Canada*, 1996, Catalogue 91-209, (Ottawa: Statistics Canada, March 25, 1998). Reprinted by permission of Statistics Canada.

Figure 21.1: "Native Languages and Language Families of Canada," from Rod Beaujot and Don Kerr, *Population Change in Canada*, (Don Mills: Oxford University Press, 2004) based on Ives Goddard, *Languages: Handbook of North American Indians*, Volume 17, 1996. Reprinted by permission of the Smithsonian Institution.

Figure 21.3: Mary Jane Norris, "Percentage Distribution by Age Group and Sex of Total Canadian, Aboriginal Ancestry, and Aboriginal Identity Populations, Canada, 1996," from *Visions of the Heart: Canadian Aboriginal Issues*, 2nd Edition.

TABLES

Table 2.1: Council of Europe, "Mean Age of Women at Birth of First Child, Selected Countries: 1965 to 1996," from *Recent Demographic Developments in Europe*; and United Nations, from *Patterns of Fertility in Low-Fertility Settings*, (1992). Reprinted by permission of Council of Europe.

Table 2.2: Christopher Prinz and Wolfgang Lutz, "Population Size (in Millions) for Twenty European Countries, 1990 and 2050," from *The Future of Europe's Population*. Reprinted by permission of Council of Europe.

Table 2.3: Statistics Canada, "Projected Population (in Millions) for Canada under Four Alternate Scenarios, 1998 to 2051," from Author's Calculations using Statistics Canada's 1998-based Population Projection, 1998.

Table 5.1: "Comparison of Fertility Rates by Age Group and the Total Fertility Rate, Estimated According to the Own Children Method (Census) and Vital Statistics, Women Born in Canada and Abroad, Canada, 1996-2001," adapted from Statistics Canada publication *Report on the Demographic Situation in Canada — 2002*, Catalogue 91-209, (Ottawa: Statistics Canada, December 22, 2003), 132. Reprinted by permission of Statistics Canada.

Table 5.2: "Total Fertility Rate of Canadian-born Women and Canadian Women Born Abroad by Region of Birth, Canada 1976-1981 to 1996-2001," adapted from Statistics Canada publication *Report on the Demographic Situation in Canada —2002*, Catalogue 91-209, (Ottawa: Statistics Canada, December 22, 2003), 136. Reprinted by permission of Statistics Canada.

Table 5.3: "Total Fertility Rate of Immigrant Women Admitted During the Five Years Preceding the Census According to Whether the Child was Born in Canada or Abroad, Canada, 1981 to 2001," adapted from Statistics Canada publication *Report on the Demographic Situation in Canada — 2002*, Catalogue 91-209, (Ottawa: Statistics Canada, December 22, 2003), 142. Reprinted by permission of Statistics Canada.

Table 5.4: "Age Specific Fertility Rate and Total Fertility Rate by Generation, Canada, 1996-2001," adapted from Statistics Canada publication *Report on the Demographic Situation in Canada —2002*, Catalogue 91-209, (Ottawa: Statistics Canada, December 22, 2003), 145. Reprinted by permission of Statistics Canada.

Table 6.1: "Leading Causes of Death, Canada, 1921-25 and 1996-97," from Statistics Canada *Canadian Social Trends*, Catalogue 11-008, No. 59, (Ottawa: Statistics Canada, Winter 2000), 13. Reprinted by permission of Statistics Canada.

Table 6.2: "Incidents of Selected Health Problems by Age and Sex, Canada, 1978-79 and 1996-97," adapted from Statistics Canada *Canadian Social Trends*, Catalogue 11-008, No. 59, (Ottawa: Statistics Canada, Winter 2000), 16. Reprinted by permission of Statistics Canada.

Table 7.1: "Contribution (in %) by Age Groups to Gains in Life Expectancy at Birth, Both Sexes, Quebec, 1921-24 to 1995-99," From *Base de donnees sur la longevite canadienne (BDLC)*. Reprinted by permission of Département de Démographie.

Table 11.1: H. Zlotnik, "Migrant Origins by Region, 1965 to 1990," from *Trends of International Migration Since 1965: What Existing Data Reveal. International Migration 37*(1), 1999. Reprinted by permission of Blackwell Publishing.

Table 11.2: United Nations High Commissioner for Refugees, "Populations in Need of UNHCR Assistance (January 1, 2001)," from *Global Appeal 2002*, (2002).

Table 13.1: "Low-income Rates by Immigration Status, Canada, 1980-2000," adapted from Statistics Canada publication *The Rise in Low-Income among Immigrants in Canada*, Catalogue 11F0019MIE2003198. Reprinted by permission of Statistics Canada.

Table 13.2: "Percentage Change in the Low-income Rate by Source Region, Canada, 1980-2000," adapted from Statistics Canada publication *The Rise in Low-Income among Immigrants in Canada*, Catalogue 11F0019MIE2003198, Reprinted by permission of Statistics Canada.

Table 13.3: "Low-income Rates Among Recent Immigrants Aged 25 to 65 by Education Level, Canada, 1990 and 2000," adapted from Statistics Canada publication *The Rise in Low-Income among Immigrants in Canada*, Catalogue 11F0019MIE2003198. Reprinted by permission of Statistics Canada.

Table 14.2: "Percentage of Primary Household Maintainers Below LICO, 2001," CERIS Data, 2004, Metropolis Core Tables, Part 3, Table 2. Reprinted by permission of Statistics Canada.

Table 18.1: "Net Migration by Province, Canada, 1956-1996," adapted from the Statistics Canada publication *Population Projections for Canada, Provinces and Territories*, Catalogue 91-520, various years. Reprinted by permission of Statistics Canada.

Table 20.5: "Rates of Undercount by Age Group and Census Year, Canada," adapted from the Statistics Canada publication *Coverage (Reference Products: Technical Reports: 1991 Census of Population)*, 1991, Catalogue 92-341, (Ottawa: Statistics Canada, March 31, 1994). Reprinted by permission of Statistics Canada.

APPENDIX

Appendix by Alain Bélanger, Laurent Martel, and Eric Caron-Malenfant, "Canadian Population Estimates (1971-2005) and Projections (2005-2035)," adapted from the Statistics Canada publication *Population Projections for Canada, Provinces and Territories*, Catalogue 91-520, various years. Reprinted by permission of Statistics Canada.

Table A1: "Annual Population Estimates, July 1971 to July 2005, Canada, Provinces and Territories," adapted from the Statistics Canada publication *Annual Demographic Statistics*, 2005, Catalogue 91-213, (Ottawa: Statistics Canada, April 4, 2006). Reprinted by permission of Statistics Canada.

Table A2: "Age/Sex Distribution of the 2005 Population of Canada," adapted from the Statistics Canada publication *Annual Demographic Statistics*, 2005, Catalogue 91-213, (Ottawa: Statistics Canada, April 4, 2006). Reprinted by permission of Statistics Canada.

Table A3: "Annual Population Projections, July 2005 to July 2030, Canada, Provinces and Territories," adapted from the Statistics Canada publication *Population Projections for Canada, Provinces and Territories, 2005 to 2031*, Catalogue 91-520, (Ottawa: Statistics Canada, December 15, 2005). Reprinted by permission of Statistics Canada.

Table A4: "Age/Sex Distribution of the Projected 2031 Population of Canada, Medium Growth Scenario," adapted from the Statistics Canada publication *Population Projections for Canada, Provinces and Territories, 2005 to 2031*, Catalogue 91-520, (Ottawa: Statistics Canada, December 15, 2005). Reprinted by permission of Statistics Canada.

Figure A1: "Population Observed (1981 to 2005) and Projected (2006-2056) according to Three Scenarios", adapted from the Statistics Canada publication *Population Projections for Canada, Provinces and Territories, 2005 to 2031*, Catalogue 91-520, (Ottawa: Statistics Canada, December 15, 2005). Reprinted by permission of Statistics Canada.

Figure A2: "Age Pyramid of the Canadian Population, 2005 and 2031," adapted from the Statistics Canada publication *Population Projections for Canada, Provinces and Territories, 2005 to 2031*, Catalogue 91-520, (Ottawa: Statistics Canada, December 15, 2005). Reprinted by permission of Statistics Canada.